Reading in the Academic Environment

Mary L. Dillard

Shawnee State University

Prentice
Hall

Upper Saddle River, New Jersey 07458

Library of Congress Control Number: 2002107276

Editor in chief: Leah Jewell
Senior acquisitions editor: Craig Campanella
Marketing manager: Rachel Falk
Assistant editor: Karen Schultz
Editorial assistant: Joan Polk
Production editor: Kari Callaghan Mazzola
Project liaison: Randy Pettit
Prepress and manufacturing buyer: Ben Smith
Electronic page makeup: Kari Callaghan Mazzola and John P. Mazzola
Interior design: John P. Mazzola
Cover director: Jayne Conte
Cover design: Bruce Kenselaar
Cover art: Sergio Jose Ortega/Stock Illustration Source, Inc.

This book was set in 10/12 Meridien by Big Sky Composition
and was printed and bound by RR Donnelley & Sons Company.
The cover was printed by Phoenix Color Corp.

© 2003 by Pearson Education, Inc.
Upper Saddle River, New Jersey 07458

Printed in the United States of America
10 9 8 7 6 5 4 3 2 1

ISBN 0-13-041468-9

Pearson Education LTD., London
Pearson Education Australia PTY, Limited, Sydney
Pearson Education Singapore, Pte. Ltd
Pearson Education North Asia Ltd, Hong Kong
Pearson Education Canada, Ltd., Toronto
Pearson Educación de Mexico, S.A. de C.V.
Pearson Education—Japan, Tokyo
Pearson Education Malaysia, Pte. Ltd
Pearson Education, Upper Saddle River, New Jersey

Contents

Preface

MY DEVELOPMENTAL READING PROGRAM

My open-admissions university has mandatory testing, placement, and exit exams. Students are placed into developmental composition and developmental reading according to their placement scores. We offer two developmental reading courses, and our reading students can exit from the lower-level reading course to the higher-level one or exit to the regular freshman English program.

Students reading below the ninth-grade level are placed in the lower-level course. The upper-level course is for students placing on the ninth- and tenth-grade levels, and *Reading in the Academic Environment* is used as its text. I have found that students on the ninth- and tenth-grade levels often bottom out and have a difficult time increasing their reading skills. They can usually operate efficiently in the real world but have difficulty in the academic one. To exit our reading program, a student must score an eleventh-grade equivalency on the Nelson Denny Reading Test. This exit score may seem low, but I justify it mainly because of research on GPAs done a year after students completed their reading course. When I used the eleventh-grade equivalency exit score at a university in Louisiana where I served as developmental reading coordinator for five years, I found that those students who exited on the eleventh-grade level had a GPA less than a letter grade lower than those who exited at higher levels. Because there is no significant difference in GPAs and because of complaints about timed tests, I feel that the lower exit score is justified.

MY STUDENTS

One of the delights of going to developmental education conferences—like the National Association of Developmental Education (NADE) or the College Division of College Reading Association (CRA)—is talking with fellow teachers about my students and their problems. The students at my university are basically first-generation college students, on financial aid, from south central Ohio and Kentucky. Many of the traditional-age students had not planned on going to college and therefore did not take appropriate high-school courses; others spent their school years involved in extracurricular activities that took time from their academic studies. I have an increasing number of middle-class, white, single mothers who are coming straight from high school. I have had two students who have had babies during the quarter and returned to finish the class. Nontraditional or returning students, whose academic skills are rusty, are also present in my classes. They may have been out of school for five to twenty years before deciding to go to college. Many students, traditional and nontraditional, work full-time jobs and take a full load of classes at the same time. When I first started teaching developmental English, I was very judgmental about students who were not performing well. Now I try to find out what is going on in their lives and try to work with them.

The local culture stresses sports, beauty pageants, country and gospel music, and a sense of family. The students are mostly interested in job training, not an education, even though most of them plan to get a four-year degree. I try to build on what they bring to the classroom. I think of Louise Rosenblatt's statement that the more they know before they read, the more they learn when they read. How do we give them a rich and varied background so that they can be successful readers in their college-level courses? When their life experiences are limited, I try to introduce new ideas and types of writing to them. This is part of what the book is about.

MY DEVELOPMENTAL READING TEACHING EXPERIENCE

Besides teaching at the university level, I have taught developmental English at two church-sponsored colleges, one a four-year college and one a junior college. I have also taught developmental English at a public technical college located on a psychiatric hospital's grounds. I am a graduate of the Kellogg Institute (1984), where I found my new mission in teaching: helping the underprepared. For years I have attended NADE, CRA, and IRA conferences, where I have absorbed ideas and adapted them to meet my needs. For example, I do not remember who first used *recreational* for *pleasure* reading or *overview* instead of *preview*, but I like the terms and have made them my own. I never seem to burn out in this field because I never solve all the problems. If I ever get it right, I think I'll retire.

THE TEXTBOOK

This textbook is called *Reading in the Academic Environment* to emphasize that academic reading is different from everyday reading. It requires a different set of skills for success. Just as the academic environment is different from the everyday world, academic reading is different from everyday reading in that the level is higher, writing patterns and patterns of organization are more complex, and the density of concepts can be enormous. Textbook authors often assume background knowledge and experience on the part of the student that simply is not there. The complexity of ideas can be staggering, especially to the student with little background knowledge or interest in a subject. Along with learning the reading skills necessary for academic success, students must transfer and practice what they learn; they must practice reading difficult material on difficult subjects. Reading simple but entertaining and relevant stories or newsmagazines is highly motivational and often leads to good class discussions and high-energy sessions. Students often learn to enjoy reading and thinking in such classes. The problem with such classes is that often there is not enough *academic* writing (as opposed to mainstream writing) for students to analyze and sort out. They are not exposed to in-depth discussions of a topic, a great amount of specialized vocabulary, or complex organizational patterns and writing styles. Content-area reading provides such challenges.

The writing of this book came out of years of frustration at not being able to find a textbook appropriate for the ninth- and tenth-grade reading level of my students. I wanted to work on various levels of comprehension because of Delores Durkin's observation that we test, not teach, comprehension, and because of my observation that my students were good at answering literal-level questions but had difficulty seeing the significance of the answers. I wanted to work with degrees of knowing vocabulary words, not just matching words with definitions. I wanted to use longer passages so that a reader's understanding of anaphoric and transitional devices could be observed. I also wanted to use difficult material and teach my students about the self-esteem that comes with being able to read it. I used several good books but always found something missing. I used an ESL book and wrote my own lessons based on the readings in the book and had them printed in the university print shop. I next used readings from the ESL textbook combined with my lessons and had them custom printed in another state. When the company printing that book had difficulty getting copyrights for the reading selections, I asked my husband to write some chapters that I could use in class. Luckily for me, he has taught developmental English and helped write a developmental composition textbook with members of his English Department, so he understood what I needed. He was so concerned about my frustration over copyrights that he did not even use anything from the thirteen books he has published. From that point, the book grew and changed.

Each of the two parts of the book has introductory material on the chapters, an organizational plan, and a method for teaching. Part I contains information on comprehension, vocabulary, reading speed, the content-area chapters, and suggestions for using the chapters. Part II discusses differences in the two parts, vocabulary, and comprehension. It also contains an overview of the study skills introduced and an overview of the textbook chapters and closes with an explanation of the method for teaching incorporated in the lessons.

VOCABULARY

The workshops of Sherri Nist and Michelle Simpson have greatly influenced the way I now teach vocabulary. Anyone who has used their textbooks or attended their vocabulary workshops will remember their Conceptual Word Knowledge iceberg. For those unfamiliar with their work, their textbook *Developing Vocabulary Concepts for College Thinking* (1997, pp. 14–15) contains a good explanation. Briefly, the iceberg above the water level represents the word's definition while the part of the iceberg below represents the deeper meanings, synonyms and antonyms, examples and nonexamples, connotations, and other forms of the word.

METHOD

Two of the greatest influences on my teaching content-area reading are John E. Readence, David W. Moore, and Robert J. Rickelman's *Prereading Activities for Content Area Reading and Learning*, and an older book, John E. Readence, Thomas W. Bean, and R. Scott Baldwin's *Content Area Reading: An Integrated Approach*. Other reading specialists have also influenced me, especially Richard and Joanne Vacca, Jeanne Schumm, and Shawn Post. Bess Hinson's *New Directions in Reading Instruction* has also been very helpful.

Study Skills

I never thought much about the way study skills should be taught before Michelle Simpson invited me to be part of a College Reading Association discussion of the subject (which took place during the 1980s). Obviously, I read what she suggested before I attended the discussion. I have been thinking about it since, and with this textbook, I hope that I have learned to integrate the study skills into the content. The issue, of course, is whether to teach the skills in isolation or as part of the content. I believe that using study skills on content that students are responsible for learning is more helpful than learning a skill in isolation.

Besides the work of Michelle Simpson and Sherri Nist, two books have greatly influenced my thinking about study skills: Rona F. Flippo and David C. Caverly's *Teaching Reading and Study Strategies at the College Level* and *College Reading and Study Strategy Programs*. I based my decision on which study skills to use for this textbook on information in these two books.

Acknowledgments

Thanks to Prentice Hall's Robert Thoresen, Craig Campanella, and Joan Polk, and to Kari Callaghan Mazzola of Big Sky Composition and copy editor Dana Chicchelly for their help and support. Thanks to my students at Shawnee State and elsewhere who have shown me what they need to learn. Thanks also to the late Dr. J. Estill Alexander and to Dr. Sandra Zecchini, my mentors at the University of Tennessee, and to the many Kellogg Institute graduates and CRA, NADE, LADE, and OADE members who helped me form a mission and purpose in the developmental education field. Thanks to Gene Beckett, who trusted me to develop a good reading program, and to the members of the SSU English Department for their support of my program. Thanks to Sibylle Herrmann, Roberta Milliken, and Teresa Redoutey for years of tea and sympathy. Thanks also to the following Prentice Hall reviewers: Karen Patty-Graham, Southern Illinois University at Edwardsville; Victoria F. Sarkisian, Marist College; Nancy Meyer, DeVry Institute of Technology; AnnaMarie Schlender, Austin Community College; Wendy-Jean Frandsen, Vance-Granville Community College; Thurmond Whatley, Aiken Technical College; Barbara Fowler, Longview Community College; Dianne Ruggiero, Broward Community College; Lisa A. Barnes, Delaware County Community College. And thanks to my family for their patience and love: I would not and could not have attempted this book without Joe Dillard's compassion and patience, his constant support without being invasive, and his willingness to eat in restaurants. His love and nonjudgmental attitude make life worth living and make writing fun. My son Jody provided long-distance support and the memory of his going to first grade to learn to read.

Mary L. Dillard

Part I

Introduction

The two-fold purpose of this book is to help the student pass developmental English exit exams and to help the student read textbooks for college-level courses. In order to do both, the student needs to improve in comprehension and vocabulary development. An added concern for most students is reading faster. Information below is presented in terms of my students' questions.

WHAT ARE YOU GOING TO DO TO HELP ME?

COMPREHENSION

To help the student improve in comprehension, I have designed a three-part reading plan based on schema theory and strategies other reading specialists have developed. In simple terms, the plan consists of what readers do before they read, while they read, and after they read. In *pre-reading*, readers take time to tap their experience and prior knowledge about the featured textbook chapter topic, predict what they will read, and overview the featured textbook chapter. This is a very different approach from the common one of opening a textbook and beginning to read on page one and reading straight through the chapter. While *reading* a selection from a textbook, readers will use Reciprocal Teaching or Active Questioning as strategies for remaining active and for improving understanding as they read. In Reciprocal Teaching, they will summarize, question on higher comprehension levels, clarify important ideas, and predict. In Active Questioning, they will work on three levels of comprehension: literal, inferential, and critical/creative. In *post-reading*, the readers will come full circle by comparing what they predicted they would read to what was actually read and by looking for areas of conflict between the two that would interfere with comprehension. They will connect what they learned to what they already know, and they will be able not only to state main ideas but to discuss the significance of them. They will also incorporate what they learn into their personal lives.

VOCABULARY

To help the student increase in vocabulary knowledge, I have devised several vocabulary exercises. At the beginning of each chapter a list of ten general vocabulary words is listed in a vocabulary/metacognitive exercise. Students measure whether or not they know the words and try to match the words with their definitions. At the end of the reading plan in each chapter, I have written vocabulary lessons that include work on affixes, meaning in context, recognition of multiple meanings of words, antonyms and synonyms, and sentence writing using the words. The last vocabulary exercise, Vocabulary Extension, is designed to help students become aware of how well they know the ten words they worked with in the previous exercises. They place the ten words in four different categories of knowing, write a paragraph using five of the words, and then complete a right-brain exercise on drawing what a word means. The exercise on levels of knowing a word was developed under the influence of the vocabulary work of Drs. Michelle L. Simpson and Sherri L. Nist of the University of Georgia and on the research of Dr. Norman A. Stahl of Northern Illinois University. Through the vocabulary exercises, the readers should become aware of how well they know new words, and the readers should be able to use these new words in their own writing and speech at some level of knowing.

READING FASTER

Many times students tell me after the first class that they can read okay; they just have to learn to read faster. For those readers concerned with improving reading rate, remember that you read with your brain, not just your eyes. The more prior knowledge, experience, and interest you bring to a reading selection, the more rapidly you will read. So work on developing interest in a variety of topics, read more than you have ever read before, and use every opportunity you have to learn something new if you seriously want to read faster. No quick fix exists. Reading faster by reading down the center of the page or reading only the important words are not linguistically sound approaches.

WHAT KIND OF MATERIAL IS IN THIS BOOK?

Each of the four chapters in Part I of this book contains a complete, reproduced textbook chapter, vocabulary and metacognitive exercises, a section on prior knowledge, academic study skills, a three-part reading plan, extended reading activities, and a section called reflection.

Part I of this book consists of four complete content-area chapters reproduced from authentic textbooks with appropriate reading exercises. The reading passages are long enough so that complex reading can take place; for example, these longer passages provide opportunities to use anaphoric and transition devices and to explore specialized vocabulary, complex text structure, and writing patterns. Using the textbook chapters in their entirety also provides an opportunity to seek out the most important information in a variety of ways and to separate it from less important information. The four textbooks from which the reproduced chapters were taken are currently being used on many college campuses. In fact, you may be using one of them now if you are taking a computer, psychology, sociology, or geology course. Look for the textbooks in your campus bookstore the next time you are browsing there.

WHAT SUBJECTS ARE INCLUDED IN THE TEXTBOOK CHAPTERS?

COMPUTERS

The chapter on computers was chosen as the first one because most students will use computers in their classes regardless of their majors. Business, natural sciences, graphic arts, and engineering students may be more aware of computer use in their majors than others, but research will be conducted, papers written, and Powerpoint presentations will be made with the use of computers in most majors before a degree is granted. This chapter gives an overview of computers and is motivational. For those who fear computers, this chapter will help lessen that fear.

PSYCHOLOGY

Most students have some interest in psychology, at least at the level of pop psychology, and many will be required to take an introductory course as part of their core program or general studies. The psychology chapter was chosen with the idea in mind that freshmen often start to exert their individuality and redefine their positions within groups during the first year of college. Hopefully, this chapter will shed some light on these processes.

SOCIOLOGY

Freshmen are often living away from home for the first time and live in dorms or neighborhoods with a greater variety of people than in their hometown high schools or neighborhoods. The sociology chapter chosen for this part of the book contains the kind of information that can be useful in understanding or making friends with people from different racial and ethnic backgrounds. The chapter will also help freshmen become aware of how complex and diverse our society is.

GEOLOGY

At the writing of this book, several environmental concerns are making national headlines, and this fact has influenced the choice of environmental geology as the chapter in natural sciences. The geology chapter provides a broad background to help the student make intelligent choices on environmental issues.

DO I HAVE TO DO EVERYTHING IN THIS BOOK?

Part I is written so that you have choices. You are not expected to do everything suggested in these chapters. You and your teacher will decide which exercises will provide the most help. For example, you are given two choices for a reading plan (Reciprocal Teaching or Active Questioning) to guide you through the chapter. The chapters alternate between Active Questioning and Reciprocal Teaching, with the unused plan placed in Appendix A. You are given a vocabulary lesson and a vocabulary extension exercise at the end of the lesson. You may decide to do only one, or you may decide to do parts of each.

Remember, what work you choose to do should help you improve your vocabulary or increase your comprehension. (Sometimes I have good students choose easy exercises rather than challenging ones because making high marks on the easy ones makes them feel good. High self-esteem is an important part of the learning process, but it should not be chosen over a chance to improve reading skills or learn something new. Self-esteem also comes from knowing you can do something that is a challenge for you.) Academic Study Skills exercises are placed near the beginning of each chapter to help guide you through the selected textbook chapter. They are a part of the first step in your three-part reading plan, pre-reading. The Academic Study Skills exercises in Part I focus on helping you use the textbook aids provided by the authors. Sometimes textbooks offer so much help that they seem cluttered and a reader with little background knowledge or experience or without the concepts upon which the information is based will find it difficult to find the important information. Therefore, the Textbook Study Aids Plan in the Academic Study Skills section in Part I offers guidance in separating the important information from the merely interesting information. You may choose to do these exercises, do some, or skip them if you feel you do not need them. The Extended Reading Activities at the end of the chapters are written to help you expand and deepen your knowledge of a subject in a variety of ways and to keep you reading. You have choices. With your teacher's help, decide what will help you improve your reading. The last part of each chapter, Reflection, contains my thoughts on the chapter, and I hope you find it helpful. A friend asked why I used the term *mind revolution* for the first section of Reflection. It comes from my own freshman-year experience. I stayed out of school for a year after graduating from high school, and I only went to college through an accident of fate. Luckily, my first courses were Greek drama and introductory courses in psychology and sociology. In those three courses I was presented with ideas I didn't know existed. Some I incorporated immediately, some sat cooking on a back burner of my brain, and some I rejected. The point is that I had something new to think about and it changed my perception of the world. Later I heard a story on a humanities recording about a student at Harvard. As he was getting ready to graduate, his adviser asked what his plans were. The student said he was going home to Georgia to plant corn. Shocked, his advisor asked why he had worked so hard for a Harvard degree. The student responded that he wanted something to think about while he planted corn. That story changed my perception of education. I have never given up looking for something new to think about, and I want the same experience for my students, hence, mind revolutions.

HOW AM I GOING TO LEARN HOW TO DO THE WORK?

For more years than I would want to count, I have been influenced by the work in content area reading of John E. Readence, David W. Moore, and Robert J. Rickelman. Their research introduced me to the idea of moving from teacher-directed work to teacher modeling, to guided practice, and then to student independence. The reading plans in Part I's four chapters use this progression. The first two reading plans ask the student to answer teacher-made questions (dependence level). The last two move to a combination of teacher-made questions and guided practice. Independence comes in Part II. The above reading authorities have also influenced my inclusion of exercises based on having and activating prior knowledge, predicting, connecting new information to old, following an author's organizational patterns, and student questioning on higher comprehension levels. Because you will be moving from teacher dependency to independence gradually, you will not feel dumb. You will learn how to improve your comprehension and vocabulary in a challenging but non-threatening way.

Computers:
Information Technology in Perspective

Overview

Extended Reading Activities
Reflection
　　Mind Revolution
　　Vocabulary
　　Comprehension

VOCABULARY/METACOGNITION

The purpose of this exercise is to help you become aware of when you know the meaning of a word and to help you know when you do not know the meaning of a word. This is metacognition awareness.

On a scale of 1–5 (see below), rate your knowledge of the following vocabulary words from "Information Technology in Perspective." After matching words with definitions on page 8, check your answers and then check your number *ones* and *fives* below. Did you know when you really knew a word and when you really did not know the word?

Scale

1. I absolutely do not know.
2. I do not think I know.
3. There's a 50/50 chance I have seen or heard it.
4. I think I know it.
5. I know the word and can use it.

Words

_____ 1. Adapt
_____ 2. Facet
_____ 3. Irate
_____ 4. Vilify
_____ 5. Execute
_____ 6. Niche
_____ 7. Conventional
_____ 8. Dub
_____ 9. Gross
_____10. Myriad

Go to page 8. See if you can match the right definition with the word and then write sentences for any three words in the list.

Words	***Definitions**
_____ 1. Adapt	A. Defame
_____ 2. Facet	B. (1) Do; perform; carry out; (2) enact; (3) put to death according to law
_____ 3. Irate	
_____ 4. Vilify	C. (1) 10,000; (2) many
_____ 5. Execute	D. (1) Confer a new dignity or name upon;
_____ 6. Niche	(2) rub or dress so as to make smooth;
_____ 7. Conventional	(3) record from or on a previous sound track
_____ 8. Dub	E. Make suitable; alter to fit
_____ 9. Gross	F. Conforming to custom; conservative
_____10. Myriad	G. Angry; incensed
	H. (1) Whole, without deductions; total; (2) thick; fat; coarse; hence, vulgar, indelicate; (3) dull; dense
	I. Aspect; phase
	J. (1) a recess in a wall, as for a vase, statue, etc.; (2) a suitable place or position

*Definitions for all chapters are taken from *The New American Webster Handy College Dictionary*, third edition, unless stated otherwise.

Write three words from the list and your own sentences that show you know how to use the words. Choose words that you marked a *five* if possible.

1. Word _____

    Sentence _____

2. Word _____

    Sentence _____

3. Word _____

    Sentence _____

PRE-READING THE TEXTBOOK CHAPTER

The purpose of this *first* of three steps in your reading plan is to suggest things to do *before* you read. First, as part of your pre-reading, read the Prior Knowledge section beginning on page 9, the Academic Study Skills section's overview on page 17, and the first part of the Textbook Study Aids Plan (Pre-Reading) on page 17. When you finish, return to this page and continue your pre-reading.

TAPPING PRIOR KNOWLEDGE

Tap your experience and prior knowledge about the title of this selection by writing words and phrases that come to your mind. You are pulling up your file on the topic and focusing on what you will read. What do you already know about the subject? Do not look at your textbook at this time, as these answers will vary from person to person and won't be found in the textbook. There are no wrong answers for this part of the lesson.

PREDICTING

Predict in one sentence what you will read. Try to predict in some detail. Don't write, "I predict that I will read about information technology in perspective." What behavior, action, and/or information do you expect to read about? Predicting helps you identify your expectations of what you will read. Not reading what you have predicted will serve as a warning that you have misjudged the topic of the article and will help you adapt to what is in the chapter.

OVERVIEWING

You have already skimmed the Learning Objectives, the Summary and Key Terms, and Discussion and Problem Solving sections of the chapter in the Academic Study Skills section on page 17. Continue overviewing by paying close attention to the outline of the chapter. Note that you have four major sections with several sub-headings under each one. Add this new information to what you learned in the Prior Knowledge and Academic Study Skills sections of this lesson.

PRIOR KNOWLEDGE

This section, part of your pre-reading, presents a model to show you what will help you comprehend this chapter by using your own background knowledge. If you know much of the information listed below, you have a better background for reading this chapter. This section will suggest helpful kinds of background information and help you activate what you know; do not try to look up or learn everything listed. Ask yourself what you need to know before you read and what you already know that will help you to understand this chapter. Your instructor may want to use this section for a whole-class or small group discussion or have you read it silently.

WRITING PATTERN OVERVIEW

The writing pattern used in this chapter is basically expository, to explain or inform. Some description is also used. The authors use an informal writing style and some informal vocabulary words, such as *mainstreamers*, *techies*, *cool*, *savvy*, and *shelled out*. Generally, statements are supported by examples, not by studies or authorities in the field of computers. No references to other works appear at the end of the chapter.

DIRECTIONS FOR READING THIS SECTION

First, notice the categories of information: (a) vocabulary, (b) writing patterns, and (c) concepts and background knowledge and experience. Next, skim the sections, noting what is familiar and what is not. If a great amount is familiar and/or interesting to you, you should find reading the chapter easier than if you do not recognize anything and find the information boring.

CHAPTER SECTIONS

I. Introduction: Why This Chapter Is Important to You
    A. Vocabulary
        1. General
            a. Dynamic
            b. Mainstreamers
            c. Techies
            d. Weird
            e. Cool
            f. Colleagues
            g. Competent
    B. Recognition of Writing Patterns or Arrangement of Ideas and Devices
        1. The purpose of this section is motivational. Note the upbeat, positive tone.
        2. Broad general statement
        3. Invitation to jump on the bandwagon
    C. Concepts and Background Knowledge and Experience
        1. Grew up using a computer
        2. No fear of computers
        3. Positive attitude
        4. Own a computer
        5. Computer course
II. The Information Society
    A. Vocabulary
        1. General
            a. Reluctant
            b. Integration
            c. Adapt
            d. Manipulation
            e. Pursued
            f. Facet
            g. Revenues
            h. Simulation
            i. Generation
            j. Cornerstone
            k. Cubicle
            l. Savvy
            m. Enabling
            n. Gurus
            o. Intermediary
            p. Accumulated
            q. Dexterity

    2. Specialized
      (*Indicates word is used in the "Summary and Key Terms" section
      at the end of the chapter. Note that words are introduced in context.)

      a. Information technology (IT)*
      b. Information society*
      c. Knowledge workers*
      d. Information technology competency (IT competency)*
      e. Input*
      f. Output*
      g. Cyberspace
      h. Hardware*
      i. Software*
      j. Personal computer (PC)*
      k. Electronic mail (e-mail)*
      l. Newsgroups*
      m. Infrastructure (information superhighway)*
      n. Data*
      o. Information*
      p. Record*
      q. Master file*
      r. Spam
      s. Programs*
      t. Users*

  B. Recognition of Writing Patterns or Arrangement of Ideas and Devices
    1. Information is broken up into manageable chunks.
    2. Information is mostly in lists, not paragraphs; note format and use of bullets.
    3. Broad statements are supported with examples and an analogy.
    4. Definitions are given through context.

  C. Concepts and Background Knowledge and Experience
    1. Be familiar with the broad terms *information society* and *information technology*.
    2. See the need to be competent in computer use.
    3. Use electronic mail.
    4. Take interest in history and future of computers.
    5. Have experience with gathering data and turning it into information.

III. Networking: Bringing People Together
  A. Vocabulary
    1. General
      a. Dispersed
      b. Simultaneously
      c. Irate
      d. Vilifying

      e.   Vulnerable

      f.   Migration

      g.   Vehicle

      h.   Boon

      i.   Gratis

   2. Specialized

      a.   Computer network*

      b.   Global village

      c.   Internet (the Net)*

      d.   Internet service provider (ISP)*

      e.   Information service*

      f.   Online*

      g.   Offline*

      h.   Download*

      i.   Uploaded*

B. Recognition of Writing Patterns or Arrangement of Ideas and Devices

   1. Use of paragraph form (not lists)

   2. Statements followed by examples, including visuals

   3. Definitions in context

C. Concepts and Background Knowledge and Experience

   1. Concept of what living in a global village implies

   2. Experience in using the Internet

IV. Computers: The Essentials

A. Vocabulary

   1. General

      a.   Execute

      b.   Vary

      c.   Sophistication

      d.   Vendors

      e.   Pigeonholing

      f.   Niches

      g.   Fundamental

      h.   Destination

      i.   Aspects

      j.   Scope

      k.   Spacious

   2. Specialized

      a.   Computer*

      b.   Processor*

      c.   Computer system*

      d.   Monitor*

        e.   Printer*

        f.   Soft copy*

        g. Hard copy*

        h. Keyboard*

        i.   Point-and-draw device*

        j.   Mouse*

        k. Random-access memory (RAM)*

        l.   Integrated circuits (chips)*

        m. Disks*

        n. Peripheral devices*

        o. Mainframe computers*

        p. Microcomputers*

        q. Supercomputers*

        r.   Workstation*

        s.   Input/output (I/O)*

        t.   System software*

        u. Applications software*

  B. Recognition of Writing Patterns or Arrangement of Ideas and Devices

     1. Use of paragraphs

     2. Definitions in context

     3. Statements followed by explanations, examples, and visuals

     4. Use of analogies

  C. Concepts and Background Knowledge and Experience

     1. Concept of a computer system with its internal components and peripheral devices

     2. Familiar with data storage

     3. Familiar with variety of computers, either through use or seeing them in movies and documentaries

     4. Knowledge of systems and applications software; for example, your having installed software on a computer

V. Personal Computers to Supercomputers

  A. Vocabulary

     1. General

         a. Legitimized

         b. Versatile

         c. Interchangeably

         d. Conventional

         e. Unconventional

         f. Compact

         g. Cumbersome

         h. Miniaturized

        i.   Monochrome

        j.   Emerged

        k.   Conjunction

        l.   Shelled out

        m. Dubbed

        n.   Enhancements

        o.   Prototypes

2. Specialized

    a. Operating systems*

    b. Platform*

    c. Pocket (Palmtop) PC*

    d. Laptop (Notebook) PC*

    e. Docking station*

    f. Port replicator*

    g. Ports*

    h. Desktop PC*

    i. Tower PC*

    j. Slate computers*

    k. Pen-based PC*

    l. Speech-recognition software*

    m. Personal digital assistant or handheld PC (PDA)*

    n. Personal information management (PIM)*

    o. Network computer*

    p. Multimedia application*

    q. Floppy disk drive*

    r. CD-ROM drive*

    s. Computer-aided design (CAD)*

    t. Resolution*

    u. Enterprise-wide systems*

    v. Host computers*

    w. Terminal*

    x. Input/output–bound application*

    y. Processor-bound application*

B. Recognition of Writing Patterns or Arrangement of Ideas and Devices

  1. Paragraph form and lists combination

  2. Organized by size, small to large computers

  3. Description

  4. Definitions in context

C. Concepts and Background Knowledge and Experience

  1. Spent time browsing in a computer store

  2. Familiar with brand names and variety of computers

3. Aware of conventional and unconventional computers
4. Watch computer commercials on television
5. Own several types of computers
6. Work experience with big organization that uses mainframes and/or supercomputers
7. Took a CAD course or a science or engineering course that depends on computer knowledge

VI. A Computer System at Work
   A. Vocabulary
      1. General
         a. Suite
         b. Retrieved
         c. Gross
         d. Precious
         e. Erroneous
         f. Benchmark
      2. Specialized
         a. Local area network (LAN)*
         b. Server computer*
         c. Client computer*
         d. Milliseconds*
         e. Microseconds*
         f. Nanoseconds*
         g. Picoseconds*
         h. Backup*
   B. Recognition of Writing Patterns or Arrangement of Ideas and Devices
      1. Several short paragraphs
      2. Examples and visuals support statements; both dominate the section
      3. Definitions in context
   C. Concepts and Background Knowledge and Experience
      1. Worked with a payroll department or received a computer-printed paycheck
      2. Able to read computer program instructions
      3. Dependent on usefulness of the computer at work or school

VII. How Do We Use Computers?
   A. Vocabulary
      1. General
         a. Surpassed
         b. Domestic
         c. Innovations
         d. Debonair

                e.   Accomplices

                f.   Dubbed

        2. Specialized

                a.   Information systems*

                b.   Personal computing*

                c.   Word processing software*

                d.   Document*

                e.   Object*

                f.   Desktop publishing software*

                g.   Spreadsheet software*

                h.   Database software

                i.   Presentation software*

                j.   Communications software*

                k.   Edutainment software

  B. Recognition of Writing Patterns or Arrangement of Ideas and Devices

        1. Short paragraphs and lists with bullets

        2. Statements with examples

        3. Definitions in context

  C. Concepts and Background Knowledge and Experience

        1. Used word processing, spreadsheets, and/or databases on a PC

        2. Use an e-mail account

        3. Surf the Net; play computer games

        4. Took a class that used computer-based training or long distance learning

        5. Designed an experiment or research project that depended on the computer

VIII. Summary and Key Terms

  A. Vocabulary

        1. General

                a.   Myriad

                b.   Conversant

  B. Recognition of Writing Patterns or Arrangement of Ideas and Devices

        1. Explanation

        2. Key terms used in context in short paragraphs

IX. Discussion and Problem Solving

  A. Vocabulary

        1. General

                a.   Complexion

  B. Recognition of Writing Patterns or Arrangement of Ideas and Devices

        1. Most questions are on the inferential or critical/creative levels of comprehension

ACADEMIC STUDY SKILLS

OVERVIEW

Format   Formatting is helpful in the computer chapter as an aid to comprehension. Bold and italic print serve to alert the reader to important words and phrases. Paragraphs, or bodies of information, are fairly short or are divided into sections with several subheadings. The size of print and the use of spacing are also helpful aids.

Visuals   Reading visuals and computer instructions are both necessary in the computer chapter. The visuals provided in the chapter give further examples of concepts, increase your interest in the topics, and clarify or reinforce text. The visuals include diagrams that help clarify or reinforce text, pictures of various types of computers and peripheral devices, and pictures of various pages you might see on a computer screen.

Textbook Study Aids   The textbook from which the computer chapter was taken supplies an abundance of study aids for this chapter, which include learning objectives, a motivational introduction that invites you to jump on the bandwagon of computer competency, the numbering of chapter sections, subheadings in bold print, section self-check tests with literal true/false and multiple-choice questions, a Summary and Key Terms section in which the key terms are used in context, and a Discussion and Problem Solving section with questions on the inferential and critical/creative levels of comprehension. Two special sections provide information on topics that might be of interest to the reader: Spam and online shopping. For those students using the textbook in a regular computer class, an Internet site is provided: Long and Long Internet BRIDGE (http://www.prenhall.com/long) offers Internet exercises, an interactive study guide, and a monthly technology update.

TEXTBOOK STUDY AIDS PLAN

Following is one plan of action in using the textbook aids provided for this chapter. If it does not meet your needs or approach to studying, modify it. Directions for each section are given in the pre-reading, reading, and post-reading parts of the reading plan for this chapter.

Pre-Reading   As a part of your pre-reading exercises in the Reciprocal Teaching (or alternative Active Questioning) reading plan, read the Learning Objectives and "Why This Chapter Is Important to You" at the beginning of the chapter (page 26), the Summary and Key Terms (pages 55–58) and Discussion and Problem Solving (pages 58–59) sections at the end of the chapter. If you have never used a computer or feel that you do not know very much about them, you may wish to make an informal outline of the chapter by main and subheadings. Now return to your pre-reading plan on page 8. You will be instructed during the reading and post-reading parts of your reading plan when to return to this page.

Reading   While reading the chapter according to the Reciprocal Teaching (or alternative Active Questioning) reading plan, (a) pay careful attention to main headings and subheadings, (b) take the section tests, (c) take time to carefully look at Figures 1.3, 1.4, 1.5, and 1.7 as you read the sections in which they appear. You may want to write the figure numbers on a Post-it note so that you will remember to look at them.

Post-Reading   As part of your post-reading activities, read the special sections according to your interest in the topics, "IT Ethics: The Spam Dilemma," page 30, and "Emerging IT: Online Shopping," beginning on page 39.

RECIPROCAL TEACHING

OVERVIEW

Your first step of the three-part reading plan was pre-reading. In pre-reading, you activated your prior knowledge, predicted what you would read, and overviewed the chapter before reading.

As the second step in this three-part reading plan, you will read the chapter "Information Technology in Perspective" by using the Reciprocal Teaching reading plan as explained below. An alternative plan, Active Questioning, is in Appendix A. In both plans you break up the chapter in sections and read and think about each as you read. The purpose of both plans is to keep you reading actively.

GENERAL DIRECTIONS

The concept of Reciprocal Teaching outlined here is adapted from Palinscar and Brown, 1986. Later, in Chapter 3, "Sociology: Race and Ethnicity," you will be given an updated Reciprocal Teaching order of steps.

A. Both partners read a section under a subheading at a time. Take turns summarizing the section in as few sentences as possible. In summaries, give the main ideas; do not give your opinion.

B. Take turns asking a high level question or two on each section (inferential or critical/creative).

C. Explain or clarify difficult parts to each other. Practice repeating main ideas and supporting details in your own words.

D. Read the next subheading and predict what the section will be about. Discuss (exchange) ideas.

ASSIGNMENT

Before beginning this assignment, read the "Reading" section (at the top of this page) of your Textbook Study Aids Plan in the Academic Study Skills section. The directions below are based on the Palinscar and Brown model but give step-by-step guidance and modeling. Begin reading the textbook chapter by following the directions below.

A. Read the first section, "1.1 The Information Society," and follow the directions below.

   1. Write a summary of the first major section. To write a summary, you

must first locate the main ideas in this section of the chapter. The most important subsections with their main ideas are:

a. "Rx for Cyberphobia": The main idea seems to be that people today need to be competent in information technology.

b. "The Technical Revolution": The computer is transforming the way we communicate, do business, and learn, and the personal computer helps us change. Two examples you can use to support this statement are (a) the ability to work anywhere, and (b) the ability to communicate rapidly and broadly.

c. "Looking Back a Few Years": Great strides in computer development have taken place since the 1960s.

d. "Data: Foundation for Our Information Society": Computers aid the information society by digesting data and producing information.

e. "This Course: Your Ticket to the Computer Adventure": Like the introduction, this section is motivational.

Review Section 1.1 and the above main ideas. Add or delete information as you see fit. For example, you may wish to expand the first section to include examples of competency, or you may wish to delete the examples in the second. When you have finished, write your summary in paragraph form, combining all the main ideas in this section.

Your summary _____

_____

_____

2. Write one question about something important for this section and then answer your own question. If you cannot write a question, answer the question provided. (Example of an inferential question: Look at the list of things computer-competent people can do. Which three are the most important to you? Briefly state your reasons for their importance.)

Your question _____

Your answer to your question or the one above _____

3. Identify one difficult idea from this section and then orally explain or clarify it in your own words to your partner. If you cannot think of one on your own, explain one of the examples. (Examples: Explain the difference between data and information, or explain the difference between hardware and software.)

Your idea _____

4. Predict in one sentence what you will read in the second major section, "1.2 Networking: Bringing People Together." For example, ask yourself, "What does it mean to bring people together through the use of technology?"

Your prediction _____

    B.   Read "1.2 Networking: Bringing People Together."

        1.   Summarize this second major section. Below are listed the subheadings for the two parts with their main ideas:

           a.   "The Global Village": The global village is an outgrowth of the computer network.

           b.   "The Internet and Information Services: Going Online": The Internet is a worldwide network of computers to which we gain access through Internet service providers or a commercial information service.

Review Section 1.2 and add or delete information from the main ideas above. When you have finished, write your summary in paragraph form, combining all the main ideas.

Your summary _____

_____

_____

        2.   Write one question about something important for this section and then answer your own question. If you cannot write a question, answer the question provided. (Examples of critical/creative questions: How do you access the Internet? What is the most interesting information you have found on the Net? When you are on the Net, generally how much time do you spend?)

Your question _____

Your answer to your question or the one above _____

        3.   Identify one difficult idea from this section and then orally explain or clarify it in your own words to your partner. If you cannot think of one on your own, explain the example. (Example: Expand on what a global village means.)

Your idea _____

        4.   Predict in one sentence what you will read in the third major section of the chapter, "1.3 Computers: The Essentials." Ask yourself what is essential about the computer.

Your prediction _____

    C.   Read "1.3 Computers: The Essentials."

        1.   Summarize this third major section. Following are the major sections with their main ideas:

a. "Conversational Computerese: Basic Terms and Definitions": A computer system's four basic components are *input*, *processor*, *output*, and *storage*.

b. "Computer Systems: Commuters to Wide-Bodies": The most distinguishing characteristic of any computer system is its computing capacity. Categories of computers include the personal computer, workstation, midsize mainframe, mainframe, and supercomputer.

c. "The House of Software": Two kinds of software are system software and applications software.

Review Section 1.3 and the above material. Add or delete information from the main ideas above and then write your summary in paragraph form, combining all the main ideas.

Your summary _____

_____

_____

2. Write one question about something important for this section and then answer your own question. If you cannot write a question, answer the question provided. (Examples of inferential questions: List the variety of ways output and input can be routed. Which have you used? Which would you like to learn to use?)

Your question _____

Your answer to your question or the one above _____

3. Identify one difficult idea from this section and then orally explain or clarify it in your own words to your partner. If you cannot think of one on your own, explain one of the examples. (Examples: Explain what a computer system is, or major types of computers.)

Your idea _____

4. Predict in one sentence what you will read in the fourth major section of the chapter, "1.4 Personal Computers to Supercomputers." Ask yourself what the progression is from PCs to supercomputers.

Your prediction_____

D. Read "1.4 Personal Computers to Supercomputers."
1. Summarize this fourth major section. Below are the three subheadings for this section with their main ideas.
    a. "Personal Computers": The two basic types of computers are Wintel PCs with Microsoft Windows 9x/Me/2000 operating system and the Apple Macintosh line with Mac OS operating

system. Categories of computer systems include personal computers, workstations, mainframe computers, and supercomputer systems. Unconventional PCs include slate, personal digital assistants (PDAs), and Network computers. The typical PC, which is configured for multimedia, includes several components. Workstations, used by engineers, scientists, and researchers among others, look like PCs but are very fast.

b. "Mainframe Computers": Mainframes are associated with enterprise-wide systems and are configured differently.

c. "Supercomputers": Scientists and engineers use supercomputers and they address processor-bound applications.

Review Section 1.4 and the above material. Add or delete information and then write your summary in paragraph form, combining all the main ideas.

Your summary _____

_____

_____

2. Write one question about something important for this section and then answer your own question. If you cannot write a question, answer the question provided. (Example of an inferential question: Compare/contrast PCs with mainframes and supercomputers. What can the two big computers do that PCs cannot?)

Your question _____

Your answer to your question or the one above _____

3. Identify one difficult idea from this section and then orally explain or clarify it in your own words to your partner. If you cannot think of an idea, explain the example. (Example: Describe the conventional and unconventional PCs.)

Your idea _____

4. Predict in one sentence what you will read in the fifth major section of the chapter, "1.5 A Computer System at Work." Ask yourself what a computer system does when it is working.

Your prediction_____

E. Read "1.5 A Computer System at Work."

1. Summarize this fifth major section. Following are listed the three subheadings with their major ideas.

a. "Processing Payroll: Payday": This section gives an example of the process the computer uses to make out a payroll.

b. "What Can a Computer Do?": The computer has two operations: (a) input/output and (b) processing.

c. "The Computer's Strengths": The computer's strengths include speed, accuracy, consistency, reliability, and almost unlimited memory capability.

Review Section 1.5 and the information above. Add or delete information and then write your summary in paragraph form, combining all the main ideas.

Your summary _____

_____

_____

2. Write one question about something important for this section and then answer your own question. If you cannot write a question, answer the question provided. (Example of an inferential question: In input/output operations, what does the computer do when it reads and writes?)

Your question _____

Your answer to your question or the one above _____

3. Identify one difficult idea from this section and then orally explain or clarify it in your own words to your partner. If you cannot think of one, explain the example. (Example: Explain computation and logic operations.)

Your idea _____

4. Predict in one sentence what you will read in the sixth major section of the chapter, "1.6 How Do We Use Computers?" How many ways can you think of for using a computer?

Your prediction_____

F. Read "1.6 How Do We Use Computers?"

1. Summarize this sixth major section. Following are the six subheadings with their main ideas.

a. "Information Systems": The bulk of computer use is for information systems. They support administrative aspects of an organization.

b. "Personal Computing": A variety of domestic and business applications are used. Tools include word processing, desktop publishing, spreadsheets, databases, communication, and personal information management.

c. "Communication": Communication takes place between people, and between computers. For example, computers link us to the Internet.

d. "Science, Research, and Engineering": Scientists, researchers, and engineers use computers for experimentation, design, and development.

e. "Education and Reference": CD-ROM–based computer-based training and information-based distance learning is having a profound impact on traditional modes of education.

f. "Entertainment and Edutainment": A variety of games can be played on the computer. *Edutainment* is a coined word, a combination of *education* and *entertainment*, used to describe a category of games that are educational.

Review Section 1.6 and the information above. Add or delete information, and then write your summary in paragraph form, combining all the main ideas.

Your summary _____

_____

_____

2. Write one question about something important for this section and then answer your own question. If you cannot think of a question, answer the question provided. (Examples of critical/creative questions: List ways you have used the computer. What is the last thing you learned to do on it? What interesting discoveries have you made?)

Your question _____

Your answer to your question or the one above _____

3. Identify one difficult idea from this section and then orally explain or clarify it in your own words to your partner. If you cannot think of an idea, explain the example. (Example: Discuss the productivity tools listed.)

Your idea _____

POST-READING THE TEXTBOOK CHAPTER

OVERVIEW

In the second part of your three-part reading plan, you practiced reading your textbook chapter section by section, wrote section summaries, asked and answered questions, explained or clarified important ideas, and made predictions for what you would read in the next section.

ASSIGNMENT

In this third part of the three-part reading plan, you will find suggestions for what to do after you read. Your task is to compare what you predicted with what you actually read as an aid to comprehension, to add what you have learned to your file of information on the topic, and to think about what you have read.

A. Compare what you predicted you would read with what you actually read. Did anything you predicted cause you a problem with comprehension? What? How?

B. What did you learn from the reading that you did not know about before working on this lesson?

C. Look at the words and phrases that you listed as your prior knowledge in the pre-reading section of this lesson. Group them in the table at the bottom of the page with relevant information from "B" above. This is your new file of information on computers. (The ability to group ideas and to see relationships requires more complex comprehension than merely memorizing isolated facts.)

D. What have you learned from this chapter that is important?

E. What do you already know that you can relate to it?

F. What do you see differently as a result of reading this chapter?

G. Read the "Post-Reading" section of your Textbook Study Aids Plan in the Academic Study Skills section on page 18 for directions on using other textbook aids.

Your Headings	Words and Phrases from Pre-Reading	Relevant Information from "B"

INFORMATION TECHNOLOGY IN PERSPECTIVE

 FROM LARRY LONG/NANCY LONG, *COMPUTERS, 8/E**

Learning Objectives

Once you have read and studied this chapter, you will have learned:

- The scope of information technology understanding that you will need to be an active participant in our information society (Section 1.1).
- How local and worldwide computer networks impact businesses and society (Section 1.2).
- Essential hardware, software, and computer system terminology that will enable you to begin your information technology learning adventure with confidence (Section 1.3).
- The relative size, scope, uses, and variety of available computer systems (Section 1.4).
- The fundamental complements and capabilities of a computer system (Section 1.5).
- A variety of computer and information technology applications (Section 1.6).

Why This Chapter Is Important to You

Welcome! To the computer revolution, that is. We'll be using this space to make this book very personal—to show you why studying computers and information technology is important to you, now and in the future. We're all members of a rapidly maturing information society. In this dynamic new society, people at home and in schools, institutions, and businesses are engaged in an ever-growing partnership with computers and information technology, called IT. Whether we like it or not, for good or bad, computers and technology are part of just about everything we do, during both work and play. And the fact is, computers will play an even greater role in our lives next month and in years to come.

In the 1960s, mainstreamers considered people who had anything to do with computers, especially the techies who actually touched them, to be different, even a little weird. Through the 1970s, computer illiterate people led happy and productive lives, not knowing the difference between a system bug and a byte. Well, those days are gone.

Today we're all part of an exploding information society—you, us, and the rest of the world. Computer-knowledgeable people are considered mainstream, even cool in some circles. The rest are on the outside looking in. By reading this book and taking this course, you're telling your family, friends, and, perhaps, your colleagues at work that you want to participate—to be an insider.

It's amazing how achieving information technology competency can help you keep in touch, help you learn, help make many of life's little chores easier and more fun, help you earn more money, and that's the tip of the iceberg. Upon successful completion of this course, you will be information technology competent. In most fields, this competency is considered critical to *getting* and *keeping* a good job. Your adventure into this amazing world of technology begins right here. Have fun!

1.1 The Information Society

Where will you be and what will you be doing in the year 2010? This is a tough question even for technology experts who are reluctant to speculate more than a few months into the future. Things are changing too quickly. A stream of exciting new innovations in **information technology (IT)** continues to change what we do and how we think. We use the term IT to refer to the integration of computing technology and information processing.

Most of us are doing what we can to adapt to this new **information society** where **knowledge workers** channel their energies to provide a wealth of computer-based information services. A knowledge worker's job function revolves around the use, manipulation, and broadcasting of information. Your knowledge of computers will help you cope with and understand today's technology so you can take your place in the information society, both at the workplace and during your leisure time.

Rx for Cyberphobia: Information Technology Competency

Not too long ago, people who pursued careers in almost any facet of business, education, or government were content to leave computers to computer professionals. Today these people are knowledge workers. In less than a generation, **information technology competency (IT competency)** has emerged in virtually any career from a *nice-to-have skill* to a *job-critical skill*.

If you're afraid of computers, information technology competency is a sure cure. IT competency will allow you to be an active and effective participant in the emerging information society. You and other IT-competent people will:

- Feel comfortable using and operating a computer system.
- Be able to make the computer work for you. The IT-competent person can use the computer to solve an endless stream of life's problems, from how to pass away a couple of idle hours to how to increase company revenues.
- Be able to interact with the computer—that is, generate input to the computer and interpret output from it. **Input** is data entered to a computer system for processing. **Output** is the presentation of the results of processing (for example, a printed résumé or a tax return).
- Be comfortable in cyberspace. Cyberspace is a nonphysical world made possible by a worldwide network of computer systems. Once in cyberspace, you can communicate with one another and literally travel the virtual world, visiting Walt Disney World in Florida, the Louvre Museum in Paris, and a million other interesting places.
- Understand the impact of computers on society, now and in the future. Automation is having such a profound impact on society that we must position ourselves to act responsibly to ensure that these changes are in the right direction.
- Be an intelligent consumer of computers and computer equipment, collectively called **hardware**. Smart computer shoppers save a lot of money, usually getting what they need, not what someone else says they need.
- Be an intelligent consumer of software and other nonhardware-related computer products and services. **Software** refers to a collective set of instructions, called **programs**,

that can be interpreted by a computer. The programs cause the computer to perform desired functions, such as flight simulation (a computer game), the generation of business graphics, or word processing.

- Be conversant in the language of computers and information technology. In this book, you will learn those terms and phrases that not only are the foundation of computer terminology but also are very much a part of everyday conversation at school, home, and work.

The Technology Revolution

In an information society, the focus of commerce becomes the generation and distribution of information. A technological revolution is changing our way of life: the way we live, work, and play. The cornerstone of this revolution, the computer, is transforming the way we communicate, do business, and learn.

Personal computers, or **PCs**, offer a vast array of *enabling technologies*. Enabling technologies help us do things. For example, PCs have maps that pinpoint your location to help you navigate the streets of the world. They have presentation tools that help you make your point when you get there. Already, you need go no farther than your home computer to get the best deal on a new car, send your congressperson a message, order tickets to the theater, play chess with a grand master in Russia, or listen to a radio station in New Zealand.

- Millions of people can be "at work" wherever they are as long as they have their portable personal computers—at a client's office, in an airplane, or at home. The *mobile worker's* personal computer provides electronic links to a vast array of information and to clients and corporate colleagues.

- Increasingly, the computer helps us communicate, whether with our colleagues at work through **electronic mail (e-mail)** or with our friends through **newsgroups**. Both electronic mail and newsgroups allow us to send/receive information via computer-to-computer hookups.

- Comic strips routinely rely on cybertalk for laughs, especially Dilbert, which is set in a corporate cubicle city. In one Dilbert strip (written by Scott Adams), the clueless pointy-haired boss commented, "I don't see why our Web pages need URLs. Get rid of them." Engineer Dilbert responds with "Give me a month and I'll replace our URLs with Uniform Resource Locators." The IT-savvy reader, knowing that URLs and Uniform Resource Locators are one in the same, will laugh. Others won't get it or any other comic strip punch lines with an IT edge.

That's today. *Tomorrow*, the next wave of enabling technologies will continue to cause radical changes in our lives. For example, if you're in the market for a new home, you will be able to "visit" any home for sale in the country from the comfort of your own home or office via computer. All you will need to do is tell the computer what city to look in and then enter your search criteria (price range, house style, and so on). The electronic realtor will then list those houses that meet your criteria, provide you with detailed information on the house and surrounding area, then offer to take you on a tour of the house—inside and out. After the virtual tour, you will be able to "drive" through the neighborhood, looking left and right as you would in your automobile. Such systems may seem a bit futuristic, but virtually all of California's real estate listings can be viewed on your computer. Systems that permit neighborhood drive-throughs are under active development!

Each day new applications, such as a national multilist for real estate, as well as thousands of companies, schools, and individuals, are being added to the world's information infrastructure. The infrastructure, sometimes called the **information superhighway**, encompasses a network of electronic links that eventually will connect virtually every facet of our society, both public (perhaps the local supermarket) and private (perhaps to Aunt Minnie's recipes).

Looking Back a Few Years

To put the emerging information society into perspective, let's flash back a half century and look *briefly* at the evolution of computing.

- Fifty years ago, our parents and grandparents built ships, kept financial records, and performed surgery, all without the aid of computers. Indeed, everything they did was without computers. There were no computers!

- In the 1960s, mammoth multimillion-dollar computers processed data for those large companies that could afford them. These computers, the domain of highly specialized technical gurus, remained behind locked doors. In "the old days," business computer systems were designed so a computer professional served as an intermediary between the **user**—someone who uses a computer—and the computer system.

- In the mid-1970s, computers became smaller, less expensive, and more accessible to smaller companies and even individuals. This trend resulted in the introduction of personal computers. During the 1980s, millions of people from all walks of life purchased these miniature miracles. Suddenly, computers were for everyone!

- Today, one in two Americans has a computer at home or work more powerful than those that processed data for multinational companies during the 1960s. The widespread availability of computers has prompted an explosion of applications. At the individual level, we can use our PCs to go on an electronic fantasy adventure or hold an electronic reunion with our scattered family. At the corporate level, virtually every business has embraced information technology. Companies in every area of business are using IT to offer better services and gain a competitive advantage.

Data: Foundation for Our Information Society

Data (the plural of *datum*) are just raw facts. Data are all around us. Every day we generate an enormous amount of data. **Information** is data that have been collected and processed into a meaningful form. Simply, information is the meaning we give to accumulated facts (data). Information as we now know it, though, is a relatively new concept. Just 50 short years ago, *information* was the telephone operator who provided directory assistance. Around 1950, people began to view information as something that could be collected, sorted, summarized, exchanged, and processed. But only during the last decade have computers allowed us to begin tapping the potential of information.

Computers are very good at digesting data and producing information. For example, when you call a mail-order merchandiser, the data you give the sales representative (name, address, product number) are entered directly into the merchandiser's computer. When you run short of cash and stop at an automatic teller machine, all data you enter, including that on the magnetic stripe of your bankcard, are processed immediately by the bank's computer system. A

IT ETHICS

The Spam Dilemma

As we all know, Spam is a popular Hormel meat product. By some unlucky quirk of fate, unsolicited e-mail was given the same name—spam. To Netizens, citizens of the Internet, spam is the Internet equivalent of junk mail and those dreaded telemarketing calls. To the senders of junk e-mail, spam is simply bulk e-mail, usually some kind of advertisement and/or an invitation to try some service or product. Spam may be unsolicited religious, racial, or sexual messages, as well. Such messages can be especially irritating. Generally, Internet users loathe spamming because spammers (those who send spam) use the shotgun approach, broadcasting their message to large numbers of people. Inevitably, enough of these messages find a welcome audience, prompting spammers to send more spam.

Those who receive e-mail consider their e-mail boxes a personal and costly resource. They feel that spam wastes their time, violates their electronic mailbox, and in some cases insults their integrity. On the other hand, spammers cite free speech and the tradition of a free flow of information over the Internet as justification for broadcasting their messages. Spam renews the conflict between free speech and the individual's right to privacy.

Discussion Currently laws favor the spammers, that is, there is little an individual can do to thwart the barrage of junk mail. Do you believe legislation should be enacted to control unsolicited e-mail over the Internet? Explain.

computer system eventually manipulates your *data* to produce *information*. The information could be an invoice from a mail-order house or a bank statement.

Traditionally, we have thought of data in terms of numbers (account balance) and letters (customer name), but recent advances in information technology have opened the door to data in other formats, such as visual images. For example, dermatologists (physicians who specialize in skin disorders) use digital cameras to take close-up pictures of patients' skin conditions. Each patient's **record** (information about the patient) on the computer-based **master file** (all patient records) is then updated to include the digital image. During each visit, the dermatologist recalls the patient record, which includes color images of the skin during previous visits. Data can also be found in the form of sound. For example, data collected during noise-level testing of automobiles include digitized versions of the actual sounds heard within the car.

The relationship of data to a computer system is much like the relationship of gasoline to an automobile. Data provide the fuel for a computer system. Your car won't get you anywhere without gas, and your computer won't produce any information without data.

This Course: Your Ticket to the Computer Adventure

You are about to embark on a journey that will stimulate your imagination, challenge your every resource, from physical dexterity to intellect, and alter your sense of perspective on technology. Learning about computers is more than just education. It's an adventure!

Gaining information technology competency is just the beginning—your computer adventure lasts a lifetime. Information technology is changing every minute of the day. Every year, hundreds of new IT-related buzz words, concepts, applications, and hardware devices will confront you. Fortunately, you will have established a base of IT knowledge (information technology competency) upon which you can build and continue your learning adventure.

✔ Section Self-Check ✔

1.1.1 To be IT-competent, you must be able to write computer programs. (T/F)

1.1.2 Data are the raw facts from which information is derived. (T/F)

1.1.3 Hardware refers collectively to computers and computer equipment. (T/F)

1.1.4 The term used to describe the integration of computing technology and information processing is: (a) information technology, (b) information handling, (c) software, or (d) data tech?

1.1.5 A person whose job revolves around the use, manipulation, and dissemination of information is called: (a) an office wunderkind, (b) a knowledge worker, (c) a data expert, or (d) an info being?

1.1.6 Generally, what is the presentation of the results of processing called: (a) output, (b) printout, (c) outcome, or (d) download?

1.2 Networking: Bringing People Together

So far we know that computers are extremely good at bringing together data to produce information. Computers also bring together people, from all over the world, resulting in improved communication and cooperation.

The Global Village

In 1967 Marshall McLuhan said, "The new electronic interdependence recreates the world in the image of a global village." His insightful declaration is now clearly a matter of fact. At present, we live in a *global village* in which computers and people are linked within companies and between countries. The global village is an outgrowth of the **computer network**. Most existing computers are linked electronically to a network of one or more computers to share hardware/software resources and information. When we tap into networked computers, we can hold electronic meetings with widely dispersed colleagues, retrieve information from the corporate database, make hotel reservations, and much, much more.

On a more global scale, computer networks enable worldwide airline reservation data to be entered in the Bahamas and American insurance claims to be processed in Ireland. Securities can be traded simultaneously on the New York Stock Exchange and other exchanges around the world by people in Hong Kong, Los Angeles, and Berlin. Computer networks can coordinate the purchases of Korean electronics, American steel, and Indonesian glass to make cars in Japan, and can then be used to track sales of those cars worldwide. Lotteries are no longer confined to a state, or even the nation. Internet-based lotteries draw players from the entire world, paying huge pots to the winners.

Thanks to computer networks, we are all part of a global economy, in which businesses find partners, customers, suppliers, and competitors around the world. The advent of this global economy is changing society across the board, often in subtle ways. For example, customer service may continue to improve as companies realize how quickly an irate customer can broadcast messages vilifying a company or a particular product to millions of potential customers via the information superhighway. Computers, related hardware, and software products are especially vulnerable to such customer attacks. If a product does not stand up to advertised capabilities, the computing community will quickly expose its shortcomings to potential buyers. This same level of scrutiny will ultimately be applied to other products and services. For example, there are hundreds of newsgroups devoted exclusively to discussions of restaurants in various cities and countries. In these cities and countries, you can be sure that frequent diners know which restaurants offer good food and value and which ones do not. These and thousands of other special-topic newsgroups can be found on the Internet.

Figure 1.1   Shopping on the Internet
You can shop the electronic malls of the information superhighway to find exactly what you want, whether it's a pasta maker or a home.

The Internet and Information Services: Going Online

The Internet, also known simply as **the Net**, is a worldwide network of computers that has emerged as *the* enabling technology in our migration to a global village. It connects hundreds of thousands of networks, millions of computers, and almost a billion users in every country. Most colleges are on the Net; that is, they have an Internet account. The same is true of business. The Internet can be accessed by people in these organizations with established links to the Internet and by individuals with PCs. If you have access to a computer at work or at a college computer lab, the PCs are probably "on the Net" (see Figure 1.1). Typically, individuals gain access to the Internet by subscribing to an **Internet service provider (ISP)**. For a monthly fee, you can link your PC to the ISP's computer, thus gaining access to the Net. An ISP is a company with an Internet account that provides individuals and organizations access to, or

presence on, the Internet. Another way to get on the Net is to subscribe to a commercial **information service**, such as **America Online** (see Figure 1.2). These and other commercial information services have one or several large computer systems that offer a wide range of information services over their proprietary network, which, of course, is linked to the Net. **AOL** services include up-to-the-minute news and weather, electronic shopping, e-mail, and much, much more. The services and information provided by the Net and information services are **online**; that is, once the user has established a communications link between his or her PC, the user becomes part of the network. When online, the user interacts directly with the computers in the information network to access desired information and services. When the user terminates the link, the user goes **offline**.

Figure 1.2   America Online

America Online (AOL) is the most popular online information service and is the primary way that millions of people access the Internet. AOL has 18 channels, or interest areas, from which to choose (listed on the left of the Welcome viewing window). It also has a variety of other services. Shown here is the Welcome screen, which usually announces, "You've got mail," when you "sign on," the online interactive calendar (note the weather forecast icons), the personal address book, the buddy list (which alerts you when one of your buddies signs on so you can chat), and a chat room conversation.

The Internet emerged from a government-sponsored project to promote the interchange of scientific information. This spirit of sharing continues as the overriding theme over the Internet. For example, aspiring writers having difficulty getting read or published can make their writing available to millions of readers, including agents and publishers, in a matter of minutes. Unknown musicians also use the Internet to gain recognition. *Surfers* on the Internet (Internet users) wanting to read a story or listen to a song **download** the text or a digitized version of a song (like those on an audio CD) to their personal computer, then read it or play it through their personal computer. Downloading is simply transmitting information from a remote computer (in this case, an Internet-based computer) to a local computer (in most cases a PC). Information (perhaps a story or a song) going the other way, from a local computer to a remote computer, is said to be **uploaded**.

This spirit of sharing has prompted individuals and organizations all over the world to make available information and databases on a wide variety of topics. This wonderful distribution and information-sharing vehicle is, of course, a boon for businesses. Thousands of publishers, corporations, government agencies, colleges, and database services give Internet users access to their information—some provide information gratis and some charge a fee. Over the next few years look for more and more businesses to use the Internet to generate revenue.

Services and capabilities of the Internet and commercial information services are growing daily. For example, a hungry traveler on the Internet can now order a pizza via the Net from a large number of online pizza delivery services. It works pretty much like a telephone order, except you enter the information on your PC, and it is routed immediately to the pizza shop nearest you. Usually, the order is displayed for the pizza chef within seconds. Of course, you can't download a pizza—it has to be delivered in the traditional manner. Already you can order almost any consumer item from tulips to trucks through the electronic malls (see Figure 1.1).

Services available from the publicly available Internet and the subscription-based information services play a major role in shaping our information society. We'll discuss both in considerable detail throughout the book.

✔ Section Self-Check ✔

1.2.1 Uploading on the Internet is transmitting information from an Internet-based host computer to a local PC. (T/F)

1.2.2 A global network called the Internet links millions of computers throughout the world. (T/F)

1.2.3 Mail sent electronically is called: (a) snail mail, (b) quick mail, (c) e-mail, or (d) e-news?

1.2.4 A computer network links computers to enable the: (a) linking of terminals and HDTV hookups, (b) sharing of resources and information, (c) distribution of excess processor capabilities, or (d) expansion of processing capabilities?

1.2.5 When the user terminates the link with a commercial information service, the user goes: (a) offline, (b) on-log, (c) out-of-site, or (d) online?

1.3 Computers: The Essentials

Almost everyone in our information society has a basic understanding of what a computer is and what it can do. This book is designed to add a little depth to what you already know.

Conversational Computerese: Basic Terms and Definitions

The **computer**, also called a **processor**, is an *electronic device that can interpret and execute programmed commands for input, output, computation, and logic operations.* That's a mouthful. But computers aren't as complicated as you might have been led to believe. A **computer system** has only four basic components: *input, processor, output,* and *storage* (see Figure 1.3). Note that the processor, or computer, is just one component in a computer system. It gives the computer system its intelligence, performing all computation and logic operations. In everyday conversation people simply say "computer" when they talk about a computer system. We'll do this as well throughout this book. We'll refer specifically to the processor when discussing that part of the computer system that does the processing.

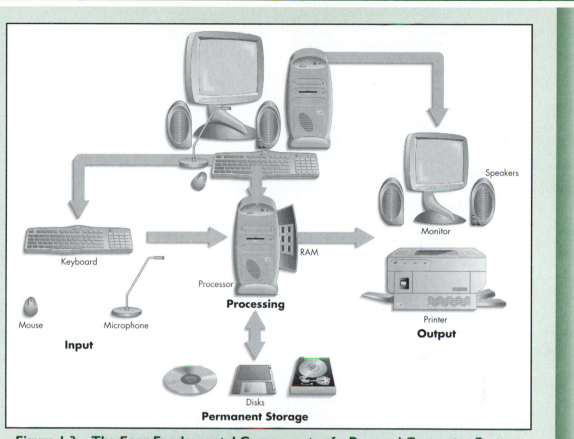

Speakers

Monitor

RAM

Processor

Processing

Keyboard

Mouse

Microphone

Input

Printer

Output

Disks

Permanent Storage

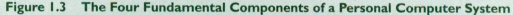

Figure 1.3   The Four Fundamental Components of a Personal Computer System

In a personal computer system, the storage and processing components are often contained in the same physical unit. In the illustration, the disk-storage medium is inserted into the unit that contains the processor.

Each of the components in a computer system can take on a variety of forms. For example, *output* (the results of processing) can be routed to a televisionlike **monitor**, audio speakers (like those on your stereo system), or a **printer** (see Figure 1.3). The output on a monitor, which is temporary, is called **soft copy**. Printers produce **hard copy**, or printed output that can be physically handled, folded, and so on. Data can be entered to a computer system for processing (input) via a **keyboard** (for keyed input), a microphone (for voice and sound input), or a **point-and-draw device**, such as a **mouse** (see Figure 1.3).

Storage of data and software in a computer system is either *temporary* or *permanent*. **Random-access memory** (**RAM**, rhymes with "ham") provides temporary storage of data and programs during processing within solid-state **integrated circuits**. Integrated circuits, or **chips**, are tiny (about .5 inch square) silicon chips into which thousands of electronic components are etched. The processor is also a chip. Permanently installed and interchangeable **disks** provide permanent storage for data and programs (see Figure 1.3). Information is read from and written to a variety of disks. Because the surface of circular, spinning disks is coated with easily magnetized elements, such as nickel, they sometimes are called magnetic disks. A computer system is comprised of its internal components (for example, RAM and special features) and its **peripheral devices** (printer, various disk-storage devices, monitor, and so on).

Computer Systems: Commuters to Wide-Bodies

Computers can be found in a variety of shapes, from cube-shaped to U-shaped to cylindrical to notebook-shaped. However, the most distinguishing characteristic of any computer system is its *size*—not its physical size, but its *computing capacity*. Loosely speaking, size, or computing capacity, is the amount of processing that can be accomplished by a computer system per unit of time. **Mainframe computers** have greater computing capacities than do personal computers, which are also called **microcomputers**. Mainframe computers vary greatly in size from midsized mainframes serving small companies to large mainframes serving thousands of people. And **supercomputers**, packing the most power, have greater computing capacities than do mainframe computers. Depending on its sophistication, a **workstation's** computing capacity falls somewhere between that of a PC and a midsized mainframe. Some vendors are not content with pigeonholing their products into one of these four major categories, so they have created new niches, such as *desktop mainframes*. In this book, we will limit our discussion to these four major categories (see Figure 1.4).

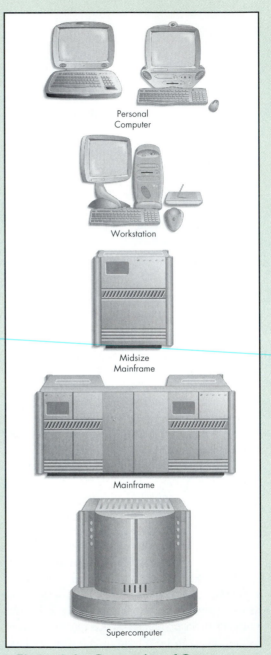

Personal
Computer

Workstation

Midsize
Mainframe

Mainframe

Supercomputer

Figure 1.4   Categories of Computers

We should emphasize that these categories are relative. What people call a personal computer system today may be called a workstation at some time in the future.

PCs, workstations, mainframes, and supercomputers are computer systems. Each offers many **input/output**, or **I/O**, alternatives—ways to enter data to the system and to present information generated by the system. All computer systems, no matter how small or large, have the same fundamental capabilities—*input*, *processing*, *output*, and *storage*. Keep this in mind as you encounter the computer systems shown in Figure 1.4 at school and at work. In keeping with conversational computerese, we will drop the word system when discussing the categories of computer systems. Keep in mind, however, that a reference to any of these categories (for example, supercomputer) implies a reference to the entire computer system.

The differences in the various categories of computers are very much a matter of scale. Try thinking of a *supercomputer* as a *wide-body jet* and a *personal computer* as a *commuter plane*. Both types of airplanes have the same fundamental capability—they carry passengers from one location to another. Wide-bodies, which fly at close to the speed of sound, can carry hundreds of passengers. In contrast, commuter planes travel much slower and carry fewer than 50 passengers. Wide-bodies travel between large international airports, across countries, and between continents. Commuter planes travel short distances between regional airports. The commuter plane, with its small crew, can land, unload, load, and be on its way to another destination in 15 to 20 minutes. The wide-body may take 30 minutes just to unload. A PC is much like the commuter plane in that one person can get it up and running in just a few minutes. All aspects of the PC are controlled by one person. The supercomputer is like the wide-body in that a number of specialists are needed to keep it operational. No matter what their size, airplanes fly and carry passengers and computers process data and produce information. Besides obvious differences in size, the various types of computers differ mostly in how they are used. Section 1.4 should give you insight into when and where a particular system might be used.

The House of Software

Software refers to any program that tells the computer system what to do. Of course, there are many different types of software. The more you understand about the scope and variety of available software, the more effective you will be as a user. Actually, understanding software is a lot like being in a big house—once you know its layout, you're able to move about the house much easier.

Once but a cottage, the house of software is now a spacious eight-room house (in a few years, it will be a mansion). Figure 1.5 (on page 38) shows the blueprint for today's house of software, with the rooms arranged by function. The entryway in the house of software consists of **system software**. When you turn on the computer, the first actions you see are directed by system software. System software programs take control of the PC on start up and then play a central role in everything that happens within a computer system by managing, maintaining, and controlling computer resources. The software from the other rooms, collectively known as **applications software**, is designed and created to perform specific personal, business, or scientific processing tasks, such as word processing, tax planning, or interactive gaming. We'll visit every room in the house by the time you finish this book.

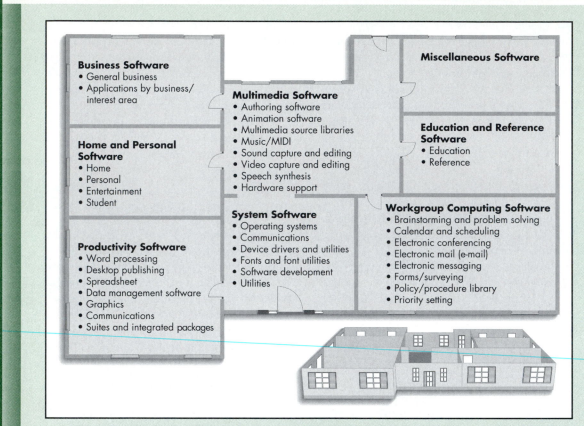

Business Software
• General business
• Applications by business/
  interest area

Home and Personal Software
• Home
• Personal
• Entertainment
• Student

Productivity Software
• Word processing
• Desktop publishing
• Spreadsheet
• Data management software
• Graphics
• Communications
• Suites and integrated packages

Multimedia Software
• Authoring software
• Animation software
• Multimedia source libraries
• Music/MIDI
• Sound capture and editing
• Video capture and editing
• Speech synthesis
• Hardware support

System Software
• Operating systems
• Communications
• Device drivers and utilities
• Fonts and font utilities
• Software development
• Utilities

Miscellaneous Software

Education and Reference Software
• Education
• Reference

Workgroup Computing Software
• Brainstorming and problem solving
• Calendar and scheduling
• Electronic conferencing
• Electronic mail (e-mail)
• Electronic messaging
• Forms/surveying
• Policy/procedure library
• Priority setting

Figure 1.5   The House of Software

This blueprint shows the layout of the house of software. The rooms are laid out to feature software in eight major areas.

✔   Section Self-Check   ✔

1.3.1 Output on a monitor is soft copy and output on a printer is hard copy. (T/F)

1.3.2 Supercomputers have greater computing capacity than mainframe computers. (T/F)

1.3.3 Only personal computers offer a variety of I/O alternatives. (T/F)

1.3.4 Applications software takes control of a PC on start up and then controls all system software activities during the computing session. (T/F)

1.3.5 A printer is an example of which of the four computer system components: (a) input, (b) output, (c) processor, or (d) storage?

1.3.6 Integrated circuits are also called: (a) slivers, (b) chips, (c) flakes, or (d) electronic sandwiches?

1.3.7 Which component of a computer system executes the program: (a) input, (b) output, (c) processor, or (d) storage?

EMERGING IT

Online Shopping: Let Your Fingers Do the Walking

How would you like to do a week's worth of grocery shopping in 10 minutes? Purchase gourmet chocolates without being tempted by the goodies in the candy counter? Book your airline and motel reservations without making a dozen calls? Check out job openings in your area of the country? Send flowers (virtual and real)? Trade stocks online? Do your banking transactions from home? Rather than loading the kids into the SUV or minivan on shopping day, you can send them out to play and do your shopping and other business from the comfort of your home. Millions of busy people have traded their shopping carts for keyboards to take advantage of the emergence of e-commerce (electronic commerce is doing any kind of business electronically over a network or the Internet). Shoppers log on to the Internet, a new channel for buying and selling goods and services.

People go online to shop for many reasons. The reason cited most often is that the stores are always open. People love the convenience of shopping anytime—day or night—and in whatever they happen to be wearing. People also go online to save time. They avoid traffic, crowds, lines, and the never-ending search for a parking place. Another reason is product availability. You may need to go to a dozen different shoe stores to find a particular style and size of sneaker. In contrast, an e-tailer would offer every style in every size for one-stop shopping. Increasingly, shoppers are noting price and service as reasons to shop electronically. Many e-tailers (online retailers) can sell for less, sometimes a lot less. They can keep a low inventory (or no inventory when items are shipped directly from the manufacturer). Plus, they avoid the real estate and personnel expenses associated with a traditional storefront. E-tailers can offer a variety of services that might not be available in a traditional store. For example, an online bookstore might notify you via e-mail when a particular book is available in paperback.

Of course, the traditional storefront has its advantages as well. Shoppers can interact with a real, live salesperson and they can take their purchases home on the same day. You can try on clothes and drive cars before you buy them. Eventually, however, forecasters predict that these advantages may not be enough as e-tailers begin to find ways to satisfy customer demands. Already, online shoppers can create three-dimensional models of themselves for when they wish to "try on" clothes. This may not be the same, but will it be enough when combined with the other conveniences of online shopping?

Currently, the most popular consumer items purchased over the Internet are books, CDs, and all computer products. However, action is rapidly increasing on everything from groceries to sneakers. Internet auction sites do a brisk business in literally thousands of different areas, including Beanie Babies, printers, and pocket knives. Online shoppers can purchase toys, electronics, greeting cards, automobiles, securities, houses, U.S. stamps, just about anything that Wal-Mart sells, and a lot more.

Popularity of Online Retailing Is Growing Fast

In a few years, according to projections, e-commerce in cyberspace will be just as significant as in-person, mail, and telephone sales. If businesses are not planning for this real-time economy, they may not be doing business to the fullest (if at all) in the twenty-first century.

Up to this point, most e-commerce is done from business-to-business. Forecasters predict U.S. online business-to-business sales to be over a trillion dollars within a few years. Online retailing (business-to-consumer) is less, but it's exploding in popularity. A variety of sources report online shopping is escalating at rates from 400 percent a year to 400 percent a month. And, the rate of growth is expected to accelerate next year. Any business that hopes to stay in business in the next millennium is offering or planning to offer its products and/or services online. If there is a demand for a product or service, there is probably a site on the Internet to meet it. These few examples should give you some insight into what we have and can expect in the near future.

Groceries Online

"Smart Shopping for Busy People"® is Peapod's slogan. Peapod, a grocer on the Internet, has made life easier for a great many people in many large cities throughout the United States. Peapod is giving us a glimpse into the future of retailing—the virtual grocery store. Peapod is a pioneer in a rapidly expanding industry that is dedicated to enabling us to buy almost anything from our PCs. Peapod subscribers go shopping at the virtual grocery store by logging on to the Peapod site on the Internet. Once online, they can shop interactively for grocery items, including fresh produce, deli, bakery, meat, and frozen products. Rather than running from aisle to aisle, you simply point and click around the screen for the items you want.

Peapod's online shopping system is linked directly to its partner stores' computer systems (for example, Safeway in San Francisco and Jewel in Chicago). When you send your shopping list to Peapod, an order is transmitted to the nearest partner store. A professionally trained shopper takes your order, grabs a shopping cart, and does your shopping for you. The professional shopper takes a fraction of the time you would take because the list is ordered by aisle and the shopper knows exactly what to get. You can redeem your coupons when the shopper/delivery person arrives with your food. Food is delivered in temperature-controlled containers. Peapod is far from alone, as others, including Wal-Mart, have begun to offer online grocery services. This is one of many interactive online approaches to shopping that can help take the hassle out of shopping.

Books and CDs Online

If you've traveled in the World Wide Web at all, you've probably run across Amazon.com and Barnesandnoble.com, two of the most well-known online stores.

These virtual stores are more than just bookstores. They offer millions of books, CDs, audiobooks, DVDs, computer games, and more, including customer reviews, personal recommendations, best-seller lists, musical chart toppers, and gift suggestions. From alternative to Zydeco, Hip-hop to Bebop, their online customers will find everything from the latest releases to hard-to-find gems in nearly 300 musical genres.

Stocks and Bonds Online

Why would you want to make online investments electronically through an online brokerage service instead of through a full-service broker? Those who do cite price and the ability to make their own trading decisions as the main reasons they go online. To date, online companies have been very competitive on price, a serious motivator to savvy investors. Generally an online trading charge is much less than that of a traditional broker (from under $10 to $30, sometimes less than 10% that of a similar trade through a traditional broker). Frequent users of online brokerage services enjoy the autonomy of having the information resources they need to do their own research.

Currently only about 4 percent of U.S. households are involved in online finance. This includes securities trading and online banking. However, online trading companies are experiencing tremendous growth in trading volume as more and more investors switch to online trading.

Online trading companies, such as E-Trade Group Inc., Charles Schwab & Co. Inc., and Datek Online Brokerage Services Corporation, are providing online discount brokerage services, including automated order placement, portfolio tracking and related market information, news, and other information services 24 hours a day, 7 days a week. Online services offer essentially the same order options as their full-service cousins, including limit, stop, and stop limit orders for all securities trading on U.S. exchanges. And, the services usually are free. The investor pays only a relatively small fee to place the order.

Online Auctions: Going. Going. Gone!

You can be part of a live auction 24 hours a day when you visit the eBay or ONSALE sites. Just enter "online auctions" into an Internet search engine and you'll be amazed at what can be traded, bought, and sold.

Every day you can experience a new set of auctions where you will find thousands of items on which to bid. eBay boasts itself as the world's largest personal online trading community with more than 1 million registered users. Individuals can use eBay to buy and sell items in more than 1000 categories, including collectibles, antiques, sports memorabilia, computers, toys, Beanie Babies, dolls, figures, coins, stamps, books, magazines, music, pottery, glass, photography, electronics, jewelry, gemstones, and much more. Users can find the unique and the interesting on eBay—everything from china to chintz chairs, teddy bears to trains, and furniture to figurines.

Even Universal Studios has online auctions of exclusive celebrity memorabilia and collectibles direct from popular movies, television shows, and entertainment in Hollywood.

The Future of Retailing

The future of online retailing and selling is very bright, but what about traditional approaches to sales? What will become of our department stores, specialty stores, bookstores, and so on? It is unlikely that any of these would disappear anytime soon; however, it's apparent that people are shopping and buying more at the virtual store and less at the bricks and mortar store. Each approach has its advantages. It looks like we'll still have the option to shop downtown or online for the foreseeable future.

1.4 Personal Computers to Supercomputers

Every 10 hours, more computers are sold than existed in the entire world 30 years ago. Back then, computers were expensive and came in one size—big. Today, computers come in a variety of sizes. In this section we discuss the capabilities and uses of the four basic categories of computers: (1) personal computers, (2) workstations, (3) mainframes, and (4) supercomputers.

Personal Computers

In 1981, IBM introduced its **IBM PC** and it legitimized the personal computer as a business tool. Shortly after that, other manufacturers began making PCs that were 100% compatible with the IBM PC; that is, they basically worked like an IBM PC. Most of today's personal computers (over 80%) evolved from these original PC-compatibles. Long removed from the IBM PC, they are also called **Wintel PCs** because they use the Microsoft *Windows 9x/Me/2000* (a collective reference to *Microsoft Windows® 95, Windows® 98, Windows® Millennium, Windows® NT,* or *Windows® 2000*) control software and an Intel Corporation or Intel-compatible processor. Each of the *Microsoft Windows 9x/Me/2000* family of **operating systems** controls all hardware and software activities on Wintel PCs.

The Wintel PC represents the dominant PC platform. A **platform** defines a standard for which software is developed. Specifically, a platform is defined by two key elements:

- The processor (for example, Intel® Pentium® II, Intel® Pentium® III, Intel® Celeron™, Intel Itaniume, Motorola® PowerPC®, AMD Athlon, and so on)
- The operating system (for example, Windows® 2000, Mac® OS X, Unix®, Linux, and so on)

Generally, software created to run on one platform is not compatible with any other platform. Most of the remaining personal computers are part of the Apple *Macintosh®* line of computers or the Apple *iMac™* line of computers. The Macintosh uses the Mac® OS operating system, and the new *iMac™* uses Apple's next-generation operating system, the *Mac® OS X*. Both are powered by Motorola® *PowerPC®* processors.

One person at a time uses a PC. The user turns on the PC, selects the software to be run, enters the data, and requests the information. The PC, like other computers, is very versatile and has been used for everything from communicating with business colleagues to controlling household appliances. Computerese is like spoken English in that more than one term can be coined to describe something. For example, the terms *personal computer, PC, microcomputer,* and *micro* are used interchangeably in practice. The personal computer is actually a family of computers, some conventional and some unconventional.

Conventional PCs: Pockets, Laptops, Desktops, and Towers

Conventional personal computers have a full keyboard, a monitor, and can function as stand-alone systems. These PCs can be categorized as *pocket PCs, laptop PCs, desktop PCs,* and *tower PCs.*

Pocket and Laptop PCs **Pocket PCs** and **laptop PCs** are light (a few ounces to about eight pounds), compact, and are called "portable" because they have batteries and can operate with or without an external power source. The pocket PC, sometimes called a **palmtop PC**, literally can fit in a coat pocket or a handbag. Laptops, which weigh from three to eight pounds, often are called **notebook PCs** because they are about the size of a one-inch-thick notebook.

The power of a PC may not be related to its size. A few laptop PCs can run circles around some tower PCs. Some user conveniences, however, must be sacrificed to achieve portability. For instance, input devices, such as keyboards and point-and-draw devices, are given less space in portable PCs and may be more cumbersome to use. This is particularly true of pocket PCs, in which miniaturized keyboards make data entry and interaction with the computer difficult and slow. The display screen on some pocket PCs is monochrome (as opposed to color) and may be difficult to read under certain lighting situations. Portable computers take up less space and, therefore, have a smaller capacity for permanent storage of data and programs. Laptop battery life can be as little as a couple of hours for older models to 20 hours for state-of-the-art rechargeable lithium batteries.

The 2-in-1 PC can be used as both a notebook and a desktop PC. It has two parts: a fully functional *notebook PC* and a **docking station**. Two-in-one PCs have a configuration that allows users to enjoy the best of both worlds—portability and the expanded features of a desktop. The notebook, which supplies the processor, is simply inserted into or removed from the docking station, depending on the needs of the user. The docking station can be *configured* to give the docked notebook PC the look and feel of a desktop PC. That is, the docking station can expand the notebook's capabilities and might include more disk storage, a CD-ROM drive, several interchangeable disk options, a full-size keyboard, a large monitor, and expansion slots into which still other features can be added to the system (for example, circuitry that would enable television programming to be viewed on the PC's monitor). Usually, docking stations provide a direct link to the corporate network.

Another notebook option, called the **port replicator**, works like the docking station in that the notebook PC is inserted into it and removed as needed. Once inserted the notebook can use the port replicator **ports** and whatever is connected to them. Ports are electronic interfaces through which devices like the keyboard, monitor, mouse, printer, and so on are connected. Port replicators also provide bigger speakers and an AC power source, and some include a network connector.

Desktop PCs and Tower PCs **Desktop PCs** and **tower PCs** are not considered portable because they rely on an outside power source and are not designed for frequent movement. Typically, the desktop PC's monitor is positioned on top of the processing component. The processing component of the tower PC is designed to sit upright, like a desktop PC's processing component standing on its end. The taller towers (over two feet) are usually placed beside or under a desk, and the smaller mini-tower may be placed in any convenient location (on a nearby shelf, on the desk, or on the floor).

Of the two, the tower has emerged as the most popular, primarily because it has a smaller *footprint* (the surface space used by the unit). The laptop, which costs about twice that of a comparable tower PC, is gaining ground. About one in three PCs sold are laptops.

The Extended PC Family: Slate PCs, PDAs, and NCs

The conventional members of the PC family have several unconventional cousins. These personal computers may be designed for special applications or for use in a particular computing environment.

Slate Computers Mobile workers in increasing numbers are using portable **slate PCs**. Slate PCs, sometimes called **pen-based PCs**, use electronic pens in conjunction with a combination monitor/drawing pad instead of keyboards. Users select options, enter data, and draw with the pen. United Parcel Service (UPS) couriers use slate PCs when they ask you to sign for packages on a pressure-sensitive display screen with an electronic stylus.

Slate computers are poised to make an entry into the world of many mobile professionals. Handwritten text is interpreted by handwriting-recognition software, then entered into the system. **Speech-recognition** software, which allows the user to enter spoken words into the system, is being integrated into high-end slate PCs. Insurance agents and claims adjusters who need to work at accident or disaster scenes have found slate computers more suitable to their input needs, which may include both text and drawings.

Personal Digital Assistants **Personal digital assistants (PDAs)**, or **handheld PCs**, may take on many forms and are called by many names, from *connected organizers* to *personal communicators* to *mobile business centers* to *Web phones*. PDAs are smaller than slate PCs, usually weighing less than half a pound. They can include a built-in cellular phone that enables the wireless sending/receiving of faxes and access to the Internet (including e-mail). Their built-in wireless communications capabilities give their users immediate access to the Internet, colleagues and clients, and needed information, virtually anytime, anywhere. PDA interaction can be via the pen (like a slate PC) or by touching the keys on an on-screen keyboard or a reduced-key keyboard.

Generally, PDAs support a variety of **personal information management** systems. A **PIM** might include appointment scheduling and calendar, e-mail, fax, phone-number administration, to-do lists, tickler files, "Post-it" notes, diaries, and so on. Some PDAs can support a variety of PC-type applications, such as spreadsheets and personal financial management. Also, PDAs are designed to be easily connected to other computers and printers for data

transfer, network access, and printing. Coca-Cola and Pepsi-Cola distributors equip their salespeople with PDAs, which enable them to manage their territories better.

Network Computers In contrast to the conventional PC, the **network computer**, or **NC**, is designed to function only when it is linked to a server computer (normally an organization's internal network of computers). The NC looks similar to a PC but with several major configuration differences. First, it has a relatively small processor and considerably less RAM than modern personal computers. Second, it does not have a permanently installed disk. And, of course, it is less expensive than a stand-alone PC.

The NC depends on a central network server computer to do much of the processing and for permanent storage of data and information. Here is the way an NC works: The network computer user has access to a wide range of applications; however, the software applications and data are downloaded as they are needed to the NC from a network's central computer. Whether or not to buy into the NC concept is one of the major debates in the information technology community. Exchanging PCs for NCs will eliminate the expensive and time-consuming task of installing and maintaining PC-based software, but it will make all NCs dependent on the server computer. If the server goes down, all NCs depending on it go down.

Configuring a PC: Putting the Pieces Together

PC users often select, configure, and install their own system. The configuration of a PC or what you put into and attach to your computer can vary enormously. Common configuration options are shown in Figure 1.6.

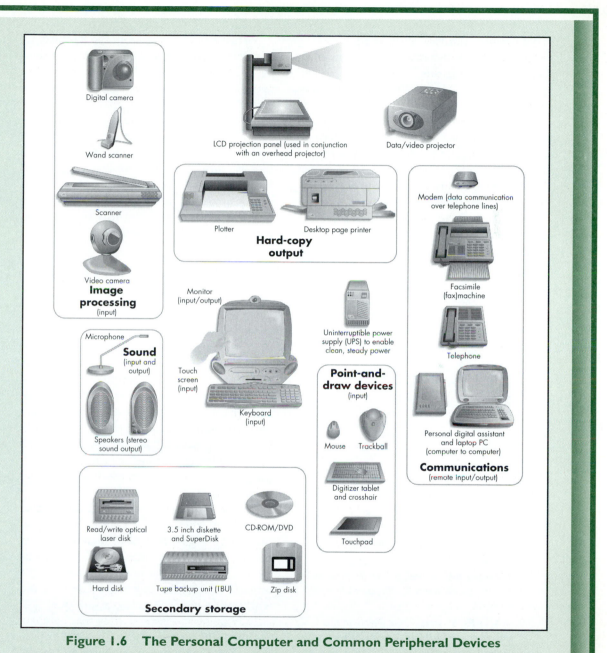

Figure 1.6   The Personal Computer and Common Peripheral Devices

A wide range of peripheral devices can be connected to a PC. Those shown here and others are discussed in detail in later chapters.

Nowadays, the typical off-the-shelf PC is configured to run multimedia applications. **Multimedia applications** integrate text, sound, graphics, motion video, and/or animation. Computer-based encyclopedias, such as Grolier's *Year 2000 Grolier Multimedia Encyclopedia*, and games, such as Broderbund's Carmen Sandiego™ series, provide a good example of multimedia applications. The encyclopedia can take you back to July 20, 1969, and let you see motion video of the Apollo 11 lunar module *Eagle* landing on the moon at the Sea of Tranquility. If you wish, you can listen to Commander Neil Armstrong proclaim, "That's one small step for [a] man, one giant leap for mankind" as he steps on the moon. Of course, the electronic encyclopedia contains supporting text that explains that he intended to say "a man." The typical PC, which is configured for multimedia (see Figure 1.3), includes the following components.

1. A microcomputer (the processor and other electronic components)
2. A keyboard for input
3. A point-and-draw device for input (usually a mouse)
4. A monitor for *soft-copy* (temporary) output
5. A printer for *hard-copy* (printed) output
6. A permanently installed high-capacity **hard-disk drive** for permanent storage of data and programs
7. A **floppy disk drive** into which an interchangeable **diskette**, or **floppy disk**, is inserted
8. A **CD-ROM drive** into which an interchangeable **CD-ROM**, which looks like an audio CD, is inserted
9. A microphone (audio input)
10. A set of speakers (audio output)

Virtually all PCs give users the flexibility to configure the system with a variety of peripheral devices (input/output and storage). A PC system is configured by linking any of a wide variety of peripheral devices to the processor component. Figure 1.6 shows the more common peripheral devices that can be configured with a PC. Many other peripherals can be linked to a PC, including video cameras, telephones, image scanners (to enter images to the system), other computers, security devices, and even a device that will enable you to watch your favorite television show on the PC's monitor.

Workstations: The Hot Rods of Computing

What looks like a PC but isn't? It's a *workstation* and it's very fast. Speed is one of the characteristics that distinguishes workstations from PCs. In fact, some people talk of workstations as "souped-up" PCs. The PC was fine for word processing, spreadsheets, and games, but for real "power users"—engineers doing **computer-aided design**, or **CAD** (using the computer in the design process), scientists and researchers who do a lot of "number crunching," graphics designers, multimedia content developers, and so on—the PC sometimes falls short.

The workstation's input/output devices also set it apart from a PC. A typical workstation will sport a large-screen color monitor capable of displaying high-resolution graphics. **Resolution** refers to the clarity of the image on the monitor's display. For pointing and drawing, the workstation user can call on a variety of specialized point-and-draw devices that combine the precision of a gun sight with the convenience of a mouse. Add-on keypads can expand the number of specialized function keys available to the user.

The capabilities of today's high-end PCs are very similar to those of low-end workstations. In a few years, the average PC will have workstation capabilities. Eventually the distinctions between the two will disappear, and we will be left with a computer category that is a cross between a PC and a workstation. Time will tell whether we call it a PC, a workstation, or something else.

Mainframe Computers: Corporate Workhorses

Mainframe computers, with their expanded processing capabilities, provide a computing resource that can be shared by many people. Mainframes are usually associated with **enterprise-wide systems**—that is, computer-based systems that service departments, plants, warehouses, and other entities throughout an organization. For example, human resources management, accounting, and inventory management tasks may be enterprise-wide systems handled by mainframe-based networks. Typically, users communicate with one or more centralized mainframes, called **host computers**, through a PC or a **terminal**. A terminal has a keyboard for input and a monitor for output. Terminals are standard equipment at airline ticket counters. Depending on the size of the organization, a dozen people or 10,000 people can share system resources (for example, information and software) by interacting with their PCs, terminals, workstations, NCs, PDAs, and other communications devices.

Until the late 1960s, all computers were mainframe computers, and they were expensive—too expensive for all but the larger companies. Large companies shelled out $1.5 million and more for mainframe computers with less power than today's $1000 PCs. In the late 1960s,

computer vendors introduced smaller, slightly "watered down" computers that were more affordable for smaller companies. The industry dubbed these small computers **minicomputers**. The term was used until recently, when the distinction between minis and mainframes began to blur. Today the term is seldom used. Smaller mainframes are called midsized computers.

Mainframe computers are *designed specifically* for the multiuser environment, in contrast to PCs and workstations, which frequently are used as stand-alone computers. Mainframes are oriented to **input/output-bound applications**; that is, the amount of work that can be performed by the computer system is limited primarily by the speeds of the I/O and storage devices. Administrative data processing jobs, such as generating monthly statements for checking accounts at a bank, require relatively little calculation and a great deal of input and output. In I/O-bound applications, the computer's processor is often waiting for data to be entered or for an output device to complete its current task.

It is unlikely that you would find two mainframe computers configured in exactly the same way. For example, a large municipal government generates a tremendous amount of *external output* (output that is directed to persons not affiliated with city government, such as utility bills and tax notices) and would require several high-speed page printers. In contrast, a software development company might enter and process all data from terminals with relatively little hardcopy output.

Supercomputers: Processing Giants

During the early 1970s, administrative data processing dominated computer applications. Bankers, college administrators, and advertising executives were amazed by the blinding speed at which million-dollar mainframes processed their data. Engineers and scientists were grateful for this tremendous technological achievement, but they were far from satisfied. When business executives talked about unlimited capability, engineers and scientists knew they would have to wait for future enhancements before they could use computers to address truly complex problems. Automotive engineers were still not able to create three-dimensional prototypes of automobiles inside a computer. Physicists could not explore the activities of an atom during a nuclear explosion. A typical scientific job involves the manipulation of a complex mathematical model, often requiring trillions of operations to resolve. During the early 1970s, some complex scientific processing jobs would tie up large mainframe computers at major universities for days at a time. This, of course, was unacceptable. The engineering and scientific communities had a desperate need for more powerful computers. In response to that need, computer designers began work on what are now known as supercomputers.

Supercomputers primarily address **processor-bound applications**, which require little in the way of input or output. In processor-bound applications, the amount of work that can be done by the computer system is limited primarily by the speed of the computer. Such applications involve highly complex or vastly numerous calculations, all of which require processor, not I/O, work.

Supercomputers are known as much for their applications as they are for their speed or computing capacity, which may be 100 times that of a large mainframe computer. These are representative supercomputer applications:

- Supercomputers enable the simulation of airflow around an airplane at different speeds and altitudes.

- Auto manufacturers use supercomputers to simulate auto accidents on video screens. (It is less expensive, more revealing, and safer than crashing the real thing.)

- Meteorologists employ supercomputers to study how oceans and the atmosphere interact to produce weather phenomena such as El Niño.

- Hollywood production studios use supercomputers to create the advanced graphics used to create special effects for movies such as *Star Wars Episode I: The Phantom Menace* and for TV commercials.

- Supercomputers sort through and analyze mountains of seismic data gathered during oil-seeking explorations.

- Medical researchers use supercomputers to simulate the delivery of babies.

All of these applications are impractical, if not impossible, on mainframes.

✔ Section Self-Check ✔

1.4.1 The power of a PC is directly proportional to its physical size. (T/F)

1.4.2 The four size categories of conventional personal computers are miniature, portable, notebook, and business. (T/F)

1.4.3 Workstation capabilities are similar to those of a low-end PC. (T/F)

1.4.4 Mainframes are usually associated with enterprise-wide systems. (T/F)

1.4.5 What has I/O capabilities and is designed to be linked remotely to a host computer: (a) terminal, (b) printer, (c) port, or (d) mouse?

1.4.6 Supercomputers are oriented to what type of applications: (a) I/O-bound, (b) processor-bound, (c) inventory management, or (d) word processing?

1.4.7 A 2-in-1 PC is in two parts, a fully functional notebook PC and a: (a) slate, (b) port hole, (c) runway, or (d) docking station?

1.4.8 What is the name given those applications that combine text, sound, graphics, motion video, and/or animation: (a) videoscapes, (b) motionware, (c) multimedia, or (d) anigraphics?

1.5 A Computer System at Work

Now that we know a little about the basic types of computer systems, let's examine what a computer can and cannot do. To get a better idea of how a computer system actually works, let's look at how it might do the processing of a payroll system.

Processing Payroll: Payday

One computer-based system makes us happy each and every payday. It's called a *payroll system*. Just about every organization that has employees and a computer maintains a computer-based payroll system. The payroll system enables input and processing of pertinent payroll-related data to produce payroll checks and a variety of reports. The payroll system walkthrough in Figure 1.7 (on page 50) illustrates how data are entered into a network of personal computer systems and how the four system components (input, processing, output, and storage) interact to produce payroll checks and information (in our example, a year-to-date overtime report).

In the walkthrough of Figure 1.7, the payroll system and other company systems are supported on a **local area network (LAN)**. A LAN connects PCs or workstations that are relatively near one another, such as in a suite of offices or a building. In most LANs, one central computer, called a **server computer**, performs a variety of functions for the other computers on the LAN, called **client computers**. One such function is the storage of data and applications software. In Figure 1.7, client PCs throughout the company are linked to a server computer. In the example, the server computer is a tower PC, but the server computer can be any type of computer, from a notebook PC to a supercomputer.

What Can a Computer Do?

Computers perform two operations: input/output operations and processing operations.

Input/Output Operations: Movement in a Computer System

Within a computer system, information is continuously moved from one part of the system to another. The processor controls this movement. It interprets information from the keyboard (a tapped key), moves it to memory and eventually to the monitor's display, the printer, or, perhaps a stored file. This movement is referred to as input/output, or I/O for short. In performing input/output operations, the computer reads from input and storage devices and then writes to output and storage devices. Before data can be processed, they must be "read" from an input device or data storage device. Typically, data are entered on a *keyboard* or via *speech recognition* (spoken words entered to the computer system), or they are retrieved from data storage, such as a magnetic disk. Once data have been processed, they are "written" to a magnetic disk or to an output device, such as a printer.

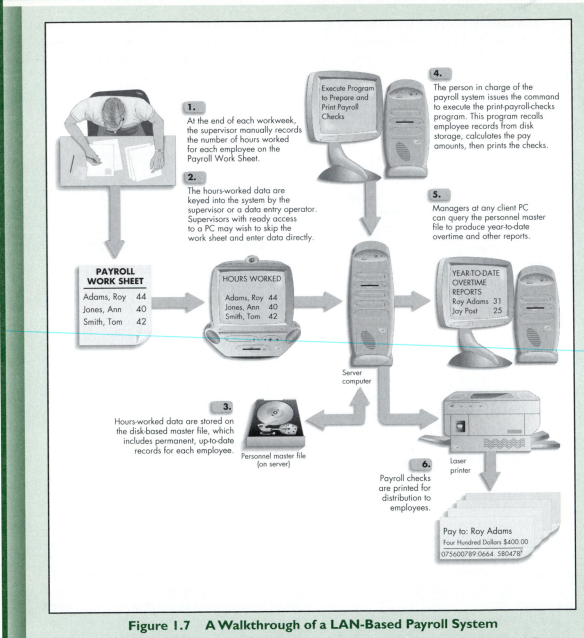

1.
At the end of each workweek, the supervisor manually records the number of hours worked for each employee on the Payroll Work Sheet.

2.
The hours-worked data are keyed into the system by the supervisor or a data entry operator. Supervisors with ready access to a PC may wish to skip the work sheet and enter data directly.

Execute Program to Prepare and Print Payroll Checks

4.
The person in charge of the payroll system issues the command to execute the print-payroll-checks program. This program recalls employee records from disk storage, calculates the pay amounts, then prints the checks.

5.
Managers at any client PC can query the personnel master file to produce year-to-date overtime and other reports.

PAYROLL WORK SHEET

Adams, Roy   44
Jones, Ann   40
Smith, Tom   42

HOURS WORKED

Adams, Roy   44
Jones, Ann   40
Smith, Tom   42

YEAR-TO-DATE OVERTIME REPORTS
Roy Adams   31
Jay Post   25

Server computer

3.
Hours-worked data are stored on the disk-based master file, which includes permanent, up-to-date records for each employee.

Personnel master file (on server)

Laser printer

6.
Payroll checks are printed for distribution to employees.

Pay to: Roy Adams
Four Hundred Dollars $400.00
075600789:0664 580478ʺ

Figure 1.7   A Walkthrough of a LAN-Based Payroll System

This step-by-step walkthrough of parts of a LAN-based payroll system (three client PCs and a server) illustrates input, storage, processing, and output.

Input/output (I/O) operations are shown in the payroll-system walkthrough example in Figure 1.7. Hours-worked data are entered by a supervisor, or "read," into the computer system (Activity 2). These data are "written" to magnetic disk storage for recall later (Activity 3). Data are "read" from the personnel master file on magnetic disk, processed (Activity 4), and "written" to the printer to produce the payroll checks (Activity 6).

Processing Operations: Doing Math and Making Decisions

Any two computers instructed to perform the same operation will arrive at the same result because the computer is totally objective. Computers can't have opinions. They can perform only *computation* and *logic operations*.

Computation Operations   Computers can add (+), subtract (−), multiply (*), divide (/), and do exponentiation (^). In the payroll system example of Figure 1.7, an instruction in a computer program tells the computer to calculate the gross pay for each employee in a computation operation. For example, these calculations would be needed to compute gross pay for Ann Jones, who worked 40 hours this week and makes $15 per hour:

Pay = 40 hours worked * $15/hour = $600

The actual program instruction that performs the above calculation might look like this:

PAY = HOURS_WORKED * PAY_RATE

The computer would then recall values for HOURS_WORKED and PAY_RATE from the personnel master file and calculate PAY.

Logic Operations   The computer's logic capability enables comparisons between numbers and between words. Based on the result of a comparison, the computer performs appropriate functions. In the example of Figure 1.7, Tom Smith and Roy Adams had overtime hours because they each worked more than 40 hours (the normal workweek). The computer must use its *logic capability* to decide if an employee is due overtime pay. To do this, hours worked are compared to 40.

Are hours worked > (greater than) 40?

For Roy Adams, who worked 44 hours, the comparison is true (44 is greater than 40). A comparison that is true causes the difference (4 hours) to be credited as overtime and paid at time and a half. The actual instruction that would perform the logical operation might look like this:

IF HOURS_WORKED > 40 THEN PAY_OVERTIME

The Computer's Strengths

In a nutshell, computers are fast, accurate, consistent, and reliable. They don't forget anything, and they don't complain.

Speed: 186 Miles per Millisecond

Computers perform various activities by executing instructions, such as those discussed in the previous section. These operations are measured in **milliseconds, microseconds, nanoseconds,** and **picoseconds** (one thousandth, one millionth, one billionth, and one trillionth of a second, respectively). To place computer speeds in perspective, consider that a beam of light travels down the length of this page in about one nanosecond. During that time a mainframe computer can perform the computations needed to complete a complex tax return.

Accuracy: Zero Errors

Computers are amazingly accurate, and their accuracy reflects great precision. Computations are accurate within a penny, a micron (a millionth of a meter), a picosecond, or whatever level of precision is required. Errors do occur in computer-based information systems, but precious few can be directly attributed to the computer system itself. Most can be traced to a program logic error, a procedural error, or erroneous data. These are *human errors*.

Consistency: All Strikes, No Balls

Baseball pitchers try to throw strikes, but often end up throwing balls. Computers always do what they are programmed to do—nothing more, nothing less. If we ask them to throw strikes, they throw nothing but strikes. This ability to produce the consistent results gives us the confidence we need to allow computers to process *mission-critical* information (information that is necessary for continued operation of an organization, a space shuttle, and so on).

Reliability: No Downtime

Computer systems are the most reliable workers in any company, especially when it comes to repetitive tasks. They don't take sick days or coffee breaks, and they seldom complain. Anything below 99.9% *uptime*, the time when the computer system is in operation, is usually unacceptable. For some companies, any *downtime* is unacceptable. These companies provide **backup** computers that take over automatically should the main computers fail.

Memory Capability: Virtually Unlimited

Computer systems have total and instant recall of data and an almost unlimited capacity to store these data. A typical mainframe computer system will have trillions of characters and millions of images stored and available for instant recall. A typical PC will have immediate access to billions of characters of data and thousands of images. To give you a benchmark for comparison, this book contains approximately 1.5 million characters and about 500 images.

✔ Section Self-Check ✔

1.5.1 On a LAN, the client computer stores all data and applications software used by the server computer. (T/F)

1.5.2 The operational capabilities of a computer system include the ability to do both logic and computation operations. (T/F)

1.5.3 A microsecond is 1000 times longer than a nanosecond. (T/F)

1.5.4 Downtime is unacceptable in some companies. (T/F)

1.5.5 In a LAN, a server computer performs a variety of functions for its: (a) client computers, (b) subcomputers, (c) LAN entity PC, or (d) work units?

1.5.6 Which of the following would be a logic operation: (a) TODAY,BIRTHDATE, (b) GROSS-TAX-DEDUCT, (c) HOURSp-WAGE, or (d) SALARY/12?

1.5.7 Spoken words are entered directly into a computer system via: (a) key entry, (b) OCR, (c) Morse code, or (d) speech recognition?

1.6 How Do We Use Computers?

The uses of computers are like the number of melodies available to a songwriter—limitless. If you can imagine it, there is a good chance that computers can help you do it. This section provides an overview of potential computer applications, which should give you a feel for how computers are affecting your life. These applications, however, are but a few of the many applications presented throughout the book.

Information Systems

The bulk of existing computer power is dedicated to **information systems**. This includes all uses of computers that support the administrative aspects of an organization, such as airline reservation systems, student registration systems, hospital patient-billing systems, and countless others. We combine *hardware*, *software*, *people*, *procedures*, and *data* to create an information system. A computer-based information system provides an organization with *data processing* capabilities and the knowledge workers in the organization with the *information* they need to make better, more informed decisions.

Personal Computing

The growth of **personal computing**, an environment in which one person controls the PC, has surpassed even the most adventurous forecasts of a decade ago. It's not uncommon for companies to have more personal computers than they do telephones.

A variety of domestic and business applications form the foundation of personal computing. Domestic applications include everything from personal finance to education to entertainment. PC software is available to support thousands of common and not-so-common personal and business applications.

A growing family of software for personal or business productivity is the foundation of personal computing in the home and in the business world. These are some of the most popular productivity tools.

- Word processing. **Word processing software** enables users to create, edit (revise), and format documents in preparation for output (for example, printing, displaying locally or over the Internet, faxing, or sending via e-mail). The term **document** is a generic reference to whatever is currently displayed in a software package's work area or to a permanent file, perhaps a disk, containing document contents (perhaps a report or an outline). Word processing documents can include anything that can be printed (for example, text and graphic images). When viewed on a computer, displayed documents can include objects other than graphic images. Generally, an **object** is anything within a document that can be selected and manipulated. For example, animations, video, and sound objects can be embedded in displayed word processing documents.

- Desktop publishing. **Desktop publishing software** allows users to produce camera-ready documents (ready to be printed professionally) from the confines of a desktop. People routinely use desktop publishing to create newsletters, advertisements, procedures manuals, and for many other printing needs.

- Spreadsheet. **Spreadsheet software** permits users to work with the rows and columns of data.

- Database. **Database software** permits users to create and maintain a database and to extract information from the database. In a database, data are organized for ease of manipulation and retrieval.

- Presentation. **Presentation software** lets you create professional-looking images for group presentations, self-running slide shows, reports, and for other situations that require the presentation of organized, visual information. The electronic images may include multimedia elements, such as sound, animation, and video.
- Communications. **Communications software** is a family of software applications that enable users to send e-mail and faxes, tap the resources of the Internet, log on to an information service, and link their PC with a remote computer.
- Personal information management. PIM software is an umbrella term that encompasses a variety of personal management and contact information programs. A particular PIM package might include calendar applications (appointment scheduling and reminders), communications applications (e-mail and fax), and databases that help you organize your phone numbers, e-mail addresses, to-do lists, notes, diary entries, and so on.

Communication

Computers are communications tools that give us the flexibility to communicate electronically with one another and with other computers. For example, we can set up our computers to send e-mail birthday greetings to our friends and relatives automatically. We can log on to a commercial information service (like America Online or CompuServe) to chat online (via keyed-in text) with one person or a group of people. Recent software innovations allow us to talk to, and see, people in remote locations, using only our PCs and a link to the Internet. Communications applications and concepts are discussed and illustrated in detail throughout the book.

Science, Research, and Engineering

Engineers and scientists routinely use the computer as a tool in *experimentation*, *design*, and *development*. There are at least as many science and research applications for the computer as there are scientists and engineers. One of these applications is computer-aided design (CAD), which involves using the computer in the design process. CAD systems enable the creation and manipulation of an on-screen graphic image. CAD systems provide a sophisticated array of tools, enabling designers to create three-dimensional objects that can be flipped, rotated, resized, viewed in detail, examined internally or externally, and much more. Photographs throughout the book illustrate a variety of CAD applications, such as automobile design and architectural design.

Education and Reference

Students at all levels, from kindergarten to professional adult education, are embracing a new approach to learning. Learning resources are being developed and delivered on CD-ROM and via the Internet to relatively inexpensive personal computers, each capable of multidimensional communication (sound, print, graphics, video, and animation). The result is a phenomenal growth of technology as an educational tool in the home, in the classroom, and in business. Computer-based education and online classes will not replace teachers, but educators agree that CD-ROM-based *computer-based training (CBT)* and information-based *distance learning* is having a profound impact on traditional modes of education. Available CBT programs can help you learn keyboarding skills, increase your vocabulary, study algebra, learn about the makeup of the atom, practice your Russian, and learn about computers. Colleges and even high schools offer thousands of courses online via distance learning. You can now get an MBA, a law degree, and bachelors degrees in most disciplines without attending a single traditional classroom lecture. These are just the tip of the CBT/distance learning iceberg.

Entertainment and Edutainment

More applications are being created that tickle our fancy and entertain us. You can play electronic golf. You can buy a computer chess opponent in the form of a board, chess pieces, and a miniature robotic arm that moves the pieces (you have to move your own pieces). You can "pilot" an airplane to Paris and battle Zorbitrons in cyberspace. Carmen Sandiego, the debonair thief of computer games and television fame, thrills children with the chase to find her and her accomplices, while teaching them history and geography. Software that combines *education* and *entertainment*, such as "Carmen Sandiego," has been dubbed *edutainment software.*

The amount of computing capacity in the world is doubling every two years. The number and sophistication of applications are growing at a similar pace. Tomorrow, there will be applications that are unheard of today.

✔ Section Self-Check ✔

1.6.1 Desktop publishing refers to the capability of producing camera-ready documents from the confines of a desktop. (T/F)

1.6.2 More computing capacity is dedicated to information systems than to CBT. (T/F)

1.6.3 The PC productivity tool that manipulates data organized in rows and columns is called a: (a) database record manager, (b) presentation mechanism, (c) word processing document, or (d) spreadsheet?

1.6.4 What type of software combines education and entertainment: (a) video games, (b) Nintendo, (c) edutainment, or (d) click-and-learn?

1.6.5 Which PC productivity tool would be helpful in writing a term paper: (a) word processing, (b) presentation, (c) spreadsheet, or (d) communications?

Summary and Key Terms

1.1 The Information Society

In an **information society, knowledge workers** focus their energies on providing a myriad of information services. The knowledge worker's job function revolves around the use, manipulation, and broadcasting of information. Learning about computers is an adventure that will last a lifetime because **information technology (IT)**, the integration of computing technology and information processing, is changing daily.

Information technology competency (IT competency) is emerging as a universal goal in the information society. IT-competent people know how to purchase, use, and operate a computer system, and how to make it work for them. The IT-competent person is also aware of the computer's impact on society and is conversant in the language of technology.

Software refers collectively to a set of machine-readable instructions, called **programs**, that causes the computer to perform desired functions. Computers and computer equipment, which accept **input** and provide **output**, are called **hardware**.

The computer revolution is transforming the way we communicate, do business, and learn. This technological revolution is having a profound impact on the business community and on our private and professional lives. For example, increasingly, we communicate with our colleagues at work through **electronic mail (e-mail)** or with our friends through **newsgroups**.

After the turn of the century, we can anticipate traveling the **information superhighway**, a network of high-speed data communications links that eventually will connect virtually every facet of our society. Today, millions of people have a **personal computer (PC)**. This widespread availability has resulted in an explosion of applications for computers.

Through the 1970s, **users** related their information needs to computer professionals who would then work with the computer system to generate the necessary information. Today, users work directly with their PCs to obtain the information they need.

Data, which all of us create and use every day, are the raw facts from which information is derived. **Information** consists of data collected and processed into a meaningful form. The data in a computer-based system are stored on the **master file**, which is made up of **records**.

1.2 Networking: Bringing People Together

We now live in a global village in which computers and people are linked within companies and between countries. Most existing computers are part of a **computer network** that shares hardware/software resources and information.

The **Internet** links almost a billion users in a global network. **The Net** can be accessed by people in organizations with established links to the Internet and by individuals with PCs often via **Internet service providers (ISPs)**. **Commercial information services**, such as **America Online (AOL)**, offer a wide range of information services, including up-to-the-minute news and weather, electronic shopping, e-mail, and much more. When the user terminates this **online** link, the user goes **offline**. Internet users can **download** text or a digitized version of a song directly to their PC, then read it or play it through their PC. Information is **uploaded** from a local computer to a remote computer.

1.3 Computers: The Essentials

The **computer**, or **processor**, is an electronic device capable of interpreting and executing programmed commands for input, output, computation, and logic operations.

Output on a computer can be routed to a **monitor** or a **printer**. The output on a monitor is temporary and is called **soft copy**. Printers produce **hard-copy** output. Data can be entered via a **keyboard** or a **mouse**, a **point-and-draw device**.

Random-access memory (RAM) provides temporary storage of data and programs during processing within solid-state **integrated circuits**, or **chips**. Permanently installed and interchangeable **disks** provide permanent storage for data and programs. A computer system can include a variety of **peripheral devices**.

The differences in the various categories of computers are very much a matter of scale. **Mainframe computers** have greater computing capacities than do PCs, or **microcomputers**. And **supercomputers** have greater computing capacities than mainframe computers. Depending on its sophistication, a **workstation's** computing capacity falls somewhere between that of a PC and a midsized mainframe. All **computer systems**, no matter how small or large, have the same fundamental capabilities—processing, storage, input, and output. Each offers many **input/output**, or **I/O**, alternatives.

System software programs take control of the PC on start up and then play a central role in everything that happens within a computer system. **Applications software** performs specific personal, business, or scientific processing tasks.

1.4 Personal Computers to Supercomputers: Capabilities and Uses

In 1981, IBM introduced its **IBM PC**, defining the original PC-compatible machine, now also called a **Wintel PC** because of its use of Windows 9x/Me/2000 **operating systems** and the Intel processors. The Apple iMac, with its Mac OS X and Motorola PowerPC processor, is the other major **platform**. Conventional personal computers come in four different physical sizes: **pocket PCs (palmtop PCs)**, **laptop PCs** (also called **notebook PCs**), **desktop PCs**, and **tower PCs**. Pocket and laptop PCs are considered portable. A 2-in-1 PC that can be used as both a notebook and a desktop has two parts: a fully functional notebook PC and a **docking station**. Two-in-one PCs allow users to enjoy the best of both worlds: portability and the expanded features of a desktop. The **port replicator** works like the docking station in that the notebook PC is inserted into it and removed as needed to enable access to the port replicator **ports** and whatever is connected to them.

Slate PCs, sometimes called **pen-based PCs**, use electronic pens instead of keyboards. **Speech-recognition** software is being integrated into high-end slate PCs. **Personal digital assistants (PDAs)**, or **handheld PCs**, are handheld personal computers that support a variety of personal information systems. PDAs support a variety of **personal information management (PIM)** systems, including appointment scheduling and to-do lists. The **network computer**, or **NC**, is designed to work only when linked to a network. The diskless NC has a relatively small processor and less RAM than modern personal computers.

Multimedia applications combine text, sound, graphics, motion video, and/or animation. The typical multimedia-configured PC includes a microcomputer; a keyboard and a point-and-draw device for input; a monitor and a printer for output; a **hard-disk drive** and a **floppy disk drive** into which an **interchangeable diskette**, or **floppy disk**, is inserted; a **CD-ROM drive** into which an interchangeable **CD-ROM** is inserted; and a microphone and a set of speakers for audio I/O.

The workstation's speed and input/output devices set it apart from a PC. A typical workstation will have a **high-resolution** monitor and a variety of specialized point-and-draw devices. A common use of workstations is for **computer-aided design (CAD)**.

Mainframe computers are usually associated with **enterprise-wide systems**; that is, computer-based systems that service entities throughout the company. Users communicate with a centralized mainframe, called a **host computer**, through their **terminals** and other communications devices. The term **minicomputer** was used until recently, when the distinction between minis and mainframes began to blur. Mainframes are oriented to **input/output-bound applications**. Supercomputers primarily address **processor-bound applications**.

1.5 A Computer System at Work

A **local area network (LAN)** connects PCs or workstations in close proximity. The LAN's **server computer** performs a variety of functions for other computers on the LAN, called **client computers**.

Computer system capabilities are either input/output or processing. Processing capabilities are subdivided into computation and logic operations.

Computers perform input/output (I/O) operations by reading from input and storage devices and writing to output devices.

The computer is fast, accurate, consistent, and reliable, and has an enormous memory capacity. Computer operations are measured in **milliseconds**, **microseconds**, **nanoseconds**, and **picoseconds**. When downtime is unacceptable, companies provide **backup** computers that take over automatically should the main computers fail.

1.6 How Do We Use Computers?

There are many applications of computers, including the following:

- Information systems. The computer is used to process data and produce business information. Hardware, software, people, procedures, and data are combined to create an **information system**.
- Personal computing. The PC is used for **personal computing** by individuals for a variety of business and domestic applications, including such productivity tools as **word processing software**, **desktop publishing software**, **spreadsheet software**, **database software**, **presentation software**, and **communications software**. An **object** is anything within a **document** that can be selected and manipulated.
- Communication. Computers are communications tools that give us the flexibility to communicate electronically with one another and with other computers.
- Science, research, and engineering. The computer is used as a tool in experimentation, design, and development.
- Education and reference. The computer interacts with students to enhance the learning process.
- Entertainment and edutainment. Every day, computer applications are being designed and created just to entertain us. Software that combines education and entertainment has been dubbed edutainment software.

Discussion and Problem Solving

1.1

a. Information technology has had far-reaching effects on our lives. How has the computer and IT affected your life?

b. What is your concept of information technology competency? In what ways do you think achieving information technology competency will affect your domestic life? Your business life?

c. At what age should information technology competency education begin? Is society prepared to provide IT education at this age? If not, why?

d. Describe the relationship between data and information. Give an example.

e. Discuss how the complexion of jobs will change as we evolve from an industrial society into an information society. Give several examples.

1.2

a. Comment on how information technology is changing our traditional patterns of personal communication.

b. If you are a current user of the Internet, describe four Internet services that have been of value to you. If not, in what ways do you think the Internet might be a benefit to you?

c. What might you want to download over the Internet?

1.3

a. List as many computer and information technology terms as you can (up to 30) that are used in everyday conversations at the office and at school.

b. Describe an ideal applications software package that might help you meet your personal or business information processing needs.

1.4

a. If you could purchase only one personal computer, which would you buy, a notebook PC or a tower PC? Why?

b. Explain circumstances that would cause you to choose a docking station over a port replicator.

c. Speculate on how one of these professionals would use a slate PC: a police officer, an insurance adjuster, a delivery person for a courier service, or a newspaper reporter.

d. Management at a large company with 1000 three-year-old PCs, all on a network, is debating whether to replace the PCs with network computers or with new PCs. Each has its advantages. Name the single most important advantage for each option.

e. Give at least two reasons that a regional bank might opt to buy two mainframe computers rather than one supercomputer.

1.5

a. Discuss the relationship between the server computer and its client computers.

b. Compare the information processing capabilities of human beings to those of computers with respect to speed, accuracy, reliability, consistency, and memory capability.

c. Within the context of a computer system, what is meant by read and write?

d. Identify and briefly describe five computation and five logic operations that might be performed by a computer during the processing of college students throughout the academic year.

1.6

a. The use of computers tends to stifle creativity. Argue for or against this statement.

b. Comment on how computers are changing our traditional patterns of recreation.

c. Of the productivity software described in this chapter, choose the two that will have (or currently have) the most impact on your productivity. Explain why you chose these two.

VOCABULARY LESSON

The purpose of this vocabulary lesson is to help you review and deepen your knowledge of the ten general vocabulary words you worked with at the beginning of this chapter.

A. Structural Analysis—Affixes and Root Words
    1. Identify the root (or base) word by underlining it: *Conventional*
    2. Circle the suffix of the following word: *Vilify*
B. Use of Context: Read the sentence written below and in your own words write a definition for the word *dub*:

> The industry *dubbed* these small computers minicomputers. The term was used until recently....

_____

C. Multiple meanings of words
    1. Circle the definition below of the word *execute* that fits the way it is used in this sentence, "The computer ... is an electronic device that can interpret and *execute* programmed commands...."
        a. Do; perform; carry out
        b. Put to death according to law
    2. Circle the definition below of the word *gross* that fits the way it is used in this sentence, "... an instruction in a computer program tells the computer to calculate the *gross* pay for each employee...."
        a. Whole, without deductions; total
        b. Thick; fat; coarse; hence, vulgar, indelicate
D. Synonyms and Antonyms: List one synonym (same meaning) and one antonym (opposite meaning) for each of the following words:

Word	**Synonym**	**Antonym**
Conventional		
Irate		
Myriad		

E. Generate Your Own Language
    1. When have you been *irate* because of poor service at a store or restaurant?
    2. What do you consider your *niche* in society?
    3. What *facet* of your job is the most interesting?
F. Word Confusion: Do not confuse *adapt*, to make suitable, and *adopt*, to receive as one's own.
    1. In most foreign countries, American electrical appliances must be *adapted* to the local current. Have you traveled to a country where you had to use an adapter? What was the experience like?
    2. What clothing fashions have you *adopted* as your own since arriving on campus?

G. Textbook Preview: The following words that appear in this chapter will appear as your vocabulary words for Part Two of this textbook, in various forms. How well do you already know them? Which ones do you use in your written and oral language?

   1. Emerged
   2. Virtual
   3. Err (Erroneous)
   4. Traditions

VOCABULARY EXTENSION

The purpose of this exercise is to help you see to what degree you know the ten general vocabulary words in this chapter. Matching a word with its definition is the beginning of knowing a word. Using the word in your speaking and writing is full knowledge.

Now that you have completed the reading lesson for this chapter, see if you have increased your vocabulary by following the directions below:

A. List the vocabulary words from this lesson that you can now use in both your speaking and writing.

B. List the vocabulary words from this lesson that you can now use in writing but are still not comfortable using in speaking.

C. List the vocabulary words from this lesson that you cannot use yet but will recognize in reading.

D. List general vocabulary words from this lesson that are still difficult to understand.

E. Use five vocabulary words from this lesson in a five-sentence paragraph on the topic of this lesson.

F. Illustrate the meaning of one of the vocabulary words from this lesson through some form of artwork or a cartoon. (This exercise is for right-brain students who enjoy drawing better than writing!)

EXTENDED READING ACTIVITIES

The purpose of this section is to give you a variety of options for independent study or investigation of the chapter topic. Reading is a skill that must be practiced each day if progress is to take place. These activities are designed to give you a variety of reading experiences through which you can improve your general vocabulary and increase your higher-level comprehension skills.

Your instructor may wish to (a) assign one or more activities to the class as a whole, (b) assign various activities to small groups, (c) assign one or more activities to individual students, or (d) let students choose to do the activities or not.

A. Weekly Reading Report: Begin keeping a weekly report of your reading. Record what you read each day for your courses and what you read for fun. Use the form at the end of this chapter if you wish. Be honest with yourself.

B. Attend a Reading Lab on Campus: If your school has a reading lab, attend it for at least thirty minutes at a time. Work on exercises that are slightly difficult for you. If you make more than 70 percent on a comprehension exercise, go to a higher level. If you make below 70 percent on several exercises, go to a lower level. Work on skills exercises that you know are helping you, not on skills exercises at which you are already proficient.

C. Read a non-fiction book.

   1. Read books about computers: The following books on computers appeared on Amazon.com's most popular and best-selling books about computers. When I entered the word *computer*, at the company site, I found that the company had 32,000 entries.

      a. David A. Jonassen, et al., *Computers and Mindtools for Schools: Engaging Critical Thinking*

      b. Russell M. Walter, *The Secret Guide to Computers for 2001, 27th Ed.*

      c. Ron White, et al., *How Computers Work: Millennium Edition*

      d. Steve Krug and Roger Black, *Don't Make Me Think! A Common Sense Approach to Web Usability*

      e. Mary Modahl, *Now or Never: How Companies Must Change Today to Win the Battle for Internet Consumers*

      f. Joel Scambray, et al., *Hacking Exposed*

   2. Read with or to your children: After logging on Amazon.com, I entered *children's books* and then *computers* and found the following interesting items:

      a. Trevor Meers and Tony Caldwell (illustrator), *Consumerguide, 101 Best Web Sites for Kids*

      b. Philippa Wingate, et al., *Internet for Beginners*

      c. Ken Leebow, et al., *300 Incredible Things for Kids on the Internet*

      d. Ted Pedersen, et al., *Make Your Own Web Page! A Guide for Kids*

      e. Nancy White, et al., *Scholastic's The Magic School Bus Gets Programmed: A Book about Computers*

D. Reading/Writing Connection: You may want to begin a college experience journal and include one of the topics below in it.

   1. Compare and contrast the advantages and disadvantages of online shopping with shopping in a real store. Use the special section in the computer chapter, "Emerging IT: Online Shopping," (starting on page 39) for background information. At the writing of this textbook, two online sources listed in the computer chapter have gone out of business: a grocery shopping site and a wine company.

   2. Describe the first time you used a computer.

   3. How does a computer save you time? How does it cost you time? Is learning to use a computer worth the effort?

    E. Use the Internet.
       1. Look up the authors' web site: http://www.prenhall/long.
       2. Research a topic for another course on the computer.
    F. Content Area Report: If you are having difficulty with another course you are taking this quarter or semester, use the Content Area Report at the end of this chapter to help you learn to use the textbook aids provided and to overview the textbook. If you have never drawn a visual, as directed to do on the form at the end of the chapter, start with a circle or rectangle at the top of your page and place the chapter title in it. On the next horizontal line, place the main chapter headings in similar circles or rectangles. Their place on the same line shows that they are equal in importance. If you wish to add one more layer of information, on a horizontal line below the one with your main headings, place subheadings (yours or the textbook's) again in circles or rectangles. Draw connecting lines among your circles or rectangles. Now you have a picture of the most important information in the chapter.

REFLECTION

MIND REVOLUTION

The Mind Revolution grew out of my awareness that too often students do not incorporate what they learn in class into their personal lives. Learning remains compartmentalized and sometimes wasted. This is an attempt to get you to see how the chapter information can be personally important. Hopefully, you will encounter a new idea in each chapter that you can incorporate into your own life, or at least have something new to think about as you go about your daily routine. Life should never be boring!

We can understand the speed with which our world is changing through technology by just reading a brief history of computers. The choice seems to be to live with them or be left behind. We not only need to learn how to let computers help us at home and at work, but we need to keep up with the field. No matter what our majors, we will all use computers in some capacity. Become more aware of how much you depend on computers in your daily life. In what ways do computers control the quality of your life, especially those computers that are out of sight controlling environmental conditions and printing your paychecks?

VOCABULARY

Specialized vocabulary is the most important vocabulary issue in this chapter. Just a brief look at the specialized vocabulary terms in the Prior Knowledge section of this reading lesson will convince us of that. The good news is that the authors have made every effort to help us learn these new terms. The terms are in bold print in the text and are repeated in context in the summary of the chapter. The sections entitled "Section Self-Check" also reinforce our learning of the vocabulary words.

Background knowledge and experience played a major role in comprehending this chapter. Your taking a computer course in high school and/or having access to computers in the lower school grades or in high school made a difference in how easy this chapter was for you. If you own your own personal computer and use it for home and work, if you have grown up with computers, or if you like to browse in computer stores or order online, this chapter was easier for you. The pictures of computers and peripheral devices may remind you of catalogs you receive. Did the pictures increase your interest in computers?

Density of concepts is not a problem at this point but could become one later in the computer textbook. If understanding new material on computers depends on remembering what you have already learned, then it is important for you to know the information in this chapter.

Weekly Reading Report

Your Name _____

Directions: The purpose of this reading report is to make you aware of how much you are reading. Please answer as accurately as possible. I strongly suggest that you record everything you read daily.

A. List each course you are currently taking under the appropriate subject and what you have read for those courses during this week.

Subjects	Chapters	Topics
English		
Math		
Social sciences		
Business/computers		
Natural sciences		
Health sciences		
Technical courses		
Other		

B. List all pleasure reading you have done this week (e.g., magazines, journals, books, newspapers). Also list the topics you read about.

_____

_____

C. List one interesting topic you read about this week. Briefly, tell why it interested you. Be specific.

_____

_____

D. Reflection. How has your reading improved? Are you spending more time reading? Thinking deeper? Reading more high-level content?

Content Area Report

Your Name _____

   A. Overview
      1. Choose a textbook for a subject you are now taking or for your major.
         a. Title: _____
         b. Author: _____
      2. Summarize the message of the preface in your own words:

         _____
         _____

      3. List the first ten chapter titles in the Table of Contents below:

         _____
         _____
         _____
         _____
         _____
         _____
         _____
         _____
         _____
         _____

      4. What pages are the index on? _____
      5. Does it have a glossary? _____
      6. Are there chapter
         a. Introductions? _____
         b. Stated objectives? _____
         c. Summaries? _____
         d. Review questions? _____
   B. Choose a chapter from the textbook.
      1. List the major headings:

         _____
         _____
         _____

      2. Give the subheadings for one major heading:

         _____
         _____

   C. Choose a paragraph and copy it on a separate sheet of paper. You may photocopy it if you wish. Write the following below the paragraph:
      1. Main idea
      2. Supporting details for the main idea
   D. Outline or draw a visual map of the chapter on the back of this paper. (See directions in Extended Reading Activities, letter F, page 63.)

2

Psychology:
Behavior in Social and Cultural Context

Overview

Extended Reading Activities
Reflection
  Mind Revolution
  Vocabulary
  Comprehension

VOCABULARY/METACOGNITION

The purpose of this exercise is to help you become aware of when you know the meaning of a word and to help you know when you do not know the meaning of a word. This is metacognition awareness.

On a scale of 1–5 (see below), rate your knowledge of the following vocabulary words from "Behavior in Social and Cultural Context." After matching words with definitions on page 68, check your answers and then check your number *ones* and *fives* below. Did you know when you really knew a word and when you really did not know the word?

Scale

1. I absolutely do not know.
2. I do not think I know.
3. There's a 50/50 chance I have seen or heard it.
4. I think I know it.
5. I know the word and can use it.

Words

_____ 1. Vulnerable (invulnerability)
_____ 2. Arbitrary (arbitrarily)
_____ 3. Convention (conventions)
_____ 4. Boycott
_____ 5. Euphoria
_____ 6. Antidote (antidotes)
_____ 7. Anguish (anguished)
_____ 8. Tangible
_____ 9. Ambiguous
_____10. Animosity

Go to page 68. See if you can match the right definition with the word and then write sentences for any three words in the list.

Words

_____ 1. Vulnerable (invulnerability)
_____ 2. Arbitrary (arbitrarily)
_____ 3. Convention (conventions)
_____ 4. Boycott
_____ 5. Euphoria
_____ 6. Antidote (antidotes)
_____ 7. Anguish (anguished)
_____ 8. Tangible
_____ 9. Ambiguous
_____ 10. Animosity

Definitions

A. (1) An assembly; (2) an agreement, esp. international; (3) a fixed custom or usage

B. Acute bodily or mental distress; extreme pain

C. (1) Capable of being touched; having corporeal existence; (2) definite or concrete; capable of being realized

D. Of doubtful purport; open to various interpretations; having a double meaning

E. A feeling or state of well-being

F. (1) A drug that counteracts the effects of a poison; (2) any remedy against disease or injurious influence

G. (1) Susceptible of being wounded, assaulted, or conquered; (2) open to reproof; (3) not resistant to evil influence

H. Combine with others to abstain from buying, using, patronizing, etc. (a business product, etc.), as a means of coercing or intimidating

I. (1) Not regulated by fixed rule or law; (2) capricious; unreasonable

J. Active enmity; hatred; ill will

Write three words from the list and your own sentences that show you know how to use the words. Choose words that you marked a *five* if possible.

1. Word _____

   Sentence _____

2. Word _____

   Sentence _____

3. Word _____

   Sentence _____

PRE-READING THE TEXTBOOK CHAPTER

The purpose of this *first* of three steps in your reading plan is to suggest things to do *before* you read. First, as part of your pre-reading, read the Prior Knowledge section beginning on page 69, the Academic Study Skills section's overview on page 74, and the first part of the Textbook Study Aids Plan on page 74. When you finish, return to this page and continue your pre-reading.

Tapping Prior Knowledge

Tap your experience and prior knowledge about the title of this selection by writing words and phrases that come to your mind. You are pulling up your file on the topic and focusing on what you will read. What do you already know about the subject? Do not look at your textbook at this time, as these answers will vary from person to person and won't be found in the textbook. There are no wrong answers for this part of the lesson.

Predicting

Predict in one sentence what you will read. Try to predict in some detail. Don't write, "I predict that I will read about behavior in social and cultural context." What behavior, action, and/or information do you expect to read about? Predicting helps you identify your expectations of what you will read. Not reading what you have predicted will serve as a warning that you have misjudged the topic of the article and will help you adapt to what is in the chapter.

Overviewing

Now you may look at your chapter. Continue overviewing by reading the Summary and "Looking Back" questions at the end of the chapter and by paying close attention to the headings. Note that you have five major sections with several subheadings under each one. Add this new information to what you learned in the Prior Knowledge and Academic Study Skills sections of this lesson.

Prior Knowledge

This section presents a model to show you what will help you comprehend this chapter by using your own background knowledge. If you know much of the information listed below, you have a better background for reading this chapter. This section will suggest information and help you activate what you know; do not try to look up or learn everything listed. Ask yourself what you need to know before you read and what you already know that will help you to understand this chapter.

Writing Pattern Overview

In the social sciences the reader can expect expository writing in which the author informs the reader. Statements are supported by examples, especially facts and numbers. References (over one hundred citations in this chapter) refer to sources that support the information in the chapter.

Directions for Reading This Section

First, notice the categories of information: (a) vocabulary, (b) writing patterns, and (c) concepts and background knowledge and experience. Next, skim the sections, noting what is familiar and what is not. If a great amount is familiar and/or interesting to you, you should find reading the chapter easier than if you do not recognize anything and find the information boring.

I.   Roles and Rules
   A. Vocabulary
      1. General
         a. Conventions
         b. Anguished
         c. Invalidated
         d. Tangible
         e. Relinquished
         f. Ambiguous
      2. Specialized
         (These words appear at the end of the chapter, under "Key Terms.")
         a. Norms
         b. Role
         c. Culture
         d. Entrapment
   B. Recognition of Writing Patterns or Arrangement of Ideas and Devices
      1. In the social sciences, look for specialized vocabulary, use of examples, and studies to support statements.
      2. Introduction
         a. Specific to general pattern
         b. Anecdote leading in to statement of thesis
         c. Statement about specific fields of psychology and focus of chapter
      3. Asks questions to engage reader
      4. Introduces concept of *social norms*, defines it, and gives examples
      5. Introduces concept of *social roles*, defines it, and gives examples
      6. Introduces concept of *culture*, defines it, and gives examples
      7. Describes background for study and "The Obedience Study" that requires the reader to understand numbers 3, 4, 5 above
      8. Describes "The Prison Study"
      9. Discussion of the two studies, the power of social roles and factors and examples of obedience
     10. Supports statements with studies
   C. Concepts and Background Knowledge and Experience
      1. Personal Experience
         a. Experience of seeing complexity of many situations
         b. Experience of questioning your own behavior and taking responsibility
         c. Ability to see social forces at work in your own life
         d. Aware of influence of advertisement on your personal choices

    2. Academic Experience
        a. Psychology course in high school
        b. See that psychology has many areas of study
        c. Have seen documentaries on cults and processes of cult persuasion
    3. Concepts
        a. Social norms, roles, culture, routinization, entrapment
        b. Understand the importance of research studies
        c. Aware of your own generation's attitudes

II. Social Influences on Beliefs
  A. Vocabulary
    1. General
        a. Intolerable
        b. Euphoria
        c. Elite
        d. Antidotes
    2. Specialized
      (*These words appear at the end of the chapter, under "Key Terms."*)
        a. Social cognition
        b. Attribution theory
        c. Fundamental attribution error
  B. Recognition of Writing Patterns or Arrangement of Ideas and Devices
    1. Introduction
        a. Broad to specific pattern
        b. States two topics of discussion for this section
        c. Introduces concept of *social cognition* and defines it in context
    2. Two main sections (subheadings are *attributions* and *attitudes*)
        a. Attributions
            (1) Introduces and explains new concepts *attribution theory* and *fundamental attribution error*; supports explanation with examples and studies
            (2) Gives examples of differences in Western and Eastern cultural influences and then supports them with a study
            (3) Explains how *just-world hypothesis* can lead to blaming the victim; supports with examples and study
        b. Attitudes
            (1) Introduces, defines, and explains *attitude*; uses studies for support; gives example of generational attitudes
            (2) Briefly introduces causes for changes in attitudes; uses brief descriptions and examples

        (3) Use of contrast pattern by showing differences in friendly and coercive persuasion

        (4) First of two main divisions introduced (*friendly persuasion*)

        (5) Explains three types, gives examples, and supports with studies

        (6) Introduces opposite (*coercive persuasion*) and the four key processes; supports with examples and studies of cults

  C. Concepts and Background Knowledge and Experience

    1. Ability to see human behavior is complex

    2. Ability to apply information to your own life and to society at large

III. Individuals in Groups

  A. Vocabulary

    1. General

      a. Dissent

      b. Invulnerability

      c. Vulnerable

      d. Boycott

    2. Specialized

      (*These words appear at the end of the chapter, under "Key Terms."*)

      a. Groupthink

      b. Diffusion of responsibility

      c. Deindividuation

  B. Recognition of Writing Patterns or Arrangement of Ideas and Devices

    1. Same pattern of introduction, explanation, use of examples and studies for support

  C. Concepts and Background Knowledge and Experience

    1. Collaborative learning experience

      a. Group dynamics course

      b. Experience of being part of a large crowd, such as sports events or concerts

      c. Stopped (or did not stop) to help a motorist with car trouble

      d. Approached by a homeless person on the street

IV. Group Conflict and Prejudice

  A. Vocabulary

    1. General

      a. Arbitrarily

      b. Cubicle

      c. Exhilarated

      d. Fomenting

      e. Animosity

    2. Specialized

      (*These words appear at the end of the chapter, under "Key Terms."*)

      a. Ethnocentrism

      b.   Social identity

      c.   Stereotype

  B.   Recognition of Writing Patterns or Arrangement of Ideas and Devices

    1.   Introduction

      a.   Introduces concept *ethnocentrism*; defines and discusses it

      b.   Follows same pattern as above; introduces concepts, explanation, examples, and studies

  C.   Concepts and Background Knowledge and Experience

    1.   Social identity

    2.   Stereotype

    3.   Prejudice

    4.   Experience of being stereotyped

    5.   Experience the prejudice of others toward you

    6.   Feel prejudice toward other groups

V.   The Question of Human Nature

  A.   Vocabulary

    1.   General

      a.   Despotic

  B.   Recognition of Writing Patterns or Arrangement of Ideas and Devices

    1.   Same general pattern: anecdote, explanation, examples, studies

  C.   Concepts and Background Knowledge and Experience

    1.   Studied human nature

    2.   People and cultures are complex and capable of both good and evil

VI. Taking Psychology with You

  A.   Vocabulary

    1.   General

      a.   Sullen

  B.   Recognition of Writing Patterns or Arrangement of Ideas and Devices

    1.   Same general pattern: anecdote, statements, and examples

  C.   Concepts and Background Knowledge and Experience

    1.   Ability to apply what you have learned

VII. Summary

  A.   Vocabulary
     None

  B.   Recognition of Writing Patterns or Arrangement of Ideas and Devices

    1.   Definitions of key terms and summary of main ideas

  C.   Concepts

    1.   Review of chapter

VIII. Key Terms
   List of terms with page numbers where they appear in the chapter

IX. Looking Back
   Mostly literal-level questions with page numbers for reference.

ACADEMIC STUDY SKILLS

OVERVIEW

Two strengths of this psychology chapter are (1) the use of good and plentiful examples of terms and concepts discussed, and (2) documentation of statements with solid research studies. Another strength is the provision of textbook aids. Each of the chapter's five sections begins with an overview. In the overview ("What's Ahead"), questions are asked that introduce the new information and whet the reader's interest. Each of the five sections contains quizzes that can serve as a review for the reader. Formatting and visuals also aid the reader.

TEXTBOOK STUDY AIDS PLAN

The following activities will help you through the pre-reading, reading, and post-reading steps of reading the textbook chapter.

Pre-Reading   As a part of your pre-reading activities, overview the following textbook aids for the chapter.

A. "What's Ahead"
1. Note the design of the section "What's Ahead" on page 85. How do bullets help this introduction to stand out in the reader's eye? Does reading questions rather than statements make this section more interesting?
2. Look at the four questions for this first section. How would you answer the questions before reading the chapter?
3. Look at the other four introductory sections on pages 93, 99, 109, and 118. Note that the format is the same. This makes this aid easy to recognize each time you encounter it. You can also expect to answer questions in each.
    a. On page 93 (second section), which of the four questions is the most difficult to answer accurately before reading the section? Which is easiest?
    b. On page 99 (third section), of the four questions asked, which can you answer before reading the section?
    c. On page 109 (fourth section), which of the five questions are too puzzling to answer? Which question is the most helpful to you before you read? Will it help you focus and think about an idea before reading?
    d. On page 118 (fifth section), you are asked two questions, one about "age-old tribal hatreds" and the other about the "banality of evil." Do you know very much about either concept before reading this section? Which of the two has more meaning for you now?
B. Outline: During the pre-reading and reading parts of your reading plan, another textbook aid you can use is the chapter outline on page 84. This can be used as an overview and then for reference throughout the chapter reading.

C. Format: Format has been used to aid the reader also. Size of print and type of print has been used uniformly to help the reader distinguish various types of information.

At this time return to your pre-reading page (page 68), the first part of your three-part reading plan. You will have instructions later in the three-part reading plan for continuing this exercise.

Reading   As you read the chapter by your Active Questioning reading plan, read and/or answer the quiz questions. At least skim through them to see what you should know when you finish reading.

A. "Quick Quizzes" appear at the end of each of the first four sections on pages 93, 99, 108, 118, and at the end of subheadings in longer sections on pages 95 and 106. All of the quizzes use the same format. Try to catch the authors' humor at the beginning of each quiz. Does having immediate access to the answers encourage you to take the quizzes?

1. On page 93 you are asked two literal questions. Could you remember the answers? For the third question, you have to read an example of a process and then identify it. Was it easier or more difficult to answer than the first two questions?

2. On page 95 you have a quiz on the first subheading, "Attributions," in the second section. For the two questions you must apply what you have learned by reading examples and labeling them. Is it fun to check yourself this way? Is it more interesting? How well did you do?

3. On page 99, the quiz is on the second half of the second section, "Attitudes," and asks you to label and apply what you have learned. How well did you do? Can you answer these questions?

4. On page 106, the question in the middle of this third section asks you to read three different situations and then label them. Can you label them correctly?

5. On page 108, the question at the end of this section asks you to apply the concepts you have learned. How well can you answer this question?

6. On page 118, the quiz at the end of the fourth section asks you to read statements and then identify the concepts involved. It also asks you to apply what you have learned. How well do you remember names of concepts? Is this a better way of learning these concepts than simply memorizing definitions for each?

7. Review all of these quizzes to see if you still know the material. Of what concepts are you now aware that you were not before reading this chapter? Have you seen news programs or documentaries on some of the subjects in this chapter? For example, the History Channel has run a documentary on cults.

B. Visuals, including figures and tables, have also been used in the text to summarize, reinforce, and give examples at key points. One helpful figure (Figure 8.1) illustrates the phenomenon of when "bystanders" will and won't help someone in distress. It can be used during this reading part of the reading plan.

At this time return to your Active Questioning reading of the chapter (page 77), the second part of your three-part reading plan. You will have instructions later in the three-part reading plan for continuing this exercise.

Post-Reading   As a post-reading activity, look at these two textbook aids: "Get Involved" and "Thinking Critically." They are two higher-level comprehension textbook aids that provide the readers with opportunities to apply what they are learning to their own lives and to think critically.

A.   Three "Get Involved" sections appear in the chapter, one in the first section (page 87), one in the third section (page 104), and the last in the fifth section (page 115). All three suggest ways to become involved in what you are reading. The first deals with being different, the second with losing yourself, and the third with investigating your own prejudices. Review the three. If you have not tried any of them, choose one now and experiment. Write your response to your new experience. How did you think and feel at the end of your experience?

B.   A "Thinking Critically" section appears in the five sections. The reader is told to ask questions (page 88), examine the evidence (page 105), question assumptions (page 116), and not to oversimplify (page 119). Are your responses to these aids different as a result of reading the entire chapter? Which of these aids was the most challenging to you? In what way?

Review and Extension   You used end-of-chapter textbook aids—including "Looking Back" questions, Key Terms, and the Summary—in your pre-reading to overview the chapter. Now use them in post-reading as a review. Another section, "Taking Psychology with You" (page 120), gives examples of cultural differences with advice on handling them that is based on information in the chapter. Read this page thoughtfully and answer these questions if you have time:

A.   French and American sales. Do you know of businesses through reading or viewing news programs that have adjusted their expectations because of differences in cultural values?

B.   Look at the other examples of shaking hands, bargaining, and prolonged gazes. Have you ever misunderstood such differences?

C.   Read the anecdote on stereotyping and then try to think of an example from your own life in which you misunderstood another person's behavior.

Active Questioning

Overview

Your first step of the three-part reading plan was pre-reading. In pre-reading, you activated your prior knowledge, predicted what you would read, and overviewed the chapter before reading.

As the second step in this three-part reading plan, you will read the chapter "Behavior in Social and Cultural Context" by using the Active Questioning reading plan as explained below. An alternative plan, Reciprocal Teaching, is in Appendix A. In both plans you break up the chapter in sections and read and think about each as you read. The purpose of both plans is to keep you reading actively.

In the Academic Study Skills section, skim the reading section on quizzes and visuals (page 75) and then use it as a guide in taking the textbook quizzes at the end of each section.

General Directions

A. The purpose for writing and answering questions on three levels of comprehension is to first get the facts and basic information to understand the meaning on a literal level.

B. From there you move to using this literal information in the chapter and your own prior knowledge to synthesize information, draw conclusions, and make judgments.

C. The last level of comprehension gives you the opportunity to incorporate the information you have learned into your own life. Answers to questions on the last two levels of comprehension take more time to process and sometimes you may feel insecure about your answers. The literal level is easier because you can copy the answer from the text. Many times you can get this answer right without really understanding what you are reading. You need to be able to do something with the literal level information, to see its importance or significance, and that is why working on the other two levels is important.

Assignment

In this first lesson using Active Questioning, you will answer my questions instead of writing your own. Later, through teacher modeling and guided practice, you will begin to write your own. Hopefully, by the end of the course, you will write and answer your own questions on all three comprehension levels without teacher help.

A. Read section one, "Roles and Rules," and answer the following questions as directed.

1. Text-explicit (literal level). A question that requires the reader to read the line. The answer will come from one line of print.

Model text-explicit question: According to the introduction of this chapter, does people's behavior depend more on (a) the situations they are in and on the values and rules of their society and culture, or (b) on their individual personality traits? (See page 85.)

Answer _____

2. Text-implicit (inferential level). A question that requires the reader to read between the lines. The answer will come from more than one line of print. You will need to make judgments and draw conclusions. Answer one of the four model text-implicit questions.

   a. Define norms as given in context and then choose two examples that are meaningful to you and explain why they are (page 85).

   b. Three criticisms of the "Obedience Study" are given. List them and then rank them in order according to the validity of the argument with number one being the most valid. Briefly defend your choices.

   c. List the four factors (pages 91–92) that cause people to obey and then rank them in order of importance to you and then again for society. Defend your choices.

   d. Read "Evaluating the Prison Study" on page 90. In the first paragraph the study is criticized as not being research. In the second paragraph the study's designers defend it. Which argument seems best? Why? Explain how reading this study has influenced you.

Answer _____

3. Experience-based (critical/creative level). A question that requires the reader to read beyond the lines. Apply what you have learned to your world. Question what you have read. Answer one of the four model experience-based questions.

   a. According to the author, we learn most of our culture's rules and values without thinking about it. Look at the examples of conversational distance and the role requirement for a "real man" and then identify and explain a rule or something of value that you learned as a part of the culture in which you grew up. What other culture would not have the same rule or value?

   b. How do you react to authority figures in your life (your parents, employer, police)? After reflecting on your own behavior with your authority figures, how do you think you would have behaved in the obedience study? Justify your response. What insights does your response show about your own ability to see forces at work in your life?

   c. Describe what emotional reaction you had to the prisoners and guards in the prison study. If you had been a part of the study, how would you have reacted as a guard? How do you know?

   d. Review the two paragraphs on pages 90–91 that describe reasons for people obeying. What rules do you always obey?

Which rules do you obey only if you are being observed?
Examples may include driving laws or living experiences in dorms.

Answer _____

B. Read the second section, "Social Influences on Beliefs," and answer the following questions as directed.
    1. Answer one of the two text-explicit questions.
        a. When we make a *dispositional attribution,* what are we identifying as the cause of action?
        b. Define *attitude* as given in context on page 95.

Answer _____

    2. Answer one of the four text-implicit questions.
        a. Explain why people who call the student guards in the "Prison Study" sadistic and the prisoners cowardly are committing the fundamental attribution error (page 94).
        b. Review the differences in Western and Eastern perspectives in attribution of behavior. Why do you think Western middle-class people tend to make dispositional attributions?
        c. Explain "just-world hypothesis" in your own words and then give an example that you have read about in which a victim was blamed for what happened to him or her.
        d. List the six key processes of coercive persuasion and then choose one and explain how you believe it would work on you. Which would not work as well?

Answer _____

    3. Answer one of the four experience-based questions.
        a. Think critically about Western and Eastern attributions. Find contradictory examples for what was stated in the text. You can give an example of a Westerner (real-life person or movie actor) blaming a situation for something that happened instead of blaming a person. You can give an example of someone from India, China, or Japan blaming a person for an act (page 94).
        b. Think about your own relationships. When do you use situational attributions and when do you use dispositional attributions (page 94)?
        c. List the three types of friendly persuasion on pages 96–97. Which has most influenced your life? What brands of goods and clothing do you buy that are endorsed by people you admire?
        d. Give an example of an attitude you have that is shared by your peers but not your parents (page 95).

Answer _____

C. Read the third section, "Individuals in Groups," and answer the following questions as directed.

1. Answer the text-explicit question: What is the process called in which responsibility for an outcome is diffused, or spread, among many people? (page 102)

Answer _____

2. Answer one of the four text-implicit questions.
    a. List the four reasons for conformity (from page 101) in order of your own conformity. Place the most important reason first. Justify your listing.
    b. Review the study (pages 104–105) on gender differences in aggressiveness and state your opinion on the topic.
    c. In the section "Anonymity and Responsibility" (page 105), a description of a crowd murder and its aftermath is described. The author asks how responsible are the murderers. What is your judgment?
    d. Look at the five steps involved in deciding to "rock the boat" (pages 106–108) and give examples from your personal or vicarious experiences to support or contradict each.

Answer _____

3. Answer one of the eight experience-based questions.
    a. On a Sunday morning, a senior church member answers a church telephone call from a woman who needs $73.00 to pay her rent or she will be kicked out of her apartment the next day. She tells the senior church member, who believes her, that she has been off welfare for five months, working as a waitress and taking care of her children alone. You are sitting in the church hall drinking coffee with friends. Two church members collect money from everyone in the church hall. So far, they have collected $57.00. How much will you give? What influences your decision?
    b. Which campus groups that you belong to make you feel a part of them? From what groups do you choose to stay away? How have you changed as a result of the influence of groups during your beginning year of college? Do the groups consist of people like you (pages 101–102)?
    c. Think about your cultural roots in terms of your own conformity. Is your culture individual-oriented or group-oriented? How has this influenced your life style and value system (page 100)?
    d. Give your own example for one of the four symptoms of groupthink, whether from your personal experience or from your vicarious experience (friends, films, chatroom) (page 101). Of the four symptoms, which would most likely cause you to conform to a group? Why?
    e. Have you read or witnessed an example of the group process called *the diffusion of responsibility*? Describe an occurrence when social loafing has taken place by members of a group you belong

to on campus (page 102). Look at the list of reasons for this occurrence (page 103) and make an educated guess at the reason for your group's social loafing. How could the social loafing be eliminated?

f.   Describe a time when you have felt deindividualized in a crowd and acted in a way that seemed uncharacteristic of your usual self. How did you feel later about your behavior?

g.   Have you ever had to wear a uniform? Did you feel deindividualized? (page 104) Describe your experience. Justify the use of or no use of school uniforms.

h.   Give examples of when members of a crowd you were a part of, conforming to the goals and norms of a situation, took part in either collective violence or collective kindness. For example, have you ever been stuck in a winter snowstorm and experienced everyone on the highway helping each other out (page 105)?

Answer _____

D.   Read the fourth section, "Group Conflict and Prejudice," and answer the following questions as directed.

1.   Answer the text-explicit question: The text states that most of us take our own rules and norms for granted, and assume they are logical, normal, and right. When, according to the text, does the trouble start (page 109)?

Answer _____

2.   Answer one of the four text-implicit questions.

a.   In order of importance to you, list the three ways stereotypes distort reality. Defend your choices (page 111).

b.   List the four sources of prejudice (page 112) and then choose one to discuss as to its importance to you.

c.   List the two ways to measure racism as listed on pages 113–115 and then evaluate them. What seems true? Not true?

d.   List the ways to classify different prejudices (page 115) and then, according to your own value system, rank the different types and justify your choices.

Answer _____

3.   Answer one of the four experience-based questions.

a.   Describe your own personality traits and then your social identity (page 109). Are you more inclined toward competition or cooperation? Can you give an example of groups that compete but also work together on your campus? For example, some fraternities compete for new members and status but work on service projects together (page 110).

b.   When have you had one of your stereotypes broken? When have you been stereotyped (page 111)?

    c.   Look at examples on page 111 of how cultural values affect how people evaluate a particular action. How do your cultural values influence how you view people who are overweight and students who are late for class?

    d.   Look at the four conditions that must be met before prejudice can be overcome (pages 116–117) in light of your campus. What prejudices exist and how can overcoming the four conditions help reduce or eliminate them?

Answer _____

  E. Read the fifth section, "The Question of Human Nature," and answer the following questions as directed.

    1.   Answer the text-explicit question: How did Wladyslaw Misiuna save Devora Salzberg's life? (See page 118.)

Answer _____

    2.   Answer the text-implicit question: Look at the examples of evil performed by a variety of people all over the world (pages 118–119). Can you think of anything about any of these groups that you know is good? What else do you know about them? In other words, can you prove that people are complex, not just good or evil?

Answer _____

    3.   Answer the experience-based question: The text states that no culture can claim to be wholly virtuous, and no culture is entirely villainous either (page 119). Think about your own culture or one you really admire or hate and list the good and evil in that culture.

Answer _____

POST-READING THE TEXTBOOK CHAPTER

OVERVIEW

In the second part of your three-part reading plan, you practiced reading your textbook chapter section by section and answered literal, inferential, and critical/creative comprehension questions.

    In this third part of the three-part reading plan, you will find suggestions for what to do after you read. Your task is to compare what you predicted with what you actually read as an aid to comprehension, to add what you have learned to your file of information on the topic, and to think about what you have read.

ASSIGNMENT

Before completing the exercise below, do the Post-Reading section of the Textbook Study Aids Plan in the Academic Study Skills section on page 76.

A. Compare what you predicted you would read with what you actually read. Did anything you predicted cause you a problem with comprehension? What? How?

B. What did you learn from the reading that you did not know about before working on this lesson?

C. Look at the words and phrases that you listed as your prior knowledge in the pre-reading section of this lesson. Group them below with relevant information in "B" above. This is your new file of information on psychology. (The ability to group ideas and to see relationships requires more complex comprehension than merely memorizing isolated facts.)

D. What have you learned from this chapter that is important?

E. What do you already know that you can relate to it?

F. What do you see differently as a result of reading the psychology chapter?

Your Headings	Words and Phrases from Pre-Reading	Relevant Information from "B"

BEHAVIOR IN SOCIAL AND CULTURAL CONTEXT

FROM CAROLE WADE/CAROL TAVRIS, *PSYCHOLOGY, 6/E*

Roles and Rules
The Obedience Study
The Prison Study
The Power of Roles
Social Influences on Beliefs
Attributions
Attitudes
Individuals in Groups
Conformity
Groupthink
The Anonymous Crowd
Disobedience and Dissent
Group Conflict and Prejudice
Group Identity: Us Versus Them
Stereotypes
Prejudice
Efforts to Reduce Prejudice
The Question of Human Nature
Taking Psychology with You
Travels Across the Cultural Divide

In a quiet suburb of Baton Rouge, Louisiana, Yoshi-hiro Hattori, a 16-year-old Japanese exchange student, went along with his friend Webb Haymaker to a Halloween party. They mistakenly stopped in front of a house covered in Halloween decorations and rang the bell. Hearing no answer, Yoshi went to see whether the party might be in the backyard. The home owner, Bonnie Peairs, opened the front door, saw Webb in a Halloween costume and then saw Yoshi running back toward her waving an object (which turned out to be a camera). She panicked and called for her husband to get his gun. Rodney Peairs grabbed a .44 Magnum and shouted, "Freeze." Yoshi, not understanding the word, did not stop. Peairs shot him in the heart, killing him instantly.

When Rodney Peairs' case came to trial, the jury acquitted him of manslaughter after only three hours of deliberation. The Japanese were appalled at this verdict. To them, it illustrated everything that is wrong with America, a nation rife with guns and violence, still growing out of its Wild-West past. The Japanese cannot imagine a country that would permit private individuals to keep guns, and the murder rate in Japan is a tiny percentage of what it is in America. In contrast, the citizens of Baton Rouge were surprised that the case came to trial at all. What is more right and natural, they asked, than protecting your family from intruders? A local man, puzzled that Peairs had even been arrested, said, "It would be to me what a normal person would do under those circumstances."

But what is normal? The shooting of Yoshihiro Hattori is a dramatic example of how external circumstances can affect behavior, and how notions of what a "normal person" would do in one culture may be considered wildly abnormal in others. In this chapter, we will see again and again that people's behavior often depends more on the situations they are in, and on the values and rules of their society and culture, than on their individual personality traits. Even acts of courage and cowardice are more often affected by circumstances than by whether a person is inherently "good" or "bad."

The fields of *social psychology* and *cultural psychology* examine the powerful influence of the social and cultural environment on the actions of individuals and groups. We report findings from these fields throughout this book: for example, in our discussions of love and sexuality, how the environmental setting affects people's responses to drugs, how emotions communicate, why friends are necessary for health, and the nature of social influence in psychotherapy. Here we will focus on the foundations of social psychology: roles, attitudes, and groups, and the conditions under which people conform or dissent. Then we will consider some of the social and cultural reasons for prejudice and conflict between groups.

What's Ahead

- How do social rules regulate behavior—and what is likely to happen when you violate them?
- Do you have to be mean or disturbed to hurt someone just because an authority tells you to?
- How can ordinary college students be transformed into sadistic prison guards?
- How can people be "entrapped" into violating their moral principles?

Roles and Rules

"We are all fragile creatures entwined in a cobweb of social constraints," social psychologist Stanley Milgram once said. The constraints he referred to are social **norms**, rules about how we are supposed to act, enforced by threats of punishment if we violate them and by promises of reward if we follow them (Kerr, 1995). Norms are the conventions of everyday life that make interactions with other people predictable and orderly; like a cobweb, they are often as invisible as they are strong. Every society has norms for just about everything in human experience: for conducting courtships, raising children, making decisions, behaving in public places. Some norms are enshrined in law, such as, "A person may not beat up another person, except in self-defense." Some are unspoken cultural understandings, such as, "A man may beat up another man who insults his masculinity." And some are tiny, unspoken regulations that people learn to follow unconsciously, such as, "You may not sing at the top of your lungs on a public bus."

In every society, people also fill a variety of social **roles,** positions that are regulated by norms about how people in those positions should behave. Gender roles define the proper behavior for a man and a woman. Occupational roles determine the correct behavior for a manager and an employee, a professor and a student. Family roles set tasks for parent and child, husband and wife. Certain aspects of every role must be carried out or there will be penalties—emotional, financial, professional. As a student, for instance, you know just what you have to do to pass your psychology course (or you should by now!).

The requirements of a social role are in turn shaped by the culture you live in. **Culture** can be defined as a program of shared rules that govern the behavior of people in a community or society, and a set of values and beliefs shared by most members of that community and passed from one generation to another (Lonner, 1995). You learn most of your culture's rules and values the way you learn your culture's language—without thinking about it.

For example, cultures differ in their rules for *conversational distance*: how close people normally stand to one another when they are speaking (Hall, 1959, 1976). Arabs like to stand close enough to feel your breath, touch your arm, and see your eyes—a distance that makes white Americans, Canadians, and northern Europeans uneasy, unless they are talking intimately with a lover. The English and the Swedes stand farthest apart when they converse; southern Europeans stand closer; and Latin Americans and Arabs stand the closest (Keating, 1994; Sommer, 1969). Knowing another culture's rules, though, does not make it any easier to change your own. Caroline Keating (1994), an American cultural psychologist, told about walking with a Pakistani colleague. The closer he moved toward her, seeking the closeness he was comfortable with, the more she moved away, seeking the distance *she* was comfortable with. "I would suddenly disappear from his view, having fallen into the street," she reported, "perhaps not 'the ugly American,' but a clumsy one!"

The same discomfort occurs when people violate a role requirement, intentionally or unintentionally; they are likely to feel uncomfortable—or other people will try to make them feel uncomfortable. For instance, in your family, whose job is it to buy gifts for parents, send greeting cards to friends, organize parties and prepare the food, remember an aunt's birthday, and call friends to see how they're doing? Chances are you are thinking of a woman. These activities are considered part of the woman's role in most cultures, and women are usually blamed if they do not carry them out (di Leonardo, 1987; Lott & Maluso, 1993).

Likewise, in your culture what are the role requirements of a "real man"? According to studies conducted with a widely used measure, the Male Role Norms Scale, traditional male norms require a man to be strong (e.g., "A man should never back down in the face of trouble"); reject qualities associated with women (e.g., "It bothers me when a man does something that I consider 'feminine'"); keep his problems to himself (e.g., "Nobody respects a man very much who frequently talks about his worries, fears, and problems"); and behave aggressively if threatened (e.g., "Fists are sometimes the only way to get out of a bad situation") (Fischer et al., 1998).

What is likely to happen to men who break these norms, for example, by revealing their fears and worries? They are frequently regarded by both sexes as being "too feminine" and poorly adjusted (Peplau & Gordon, 1985; Taffel, 1990). However, the norms of the male role, like those for females, are changing rapidly in Western cultures, as we discuss in Chapter 11. Today many men think it is normal and beneficial to express their feelings; male politicians and athletes even cry in public.

Naturally, people bring their own personalities and interests to the roles they play. Just as two actors will play James Bond differently although they are reading from the same script, you will have your own "reading" of how to play the role of student, friend, parent, or employer. Nonetheless, the requirements of a social role are pretty strong, so strong that they may even cause you to behave in ways that shatter your fundamental sense of the kind of person you are, as we will see next.

GET INVOLVED

DARE TO BE DIFFERENT

Either alone or with a friend, try a mild form of norm violation (nothing alarming, obscene, dangerous, or offensive). For example, stand backwards in line at the grocery store or cafeteria; sit right next to a stranger in the library or at a movie, even when other seats are available; sing or hum loudly for a couple of minutes in a public place; stand "too close" to a friend in conversation. Notice the reactions of onlookers, as well as your own feelings, while you violate this norm. If you do this exercise with someone else, one of you can be the "violator," and the other can note down the responses of others; then switch places. Was it easy to do this exercise? Why or why not?

The Obedience Study

A man was on trial for murder, although he personally had never killed anyone. Six psychiatrists examined him and pronounced him sane. His family life was normal and he had deep feelings of love for his wife, children, and parents. Two observers, after reviewing transcripts of his 275-hour interrogation, described him as "an average man of middle class origins and normal middle class upbringing, a man without identifiable criminal tendencies" (Von Lang & Sibyll, 1984).

The man was Adolf Eichmann, a high-ranking officer of the Nazi SS, an elite military unit of storm troopers. Eichmann supervised the deportation and death of millions of Jews during World War II. He was proud of his efficiency at his work and his ability to resist feeling pity for his victims. But when the Israelis captured him and put him on trial in 1961, he insisted that he was not anti-Semitic: He had had a Jewish mistress, and he personally arranged for the protection of his Jewish half-cousin—two dangerous crimes for an SS officer. Shortly before his execution by hanging, Eichmann said, "I am not the monster I am made out to be. I am the victim of a fallacy" (R. Brown, 1986).

The fallacy to which Eichmann referred was the widespread belief that a person who does monstrous deeds must be a monster, someone sick and evil. Is that true? In the early 1960s, Stanley Milgram (1963, 1974) designed a study that would become world famous; it was, in effect, a test of Eichmann's claim of normality.

Design and Findings

Milgram wanted to know how many people would obey an authority figure when directly ordered to violate their own ethical standards. Participants in the study, however, thought they were part of an experiment on the effects of punishment on learning. Each was assigned, apparently at random, to the role of "teacher." Another person, introduced as a fellow volunteer, was the "learner." Whenever the learner, seated in an adjoining room, made an error in reciting a list of word pairs he was supposed to have memorized, the teacher had to give him an electric shock by depressing a lever on a machine. With each error, the voltage (marked from 0 to 450) was to be increased by another 15 volts. The shock levels on the machine were labeled from SLIGHT SHOCK to DANGER—SEVERE SHOCK and, finally, ominously, XXX. In reality, the learners were confederates of Milgram and did not receive any shocks, but none of the teachers ever realized this during the study. The actor-victims played their parts convincingly: As the study continued, they shouted in pain and

THINKING CRITICALLY

ASK QUESTIONS

Jot down your best guess in answering these three questions: (1) What percentage of people are sadistic? (2) If told by an authority to harm an innocent person, what percentage of people would do it? (3) If you were instructed to harm an innocent person, would you do it or would you refuse?

pleaded to be released, all according to a prearranged script.

Before doing this study, Milgram asked a number of psychiatrists, students, and middle-class adults how many people they thought would "go all the way" to XXX on orders from the researcher. The psychiatrists predicted that most people would refuse to go beyond 150 volts, when the learner first demanded to be freed, and that only one person in a thousand, someone who was disturbed and sadistic, would administer the highest voltage. The nonprofessionals agreed with this prediction, and all of them said that they personally would disobey early in the procedure.

That is not the way the results turned out, however. Every single person administered some shock to the learner, and about two-thirds of the participants, of all ages and from all walks of life, obeyed to the fullest extent. Many protested to the experimenter, but they backed down when he merely asserted, "The experiment requires that you continue." They obeyed no matter how much the victim shouted for them to stop and no matter how painful the shocks seemed to be. They obeyed even when they themselves were anguished about the pain they believed they were causing. As Milgram (1974) noted, participants would "sweat, tremble, stutter, bite their lips, groan, and dig their fingernails into their flesh"—but still they obeyed.

More than 1,000 people at several American universities eventually went through replications of the Milgram study. Most of them, men and women equally, inflicted what they thought were dangerous amounts of shock to another person (Blass, 1993). Researchers in other countries have also found high percentages of obedience, ranging to more than 90 percent in Spain and the Netherlands (Meeus & Raaijmakers, 1995; Smith & Bond, 1993, 1994).

Milgram and his team subsequently set up several variations of the study to determine the circumstances under which people might disobey the experimenter. They found that virtually nothing the victim did or said changed the likelihood of compliance—even when the victim said he had a heart condition, screamed in agony, or stopped responding entirely as if he had collapsed.

However, people *were* more likely to disobey under the following conditions:

- *When the experimenter left the room.* Many people then subverted authority by giving low levels of shock but reporting that they had followed orders.
- *When the victim was right there in the room,* and the teacher had to administer the shock directly to the victim's body.
- *When two experimenters issued conflicting demands* to continue the experiment or to stop at once. In this case, no one kept inflicting shock.
- *When the person ordering them to continue was an ordinary man,* apparently another volunteer, instead of the authoritative experimenter.

- *When the subject worked with peers who refused to go further.* Seeing someone else rebel gave subjects the courage to disobey.

Obedience, Milgram concluded, was more a function of the situation than of the particular personalities of the participants. "The key to [their] behavior," Milgram (1974) summarized, "lies not in pent-up anger or aggression but in the nature of their relationship to authority. They have given themselves to the authority; they see themselves as instruments for the execution of his wishes; once so defined, they are unable to break free."

Evaluating the Obedience Study

The Milgram study has had its critics. Some consider it unethical because people were kept in the dark about what was really happening until the session was over (of course, telling them in advance would have invalidated the study) and because many suffered emotional pain (Milgram countered that they would not have felt pain if they had simply disobeyed the instructions). Others question the conclusion that personality traits always have less influence on behavior than the demands of the situation; certain traits, such as hostility and rigidity, do increase obedience to authority in real life (Blass, 1993).

Some psychologists also object to the parallel Milgram drew between the behavior of the study's participants and the brutality of the Nazis and others who have committed acts of barbarism in the name of duty. As John Darley (1995) noted, the people in Milgram's study obeyed only when the experimenter was hovering right there, and many of them felt enormous discomfort and conflict. In contrast, the Nazis acted without direct supervision by authorities, without external pressure, and without feelings of anguish.

Nevertheless, this study has had a tremendous influence on public awareness of the dangers of uncritical obedience. As Darley himself observed, "Milgram shows us the beginning of a path by means of which ordinary people, in the grip of social forces, become the origins of atrocities in the real world."

The Prison Study

Imagine that one day, as you are walking home from school, a police car pulls up. Two uniformed officers get out, arrest you, and take you to a prison cell. There you are stripped of your clothes, sprayed with a delousing fluid, assigned a prison uniform, photographed with your prison number, and put behind bars. You feel a little queasy but you are not panicked; you have agreed to play the part of prisoner for a two-week study, and your arrest is merely part of the script. Your prison cell, while apparently authentic, is located in the basement of a university building. So began an effort to discover what happens when ordinary college students take on the roles of prisoners and guards (Haney, Banks, & Zimbardo, 1973).

Design and Findings

The young men who volunteered for this experience were paid a nice daily fee. They were randomly assigned to be prisoners or guards, but other than that, they were given no instructions about how to behave. The results were dramatic. Within a short time, the prisoners became distressed, helpless, and panicky. They developed emotional symptoms and physical ailments. Some became apathetic; others became rebellious. After a few days, half of the prisoners begged to be let out. They were more than willing to forfeit their pay to gain an early release.

Within an equally short time, the guards adjusted to their new power. Some tried to be nice, helping the prisoners and doing little favors for them. Some were "tough but fair," holding strictly to "the rules." But about a third became tyrannical. Although they were free to use any method they liked to maintain order, they almost always chose to be harsh and abusive, even when the prisoners were not resisting in any way. One guard, unaware that he was being observed by the researchers, paced the corridor while the prisoners were sleeping, pounding his nightstick into his hand. Another put a prisoner in solitary confinement (a small closet) and tried to keep him there all night. He concealed this information from the researchers, who, he thought, were "too soft" on the prisoners. Not one of the less actively cruel guards, by the way, ever intervened or complained about the behavior of their more abusive peers.

The researchers, who had not expected such a speedy and terrifying transformation of mentally healthy students, ended this study after only six days. The prisoners were relieved by this decision, but most of the guards were disappointed. They had enjoyed their short-lived authority.

Evaluating the Prison Study

Critics maintain that you cannot learn much from such an artificial setup. They argue that the volunteers already knew, from movies, TV, and games, how they were supposed to behave. The guards acted their parts to the hilt in order to have fun and please the researchers. Their behavior was no more surprising than if they had been dressed in football gear and had then been found to be willing to bruise each other in a game. The prison study made a great story, say

some critics, but it wasn't *research*. That is, the researchers did not carefully investigate relationships between factors; for all the study's drama, it provided no new information (Festinger, 1980).

Craig Haney and Philip Zimbardo, who designed the prison study, respond that this dramatization illustrated the power of roles in a way that no ordinary lab experiment ever could. If the guards were just having fun, why did they lose sight of the "game" and behave as if it were a real job? Twenty-five years after the prison study was done, Haney and Zimbardo (1998) noted how much it contributed to understanding the behavior of real prisoners and guards in prisons, and also to increasing public awareness of how situations can outweigh personality and private values in influencing behavior.

The Power of Roles

The two imaginative studies we have described vividly demonstrate the power of social roles and obligations to influence the behavior of individuals. When people in the Milgram study believed they had to follow the legitimate orders of authority, most of them put their private values and personality traits aside. The behavior of the prisoners and guards varied—some prisoners were more rebellious than others, some guards were more abusive than others—but ultimately what the students did depended on the roles they were assigned.

Obedience, of course, is not always harmful or bad. A certain amount of routine compliance with rules is necessary in any group, and obedience to authority has many benefits for individuals and society. A nation could not operate if all its citizens ignored traffic signals, cheated on their taxes, dumped garbage wherever they chose, or assaulted each other. An organization could not function if its members came to work only when they felt like it. But obedience also has a darker aspect. Throughout history, the plea "I was only following orders" has been offered to excuse actions carried out on behalf of orders that were foolish, destructive, or illegal. The writer C. P. Snow once observed that "more hideous crimes have been committed in the name of obedience than in the name of rebellion."

Most people follow orders because of the obvious consequences of disobedience: They can be suspended from school, fired from their jobs, or arrested. They may also obey because of what they hope to gain: being liked, getting certain advantages or promotions from the authority, learning from the authority's greater knowledge or experience. Primarily, though, people obey because they are deeply convinced of the authority's legitimacy—that is, they obey not in hopes of gaining some tangible benefit, but because they like and respect the authority and value the relationship (Tyler, 1997).

But what about all those obedient people in Milgram's study who felt they were doing wrong and who wished they were free, but who could not untangle themselves from the cobweb of social constraints? Why do people obey when it is not in their interests, or when obedience requires them to ignore their own values or even commit a crime?

To answer this question, Herbert Kelman and Lee Hamilton (1989) studied "crimes of obedience," ranging from military massacres of civilians in the Vietnam War to political crimes committed by American presidents, such as Watergate (in which Richard Nixon and his advisers tried to cover up the attempted theft of files from Democratic headquarters) and the Iran-Contra scandal (in which Ronald Reagan's administration illegally sold arms to Iran in order to unlawfully fund the Contra forces in Nicaragua). They and other researchers draw our attention to several factors that cause people to obey when they would rather not:

Investing the Authority Investing the authority, rather than oneself, with responsibility allows people to absolve themselves of accountability for their own actions. In Milgram's study, many of those who administered the highest levels of shock relinquished responsibility to the experimenter. A 37-year-old welder explained that the experimenter was responsible for any pain the victim might suffer "for the simple reason that I was paid for doing this. I had to follow orders." In contrast, individuals who refused to give high levels of shock took responsibility for their actions and refused to grant the authority legitimacy. "One of the things I think is very cowardly," said a 32-year-old engineer, "is to try to shove the responsibility onto someone else. See, if I now turned around and said, 'It's your fault . . . it's not mine,' I would call that cowardly" (Milgram, 1974).

Routinization Routinization is the process of defining the activity in terms of routine duties and roles so that the behavior becomes normalized, a job to be done, with little opportunity to raise doubts or ethical questions. In the Milgram study, some people became so fixated on the "learning task" that they shut out any moral concerns about the learner's demands to be let out of the experiment. Routinization is typically the mechanism by which governments enlist citizens to aid and abet programs of genocide. German bureaucrats kept meticulous records of every Nazi victim, and in Cambodia the Khmer Rouge recorded the names and histories of the millions of victims they tortured and killed. "I am not a violent man," said Sous Thy, one of the clerks who recorded these names, to a reporter from the *New York Times*. "I was just making lists."

The Rules of Good Manners   The rules of good manners protect people's feelings and make relationships and civilization possible. But once people are caught in what they perceive to be legitimate roles and are obeying a legitimate authority, good manners ensnare them into further obedience. Most people do not like to rock the boat, appear to doubt the experts, or be rude, because they know they will be disliked for doing so (Collins & Brief, 1995).

Most people learn the language of manners ("please," "thank you," "I'm sorry for missing your birthday"), but they literally lack the words to justify disobedience and rudeness toward an authority they respect. In the Milgram study, many people could not find the words to justify walking out, so they stayed. One woman kept apologizing to the experimenter, trying not to offend him with her worries for the victim: "Do I go right to the end, sir? I hope there's nothing wrong with him there." (She did go right to the end.) A man repeatedly protested and questioned the experimenter, but he, too, obeyed, even when the victim had apparently collapsed in pain. "He thinks he is killing someone," Milgram (1974) commented, "yet he uses the language of the tea table."

Entrapment   Entrapment is a process in which individuals escalate their commitment to a course of action in order to justify their investment in it (Brockner & Rubin, 1985). The first steps of entrapment pose no difficult choices, but one step leads to another, and before you realize it, you have become committed to a course of action that poses problems. In Milgram's study, once subjects had given a 15-volt

shock, they had committed themselves to the experiment. The next level was "only" 30 volts. Because each increment was small, before they knew it most people were administering what they believed were dangerously strong shocks. At that point, it was difficult to explain a sudden decision to quit. Participants who resisted early in the study, questioning the procedure, were less likely to become entrapped by it and more likely to eventually disobey (Modigliani & Rochat, 1995).

Everyone, individuals and nations alike, is vulnerable to the sneaky process of entrapment. You start dating someone you like moderately; before you know it, you have been together so long that you can't break up, although you don't want to become committed, either. Government leaders start a war they think will end quickly. Years later, the nation has lost so many soldiers and so much money that the leaders believe they cannot retreat without losing face.

A chilling study of entrapment was conducted with 25 men who had served in the Greek military police during the authoritarian regime that ended in 1974 (Haritos-Fatouros, 1988). A psychologist who interviewed the men identified the steps used in training them to use torture when questioning prisoners. First, the men were ordered to stand guard outside the interrogation and torture cells. Then, they stood guard in the detention rooms, where they observed the torture of prisoners. Then, they "helped" beat up prisoners. Once they had obediently followed these orders and became actively involved, the torturers found their actions easier to carry out.

Many people expect solutions to moral problems to fall into two clear categories, with right on one side and wrong on the other. Yet in everyday life, as in the Milgram study, people often set out on a path that is morally ambiguous, only to find that they have traveled a long way toward violating their own principles. From Greece's torturers to the Khmer Rouge's dutiful clerks, from Milgram's well-meaning volunteers to all of us in our everyday lives, people face the difficult task of drawing a line beyond which they will not go. For many, the demands of the external role defeat the inner voice of conscience.

QUICK QUIZ

Step into your role as student to answer these questions:

1. About what percentage of the people in Milgram's obedience study administered the highest levels of shock? (a) two-thirds, (b) one-half, (c) one-third, (d) one-tenth

2. Which of the following actions by the "learner" reduced the likelihood of being shocked by the "teacher" in Milgram's study? (a) protesting noisily, (b) screaming in pain, (c) complaining of having a heart ailment, (d) nothing he did made a difference

3. A friend of yours, who is moving, asks you to bring over a few boxes. Since you are there anyway, he asks you to fill them with books. Before you know it, you have packed up his entire kitchen, living room, and bedroom. What social-psychological process is at work here?

Answers:

1. a 2. d 3. entrapment

WHAT'S AHEAD

- What is one of the most common mistakes people make when they explain the behavior of others?
- Why would a person blame victims of rape or torture for having brought their misfortunes on themselves?
- What is the "Big Lie," and why does it work so well?
- What is the difference between ordinary techniques of persuasion and the coercive techniques used by cults?

Social Influences on Beliefs

Social psychologists are interested not only in what people do in social situations, but also in what goes on in their heads while they are doing it. Researchers in the area of **social cognition** examine how the social environment influences people's thoughts, beliefs, and memories, and how people's perceptions of themselves and others affect their relationships (A. Fiske & Haslam, 1996). We will consider two important topics in this area: explanations about behavior and the formation of attitudes.

Attributions

People read detective stories to find out *who* did the dirty deed, but in real life we also want to know *why* people do things—was it because of a terrible childhood, a mental illness, possession by a demon, or what? According to **attribution theory,** the explanations we make of our behavior and the behavior of others generally fall into two categories. When we make a *situational attribution*, we are identifying the cause of an action as something in the situation or environment: "Joe stole the money because his family is starving." When we make a *dispositional attribution*, we are identifying the cause of an action as something in the person, such as a trait or a motive: "Joe stole the money because he is a born thief."

When people are trying to find reasons for someone else's behavior, they reveal a common bias: They tend to overestimate personality traits and underestimate the influence of the situation (Forgas, 1998; Nisbett & Ross, 1980). In terms of attribution theory, they tend to ignore situational attributions in favor of dispositional ones. This tendency has been called the **fundamental attribution error.** Were the hundreds of people who obeyed Milgram's experimenters sadistic by nature? Were the student guards in the prison study sadistic and the prisoners cowardly? Those who think so are committing the fundamental attribution error.

People are especially likely to overlook situational attributions when they are in a good mood and not inclined to think about other people's motives critically, or when they are distracted and preoccupied and don't have time to stop and ask themselves, "Why, exactly, *is* Aurelia behaving like a dork today?" (Forgas, 1998). Instead, they leap to the easiest attribution, which is dispositional: Aurelia simply has a dorky personality.

The fundamental attribution error is especially prevalent in Western nations, where middle-class people tend to believe that individuals are responsible for their own actions. In countries such as India, where everyone is embedded in caste and family networks, and in Japan, China, and Hong Kong, where people are more group oriented than in the West, people are more likely to be aware of situational constraints on behavior

(Choi, Nisbett, & Norenzayan, 1999; Morris & Peng, 1994). Thus, if someone is behaving oddly, makes a mistake, or plays badly in a soccer match, a person from India or China, unlike a Westerner, is more likely to make a situational attribution of the behavior ("He's under pressure") than a dispositional one ("He's incompetent").

Westerners do not always prefer dispositional attributions, however. When it comes to explaining their *own* behavior, they often reveal a **self-serving bias:** They tend to choose attributions that are favorable to them, taking credit for their good actions (a dispositional attribution) but letting the situation account for their bad or embarrassing actions. For instance, most Westerners, when angry, will say, "I am furious for good reason—this situation is intolerable." They are less likely to say, "I am furious because I am an ill-tempered grinch." On the other hand, if they do something admirable, such as donating to charity, they are likely to attribute their motives to a personal disposition ("I'm so generous") instead of the situation ("That guy on the phone pressured me into it").

People's attributions are also affected by the need to believe that the world is fair, that good people are rewarded and bad guys punished. According to the **just-world hypothesis,** the belief in a just world helps people make sense out of senseless events and feel safe in the presence of threatening events (Lerner, 1980). Unfortunately, this belief also leads to a dispositional attribution called *blaming the victim.* If a friend loses his job, if a woman is raped, if a prisoner is tortured, it is reassuring to think that they all must have done something to deserve what happened or to provoke it. This kind of attribution was apparent in the Milgram study, when many of the "teachers" made comments such as, "[The learner] was so stupid and stubborn he deserved to get shocked" (Milgram, 1974).

Of course, sometimes dispositional (personality) attributions do explain a person's behavior. The point to remember is that attributions, whether they are accurate or not, have tremendously important consequences for emotions and actions, for legal decisions, and for everyday relations. Happy couples, for example, tend to attribute their partners' occasional lapses to something in the situation ("Poor Harold is under a lot of stress at work"), whereas unhappy couples tend to make dispositional attributions ("Harold is just a selfish skunk")(Fincham & Bradbury, 1993; Karney et al., 1994). Your attributions about your partner, your parents, and your friends will make a big difference in how you get along with them—and how long you will put up with their failings.

QUICK QUIZ

To what do you attribute your success in answering these questions?

1. What kind of attribution is being made in each case, situational or dispositional? (a) A man says, "My wife has sure become a grouchy person." (b) The same man says, "I'm grouchy because I've had a bad day at the office." (c) A woman reads that unemployment is high in inner-city communities. "Well, if those people weren't so lazy, they would find work," she says.

2. What principles of attribution theory are suggested by the items in the preceding question?

Answers:

1. a. dispositional   b. situational   c. dispositional
2. Item *a* illustrates the fundamental attribution error; *b*, the self-serving bias; and *c*, blaming the victim, possibly because of the just-world hypothesis.

Attitudes

People hold attitudes about all sorts of things—politics, people, food, children, movies, sports heroes, you name it. An *attitude* is a relatively stable opinion containing both a cognitive element (perceptions and beliefs about the topic) and an emotional element (feelings about the topic, which can range from negative and hostile to positive and warm).

Most people think that their attitudes are based on thinking, a result of reasoned conclusions about how things work. Sometimes, of course, that's true! But some attitudes are a result of not thinking at all. They are a result of conformity, habit, rationalization, economic self-interest, and many subtle social and environmental influences. For example, some attitudes arise because of the shared experiences of an age group or generation. Each generation has its own defining social and political events, economic interests, job and marital opportunities, and other shared concerns, and therefore its own characteristic attitudes. (That is why people speak of the Depression generation, the Baby Boomers, and "Generation X.") The ages of 16 to 24 appear to be critical for the formation of a "generational identity" that lasts throughout adulthood; the experiences that occur during these years make deeper impressions and exert more lasting influence than those that happen later in life (Inglehart, 1990; Schuman & Scott, 1989). For example, Americans who were young adults during the Depression (1930s), World War II (1940s), the civil-rights movement (1950s-1960s), the Vietnam War (1965-1973), or the rebirth of the women's rights movement (1970s) regard these events as major influences on their political philosophy, values, attitudes, and ambitions. What do you think might be the critical generational events affecting the attitudes of your generation?

Attitudes and behavior influence each other. Often, attitudes dispose people to behave in certain ways; if you have a positive attitude toward martial-arts movies, you'll go to as many as you can, and if you hate them, you'll stay away from them. But new behavior can also change attitudes. Suppose your friend drags you unwillingly to a Jackie Chan movie, and you discover that you like it. Your attitude toward martial-arts movies will change accordingly.

Attitudes also change because of the need for consistency. In Chapter 9, we discuss *cognitive dissonance,* the uncomfortable feeling that occurs when two attitudes, or an attitude and behavior, are in conflict (are dissonant). Cognitive dissonance will occur, for example, if you learn that a male athlete you admire has been arrested for rape. To restore consistency, you will need to lose your admiration for the man, rationalize his behavior, or decide that his accuser is lying.

Our attitudes are also influenced constantly by other people. Sometimes people persuade us to change our minds using reasoned argument; sometimes they use subtle manipulation; and sometimes they use outright coercion.

Friendly Persuasion

All around you, every day, advertisers, politicians, and friends are trying to influence your attitudes. One weapon they use is the drip, drip, drip of a repeated idea. Repeated exposure even to a nonsense syllable such as *zug* is enough to make a person feel more positive toward it (Zajonc, 1968). The effectiveness of familiarity has long been known to politicians and advertisers: Repeat something often enough, even the basest lie, and eventually the public will believe it—which is why Hitler's propaganda minister, Joseph Goebbels, called this technique the "Big Lie." Its formal name is the **validity effect**.

In a series of experiments, Hal Arkes and his associates demonstrated how the validity effect operates (Arkes, 1993; Arkes, Boehm, & Xu, 1991). In a typical study, people read a list of statements, such as "Mercury has a higher boiling point than copper" or "Over 400 Hollywood films were produced in 1948." They had to rate each statement for its validity, on a scale of 1 (definitely false) to 7 (definitely true). A week or two later, they again rated the validity of some of these statements and also rated others that they had not seen previously. The result: Mere repetition increased the perception that the familiar statements were true. The same effect also occurred for other kinds of statements, including unverifiable opinions (e.g., "At least 75 percent of all politicians are basically dishonest"), opinions that subjects initially felt were true, and even opinions they initially felt were false. "Note that no attempt has been made to persuade," said Arkes (1993). "No supporting arguments are offered. We just have subjects rate the statements. Mere repetition seems to increase rated validity. This is scary."

Another effective technique for influencing people's attitudes is to have arguments presented by someone who is considered admirable, knowledgeable, or beautiful; this is why advertisements are full of sports heroes, experts, and fashion models (Cialdini, 1993). Persuaders may also try to link their message with a good feeling. In one classic study, students who were given peanuts and Pepsi while listening to a speaker's point of view were more likely to be convinced by it than were students who listened to the same words without the pleasant munchies and soft drinks (Janis, Kaye, & Kirschner, 1965). This finding has been replicated many times (Pratkanis & Aronson, 1992) and may explain why so much business is conducted over lunch, and so many courtships over dinner!

In sum, here are three good ways to influence attitudes:

1. Repetition of an idea or assertion (the validity effect)
2. Endorsement by an admired or attractive person
3. Association of the message with a good feeling

In contrast, the emotion of fear can cause people to resist arguments that are in their own best interest (Pratkanis & Aronson, 1992). Fear tactics are often used to try to persuade people to quit smoking or abusing other drugs, drive only when sober, use condoms, check for signs of cancer, and prepare for earthquakes. However, fear works only if people become moderately anxious, not scared to death, *and* if the message also provides information about how to avoid the danger (Leventhal & Nerenz, 1982). When messages about a future disaster are too terrifying and when people believe that they can do nothing to avoid it, they tend to deny the danger. (This finding makes us curious about how the recent antismoking ads will do—the ones that inform men that smoking is a leading cause of impotence. Do you think they will work?)

Coercive Persuasion

Some manipulators use harsher tactics, not just hoping that people will change their minds but attempting to force them to. These tactics are sometimes referred to as *brainwashing,* a term first used during the Korean War to describe techniques used on American prisoners of war to get them to collaborate with their Chinese Communist captors and to endorse anti-American propaganda. Most psychologists, however, prefer the phrase *coercive persuasion.*

"Brainwashing" implies that a person has a sudden change of mind and is unaware of what is happening; it sounds mysterious and powerful. In fact, the methods involved are neither mysterious nor unusual. The difference between "persuasion" and "brainwashing" is often only a matter of degree and the observer's bias, just as a group that is a crazy cult to one person may be a group of devoutly religious people to another.

How, then, might we distinguish coercive persuasion from its more benign form? Persuasion techniques become coercive when they suppress an individual's ability to reason, think critically, and make choices in his or her own best interests. Studies of religious, political, and other cults have identified some of the key processes of coercive persuasion (Galanter, 1989; Mithers, 1994; Ofshe & Watters, 1994; Singer, Temerlin, & Langone, 1990; Zimbardo & Leippe, 1991):

The Person Is Put under Physical or Emotional Distress The individual may not be allowed to eat, sleep, or exercise; may be isolated in a dark room with no stimulation or food; or may be induced into a trancelike state through repetitive chanting, hypnosis, or fatigue.

The Person's Problems are Reduced to One Simple Explanation, Which Is Repeatedly Emphasized There are as many simplistic explanations as there are cults, but here are some real examples: Are you afraid or unhappy? It all stems from the pain of being born. Are you worried about homeless earthquake victims? It's not your problem; victims are responsible for everything that happens to them. Are you struggling financially? It's your fault for not fervently wanting to be rich. Members may also be taught to blame their problems on particular enemies: Jews, blacks, whites, nonbelievers.

The Leader Offers Unconditional Love, Acceptance, and Attention   The new recruit may be given a "love bath" from the group—constant praise, support, applause, and affection. Euphoria and well-being are intense because they typically follow exhaustion and fatigue. In exchange, the leader demands everyone's adoration and obedience.

A New Identity Based on the Group Is Created   The recruit is told that he or she is part of the chosen, the elite, or the saved. To foster this new identity, many cults require their members to wear special clothes or eat special diets, and they assign each member a new name. All members of the Philadelphia group MOVE were given the last name "Africa"; all members of the Church of Armageddon took the last name "Israel."

The Person Is Subjected to Entrapment   At first, the new member agrees only to do small things, but gradually the demands increase: for example, to spend a weekend with the group, then another weekend, then take weekly seminars, then advanced courses. During the Korean War, the Chinese first got the American POWs to agree with mild remarks, such as "The United States is not perfect." Then the POWs had to add their own examples of American imperfections. At the end, they were signing their names to anti-American broadcasts (Schein, Schneier, & Barker, 1961).

The Person's Access to Information Is Severely Controlled   As soon as a person is a committed believer or follower, the group limits the person's choices, denigrates critical thinking, makes fun of doubts, and insists that any private distress is due to lack of belief in the group. Total conformity is demanded. The person may be physically isolated from the outside world and thus from antidotes to the leader's ideas. In many groups, members are encouraged or required to break all ties with their parents, who are the most powerful link to the members' former world and thus the greatest threat to the leader's control.

You could see these strategies in operation in the Heaven's Gate cult, which made the news a few years ago when its leader, Marshall Applewhite, and all 38 of his followers committed suicide. Applewhite had offered members a new identity (extraterrestrials in human bodies) and a simplistic solution to their problems (suicide would free them to travel to heaven in a spaceship hiding in the tail of a comet). He encouraged members to sever their relationships with friends and relatives, had them dress alike, and censored all dissenting opinions. Applewhite entrapped his followers in an escalating series of obligations and commitments. He never said to new recruits, "If you follow me, you will eventually give up your marriages, your homes, your children, and your lives"; but by the end, that is just what they did.

Some people may be more vulnerable than others to coercive tactics. But these techniques are powerful enough to overwhelm even strong individuals; by all accounts, Applewhite's followers were pleasant people without serious mental disorders, and many were well educated. The first step in increasing people's resistance to coercive persuasion, therefore, is to dispel their illusion of invulnerability to these tactics (Sagarin, Cialdini, & Rice, 1998).

Quick Quiz

Now, how can we persuade you to take this quiz without using coercive techniques?

1. Candidate Carson spends 3 million dollars to make sure his name is seen and heard frequently, and to repeat unverified charges that his opponent is a thief. What psychological process is he relying on to win?
2. Your best friend urges you to join a "life-renewal" group called "The Feeling Life." Your friend has been spending increasing amounts of time with her fellow Feelies, and you have some doubts about them. What questions would you want to have answered before joining up?

Answers:

1. the validity effect   2. A few things to consider: Is there an autocratic leader who tolerates no dissent or criticism, while rationalizing this practice as a benefit for members? ("Doubt and disbelief are signs that your feeling side is being repressed.") Have long-standing members cut off ties with their families and given up their interests and ambitions for this group? Does the leader offer simple but unrealistic promises to repair your life and all that troubles you? Are members required to make extreme personal sacrifices and donate large amounts of money to the group?

What's Ahead

- Why do people in groups often go along with the majority even when the majority is dead wrong?
- How can "groupthink" lead to bad, even catastrophic, decisions?
- In an emergency, are you more likely to get help when there are lots of strangers in the area or only a few?
- What enables some people to disagree with a group, take independent action, or blow the whistle on wrongdoers?

Individuals in Groups

In March 1998, a man named Larry Froistad admitted to his Internet support group that he had killed his 5-year-old daughter, Amanda, three years earlier. "When she was asleep," he wrote on e-mail, he got drunk, set the house on fire, "listened to her scream twice, climbed out the window and set about putting on a show of shock and surprise and grief to remove culpability from myself." Of the more than 200 members of his online support group, only 3 called the police; Froistad was arrested and pleaded guilty. When members learned that the matter had been reported to the police, many of them became enraged—not at the man who had cold-bloodedly murdered his child, but at the "meddlesome rat fink" who turned him in. "Frankly, I'm offended," wrote one. "This is a SUPPORT group."

The members of Froistad's group were caught between two sets of norms and values:

You are supposed to report a murderer to the police, but you are also supposed to be loyal to members of your "support" group. If you were in such a situation, what do you think you would do?

As we will see, all of us act differently when we are with a bunch of other people than when we are on our own, regardless of whether the group has convened to solve problems and make decisions, has gathered to have fun, consists of anonymous bystanders or anonymous members of an Internet chat room, or is just a loose collection of individuals waiting around in a room. The decisions we make and the actions we take, in groups, often depend less on our personal desires than on the structure and dynamics of the group itself.

Conformity

One thing people in groups do is conform, taking action or adopting attitudes as a result of real or imagined group pressure.

Suppose that you are required to appear at a psychology laboratory for an experiment on perception. You join seven other students seated in a room. You are shown a 10-inch line and asked which of three other lines is identical to it:

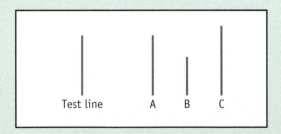

The correct answer, line A, is obvious, so you are amused when the first person in the group chooses line B. "Bad eyesight," you say to yourself. "He's off by 2 whole inches!" The second

person also chooses line B. "What a dope," you think. But by the time the fifth person has chosen line B, you are beginning to doubt yourself. The sixth and seventh students also choose line B, and now you are worried about *your* eyesight. The experimenter looks at you. "Your turn," he says. Do you follow the evidence of your own eyes or the collective judgment of the group?

This was the design for a series of famous studies of conformity conducted by Solomon Asch (1952, 1965). The seven "nearsighted" students were actually Asch's confederates. Asch wanted to know what people would do when a group unanimously contradicted an obvious fact. He found that when people made the line comparisons on their own, they were almost always accurate. But in the group, only 20 percent of the students remained completely independent on every trial, and often they apologized for not agreeing with the group. One-third conformed to the group's incorrect decision more than half the time, and the rest conformed at least some of the time. Whether they conformed or not, the students often felt uncertain of their decision. As one participant later said, "I felt disturbed, puzzled, separated, like an outcast from the rest."

Asch's experiment has been replicated many times over the years, in the United States and other countries. According to a meta-analysis of 133 studies, conformity in America has declined since the 1950s, when Asch first did his work, suggesting that conformity rises or falls according to changing social norms. Conformity also reflects cultural norms. People in individual-oriented cultures, such as the United States, are less conformist than are people in group-oriented cultures, where social harmony is considered more important than individual assertiveness. But regardless of culture, we are all more likely to conform when the group consists of people like us—in age, sex, and ethnicity—and as the group's size increases (Bond & Smith, 1996).

People conform for all sorts of reasons. Some do so because they identify with group members and want to be like them in dress, attitudes, or behavior. Some want to be liked and know that disagreeing with a group can make them unpopular. Some believe the group has knowledge that is superior to their own. And some conform out of pure self-interest, to keep their jobs, win promotions, or win votes. For their part, groups are often uncomfortable with nonconformists, and their members will try to persuade a rebel to conform. If pleasant persuasion fails, the group may punish, isolate, or reject the person altogether (Moscovici, 1985).

Like obedience, conformity has both its positive and its negative sides. Society runs more smoothly when people know how to behave in a given situation and when they share the same attitudes. But conformity can also suppress critical thinking and creativity. In a group, many people will deny their private beliefs, agree with silly notions, and violate their own values (Cialdini, 1993).

Groupthink

Close, friendly groups usually work well together. But they face the problem of getting the best ideas and efforts of their members while avoiding an extreme form of conformity called **groupthink,** the tendency to think alike and suppress dissent. According to Irving Janis (1982, 1989), groupthink occurs when a group's need for total agreement overwhelms its need to make the wisest decision. The symptoms of groupthink include:

- *An illusion of invulnerability.* The group believes it can do no wrong and is 100 percent correct in its decisions.

- *Self-censorship.* Dissenters decide to keep quiet rather than rock the boat, offend their friends, or risk being ridiculed.

- *Direct pressure on dissenters to conform.* The leader teases or humiliates dissenters or otherwise pressures them to go along.

- *An illusion of unanimity.* By discouraging dissent, leaders and group members create an illusion of consensus. They may even explicitly deny suspected dissenters the chance to say what they think.

Throughout history, groupthink has led to disastrous decisions in military and civilian life. One example occurred in 1961, when President John F. Kennedy, after meeting with his advisers, approved a CIA plan to invade Cuba at the Bay of Pigs and overthrow the government of Fidel Castro; the invasion was a humiliating defeat. Another occurred in the mid-1960s, when President Lyndon Johnson and his cabinet escalated the war in Vietnam in spite of obvious signs that further bombing and increased troops were not bringing the war to an end. And a third example occurred in 1986, when NASA officials made the fatal decision to launch the space shuttle *Challenger,* which exploded shortly after take off. Apparently, they insulated themselves from the objections of dissenting engineers who tried to warn them that the rocket was unsafe (Moorhead, Ference, & Neck, 1991).

Groupthink can occur in any setting, even in hospitals. For example, throughout the 1990s, psychiatrists at mental hospitals in Texas, Illinois, and elsewhere persuaded many patients that they were victims of ritual abuse by satanic cults despite a complete absence of evidence that the cults even existed (Kaczynski, 1997). The psychiatrists favoring this interpretation of their patients' problems refused to consider alternative explanations from "outsiders" and suppressed dissent from staff nurses and other physicians. It took a wave of successful malpractice suits to break this epidemic of psychiatric groupthink.

Janis (1982) examined the records of historical military decisions and identified typical features of groups that are vulnerable to groupthink: Their members feel that they are part of a tightly connected team; they are isolated from other viewpoints; they feel under pressure from outside forces; and they have a strong, directive leader. (Do you notice the similarities between these conditions and those of coercive cults?)

Fortunately, groupthink can be counteracted by creating conditions that explicitly encourage and reward the expression of doubt and dissent and by basing decisions on majority rule instead of unanimity (Kameda & Sugimori, 1993). President Kennedy apparently learned this lesson from the Bay of Pigs decision. In his next political crisis, provoked by missiles placed in Cuba by the then-Soviet Union in 1962, Kennedy brought in outside experts to advise his inner circle, often absented himself from the group so as not to influence their discussions, and encouraged free debate between the "hawks" and the "doves" (Aronson, Wilson, & Akert, 1999). The crisis, one of the most dangerous in post-World War II history, was resolved peacefully.

Of course, it is easy to see after the fact how conformity contributed to a bad decision or open debate to a good one, as Janis did. Predicting whether a group will make good or bad decisions in the future is far more complicated; you have to know a lot more about the history, structure, and purpose of the group (Aldag & Fuller, 1993). Nevertheless, according to many laboratory studies and analyses of historical events, Janis put his finger on a phenomenon that many of us have experienced: individual members of a group suppressing their real opinions and doubts so as to be good team players.

The Anonymous Crowd

If you were in trouble—say, being mugged or having a sudden appendicitis attack—on a city street or in another public place, do you think you would be more likely to get help if (1) one other person was passing by, (2) several other people were in the area, or (3) dozens of people were in the area?

Diffusion of Responsibility

Most people think that the more people who are available to help, the more likely it is that someone will step forward. But that is not how people operate. On the contrary, the more people there are around you, the *less* likely it is that one of them will come to your aid. The reason has to do with a common group process called the **diffusion of responsibility,** in which responsibility for an outcome is diffused, or spread, among many people. In crowds, individuals often fail to take action because they believe that someone else will do so.

The many reports of *bystander apathy* in the news reflect the diffusion of responsibility. When others are near, people fail to call the police when they see a woman being attacked on the street, they fail to report that a child in their neighborhood is being neglected and beaten by a parent, or they stand frozen to the spot as a store clerk is robbed and beaten by an assailant—even after the assailant flees. People are more likely to come to a stranger's aid if they are the only ones around to help, because responsibility cannot be diffused (see Figure 8.1).

In work groups, the diffusion of responsibility sometimes takes the form of *social loafing*: Each member of a team slows down, letting others work harder (Karau & Williams, 1993; Latané, Williams, & Harkins, 1979). Social loafing

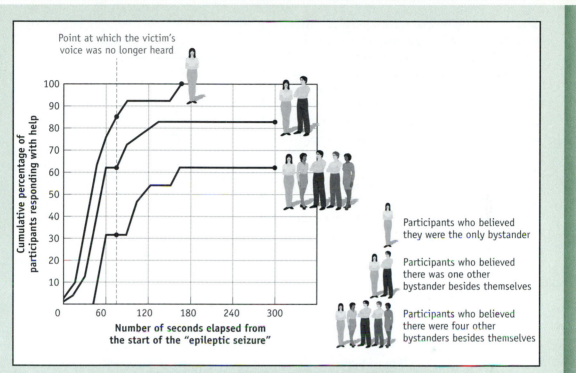

Point at which the victim's voice was no longer heard

Cumulative percentage of participants responding with help (y-axis: 0, 10, 20, 30, 40, 50, 60, 70, 80, 90, 100)

Number of seconds elapsed from the start of the "epileptic seizure" (x-axis: 0, 60, 120, 180, 240, 300)

Participants who believed they were the only bystander

Participants who believed there was one other bystander besides themselves

Participants who believed there were four other bystanders besides themselves

Figure 8.1   When Will Bystanders Help?

When people believed they were the only one hearing a student having an epileptic seizure in the next room, most of them went to help him immediately, and all of them did so within a few minutes. When they believed another bystander also heard the need for help, however, they were less likely to intervene. And when they believed that four other bystanders were listening, they were even less likely to help (from Darley & Latane, 1968).

occurs when individual group members are not accountable for the work they do; when people feel that working harder would only duplicate their colleagues' efforts; when workers feel that others are getting a "free ride"; or when the work itself is uninteresting (Shepperd, 1995). When the challenge of the job is increased or when each member of the group has a different, important job to do, the sense of individual responsibility rises and social loafing declines (Harkins & Szymanski, 1989; Williams & Karau, 1991).

Deindividuation

The most extreme instances of the diffusion of responsibility occur in large, anonymous mobs or crowds—whether they are cheerful ones, such as sports spectators, or angry ones, such as rioters. In situations like these, people often lose all awareness of their individuality and seem to "hand themselves over" to the mood and actions of the crowd, a state called **deindividuation** (Festinger, Pepitone, & Newcomb, 1952). You are more likely to feel deindividuated in a large city, where no one recognizes you, than in a small town, where it is hard to hide. Sometimes organizations actively promote the deindividuation of their members in order to enhance conformity and allegiance to the group. This is an important function of uniforms or masks, which eliminate each member's distinctive identity.

Deindividuation has long been considered a prime reason for mob violence. According to this explanation, because deindividuated people in crowds "forget themselves" and do not feel accountable for their actions, they are more likely to violate social norms and laws than they would on their own: breaking store windows, looting, getting into fights, rioting at a sports event. Their usual inhibitions against aggressiveness are weakened.

Many studies have indeed found that deindividuation increases a person's willingness to harm a stranger, cheat, or break the law (Aronson, Wilson, & Akert, 1999). Deindividuation even eliminates gender differences in aggressiveness, in spite of the common belief that women are "naturally" less aggressive than men. In two studies, men behaved more aggressively than women in a competitive video war game when they were individuated—that is, when their names and background information about them were spoken aloud, heard by all participants, and recorded publicly by the experimenter. But when the men and women believed they were anonymous to their fellow students and to the experimenter—that is, when they were deindividuated—they did not differ in how aggressively they played the game (Lightdale & Prentice, 1994).

But deindividuation does not always make people more combative. Sometimes it makes them more friendly; think of all the chatty, anonymous people on buses and planes who

reveal things to their seatmates they would never tell anyone they knew. What really seems to be happening when people are in large crowds or anonymous situations is not that they become mindless or uninhibited, but that they are simply more likely to conform to the norms of the *specific situation* (Postmes & Spears, 1998). College students who go on wild sprees during spring break may be violating the local laws and norms of Palm Springs or Key West, not because their "aggressiveness" has been released but because they are conforming to the "let's party!" norms of their fellow students.

Two classic experiments illustrate the power of the situation to influence what deindividuated people will do. In one, women who wore Ku Klux Klan-like disguises that completely covered their faces and bodies delivered twice as much apparent electric shock to another woman as did women who were not only undisguised but also wore large name tags (Zimbardo, 1970). In a second, women who were wearing nurses' uniforms gave *less* shock than did women in regular dress (Johnson & Downing, 1979). Evidently, the KKK disguise was a signal to behave aggressively; the nurses' uniforms were a signal to behave nurturantly.

In real life, too, members of crowds, conforming to the goals and norms of the situation, can be induced to take part in either collective violence or collective kindness. Peer pressure and conformity to an angry mob can induce people to commit hate crimes, such as violence against gay men or lesbians, lynchings or attacks on black people or Jews, and the rape of women by gangs of civilians or soldiers (Franklin, 1998; Green, Glaser, & Rich, 1998). On the other hand, when collective norms are positive, anonymous members of a community will behave in constructive ways. When Swissair Flight 111 crashed over Halifax, Nova Scotia, in 1998, killing 229 people, the entire community—which holds a group norm about the importance of helping one another in that tough terrain—turned out to join in the rescue effort and comfort families in distress.

Anonymity and Responsibility

Deindividuation has important legal as well as psychological implications. Should individuals in a crowd be held accountable for their harmful "deindividuated" behavior? Consider a trial held in South Africa in the late 1980s, in which six black residents of an impoverished township were accused of murdering an 18-year-old black woman who was having an affair with a hated black police officer. The woman was "necklaced"—a tire was placed around her neck and set afire—during a community protest against the police. The crowd danced and sang as she burned to ashes.

The six men were convicted of murder, but their sentence was commuted to 20 months of prison when a British social psychologist, Andrew Colman (1991), testified that deindividuation should reduce the "moral blameworthiness" of their behavior. The young men were swept up in the mindless behavior of the crowd, he argued, and hence not fully responsible for their actions. Do you agree? An African social scientist, Pumla Gobodo-Madikizela (1994), did not. She interviewed some of the men accused of the necklacing and found they were not so mindless after all. Some were tremendously upset, were well aware of their actions, had debated the woman's guilt, thought about running away, and consciously tried to rationalize their behavior. Moreover, she argued, we must remember that in every crowd, some people do not go along; they remain mindful of their own values and norms.

And so, should the deindividuation excuse, like the "I was only following orders" excuse, exonerate a person of responsibility for looting, rape, or murder? If so, to what degree? What do you think?

THINKING CRITICALLY

EXAMINE THE EVIDENCE

How mindless are "mindless" crowds? Should deindividuation be considered a legitimate excuse for people who loot, rape, or commit murder because the mob is doing it?

QUICK QUIZ

On your own, take responsibility for identifying which phenomenon discussed in the previous section is illustrated in the following situations:

1. The president's closest advisers are afraid to disagree with his views on arms negotiations.
2. You are at a Halloween party wearing a silly gorilla suit. When you see a chance to play a practical joke on the host, you do it.
3. Walking down a busy street, you see that fire has broken out in a store window. "Someone must have called the fire department," you say.

Answers:

1. groupthink 2. deindividuation 3. diffusion of responsibility

Disobedience and Dissent

We have seen how social roles, norms, and pressures to obey authority and conform to one's group can cause people to behave in ways they might not otherwise do. Yet, throughout history, men and women have disobeyed orders they believed to be immoral and have gone against prevailing cultural beliefs; their actions have changed the course of history. In 1956 in Montgomery, Alabama, Rosa Parks refused to give up her seat and move to the back of a bus, as the segregation laws of the time required. She was arrested, fingerprinted, and convicted of breaking the law. Her calm defiance touched off a boycott in which black citizens refused to ride city buses. It took them over a year, but they won— and the civil rights movement began.

Dissent and *altruism*, the willingness to take selfless or dangerous action on behalf of others, are in part a matter of personal convictions and conscience. However, just as there are situational reasons for obedience and conformity, so there are situational influences on a person's decision to speak up for an unpopular opinion, choose conscience over conformity, or help a stranger in trouble. Here are some of the steps involved in deciding to "rock the boat," and some social and cultural factors involved in them (Aronson, Wilson, & Akert, 1999):

You Perceive the Need for Intervention or Help   It may seem obvious, but before you can take independent action, you must realize that such action is necessary. Sometimes people willfully blind themselves to wrongdoing to justify their own inaction ("I'm just minding my business here"). But blindness to the need for action also occurs when people have too many demands on their attention. Workers who must juggle many pressures from work and family cannot stop to make a fuss about every problem or bureaucratic misdeed they notice. Likewise, residents of densely populated cities cannot stop to offer help to everyone who seems to need it; they would never do anything else (Levine et al., 1994).

Whether you even interpret a situation as requiring your aid also depends on cultural rules (see Figure 8.2). In northern European nations and in the United States, husband-wife disputes are considered strictly private; neighbors intervene at their peril. In one field study, bystanders observed a (staged) fight between a man and a woman. When the woman yelled, "Get away from me; I don't know you!" two-thirds of the bystanders went to help her. When she shouted, "Get away from me; I don't know why I ever married you!" only 19 percent tried to help (Shotland & Straw, 1976). In Mediterranean and

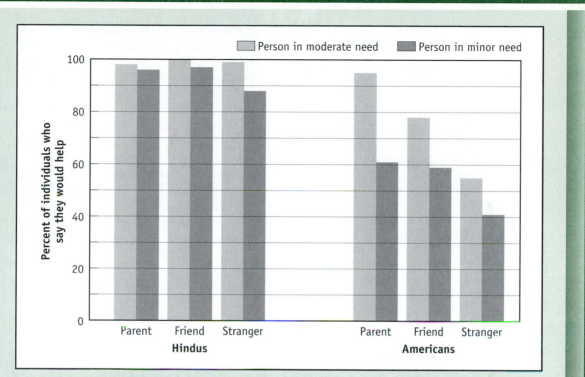

Figure 8.2   Culture and the Obligation to Help

Community-oriented Hindus in India believe that people are obligated to help anyone who needs it—parent, friend, or stranger—even if the need is minor. In contrast, individualistic Americans do not feel as strongly obligated to help friends and strangers, or even parents, who merely have "minor" needs. People in both cultures, however, share a sense of obligation to help anyone in a life-threatening situation (Miller, Bersoff, & Harwood, 1990).

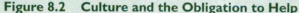

Latin cultures, however, a dispute between any two people is considered fair game for anyone who is passing by. In fact, two people in a furious dispute might even rely on bystanders to intervene (Hall & Hall, 1990).

You Decide to Take Responsibility   When you are in a large crowd of observers or in a large organization, it is easy to avoid action because of the diffusion of responsibility. Even when you might like to help a stranger in trouble, in some places it is impossible to help everyone who

needs it, as in cities where homeless persons number in the thousands. The decision to take responsibility also depends on the degree of risk involved. It is easier to be a whistle-blower or to protest a company policy when you know you can find another job, but what if jobs in your field are scarce and you have a family to support?

You Decide That the Costs of Doing Nothing Outweigh the Costs of Getting Involved   The cost of helping or protesting might be embarrassment and wasted time or, more seriously, lost income, loss of friends, and even physical danger. The cost of not helping or remaining silent might be guilt, blame from others, loss of honor, or, in some tragic cases, the injury or death of others. Three employees of Rockwell International weighed these two sets of costs and ended up trying to convince NASA that the space shuttle *Challenger* was unsafe. The NASA authorities (perhaps influenced by groupthink, as we noted earlier) weighed the costs differently, and refused to postpone the launch. The price of their decision was an explosion that caused the deaths of the entire crew.

You Have an Ally   In Asch's conformity experiment, the presence of one other person who gave the correct answer was enough to overcome agreement with the majority. In Milgram's experiment, the presence of a peer who disobeyed the experimenter's instruction to shock the learner sharply increased the number of people who also disobeyed. One dissenting member of a group may be viewed as a troublemaker, but several are a coalition. An ally reassures a person of the rightness of the protest, and their combined efforts may eventually persuade the majority (Wood et al., 1994).

You Become Entrapped   Once having taken the initial step of getting involved, most people will increase their commitment. In one study, nearly 9,000 federal employees were asked whether they had observed wrongdoing at work, whether they had told anyone about it, and what had happened if they had told. About half of the sample had observed some serious cases of wrongdoing, such as stealing federal funds, accepting bribes, or creating a situation that was dangerous to public safety. Of that half, 72 percent had done nothing at all, but the other 28 percent had reported the problem to their immediate supervisors. Once they had taken that step, a majority of the whistle-blowers eventually took the matter to higher authorities (Graham, 1986).

As you can see, certain social and cultural factors make altruism, disobedience, and dissent more likely to occur, just as other factors suppress them. This is why people are so often inconsistent across situations: A woman may be forthright about her opinions on her job, yet conform to the opinions of others when she serves on a jury; a man might leap into a frozen river on Tuesday to rescue a child, yet keep silent on Wednesday when his employer orders him to ignore worker-safety precautions at a factory because they are too expensive. How do you think you would behave if you were faced with a conflict between social pressure and conscience? Would you call 911 if you saw someone being injured in a fight or voice your true opinion in class even though everyone else seemed to disagree with you? What aspects of the situation and your culture's norms would influence your responses?

QUICK QUIZ

Imagine that you are chief executive officer of a new electric-car company. To improve productivity and satisfaction, you want your employees to feel free to offer their suggestions and criticisms and to inform managers if they find any evidence that your cars are unsafe, even if that means delaying production. What concepts from this chapter could you use in setting company policy?

Answers:

Some possibilities: Encourage and acknowledge deviant ideas, and do not require unanimity of group decisions (to avoid groupthink); reward individual innovation and suggestions by paying attention to them and implementing the best ones (to avoid social loafing and deindividuation); stimulate commitment to the task (building a car that will solve the world's pollution problem); establish a written policy to protect whistle-blowers. What else can you think of?

What's Ahead

- How difficult is it to create "us–them" thinking?
- How do stereotypes benefit us, and how do they distort reality?
- Is prejudice more likely to be a cause of competition and war or a result of them?
- Why do well-meaning people sometimes get caught up in a "cycle of distrust" with other ethnic groups?
- Why isn't mere contact between cultural groups enough to reduce prejudice between them? What does work?

Group Conflict and Prejudice

So far, we have been discussing the effects of groups on their members. But a lot of human mischief and misery occurs when groups compete and conflict with one another, and especially when groups are operating on the basis of different cultural rules. Most of us take our own rules and norms for granted, and assume they are logical, normal, and right. The trouble starts when we assume that other people's customs are irrational, peculiar, and wrong.

Ethnocentrism, the belief that one's own culture or ethnic group is superior to all others, is universal, probably because it aids survival by making people feel attached to their own group and willing to work on the group's behalf. Ethnocentrism is even embedded in some languages: The Chinese word for China means "the center of the world" and the Navajo and the Inuit both call themselves simply "The People." But does the fact that we feel good about our own culture, nationality, gender, or school mean that we have to regard other groups as inferior? Social and cultural psychologists strive to identify the conditions that promote harmony or conflict, understanding or prejudice, between groups.

Group Identity: Us versus Them

Each of us develops a personal identity that is based on our particular traits and unique history. But we also develop **social identities** based on the groups we belong to, including our national, ethnic, religious, and occupational groups (Brewer & Gardner, 1996; Hogg & Abrams, 1988; Tajfel & Turner, 1986). Social identities are important because they give us a feeling of place and position in the world. Without them, most of us would feel like loose marbles rolling around in an unconnected universe.

Being in a group confers an immediate social identity: Us. As soon as people have created a category called "us," however, they invariably perceive everybody else as "not-us." This in-group solidarity can be manufactured in a minute in a laboratory, as Henri Tajfel and his colleagues (1971) first demonstrated in a classic experiment with British schoolboys. Tajfel showed the boys slides with varying numbers of dots on them and asked the boys to guess how many dots there were. The boys were arbitrarily told they were "overestimators" or "underestimators" and were then asked to work on another task. In this phase, they had the chance to award points to other boys identified as overestimators or underestimators. Although each boy worked alone in his own cubicle, almost every single one assigned far more points to boys he thought were like him, an overestimator or an underestimator. As the boys emerged from their rooms, they were asked, "Which were you?"— and the answers received a mix of cheers and boos from the others.

Us-them social identities are strengthened when two groups compete with one another. Competition can be great fun, of course; during an exciting basketball game or Olympic event, participants and spectators alike are exhilarated. Moreover, competition in business and science can lead to better services and products and new inventions. Yet, competition has psychological hazards. It often decreases work motivation; it makes people feel insecure and anxious, even if they win; it makes people angry and frustrated if they lose; it fosters jealousy and hostility. After reviewing the huge number of studies on its effects, Alfie Kohn (1992) concluded that "the phrase *healthy competition* is a contradiction in terms."

Years ago, Muzafer Sherif and his colleagues used a natural setting, a Boy Scout camp called Robbers Cave, to demonstrate the effects of competition on hostility and conflict between groups (Sherif, 1958; Sherif et al., 1961). Sherif randomly assigned 11- and 12-year-old boys to two groups, the Eagles and the Rattlers. To build a sense of in-group identity and team spirit, he had each group work together on projects such as making a rope bridge and building a diving board. Sherif then put the Eagles and Rattlers in competition for prizes. During fierce games of football, baseball, and tug-of-war, the boys whipped up a competitive fever that soon spilled off of the playing fields. They began to raid each other's cabins, call each other names, and start fistfights. No one dared to have a friend from the rival group. Before long, the Rattlers and the Eagles were as hostile toward each other as any two gangs fighting for turf or any two nations fighting for dominance. Their hostility continued even when they were just sitting around together watching movies.

Then Sherif decided to try to undo the hostility he had created and make peace between

the Eagles and Rattlers. He and his associates set up a series of predicaments in which both groups needed to work together to reach a desired goal. The boys had to cooperate to get the water supply system working. They had to pool their resources to get a movie they all wanted to see. When the staff truck "accidentally" broke down on a camping trip, they all had to join forces to pull the truck up a steep hill and get it started again.

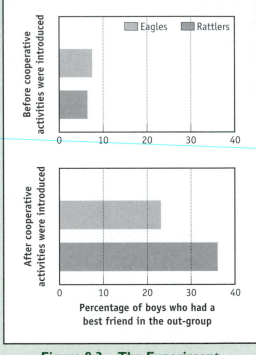

Figure 8.3   The Experiment at Robbers Cave

In this study, competitive games fostered hostility between the Rattlers and the Eagles. Few boys had a best friend from the other group (top). But after the boys had to cooperate to solve various problems, the percentage who made friends across "enemy lines" shot up (bottom) (Sherif et al., 1961).

This policy of *interdependence in reaching mutual goals* was highly successful in reducing the boys' competitiveness and hostility; the boys eventually made friends with their former enemies (see Figure 8.3). Interdependence has a similar effect in adult groups. The reason is that cooperation causes people to think of themselves as members of one big group instead of two opposed groups, *us* and *them* (Gaertner et al., 1990).

Stereotypes

If you are like most people, you can think of a million ways that members of your family vary—Harold is stodgy, Ruth is prissy, Fatima is outgoing. But if you have never met a person from Turkey or Tibet, you are likely to *stereotype* Turks and Tibetans. A **stereotype** is a summary impression of a group of people in which all members of the group are viewed as sharing a common trait or traits. Stereotypes may be negative, positive, or neutral. There are stereotypes of people who drive Jeeps or BMWs, of men who wear earrings and of women who wear business suits, of engineering students and art students, of feminists and fraternity members.

Stereotypes play an important role in human thinking. They help us quickly process new information and retrieve memories. They allow us to organize experience, make sense of differences among individuals and groups, and predict how people will behave. They are, as some psychologists have called them, useful "tools in the mental toolbox"—energy-saving devices that allow us to make efficient decisions (Macrae, Milne, & Bodenhausen, 1994).

Although stereotypes reflect real differences among people, however, they also distort that reality in three ways (Judd et al., 1995). First, *they exaggerate differences between groups*, making the stereotyped group seem odd, unfamiliar, or dangerous, not like "us." Second, *they produce selective perception*; people tend to see only the evidence that fits the stereotype and reject any perceptions that do not fit. Third, *they underestimate differences within other groups*. People realize that their own groups are made up of all kinds of individuals, but stereotypes create the impression that all members of other groups (say, all Texans or all teenagers) are the same.

Some stereotypes stem from a person's cultural values. For example, as discussed in Chapter 3, white Americans tend to have strongly negative stereotypes about fat people because of a cultural ideology that individuals are responsible for what happens to them and for how they look. In contrast, Mexicans (in Mexico and the United States) and African-Americans are significantly more accepting of heavy people (Crandall & Martinez, 1996; Hebl & Heatherton, 1998).

Cultural values also affect how people evaluate a particular action (Taylor & Porter, 1994). For example, Chinese students in Hong Kong, where communalism and respect for elders are valued, think that a student who comes late to class or argues with a parent about grades is being selfish and disrespectful of adults. But Australian students, who value individualism, think that the same behavior is perfectly appropriate (Forgas & Bond, 1985). You can see how the Chinese might form negative stereotypes of "disrespectful" Australians, and how the Australians might form negative stereotypes of the "spineless" Chinese. And it is a small step from negative stereotypes to prejudice.

Prejudice

A *prejudice* consists of a negative stereotype and a strong, unreasonable dislike or hatred of a group or its individual members. Feelings of prejudice violate the spirit of critical thinking because they resist rational argument and evidence. In his classic book *The Nature of Prejudice*, Gordon Allport (1954/1979) described the responses characteristic of a prejudiced person when confronted with evidence contradicting his or her beliefs:

> Mr. X: The trouble with Jews is that they only take care of their own group.
>
> Mr. Y: But the record of the Community Chest campaign shows that they give more generously, in proportion to their numbers, to the general charities of the community, than do non-Jews.
>
> Mr. X: That shows they are always trying to buy favor and intrude into Christian affairs. They think of nothing but money; that is why there are so many Jewish bankers.
>
> Mr. Y: But a recent study shows that the percentage of Jews in the banking business is negligible, far smaller than the percentage of non-Jews.
>
> Mr. X: That's just it; they don't go in for respectable business; they are only in the movie business or run night clubs.

Notice that Mr. X does not respond to Mr. Y's evidence; he just moves along to another reason for his dislike of Jews. That is the slippery nature of prejudice. It is based on faulty generalizations about an entire group; it is not grounded in the prejudiced person's direct experience with that group; and, unlike mere misconceptions about a group that can be modified with information, it is resistant to change (Herek, 1998).

The Origins of Prejudice

Prejudice is a universal human experience because it has so many sources—psychological, social, economic, and cultural.

Psychologically, prejudice often serves to ward off feelings of doubt and fear. Prejudiced persons may transfer their worries onto the target group; thus, a person who has doubts or anxieties about his own sexuality may develop a hatred of gay people. Prejudice also allows people to use the target group as a scapegoat: "Those people are the source of all my troubles." And, as research from many nations has confirmed, prejudice is a tonic for low self-esteem: People puff up their own low self-worth by disliking or hating groups they see as inferior (Islam & Hewstone, 1993; Stephan et al., 1994; Tajfel & Turner, 1986).

Not all prejudices have deep-seated psychological roots, however. Some prejudices are acquired through groupthink and social pressures to conform to the views of friends, relatives, or associates. Some prejudices are passed along mindlessly from one generation to another, as when parents communicate to their children that "We don't associate with people like that." And some are acquired uncritically from advertising, TV shows, and news reports that contain derogatory images and stereotypes of certain groups.

Prejudice also has important economic functions. It makes official forms of discrimination seem legitimate, by justifying the majority group's dominance, status, or greater wealth (Sidanius, Pratto, & Bobo, 1996). Historically, for example, white men in positions of power have justified their exclusion of women, blacks, and other minorities from the workplace and politics by claiming that those minorities were inferior, irrational, and incompetent (Gould, 1996). But any majority group—of any ethnicity, gender, or nationality—that discriminates against a minority will call upon prejudice to legitimize its actions (Islam & Hewstone, 1993).

Although it is widely believed that prejudice is the primary cause of conflict and war, prejudice is actually more often a *result* of conflict and war; it *legitimizes* them. When any two groups are in direct competition for jobs, or when people are worried about their incomes and the stability of their communities, prejudice between them increases (Doty, Peterson, & Winter, 1991). Social psychologist Elliot Aronson (1999b) traced the rise and fall of attitudes toward Chinese immigrants in the United States in the nineteenth century, as reported in newspapers of the time. When the Chinese were working in the gold mines and potentially taking jobs from white laborers, whites described them as depraved, vicious, and bloodthirsty. Just a decade later, when the Chinese began working on the transcontinental railroad—doing difficult and dangerous jobs that few white men wanted—prejudice against them declined. Whites described them as hardworking, industrious, and law-abiding. Then, after the railroad was finished and the Chinese had to compete with Civil War veterans for scarce jobs, white attitudes changed again. Whites now considered the Chinese to be "criminal," "crafty," "conniving," and "stupid" (Aronson, 1999b). (The white newspapers did not report the attitudes of the Chinese.)

Finally, prejudice toward other groups also serves cultural purposes, bonding people to their own ethnic or national group and its ways; indeed this may be a major evolutionary reason for the universal persistence of prejudice (Fishbein, 1996). In this respect, prejudice is the flip side of ethnocentrism; it is not only that we are good, but also that they are bad, lazy, or dumb.

When two nations are at war, prejudice toward the enemy allows each side to continue feeling righteous about its cause. Each side portrays the other in stereotyped ways to demonize and dehumanize the enemy, making it seem that the enemy deserves to be killed (Aronson, 1999b). Fomenting prejudice against the perceived enemy—calling them traitors, heathens, vermin, subhuman, baby-killers, brutes, or monsters—legitimizes the attackers' motives for war.

The Varieties of Prejudice

If you ask people directly about their attitudes, you may conclude that prejudice in the United States and Canada is declining. White attitudes toward integration have become steadily more favorable, and the belief that blacks are inferior to whites has become much less prevalent (Plant & Devine, 1998). Men and women are also more likely to endorse gender equality; the number of men openly expressing prejudice toward women executives declined from 41 percent in 1965 to only 5 percent in 1985 (Tougas et al., 1995), and between 1970 and 1995 antiwoman attitudes in general dropped sharply (Twenge, 1997).

However, some social scientists believe that these statistics are misleading. Overt attitudes, they say, are not necessarily an accurate measure of prejudice, because many people know they should not admit their prejudices (Bell, 1992; Plant & Devine, 1998). These observers maintain that racial animosity and sexism are undiminished. Prejudice toward blacks, they argue, lurks behind a mask of *symbolic racism*, in which whites focus not on dislike of black individuals but on issues such as "reverse discrimination," "hard-core criminals," or "welfare abuse." In this view, such issues have become code words for the continuing animosity that many whites feel toward blacks.

The way to measure racism, according to this argument, is by using unobtrusive measures rather than direct attitude questionnaires. One method is to observe people's

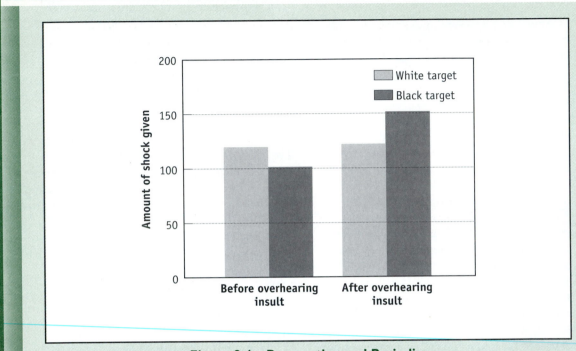

Figure 8.4   Provocation and Prejudice

When white students were insulted, they gave much higher levels of shock to blacks than they did when not angry (Rogers & Prentice-Dunn, 1981). Studies of the majority's behavior toward other minorities, such as Jews, gays, and French Canadians, find the same results.

unconscious behavior when they are with a possible object of prejudice. Do they sit farther away than they normally would; reveal involuntary, negative facial expressions; or have other signs of physical tension (Fazio et al., 1995; Vanman et al., 1997)? In such cases, however, it is difficult to say whether you are identifying "real" prejudice or merely discomfort and unfamiliarity with the target.

Another method is to observe how people who say they are unprejudiced actually behave when they are emotionally upset (Jones, 1991). In one such experiment, students thought they were giving shock to other subjects in a study of biofeedback. White students initially showed *less* aggression toward blacks than toward whites. But as soon as the white students were angered by overhearing derogatory remarks about themselves, they showed *more* aggression toward blacks than toward whites (Rogers & Prentice-Dunn, 1981). (See Figure 8.4.)

In another study, English-speaking Canadians who had been put through a frustrating experience with failure rated members of the outgroup (French-speaking Canadians) more negatively than did those who had not been frustrated (Meindl & Lerner, 1985). And in studies with non-Jewish students and heterosexuals, students who had received a blow to their self-esteem evaluated Jews or gay men more harshly than other students did (Fein & Spencer, 1997). Findings like these imply that people are willing to control negative feelings toward their customary targets of prejudice under normal conditions. But as soon as they are angry, frustrated, provoked, or suffer a loss of self-esteem, their real prejudice reveals itself.

One complication in measuring prejudice is that not all people are prejudiced in the same way. Some people are unapologetically racist, sexist, or antigay; others have a patronizing sense of superiority over other groups but are not explicitly hostile toward them; still others feel guilty about harboring negative feelings toward other groups. Gordon Allport (1954/1979) observed that "defeated intellectually, prejudice lingers emotionally." That is, a person might realize that a prejudice is unwarranted, yet still feel

uncomfortable with members of certain groups. Should we put this person in the same category as one who is an outspoken bigot or who actively discriminates against others because of their sex, culture, sexual orientation, weight, disability, or skin color? What if a person is ignorant of another culture and mindlessly blurts out a remark that reflects that ignorance? Does that count as prejudice or mere thoughtlessness? Can women be sexist and blacks be racist, or do "sexism" and "racism" apply only to institutional practices by those in power? Because people differ in their definitions of *racist*, *sexist*, and *prejudiced*, their conclusions about prejudice will also differ.

Efforts to Reduce Prejudice

Given the many sources and definitions of prejudice, no one method of reducing it is likely to work in all situations (Monteith, 1996). That is why social and cultural psychologists have designed different programs to try to reduce misunderstanding and prejudice, depending on the origins of a given conflict and the factors that are supporting it.

For example, according to Patricia Devine (1995), different strategies should be used with people who are trying to break their "prejudice habit" than with people who are comfortable with their bigotry. She has been working with people who are making an effort to put old prejudices aside, but who are unfamiliar or uncomfortable with members of another group. In such situations, a "cycle of distrust" and animosity can emerge even when individuals start off with the best intentions to get along. Some majority group members, although highly motivated to work well with minorities, may be self-conscious and anxious about doing the wrong thing. Their anxiety makes them behave

GET INVOLVED

PROBING YOUR PREJUDICES

Are you prejudiced toward a specific group of people? Is it a group defined by gender, ethnicity, sexual orientation, nationality, religion, physical appearance, or political views? Write down your deepest thoughts and feelings about this group. Take as long as you want, and do not censor yourself or say what you think you ought to say. Now reread what you have written. Which of the many sources of prejudice discussed in the text might be contributing to your views? Do you feel that your attitudes toward the group are legitimate, or are you uncomfortable about having them?

awkwardly; for instance, by blurting out dumb remarks and avoiding eye contact with minority-group members. The minority members, based on their own history of discrimination, may interpret the majority-group members' behavior as evidence of hostility and respond with withdrawal, aloofness, or anger. The majority members, not understanding that their own anxieties have been interpreted as evidence of prejudice, regard the minority members' behavior as unreasonable or mysterious, so they reciprocate the hostility or withdraw. This behavior confirms the minority members' suspicions about the majority's true feelings and prejudices (Devine, Evett, & Vasquez-Suson, 1996).

By understanding this cycle, Devine argues, people can learn to break it. Majority members can become aware of the discrepancy between their intentions and their actual behavior. They can learn to reduce their discomfort with people unlike themselves and acquire the skills that will lessen their anxiety. But minorities must become part of the solution too—for example, by recognizing their possible biases in seeing the majority members' behavior only in a negative light. Both sides, Devine (1995) emphasizes, should remember that reducing prejudice is a *process* and does not happen overnight. It is important, she argues, to reward people who are making an effort to change their biases, instead of condemning them for not being perfect.

What happens, however, when two groups really do bear enormous animosity toward each other? How then might their conflicts be reduced? Sociocultural researchers emphasize the importance of changing people's circumstances, rather than waiting around for individuals to undergo a moral or psychological conversion. They have identified four conditions that must be met before conflict and prejudice between groups can be overcome (Dovidio, Gaertner, & Validzic,

---

THINKING CRITICALLY

QUESTION ASSUMPTIONS

"If only people got to know one another, they could get along." What is wrong with this popular assumption?

1998; Fishbein, 1996; Fisher, 1994; Pettigrew, 1997; Rubin, 1994; Staub, 1996):

Both Sides Must Have Equal Legal Status, Economic Opportunities, and Power   This requirement is the spur behind efforts to change laws that permit discrimination. Integration of public facilities in the American South would never have occurred if civil-rights advocates had waited for segregationists to have a change of heart. Women would never have gotten the right to vote, attend college, or do "men's work" without persistent challenges to the laws that permitted gender discrimination. Laws, however, do not necessarily change attitudes if all they do is produce unequal contact between groups or if competition for jobs continues.

The Larger Culture—Authorities and Community Institutions—Must Endorse Egalitarian Norms and Thereby Provide Moral Support and Legitimacy for Both Sides   The larger culture must establish norms of equality and support them in the actions of its officials—teachers, employers, the judicial system, government officials, and the police.

Both Sides Must Have Opportunities to Work and Socialize Together, Formally and Informally   According to the *contact hypothesis*, prejudice declines when people have the chance to get used to one another's rules, food, music, customs, and attitudes. By making friends with one another, people of different groups and cultures can discover their shared interests and shared humanity (Pettigrew, 1997).

The contact hypothesis has been supported by many studies in the laboratory and in the real world. Researchers have examined newly integrated housing projects in the American South during the 1950s and 1960s; relationships between German and immigrant Turkish children in German schools; young people's attitudes toward and contact with the elderly; healthy people's attitudes toward the mentally ill; nondisabled children's attitudes toward the disabled; and straight people's prejudices toward gay men and lesbians (Fishbein, 1996; Herek, 1998; Herek & Capitanio, 1996; Pettigrew, 1997; Wilner, Walkley, & Cook, 1955). These studies confirm that when people make friends with members of another group, they tend to become less prejudiced toward the group as a whole.

Nevertheless, contact and friendship alone are not enough to reduce prejudice and achieve harmony between groups (Fishbein, 1996). This is sadly apparent at multiethnic high schools, where ethnic groups often form cliques and gangs, fighting other groups and defending their own ways.

Both Sides Must Cooperate, Working Together for a Common Goal This enterprise reduces us-them thinking and creates an encompassing social identity ("We're all in this together"). This fourth key to reducing prejudice is one of the most powerful (Fishbein, 1996). Researchers learned this by setting up cooperative situations in schools, businesses, and communities, requiring formerly antagonistic groups to work together for a common goal—the Eagles and the Rattlers solution.

In schools, psychologists have experimented with variations on *cooperative learning*, in which the success of any individual child rests on the success of the whole group. For example, years ago, researchers were able to reduce ethnic conflict among white, Chicano, and black children in Texas elementary schools by designing a "jigsaw method" to build cooperation (Aronson et al., 1978). Classes were divided into groups of six students of mixed ethnicity, and every group worked together on a task that was broken up like a jigsaw puzzle. Each child needed the contributions of the others to put the assignment together; for instance, each child might be given one paragraph of a six-paragraph biography and be asked to learn the whole story. The cooperative students, in comparison to classmates in regular classes, had greater self-esteem, liked their classmates better, showed a decrease in stereotyping and prejudice, and improved their grades.

These findings, and studies of other kinds of cooperative learning, have been replicated in many classrooms (Aronson & Patnoe, 1997; Vanman et al., 1997; Wolfe & Spencer, 1996). However, cooperation does not work when members of a group have unequal status, blame one another for loafing or "dropping the ball," or perceive that their teachers or employers are playing favorites.

Each of these four approaches to reducing prejudice is important, but none is sufficient on its own. Perhaps one reason that group conflicts are so persistent is that all four conditions are rarely met at the same time.

QUICK QUIZ

Try to overcome your prejudice against quizzes by taking this one.

A. Which concept—ethnocentrism, stereotyping, or prejudice—is illustrated by each of the following statements?
   1. Juan believes that all Anglos are uptight and cold, and he won't listen to any evidence that contradicts his belief.
   2. John knows and likes the Mexican minority in his town, but he privately believes that Anglo culture is superior.
   3. Jane believes that Honda owners are thrifty and practical. June believes that Honda owners are stingy and dull.
B. What strategy does the Robbers Cave study suggest for reducing hostility between groups?
C. Surveys find that large percentages of African-Americans, Asian-Americans, and Latinos hold negative stereotypes of one another and resent other minorities, too. What are some reasons that people who have themselves been victims of stereotyping and prejudice would hold the same attitudes toward others?

Answers:

A. 1. prejudice 2. ethnocentrism 3. stereotyping B. fostering interdependence in reaching mutual goals C. their own insecurity and low self-esteem; socialization by parents and messages in the larger society; conformity with relatives and friends who share these prejudices; competition for jobs; ethnocentrism

WHAT'S AHEAD

- Are "age-old tribal hatreds" the best explanation for war and genocide?
- What is the "banality of evil," and what does it tell us about human nature?

The Question of Human Nature

In 1942, Wladyslaw Misiuna, a Polish teenager, was ordered by the Germans to supervise inmates at a concentration camp. One day, an inmate named Devora Salzberg came to see him about an infection that had covered her arms with open lesions. Misiuna knew that he could never get a doctor to the camp to treat her. So he infected himself with her blood, contracted the lesions himself, and went to a doctor. Then he shared with Devora the medication he was given. Both were cured, and both survived the war (Fogelman, 1994).

Heroes like Misiuna represent the greatest good in humanity. In contrast, the Nazis have come to symbolize the evil in human nature, because they systematically exterminated millions of Jews, Gypsies, homosexuals, disabled people, and anyone else not deemed to be of the "pure" Aryan "race." But the Nazis were not a strange historical oddity; torture, genocide, and massacres are all too common in history. Americans and Canadians slaughtered native peoples in North America, Turks slaughtered Armenians, the Khmer Rouge slaughtered millions of fellow Cambodians, the Spanish conquistadors slaughtered native peoples in Mexico and South America, Idi Amin waged a reign of terror against his own people in Uganda, the Japanese slaughtered Koreans and Chinese, Iraqis slaughtered Kurds, despotic political regimes in Argentina and Chile killed thousands of dissidents and rebels. In recent years in Rwanda, hundreds of thousands of Tutsis have been shot or hacked to death with machetes by members of the rival Hutu tribe; and in the former Yugoslavia, Bosnian Serbs have massacred Bosnian Muslims in the name of "ethnic cleansing."

Many people believe that these outbreaks of horrifying violence are a result of inner aggressive drives or, in the case of Rwanda and Yugoslavia, "age-old tribal hatreds." But in fact, policies of genocide against a perceived outside enemy are almost always generated by governments that feel weakened and vulnerable (Smith, 1998; Staub, 1996). Governments then rely on the social psychological processes discussed in this chapter—including obedience to authority, conformity, rationalization, groupthink, deindividuation, and prejudice—to carry out their policies.

That is why, from the standpoint of social and cultural psychology, all human beings, like all cultures, contain the potential for good *and* bad; how most of us actually behave in a given situation depends more on human social organization than on human nature. The philosopher Hannah Arendt (1963), who covered the trial of Adolf Eichmann, used the phrase *the banality of evil* to describe how it was possible for Eichmann and other ordinary people in Nazi Germany to commit the monstrous acts they did. (*Banal* means "commonplace" or "unoriginal.")

The compelling evidence for the banality of evil is, perhaps, the hardest lesson in psychology. Most people want to believe that only evil people, who are bad down to their bones, do harm others; or that only evil cultures, which do not have one good custom to recommend them, start wars. It is reassuring to divide the world into those who are good or bad, kind or cruel, moral or immoral. But research from social and cultural psychology knocks us off our ethnocentric pedestal. No culture can claim to be wholly virtuous, and no culture is entirely villainous either. Throughout history, as circumstances have changed, societies have changed from being warlike to being peaceful, and vice versa.

Of course, some people do stand out as being unusually heroic or unusually sadistic. But as we have seen, good people can do terribly disturbing things when norms and roles encourage or require them to do so—when the situation takes over and they do not stop to think critically. Otherwise healthy people may join self-destructive cults, inflict pain on others if ordered to, and go along with a violent crowd.

The research discussed in this chapter suggests that ethnocentrism and prejudice will always be with us, as long as differences exist among groups. But it can also help us formulate realistic yet nonviolent ways of living in a diverse world. By identifying the conditions that create the banality of evil, perhaps we can create others that foster the "banality of virtue"—everyday acts of kindness, selflessness, and generosity.

THINKING CRITICALLY

DON'T OVERSIMPLIFY

Many people like to divide individuals and nations into those that are "good" and those that are "evil." What is wrong with thinking this way?

TAKING PSYCHOLOGY WITH YOU

Travels across the Cultural Divide

A French salesman worked for a company that was bought by Americans. When the new American manager ordered him to step up his sales within the next three months, the employee quit in a huff, taking his customers with him. Why? In France, it takes years to develop customers; in family-owned businesses, relationships with customers may span generations. The American wanted instant results, as Americans often do, but the French salesman knew this was impossible and quit. The American view was, "He wasn't up to the job; he's lazy and disloyal, so he stole my customers." The French view was, "There is no point in explaining anything to a person who is so stupid as to think you can acquire loyal customers in three months" (Hall & Hall, 1987).

Both men were committing the fundamental attribution error: assuming the other person's behavior was due to personality rather than the situation—in this case, a situation governed by cultural rules. Many corporations now realize that such rules are not trivial and that success in a global economy depends on understanding them. You, too, can benefit from the psychological research on cultures, whether you plan to do business abroad, visit as a tourist, or just want to get along better in your own society.

Be Sure You Understand the Other Culture's Rules, Manners, and Customs

If you find yourself getting angry over something a person from another culture is doing, try to find out whether your expectations and perceptions of that person's behavior are appropriate. For example, Koreans typically do not shake hands when greeting strangers, whereas most North Americans and Europeans do. People who shake hands as a gesture of friendship and courtesy are likely to feel insulted if another person refuses to do the same unless they understand this cultural difference.

Here is another example: Suppose you are shopping in the Middle East or Latin America. If you are not used to bargaining, the experience is likely to be exasperating. Because you do not know the unstated rules, you will not know whether you got taken or got a great buy. On the other hand, if you are from a culture where people bargain for everything, you will feel just as exasperated if a seller offers you a flat price. "Where's the fun in this?" you'll say. "The whole human transaction of shopping is gone!" It will help to find a cultural translator who can show you the ropes.

When in Rome, Do as the Romans Do—as Much as Possible

Most of the things you really need to know about a culture are not to be found in the guidebooks or travelogues. To learn the unspoken rules of a culture, look, listen, and observe. What is the pace of life like? Do people regard brash individuality as admirable or embarrassing? When customers enter a shop, do they greet and chat with the shopkeeper or ignore the person as they browse?

Remember, though, that even when you know the rules, you may find it difficult to carry them out, as we noted in discussing conversational distance. For example, cultures differ in their tolerance for prolonged gazes (Keating, 1994). In the Middle East, two men will look directly at one another as they talk, but such direct gazes would be deeply uncomfortable to most Japanese and a sign of insult or confrontation to some African-Americans. Knowing this fact about gaze rules can help people accept the reality of different customs, but most of us will still feel uncomfortable trying to change our own ways.

Avoid Stereotyping

Try not to let your awareness of cultural differences cause you to overlook individual variations within cultures. During a dreary Boston winter, social psychologist Roger Brown (1986) went to the Bahamas for a vacation. To his surprise, he found the people he met unfriendly, rude, and sullen. He decided that the reason was that Bahamians had to deal with spoiled, demanding foreigners, and he tried out this hypothesis on a cab driver. The cab driver looked at Brown in amazement, smiled cheerfully, and told him that Bahamians don't mind tourists—just *unsmiling* tourists.

And then Brown realized what had been going on. "Not tourists generally, but this tourist, myself, was the cause," he wrote. "Confronted with my unrelaxed wintry Boston face, they had assumed I had no interest in them and had responded noncommittally, inexpressively. I had created the Bahamian national character. Everywhere I took my face it sprang into being. So I began smiling a lot, and the Bahamians changed their national character. In fact, they lost any national character and differentiated into individuals."

Wise travelers can use their knowledge of cultural differences to expand their understanding of human behavior, while avoiding the trap of stereotyping. Sociocultural research teaches us to appreciate the countless explicit and implicit cultural rules that govern our behavior, values, and attitudes, and those of others. Yet, we should not forget Roger Brown's lesson that every human being is an individual: one who not only reflects his or her culture, but also shares the common concerns of all humanity.

Summary

Roles and Rules

Social psychology is the study of people in social context, including the influence of *norms*, *roles*, and groups on behavior and cognition. Roles and norms are affected by one's *culture*.

Two classic studies illustrate the power of roles to affect individual actions. In Milgram's obedience study, most people in the role of "teacher" inflicted what they thought was extreme shock on another person because of the authority of the experimenter. In Zimbardo's prison study, college students quickly fell into the role of "prisoner" or "guard."

Obedience to authority contributes to the smooth running of society, but obedience can also lead to actions that are deadly, foolish, or illegal. People obey orders because they can be punished if they do not, out of respect for authority, and to gain advantages. Even when they would rather not obey, they may do so because they believe the authority is *legitimate*; because the role is *routinized* into duties that are performed mindlessly; because they are embarrassed to break the rules of good manners and lack the words to protest; or because they have been *entrapped*.

Social Influences on Beliefs

According to *attribution theory*, people are motivated to search for causes to which they can attribute their own and other people's behavior. Their attributions may be *situational or dispositional*. The *fundamental attribution error* occurs when people overestimate personality traits as a cause of behavior and underestimate the influence of the situation. A *self-serving bias* allows people to excuse their mistakes by blaming the situation yet also take credit for their good deeds. According to the *just-world hypothesis*, most people need to believe that the world is fair and that people get what they deserve. To preserve this belief, they may blame victims of abuse or injustice for provoking or deserving it, instead of blaming the perpetrators.

People hold many *attitudes*, which include cognitions and feelings about a subject. One important influence on attitudes is the shared experiences of a person's age group or generation. Another influence is the *validity effect*: Simply hearing a statement over and over again makes it seem more believable. Techniques of attitude change include associating a product or message with someone who is famous, attractive, or expert; and linking the product with good feelings. Fear tactics tend to backfire.

Some methods of attitude change are intentionally manipulative. Tactics of *coercive persuasion* include causing the person extreme distress, defining problems simplistically, offering the appearance of unconditional love and complete acceptance of the person in exchange for unquestioning loyalty, creating a new identity for the person, using entrapment, and controlling the person's access to outside information.

Individuals in Groups

In groups, individuals often behave differently than they would on their own. They may conform to social pressure because they identify with a group, trust the group's judgment or knowledge, hope for personal gain, or wish to be liked. But they also may conform mindlessly and self-destructively, violating their own preferences and values because "everyone else is doing it."

Groups that are strongly cohesive, are isolated from other views, are under outside pressure, and have strong leaders are vulnerable to *groupthink*, the tendency of group members to think alike, censor themselves, actively suppress disagreement, and feel that their decisions are invulnerable. Groupthink often produces faulty decisions because group members fail to seek disconfirming evidence for their ideas. However, groups can be structured to counteract groupthink.

Diffusion of responsibility in a group can lead to inaction on the part of individuals, such as *bystander apathy* or, in work groups, *social loafing*. The diffusion of responsibility is especially likely to occur under conditions that promote *deindividuation*, the loss of awareness of one's individuality. Deindividuation increases when people feel anonymous, as in a large group or crowd, or when they are wearing masks or uniforms. In some situations, crowd norms lead deindividuated people to behave aggressively, but in others, crowd norms foster helpfulness and *altruism*.

The willingness to speak up for an unpopular opinion, blow the whistle on illegal or immoral practices, or help a stranger in trouble is partly a matter of personal belief and conscience. But several social and situational factors are also important. These include seeing a need for help, deciding to take responsibility, deciding that the costs of not doing anything are greater than the costs of getting involved, having an ally, and becoming entrapped in a commitment to help or to dissent.

Group Conflict and Prejudice

Ethnocentrism, the belief that one's own group or nation is superior to all others, promotes *"us-them" thinking*. People develop *social identities* based on their group affiliations, including nationality, ethnicity, religion, and other social memberships. As soon as people see themselves as "us" (members of an in-group), they tend to define anyone different as "them." Dividing the world into us and them is often fueled by competition. Conflict and hostility between groups can be reduced by teamwork and by *interdependence* in working for mutual goals.

Stereotypes help people rapidly process new information, organize experience, and predict how others will behave. But they distort reality by (1) emphasizing differences between groups, (2) underestimating the differences within groups, and (3) producing selective perception. Cultural values and rules determine how people from different cultures see and interpret the same event.

A *prejudice* is an unreasonable negative feeling toward a category of people. People acquire prejudices through childhood socialization, media images, and conformity and groupthink. Prejudice wards off feelings of anxiety and doubt, provides a simple explanation of complex problems, and bolsters self-esteem when a person feels threatened. Prejudice also justifies a majority group's economic interests and dominance, and, in extreme cases, legitimizes group conflict and war. During times of economic insecurity and competition for jobs, prejudice rises significantly.

Prejudice occurs in many varieties and degrees. As a result, people disagree about how to define racism, sexism, and other prejudices, and on whether racism and other prejudices are declining or have merely taken new forms (such as *symbolic racism*).

Efforts to reduce prejudice and group conflict must take into account the origins of the conflict and the factors that support it. In groups where members of majority and minority groups are unfamiliar with one another's ways, it is important to break the *cycle of distrust*, by not inferring prejudice or hostility when none is intended.

Four important conditions are required for reducing prejudice and conflict between groups: Both sides must have equal legal status, economic standing, and power; both sides must have the legal and moral support of authorities and the larger culture; both sides must have opportunities to work and socialize together (the *contact hypothesis*); and both sides must work together for a common goal.

The Question of Human Nature

Although many people believe that only bad people do bad deeds, the principles of social and cultural psychology show that under certain conditions, good people are often induced to do bad things too. All of us, depending on circumstances, are susceptible to obedience and conformity, bystander apathy, groupthink, deindividuation, ethnocentrism, stereotyping, and prejudice. All of us are subject to the same social and cultural forces that foster tolerance or animosity, conformity or dissent, courage or cowardice.

Key Terms

social psychology (p. 85)

cultural psychology (p. 85)

norms (social) (p. 85)

role (p. 85)

Looking Back

Vocabulary Lesson

The purpose of this vocabulary lesson is to help you review and deepen your knowledge of the ten general vocabulary words you worked with at the beginning of this chapter.

A. Structural Analysis—Affixes and Root Words
   1. Circle the prefix of the following word: *Invulnerability*
   2. Find the dictionary definitions of the root word of *invulnerability* and write the definition by the words.
   3. How does the prefix change the meaning of the word?
   4. Underline the suffix of the following word: *Arbitrarily*
   5. Find the dictionary definition for the root word of *arbitrarily* and write the definition by the word.
   6. How does the suffix change the meaning of the word?

B. Use of Context: Read the first paragraph of the first section of "Roles and Rules" on page 85 in which the word *conventions* appears ("Norms are the *conventions* of everyday life that make interactions with other people predictable and orderly...."). In your own words write a definition for *conventions* below:

   _____

C. Multiple Meanings of Words
   1. Circle the definition below of the word *convention* that fits the way it is used in paragraph one of "Roles and Rules" on page 85.
      a. An assembly
      b. An agreement, esp. international
      c. A fixed custom or usage

D. Synonyms and Antonyms: List one synonym (same meaning) and one antonym (opposite meaning) for the following word:

Word	Synonym	Antonym
Euphoria		

E. Generate Your Own Language
   1. When Amy gave an *ambiguous* response to Carlos' invitation to the party, did Carlos have a clear or cloudy idea of whether or not she would go?
   2. If you decided to *boycott* a certain brand of clothing, on what grounds would you base your decision?
   3. Describe the last time you *anguished* over something you did to someone else.
   4. What *tangible* rewards do you receive when you exercise and eat healthy food?
   5. How do you show your *animosity* toward other people?

F. Word Confusion: Write a sentence that shows you know the difference between *antidotes* and *anecdotes*.

G. Textbook Vocabulary Preview: The following words that appear in this chapter will be some of your vocabulary words for Part Two of this textbook. How well do you already know them? Which ones do you use in your written and oral language?

1. Traditional

2. Virtually

3. Bigot

4. Egalitarian

5. Unanimous (unanimity, unanimously)

6. Consistent (consistency)

VOCABULARY EXTENSION

The purpose of this vocabulary exercise is to help you see to what degree you know the ten general vocabulary words in this chapter. Matching a word with its definition is the beginning of knowing a word. Using the word in your speaking and writing is full knowledge. See if you have increased your vocabulary by following the directions below:

A. List the vocabulary words from this lesson that you can now use in both your speaking and writing.

B. List the vocabulary words from this lesson that you can now use in writing but are still not comfortable using in speaking.

C. List the vocabulary words from this lesson that you cannot use yet but will recognize in reading.

D. List general vocabulary words from this lesson that are still difficult to understand.

E. Use *five* vocabulary words from this lesson in a five-sentence paragraph on the topic of this lesson.

F. Illustrate the meaning of *one* of the vocabulary words from this lesson through some form of artwork or a cartoon. (This exercise is for right-brain students who enjoy drawing better than writing!)

EXTENDED READING ACTIVITIES

The purpose of this section is to give you a variety of options for independent study or investigation of the chapter topic. Reading is a skill that must be practiced each day if progress is to take place. These activities are designed to give you a variety of reading experiences through which you can improve your general vocabulary and increase your higher-level comprehension skills.

Your instructor may wish to (a) assign one or more activities to the class as a whole, (b) assign various activities to small groups, (c) assign one or more activities to individual students, or (d) let students choose to do the activities or not.

A. Weekly Reading Report: In the first chapter of this textbook, you were given the opportunity to begin keeping a weekly report of your reading. Record what you read each day for your courses and what you read for fun. Photocopy the Weekly Reading Report form in Appendix C if you wish to continue keeping this report.

B. Attend a Reading Lab on Campus: In the first chapter of this textbook, it was suggested that you attend a reading lab on campus if your school has one. If you decide to attend, do so for at least thirty minutes at a time.

C. Read an Adult Novel. If you wish to write a report on one of these novels, a novel report form is in Appendix C.
    1. Shirley Jackson, *The Lottery*
    2. Alice Hoffman, *Practical Magic*
    3. Annie Proulx, *Postcards*
    4. Anne Tyler, *Dinner at the Homesick Restaurant*
    5. Jane Smiley, *Duplicate Keys*

D. Reading/Writing Connection: Use one of the experience-based questions that you did not answer in the Active Questioning lesson for an entry in your college experience journal.

E. Use the Internet
    1. Do a search on the International Tribunal from WWII and present-day war criminals.
    2. Do a search on ethnocentrism.
    3. Do research on prejudice against Jews, Japanese, and African Americans.

F. Vocabulary Journal: Begin keeping a vocabulary journal by recording five words a week of which you have beginning knowledge but not complete use. Record the word, its source, a sentence or phrase in which it was used, what you think the word means, and then a dictionary definition that shows its meaning as it is used in the sentence. The words can come from academic or pleasure reading. Use the form at the end of this chapter if you wish.

G. Research: This is the first chapter you have studied in this textbook that relies on research studies for support of main ideas. For example, in the first section of the chapter, "Roles and Rules," the authors cite twenty-six studies by giving the last names of the authors and dates of publication in parentheses. These studies, listed in the bibliography of the psychology textbook, are printed in professional journals, in books of articles edited by professionals, and as books. The manuscript style used by all of the studies is that published by the American Psychological Association.
    1. Look up one of the studies listed on page 128 and write a summary of the main ideas. Next, write your personal response to the study.

a. Collins, Barry E., & Brief, Diana E. (1995). Using person-perception vignette methodologies to uncover the symbolic meanings of teacher behaviors in the Milgram paradigm. *Journal of Social Issues, 51,* 89–106.

b. Darley, John M. (1995). Constructive and destructive obedience: A taxonomy of principal agent relationships. In A.G. Miller, B.E. Collins, & D.E. Brief (eds.), Perspectives on obedience to authority: The legacy of the Milgram experiments. *Journal of Social Issues, 51*(3), 125–154.

c. di Leonardo, Micaela (1987). The female world of cards and holidays: Women, families, and the work of kinship. *Signs, 12,* 1–20.

d. Fischer, Ann R.; Tokar, David M.; Good, Glen E.; & Snell, Andrea F. (1998). More on the structure of male role norms. *Psychology of Women Quarterly, 22,* 135–155.

e. Haney, Craig; Banks, Curtis; & Zimbardo, Philip (1973). Interpersonal dynamics in a simulated prison. *International Journal of Criminology and Penology, 1,* 69–97.

f. Haney, Craig & Zimbardo, Philip (1998). The past and future of U.S. prison policy: Twenty-five years after the Stanford Prison Experiment. *American Psychologist, 53,* 709–727.

g. Haritos-Fatouros, Mika (1988). The official torturer: A learning model for obedience to the authority of violence. *Journal of Applied Social Psychology, 18,* 1107–1120.

h. Meeus, Wm. H.J., & Raaijmakers, Quinten A.W. (1995). Obedience in modern society: The Utrecht studies. In A.G. Miller, B.E. Collins, & D.E. Brief (eds.), Perspectives on obedience to authority: The legacy of the Milgram experiments. *Journal of Social Issues, 51* (3), 155–175.

i. Milgram, Stanley (1963). Behavioral study of obedience. *Journal of Abnormal and Social Psychology, 67,* 371–378.

j. Taffel, Ronald (1990, September/October). The politics of mood. *Family Therapy Networker,* 49–53, 72.

k. Tyler, Tom R. (1997). The psychology of legitimacy: A relational perspective on voluntary deference to authorities. *Personality and Social Psychology Review, 1,* 323–345.

2. Analyze the manuscript style of the above entries. Pretend you do not have access to an APA style manual in your library.

a. What words do you capitalize?

b. Where do you put commas?

c. Where do you put semicolons?

d. Where do periods go?

e. What is italicized?

f. How are multiple authors listed?

g. What do all the numbers at the end of the entries mean?

3. Play detective with the above entries.
   a. Which is the oldest entry?
   b. Which are the latest entries?
   c. How many studies were published in 1995?
   d. How many entries are published in the *Journal of Social Issues*?
   e. Which entry has the most authors?

Reflection

Mind Revolution

The Mind Revolution grew out of my awareness that too many times students do not incorporate what they learn in class into their personal lives. Learning remains compartmentalized and sometimes wasted. This is an attempt to get you to see how the chapter information can be personally important. Hopefully, you will encounter a new idea in each chapter that you can incorporate into your own life, or at least have something new to think about as you go about your daily routine. Life should never be boring!

The influence of society and cultural values on individual behavior will probably be the most important information to those readers who grew up in Western middle-class homes that emphasized personal responsibility. For readers from homes that are part of a group-oriented culture, the difference in perception of the various cultures and the reliance on personal responsibility may be an awakening experience. Hopefully, understanding that cultures influence how people perceive action differently will help people in understanding each other.

Vocabulary

No great problems seem to exist with general vocabulary words. Specialized vocabulary was well defined, explained, and reinforced.

Comprehension

The textbook organization helped with comprehension. The textbook is arranged topically; in other words, each chapter stands alone. New concepts are defined and explained in each chapter. References to previous chapters exist but the authors do not assume prior knowledge on the part of the reader.

The density of concepts was fairly easy to follow because of the textbook aids and examples used. The reader's background information and experience may have caused trouble for the reader. Seeing the world as simplistic, in black and white terms, could have created difficulty. A reader who believes that people are totally responsible for their own actions could have difficulty with truly understanding that society and culture play an important part in what an individual does. Not understanding the influence of social forces on people's lives because of limited academic background or experience could have caused difficulty with understanding. Another area of personal background experience that could have led to difficulty in understanding could be not seeing through one's own prejudices. Not having thought about personal prejudices before reading this chapter could limit understanding. An unwillingness to explore other cultures as a way to enrich one's own life could also limit understanding.

The authors assumed limited knowledge on the part of the reader and therefore helped the reader learn new concepts. They were well aware of which concepts in their field a freshman would not know and spent a great deal of effort in making them clear.

Weekly Vocabulary Journal

Your Name _____

Directions: The purpose of this vocabulary journal is to help you deepen your knowledge of words you vaguely know. The directions are as follows: (1) Skim your own pleasure and school (academic) reading to find words you know vaguely but feel you cannot define adequately. (2) Write the words in the context in which they were found. In other words, write at least the phrase or sentence in which the word was used. Give the source for the word. (3) Write what you think the word means as it is used. (4) Check your guess against a dictionary definition and write the dictionary definition down. If you cannot find the word in your dictionary, check your spelling, look for the root word, or use a larger dictionary.

A. Word: _____

    1. Source: _____

    2. Sentence in which word is used: _____

    3. What word means in sentence: _____

    4. Dictionary definition: _____

B. Word: _____

    1. Source: _____

    2. Sentence in which word is used: _____

    3. What word means in sentence: _____

    4. Dictionary definition: _____

C. Word: _____

    1. Source: _____

    2. Sentence in which word is used: _____

    3. What word means in sentence: _____

    4. Dictionary definition: _____

D. Word: _____

    1. Source: _____

    2. Sentence in which word is used: _____

    3. What word means in sentence: _____

    4. Dictionary definition: _____

E. Word: _____

    1. Source: _____

    2. Sentence in which word is used: _____

    3. What word means in sentence: _____

    4. Dictionary definition: _____

Sociology:
Race and Ethnicity

Vocabulary Extension
Extended Reading Activities
Reflection
Mind Revolution
Vocabulary
Comprehension

VOCABULARY/METACOGNITION

The purpose of this exercise is to help you become aware of when you know the meaning of a word and to help you know when you do not know the meaning of a word. This is metacognition awareness.

On a scale of 1–5 (see below), rate your knowledge of the following vocabulary words from "Race and Ethnicity." After matching words with definitions on page 134, check your answers and then check your number *ones* and *fives* below. Did you know when you really knew a word and when you really did not know the word?

Scale

1. I absolutely do not know.
2. I do not think I know.
3. There's a 50/50 chance I have seen or heard it.
4. I think I know it.
5. I know the word and can use it.

Words

_____ 1. Continuum
_____ 2. Subtle
_____ 3. Blatant
_____ 4. Miscegenation
_____ 5. Detriment
_____ 6. Succumbed
_____ 7. Fostered
_____ 8. Plummeting
_____ 9. Overt
_____10. Xenophobia

Go to page 134. See if you can match the right definition with the word and then write sentences for any three words in the list.

Words	Definitions
_____ 1. Continuum	A. (1) A continuous whole; (2) continuity
_____ 2. Subtle	B. (1) Offensively loud-voiced, noisy; (2) obtrusive
_____ 3. Blatant	C. An injury or loss, or that which causes it
_____ 4. Miscegenation	D. (1) Nourish, bring up; (2) cherish; (3) promote the growth of or development of
_____ 5. Detriment	
_____ 6. Succumb (succumbed)	E. Plain to the view; open
_____ 7. Foster (fostered)	F. Fear or hatred of foreigners
_____ 8. Plummet (plummeting)	G. Plunge straight down
_____ 9. Overt	H. (1) Give way under pressure, yield; (2) die
_____10. Xenophobia	I. Interbreeding between races
	J. (1) Delicate, refined; (2) artful, crafty; (3) discerning, discriminating, shrewd

Write three words from the list and your own sentences that show you know how to use the words. Choose words that you marked a *five* if possible.

1. Word _____

   Sentence _____

2. Word _____

   Sentence _____

3. Word _____

   Sentence _____

PRE-READING THE TEXTBOOK CHAPTER

The purpose of this *first* of three steps in your reading plan is to suggest things to do *before* you read. First, as part of your pre-reading, read the Prior Knowledge section beginning on page 135, the Academic Study Skills section's overview on page 139, and the first part of the Textbook Study Aids Plan (Pre-Reading) on page 139. When you finish, return to this page and continue your pre-reading.

TAPPING PRIOR KNOWLEDGE

Tap your experience and prior knowledge about the title of this selection by writing words and phrases that come to your mind. You are pulling up your file on the topic and focusing on what you will read. What do you already know about the subject? Do not look at your textbook at this time, as these answers will vary from person to person and won't be found in the textbook. There are no wrong answers for this part of the lesson.

PREDICTING

Predict in one sentence what you will read. Try to predict in some detail. Don't write, "I predict that I will read about race and ethnicity." What behavior, action, and/or information do you expect to read about? Predicting helps you identify your expectations of what you will read. Not reading what you have predicted will serve as a warning that you have misjudged the topic of the article and will help you adapt to what is in the chapter.

OVERVIEWING

Overview the chapter by turning to the Textbook Study Aids Plan in the Academic Study Skills section of this chapter on page 139 and following the directions for Pre-Reading. Note that you have four major sections with several subheadings under each one. Add the new information you learn to what you learned in the Prior Knowledge section of this lesson.

PRIOR KNOWLEDGE

This section, part of your pre-reading, presents a model to show you what will help you comprehend this chapter by using your own background knowledge. If you know much of the information listed below, you have a better background for reading this chapter. This section will suggest helpful kinds of background information and help you activate what you know; do not try to look up or learn everything listed. Ask yourself what you need to know before you read and what you already know that will help you to understand this chapter.

WRITING PATTERN OVERVIEW

In the social sciences, as noted in the psychology chapter, the reader can expect expository writing in which the author explains and informs the reader. Statements are supported by examples, especially facts and numbers. References, over sixty citations in this chapter, refer to sources that support the information in the chapter.

VOCABULARY

The specialized vocabulary appears in the first sections of the chapter and then tapers off. The author defines the words in context and then elaborates on the definitions. Most general vocabulary words are common words found in general reading materials.

DIRECTIONS FOR READING THIS SECTION

First, notice the categories of information: (a) vocabulary, (b) writing patterns, and (c) concepts and background knowledge and experience. Next, skim the sections, noting what is familiar and what is not. If a great amount is familiar and/or interesting to you, you should find reading the chapter easier than if you do not recognize anything and find the information boring.

CHAPTER SECTIONS

I.   The Social Meaning of Race and Ethnicity
   A.   Vocabulary
      1.   General
         a.   Intermingled
         b.   Hierarchy
         c.   Irrational
         d.   Continuum
         e.   Embedded
         f.   Innately
         g.   Subtle
         h.   Blatant
         i.   Inherent
         j.   Perpetuates
      2.   Specialized
         a.   Race
         b.   Ethnicity
         c.   Prejudice
         d.   Racism
         e.   Scapegoat
         f.   Discrimination
         g.   Institutional prejudice and discrimination
   B.   Recognition of Writing Patterns or Arrangement of Ideas and Devices
      1.   Expository writing
      2.   Definitions in context (words in bold print and definition in italic print); explanations, including examples, follow the definitions
      3.   Use of cause/effect pattern
      4.   Facts with sources (thirteen references)
      5.   Anecdotes used to illustrate a point
      6.   References to visuals to reinforce text
   C.   Concepts and Background Knowledge and Experience
      1.   Personal Experience
         a.   Recognize prejudice and stereotypes in our own lives
         b.   Understand why people are prejudiced
      2.   Academic Experience
         a.   Recognize institutional prejudice and discrimination
         b.   This chapter will give you concept and background knowledge for reading four chapters in Part Two of this textbook: (a) "Some Problems with Columbus's 'Discovery' of America," (b) "American English: Does It Have a History?" (c) "Ethnicity and the National Pastime," and (d) "Behavior in Social and Cultural Context."

    3. Concepts
       a. Clear understanding of the difference between *race* and *ethnicity*
       b. Understand why the three-part racial classification is misleading
       c. Understand the significance of societies ranking people in racial hierarchies and then claiming that one is better that the others
       d. Know the U.S. population is genetically and ethnically mixed and varied (interracial births are increasing.)
       e. People in the U.S. have been given minority standing based on race and ethnicity and can carry a subordinate role, though not all are disadvantaged.

II. Majority and Minority: Patterns of Interaction
    A. Vocabulary
       1. General
          a. Detriment
          b. Hypersegregation (defined in context)
          c. Rallied
          d. Ultimately
          e. Ethnocentrism
          f. Succumbed
       2. Specialized
          a. Pluralism
          b. Assimilation
          c. Miscegenation
          d. Segregation
          e. Genocide
    B. Recognition of Writing Patterns or Arrangement of Ideas and Devices
       1. Definitions in context
       2. Explanations with examples, some historical
       3. Facts with sources
       4. Eight references for support
    C. Concepts and Background Knowledge and Experience
       1. Personal Experience
          a. Experience of assimilation; changed styles of dress, values, religion, language, and/or friends
          b. Visited or lived in an ethnic village, such as New York's Chinatown
          c. Read biography or viewed television documentary on Rosa Parks
       2. Academic Experience
          a. High school history or sociology course in which segregation and/or genocide were studied

      b.   Studied or saw documentaries on Adolf Hitler, Josef Stalin, Pol Pot, Hutus killing Tutsis in Rwanda, Serbs killing Bosnians

   3.   Concepts

      a.   Understand the difference between *pluralism* and *assimilation*, and what you gain and lose with each

      b.   Understand what harm segregation has done and that it still exists

      c.   Understand the horror of genocide and know what groups have suffered historically and also that it continues

III. Race and Ethnicity in the United States

   A. Vocabulary

     1. General

       a.   Refuse (page 157) (multiple meanings)

       b.   Subjugation

       c.   Indigenous

       d.   Wards

       e.   Fostered

       f.   Windfalls

       g.   Dilemma

       h.   Aloof

       i.   Shunned

       j.   Plummeting

       k.   Overt

       l.   Enclaves

       m. Internment

       n.   Entrepreneurial

       o.   Fared

   B. Recognition of Writing Patterns or Arrangement of Ideas and Devices

     1. The same patterns as in previous sections

     2. Large amount of numbers and dates

     3. Section summary

     4. Use of quotes

     5. Chronological historical background

     6. Over forty different references to sources for support

   C. Concepts and Background Knowledge and Experience

     1. Personal Experience

       a.   Know that not all people of a group are alike

     2. Academic Experience

       a.   Know subcategories within groups

     3. Concepts

       a.   Be familiar with the various groups of people that make up U.S. society

IV. Race and Ethnicity: Looking Ahead
    A. Vocabulary
        1. General
            a. Xenophobia (Greek roots)
    B. Recognition of Writing Patterns or Arrangement of Ideas and Devices
        1. Expository writing continues
        2. Continued use of statements, explanation, examples
        3. Many dates used
        4. A summary
        5. No references
    C. Concepts and Background Knowledge and Experience
        1. Personal Experience
            a. Know how immigrants add to the richness of U.S. culture
        2. Academic Experience
            a. Know who the new arrivals are and problems encountered by them
        3. Concepts
            a. History of immigration

ACADEMIC STUDY SKILLS

OVERVIEW

Using textbook study aids continues to be the main focus of the study skills activities of Part I of this textbook.

TEXTBOOK STUDY AIDS PLAN

Follow the pre-reading, reading, and post-reading directions.

Pre-Reading   As part of the pre-reading activities you do before reading the textbook chapter, skim through the Chapter Outline on page 146 and the Summary, Key Concepts, Critical-Thinking Questions, and Learning Exercises on pages 170–172. This will give you an overview of the chapter.

Also, as part of your pre-reading activities, study the following visual aids carefully: Table 10-1 (page 149), Figure 10-1 (page 154), Table 10-2 (page 159), Table 10-3 (page 161), Table 10-4 (page 163), and Table 10-5 (page 166).

Now return to your pre-reading plan on page 134. You will be instructed during the reading and post-reading parts of your three-part reading lesson to return to this page.

Reading   While you are reading the various sections of this chapter, review the tables and figures as you are instructed in the text. Did you know there were so many racial and ethnic categories in the United States before you read Table 10-1?

Had you thought about categories of bigots and liberals or how you would catego-rize yourself before looking at Figure 10-1? Tables 10-2, 10-3,10-4, and 10-5 help you compare/contrast the social standing of several groups of Americans. Did anything especially get your attention? Now go to the Reciprocal Teaching reading plan below.

Post-Reading   As part of your post-reading activities, read the inserted sections of the chapter, "Critical Thinking" on pages 151–152 and "Controversy & Debate" on page 168. If you are interested in the issues in these sections, you may want to respond to one or both of them by following the directions in the writing prompts in the Extended Reading Activities section on page 175.

Understanding the chapter information helps you to make an informed stand on the issues in these special sections. The purpose for reading them last is to help you stay focused on the most important information in the chapter first; next, you can relax and enjoy these extensions of the main text.

RECIPROCAL TEACHING

OVERVIEW

Your first step of the three-part reading plan was pre-reading, in which you acti-vated your prior knowledge and experience, predicted what you would read, and overviewed the chapter before reading.

As the second step in this three-part reading plan, you will read the chapter "Race and Ethnicity" by using the new version of the Reciprocal Teaching reading plan as explained below. An older version was used in Chapter 1. An alternative plan to Reciprocal Teaching, Active Questioning, is in Appendix A. In both the Reciprocal Teaching reading plan and Active Questioning you break up the chap-ter in sections and read and think about each as you read. The purpose of both plans is to keep you reading actively.

GENERAL DIRECTIONS

The following Reciprocal Teaching lesson is based on an updated version that ap-pears in Bess Henson, ed., *New Directions in Reading Instruction Revised* (Newark, DE: IRA, 2000, p. 23). In the old model used in Chapter 1, the steps are to summarize, question, clarify, and predict. In the new model the steps are to predict, question, clarify, and summarize. Try this lesson based on the new version and then decide which version works best for you. In the first Reciprocal Teaching reading plan (Chapter 1) you were given a great deal of guidance in following the four steps. In the plan below, you are also given guidance in keeping with the plan of this text-book. To begin with, you will work with teacher models, then move to guided practice through a combination of teacher models and opportunities for you to write your own responses, and then to total independence on your part in Part II in generating your own questions without teacher modeling or guidance. In this lesson you are at the stage of teacher modeling and guided practice.

ASSIGNMENT

Before beginning this assignment, read the "Reading" section (pages 139–140) of the Textbook Study Aids Plan in the Academic Study Skills section and then return to this page. Begin reading the textbook chapter, "Race and Ethnicity," by following the directions below.

    A. The Social Meaning of Race and Ethnicity

        1. Predict what you will read in the first section, "The Social Meaning of Race and Ethnicity." Model prediction: "I predict that I will read how race and ethnicity affect one's place in society and some of the problems that occur." What can you add or delete to this prediction to make it yours?

Your prediction _____

_____

        2. After reading this section, write one question about an important concept and then answer your own question. If you cannot write a question, answer one of the model questions provided. Model questions: (1) What minorities live in your community? Are the dominant members of your community prejudiced against them? How do you know? (2) Are you aware of stereotyping of your racial or ethnic group? If so, describe it. If not, describe the stereotype of another racial or ethnic group. (3) Review the four theories of prejudice and choose one that best fits the prejudice you have experienced or observed in your community. Justify your choice.

Your question _____

Your answer to your question or the one above _____

        3. Identify one difficult idea from this section and then orally explain or clarify it in your own words to your partner. If you can discuss or explain an idea in your own words, then you know that you understand it. If you have to keep using the author's words, then you do not know it. If you cannot think of an idea to explain, then use one of the model ideas provided. Model ideas: (1) explain why sociologists find the nineteenth-century, three-part racial classification misleading (page 147), (2) explain why prejudice, stereotyping, and racism are harmful (pages 150–153), (3) explain the four theories of prejudice in your own words (pages 153–154), (4) explain institutional prejudice and discrimination (page 155).

Your idea _____

        4. Write a summary of the first major section by using the following information, which provides the main ideas. Model summary: This first section of the chapter gives definitions of key concepts: race, ethnicity, minorities, prejudice, stereotypes, racism, and

discrimination (including institutional). It also describes four theories of prejudice. See numbers one through three of the textbook chapter summary on page 170 for guidance and combine the information with the model summary. Add and/or delete information as you find necessary.

Your summary _____

_____

_____

    B.   Majority and Minority: Patterns of Interaction
       1.   Predict what you will read in the second section, "Majority and Minority: Patterns of Interaction." Model prediction: "I will read about the interaction of minority and majority groups of people, what they do and think about each other." What can you add or delete to this prediction to make it yours?

Your prediction_____

_____

       2.   After reading this section, write one question about something important and then answer your own question. If you cannot write a question, answer one of the model questions provided. Model questions: (1) Give examples of pluralism and assimilation in your community. (2) What are the disadvantages of the hypersegregation of some African Americans in some inner cities? (3) What are the advantages and disadvantages for religious or other groups who segregate themselves? What are the advantages and disadvantages of private schools and home schooling?

Your question _____

Your answer to your question or the one above _____

       3.   Identify one difficult idea from this section and then orally explain or clarify it in your own words to your partner. If you can discuss or explain an idea in your own words, then you know that you understand it. If you have to keep using the author's words, then you do not know it. If you cannot think of an idea to explain, then use the model idea provided. Model idea: Explain the difference between and significance of *de jure* (by law) and *de facto* (in fact) segregation.

Your idea _____

       4.   Write a summary of the second major section by using the following information, which provides the main ideas. Model summary: The second section of this chapter discusses four patterns of interaction between majority and minority groups: pluralism, assimilation, segregation, and genocide. Look at number four of the textbook chapter summary (page 170) for guidance and combine the

information with the model summary. Add and/or delete
information as you find necessary.

Your summary _____

_____

_____

    C. Race and Ethnicity in the United States

        1. Predict what you will read in the third section of the chapter, "Race
and Ethnicity in the United States." Model prediction: "Since the
U.S. is a multiethnic society, I believe that I will read about the
many ethnic and racial groups that make up our society." What can
you add or delete to this prediction to make it yours?

Your prediction_____

_____

        2. After reading this section, write one question about something
important and then answer your own question. If you cannot write
a question, answer the model question provided. Model question:
Read the descriptions of the various groups listed in this section and
identify the background of your group's (or class's) members. How
many members have mixed racial and ethnic backgrounds? To what
degree do members identify with racial and ethnic groups? How
much history of heritage has been preserved?

Your question _____

Your answer to your question or the one above _____

        3. Identify one difficult idea from this section and then orally explain
or clarify it in your own words to your partner. If you can discuss or
explain an idea in your own words, then you know that you
understand it. If you have to keep using the author's words, then
you do not know it. If you cannot think of an idea to explain, then
use one of the model ideas provided. Model ideas: (1) the
differences between WASPs and white ethnic Americans, (2) the
differences among groups of Asian Americans, (3) the differences
among groups of Hispanic Americans

Your idea _____

        4. Write a summary of the third major section by using the information
provided, which contains the main ideas. Model summary: The third
section of this chapter describes various groups that make up U.S.
society: Native Americans, WASPs, African Americans, Asian
Americans, Hispanics, and white ethnics. Read numbers five through
ten of the textbook chapter summary for guidance (pages 170–171)
and combine the information with the model summary. Add and/or
delete information as you find necessary.

Your summary _____

_____

_____

   D. Race and Ethnicity: Looking Ahead
      1. Predict what you will read in the fourth section of the chapter, "Race and Ethnicity: Looking Ahead." Model prediction: "I believe that I will read about the future of race and ethnic groups and their relationship with each other." What can you add to or delete from this prediction to make it yours?

Your prediction _____

_____

      2. After reading this section, write one question about something important and then answer your own question. If you cannot write a question, answer the model question provided. Model question: List the three recent examples of hostility toward foreigners (xenophobia) listed in the textbook and then explain the fears underlying those examples. Relate this type of hostility to similar hostility in your community.

Your question _____

Your answer to your question or the one above _____

      3. Identify one difficult idea from this section and then orally explain or clarify it in your own words to your partner. If you can discuss or explain an idea in your own words, then you know that you understand it. If you have to keep using the author's words, then you do not know it. If you cannot think of an idea to explain, then use the model idea provided. Model idea: Give a historical summary of immigration to the United States in your own words.

Your idea _____

      4. Write a summary of the fourth major section by using the information provided, which contains the main ideas. Model summary: This last section of the chapter gives a brief historical summary of U.S. immigration with some description of the types of immigrants and the problems they encountered. Read number eleven of the textbook chapter summary (page 171) for guidance and combine the information with the model summary. Add and/or delete information as you find necessary.

Your summary _____

_____

_____

POST-READING THE TEXTBOOK CHAPTER

OVERVIEW

In the second part of your three-part reading plan, you practiced reading your textbook chapter section by section, made predictions for what you would read in the next section, asked and answered questions, explained or clarified important ideas, and wrote section summaries.

In this third part of the three-part reading plan, you will find suggestions for what to do after you read. Your task is to compare what you predicted with what you actually read as an aid to comprehension, to add what you have learned to your file of information on the topic, and to think about what you have read.

ASSIGNMENT

A. Compare what you predicted you would read with what you actually read. Did anything you predicted cause you a problem with comprehension? What? How?

B. What did you learn from the reading that you did not know about before working on this lesson?

C. Look at the words and phrases that you listed as your prior knowledge on page 134. Group them below with relevant information in "B" above. This is your new file of information on sociology. (The ability to group ideas and to see relationships requires more complex comprehension than merely memorizing isolated facts.)

D. What have you learned from this chapter that is important?

E. What do you already know that you can relate to it?

F. What do you see differently as a result of reading the chapter?

G. Now return to the Textbook Study Aids Plan in the Academic Study Skills section of this chapter, page 140, and follow the directions for Post-Reading.

Your Headings	Words and Phrases from Pre-Reading	Relevant Information from "B"

RACE AND ETHNICITY ◄

FROM JOHN J. MACIONIS, *SOCIETY: THE BASICS, 5/E**

Chapter Outline

On a bright, early fall day almost fifty years ago, in the city of Topeka, Kansas, a minister and his nine-year-old daughter walked, hand in hand, to the public elementary school four blocks from their home. But school officials refused to admit Linda Brown. Instead, they required that she attend another school two miles away, which meant a daily six-block walk to a bus stop where she sometimes waited half an hour for the bus. In bad weather, the child could be soaking wet by the time the bus came; one day she became so cold at the bus stop that she walked back home. Why, she asked her parents, could she not attend the school that was close by?

The answer—difficult for loving parents to give their child—was Linda Brown's introduction to a harsh fact: Skin color made her a second-class citizen in the United States. The injustice of separate schools for black and white children led the Browns and others to file a lawsuit on behalf of Linda Brown and other children, and, in 1954, Linda Brown's question was put to the Supreme Court of the United States. In Brown v. the Board of Education of Topeka, the Supreme Court ruled unanimously that racially segregated schools inevitably provide African Americans with inferior schooling, thus striking down a ruling, dating back to 1896, that permitted "separate but equal" education for the two races.

Many greeted the Supreme Court's decision as a turning point in U.S. education. Yet, as the new century begins, most U.S. children still attend racially imbalanced schools. Although our society is officially committed to the notion that all people are created equal, race and ethnicity continue to guide the lives of men, women, and children in all sorts of ways.

The pattern of inequality and conflict based on color and culture is even more striking in other parts of the world. Since the fall of the former Soviet Union, Ukrainians, Moldavians, Azerbaijanis, and a host of other ethnic peoples in Eastern Europe have struggled to recover their cultural identity. In the Middle East, Arabs and Jews are trying to overcome deep-rooted tensions, as are Protestants and Catholics in Northern Ireland. In dozens of the world's nations, color and culture often flare in violent confrontation.

An irony of the human condition is that color and culture—a source of great pride—also cause us to degrade ourselves with hatred and violence. This chapter examines the meaning of race and ethnicity, explains how these social constructs have shaped our history, and suggests why they continue to play such a central part—for better or worse—in the world today.

The Social Meaning of Race and Ethnicity

People frequently confuse the terms "race" and "ethnicity." For this reason, we begin with important definitions.

Race

A **race** is *a category of men and women who share biologically transmitted traits that members of a society deem socially significant.* People classify each other racially based on physical characteristics such as skin color, facial features, hair texture, and body shape.

Racial diversity appeared among our human ancestors as the result of living in different regions of the world. In regions of intense heat, for example, people developed darker skin (from the natural pigment, melanin) as protection from the sun; in moderate climates, people developed lighter skin. Such traits are—literally—only skin deep, because *every* human being the world over is a member of the same biological species.

The striking variety of racial traits found today is also the product of migration, in that genetic characteristics once common to a single place are now found in many lands. Especially pronounced is the racial mix in the Middle East (that is, western Asia), historically a "crossroads" of migration. Greater racial uniformity, by contrast, characterizes more isolated peoples, such as the island-dwelling Japanese. But every population has some genetic mixture, and increasing contact among the world's people ensures even more racial blending in the future.

Racial Types

Nineteenth-century biologists developed a three-part racial classification. They called people with light skin and fine hair *Caucasoid;* people with dark skin and coarse hair, *Negroid;* and people with yellow or brown skin and distinctive folds on the eyelids, *Mongoloid.*

Sociologists consider such terms misleading at best, since we know that no society contains biologically "pure" people. The skin color of people we might call "Caucasoid" (or "Indo-European," "Caucasian," or more commonly, "white people") ranges from very light (typical in Scandinavia) to very dark (in southern India). The same variation exists among so-called

"Negroids" (Africans, or, more commonly, "black people") and "Mongoloids" (that is, "Asians"). In fact, many "white people" (say, in southern India) actually have darker skin than many "black" people (like the Negroid aborigines of Australia).

The population of the United States, too, is genetically mixed. Over many generations and throughout the Americas, the genetic traits of Negroid Africans, Caucasoid Europeans, and Mongoloid Native Americans (whose ancestors came from Asia) have intermingled. Many "black people," therefore, have a significant Caucasoid ancestry, and many "white people" have some Negroid genes. In short, whatever people may think, race is no black-and-white issue.

Why, then, do people make so much of race? The reason is that societies rank people into a racial hierarchy, claiming that one category is inherently "better" than another, although no sound scientific evidence supports such beliefs. But because so much is at stake, societies construct racial meanings that may seem extreme. Earlier in this century, for example, many southern states labeled as "colored" anyone with as little as one-thirty-second African ancestry (that is, one African American great-great-great-grandparent). Today, with less caste distinction in the United States, the law allows parents to declare the race of a child as they may wish.

A Trend toward Mixture

The number of officially recorded interracial births has doubled in the last fifteen years to 150,000, about 4 percent of all births. Moreover, when completing their 1990 census forms, almost 10 million people described themselves by checking more than one racial category. As time goes on, biologically speaking, the concept of race has less and less meaning in the United States.

Ethnicity

Ethnicity is *a shared cultural heritage.* Members of an *ethnic category* may have common ancestors, language, and religion that confer a distinctive social identity. The United States is a multiethnic society that favors the English language; even so, some 30 million people speak Spanish, Italian, German, French, or some other tongue in their homes. Similarly, the United States is a predominantly Protestant society, but most people of Spanish, Italian, and Polish ancestry are Roman Catholic, while many others of Greek, Ukrainian, and Russian descent belong to the Eastern Orthodox church. More than 6 million Jewish Americans (with ancestral ties to various nations) share a religious history. Similarly, some 6 million men and women are Muslim and now outnumber Episcopalians (Blank, 1998).

Race and ethnicity, then, are quite different: One is biological, the other cultural. But the two may go hand in hand. Japanese Americans, for example, have distinctive physical traits and—for those who maintain a traditional way of life—a distinctive culture as well. Table 10-1 presents the broad sweep of racial and ethnic diversity in the United States, as recorded by the 1990 census.

People can fairly easily modify their ethnicity: Immigrants may discard their cultural traditions over time or, like many people of Native American descent in recent years, try to revive their heritage (Nagel, 1994; Spencer, 1994). Assuming people mate with others like themselves, however, racial distinctiveness persists over generations.

Finally, ethnicity involves even more variability and mixture than race does, for most people identify with more than one ethnic background. Golf star Tiger Woods, for example, describes himself as one-eighth white, one-eighth American

Table 10-1   Racial and Ethnic Categories in the United States, 1990

Racial or Ethnic Classification	Approximate U.S. Population	Percent of Total Population
African descent	29,986,060	12.1%
Hispanic descent*	22,354,059	9.0
Mexican	13,495,938	5.4
Puerto Rican	2,727,754	1.1
Cuban	1,043,932	0.4
Other Hispanic	5,086,435	2.1
Native American descent	1,959,234	0.8
American Indian	1,878,285	0.8
Eskimo	57,152	<
Aleut	23,797	<
Asian or Pacific Islander descent	7,273,662	2.9
Chinese	1,645,472	0.7
Filipino	1,406,770	0.6
Japanese	847,562	0.3
Asian Indian	815,447	0.3
Korean	798,849	0.3
Vietnamese	614,547	0.2
Hawaiian	211,014	<
Samoan	62,964	<
Guamanian	49,345	<
Other Asian or Pacific Islander	821,692	0.3
European descent	200,000,000	80.0
German	57,947,000	23.3
Irish	38,736,000	15.6
English	32,652,000	13.1
Italian	14,665,000	5.9
French	10,321,000	4.1
Polish	9,366,000	3.8
Dutch	6,227,000	2.5
Scotch-Irish	5,618,000	2.3
Scottish	5,314,000	2.1
Swedish	4,681,000	1.9
Norwegian	3,869,000	1.6
Russian	2,953,000	1.2
Welsh	2,034,000	0.8
Danish	1,635,000	0.6
Hungarian	1,582,000	0.6

*People of Hispanic descent may be of any race. Many people also identify with more than one ethnic category. Thus, figures total more than 100 percent. White people represent 80 percent of the U.S. population.

< Indicates less than 1/10 of 1 percent.

Source: U.S. Bureau of the Census (1998).

Indian, one-fourth black, one-fourth Thai, and one-fourth Chinese (White, 1997).

Minorities

As Chapter 9 ("Sex and Gender") described, a *minority* is a category of people that is both set apart by physical or cultural traits and socially disadvantaged. Distinct from the dominant majority, in other words, minorities are set apart and subordinated.

Both race and ethnicity are bases for minority standing. As shown in Table 10-1, white people of non-Hispanic background (80 percent of the total) continue to predominate numerically. But the absolute numbers and share of population for virtually every minority is growing rapidly so that, within a century, minorities will likely be a majority of the U.S. population. In 1990, a minority-majority was already a reality in 186 U.S. counties (6 percent of the total).

Minorities have two major characteristics. First, they share a *distinctive identity*. Because race is highly visible (and virtually impossible for a person to change), most minority men and women are keenly aware of their physical appearance. The significance of ethnicity (which people *can* change) is more variable. Throughout U.S. history, some people (such as Reform Jews) have downplayed their historic ethnicity, while others (including many Orthodox Jews) have maintained distinctive cultural traditions and even formed their own neighborhoods.

A second characteristic of minorities is *subordination*. As the remainder of this chapter shows, U.S. minorities typically have lower income, lower occupational prestige, and limited schooling. This fact suggests that class, race, and ethnicity, as well as gender, are not mutually exclusive issues but overlapping and reinforcing dimensions of social stratification.

Of course, not all members of any minority category are disadvantaged. Some Latinos, for example, are quite wealthy; certain Chinese Americans are celebrated business leaders; and African Americans are included among our nation's leading scholars. But even the greatest success rarely allows individuals to transcend their minority standing (Benjamin, 1991). That is, race or ethnicity often serves as a *master status* (described in Chapter 4, "Social Interaction in Everyday Life") that overshadows personal accomplishments.

Finally, minorities are usually a small proportion of a society's population. But not always. For example, black South Africans are disadvantaged even though they are a numerical majority in their country. In the United States, women represent slightly more than half the population but are still struggling to obtain opportunities and privileges enjoyed by men.

Prejudice and Stereotypes

November 19, 1994, Jerusalem, Israel. We are driving along the outskirts of this historic city—a holy place to Jews, Christians, and Muslims—when Razi, our taxi driver, spots a small group of Ethiopians at a street corner. "Those people over there," he begins, "they are different. They don't drive cars. They don't want to improve themselves. Even when our country offers them schooling, they don't take it." He shakes his head and pronounces the Ethiopians "socially incorrigible."

Prejudice is *a rigid and irrational generalization about an entire category of people.* Prejudice is irrational to the extent that people hold inflexible attitudes supported by little or no direct evidence. Prejudice may target people of a particular social class, sex, sexual orientation, age, political affiliation, race, or ethnicity.

CRITICAL THINKING

Does Race Affect Intelligence?

Are Asian Americans smarter than white people? Is the typical white person more intelligent than the average African American? Throughout the history of our nation, we have painted one category of people as more intellectually gifted than another. Moreover, people have used such thinking to justify the privileges of the allegedly superior category or to bar supposedly inferior people from entering this country.

Scientists know that the distribution of human intelligence forms a "bell curve," as shown in the figure below. By convention, average intelligence is defined as an intelligence quotient (IQ) score of 100 (technically, an IQ score is mental age, as measured by a test, divided by age in years, with the result multiplied by one hundred; thus, an eight-year-old who performs like a ten-year-old has an IQ of $10/8 = 1.25 ¥ 100 = 125$).

In a controversial study of intelligence and social inequality, Richard Herrnstein and Charles Murray (1994) claim that overwhelming evidence shows that race is related to measures of intelligence. More specifically, they say the average IQ of people with European ancestry is 100, the average for people of East Asian ancestry is 103, and for people of African descent, the average is 90.

Of course, assertions of this kind are explosive because they fly in the face of our democratic and egalitarian sentiments, which say that no racial type is inherently "better" than another. In response, critics charge that intelligence tests are not valid, or they question whether what we call "intelligence" has much real meaning.

Most social scientists acknowledge that IQ tests do measure something real and important, and they agree that some *individuals* have more intellectual aptitude than others. But they reject the notion that any *category* of people, on average, is smarter than any other. Categories of people may show small differences in measured intelligence, but the crucial question is *why*.

Thomas Sowell, an African American social scientist, links racial differences in measured intelligence not to biology but to people's environment. In some skillful sociological detective work, Sowell traced IQ scores for various racial and ethnic categories throughout this century. He found that, on average, immigrants from European nations such as Poland, Lithuania, Italy, and Greece, as well as Asian countries including China and Japan, scored ten to fifteen points below the U.S. average. Sowell's

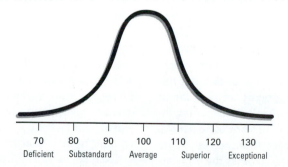

70	80	90	100	110	120	130
Deficient	Substandard		Average		Superior	Exceptional

more critical discovery, however, was that people in these same categories *today* have IQ scores that are average or above average. Among Italian Americans, for example, average IQ jumped almost ten points in fifty years; among Polish and Chinese Americans, the jump was almost twenty points.

Because genetic changes occur over thousands of years and these people largely intermarried among themselves, biological factors cannot explain such a rise in IQ scores. Rather, the evidence points to changing cultural patterns as the cause. As immigrants settled in the United States, their new surroundings improved their intellectual performance.

Sowell found the same pattern applies to African Americans. Historically, African Americans living in the North have outscored those living in the South on IQ tests by about ten points. Among African Americans who migrated from the South to the North after 1940, IQ scores soon rose, as they did among earlier immigrants. Thus, if environmental factors are the same for various categories of people, racial IQ differences largely disappear.

What these test score differences do tell, Sowell continues, is that *cultural patterns* matter. Asians who score high on tests are no smarter than other people, but they have been raised to value learning and pursue excellence. For their part, African Americans are no less intelligent than anyone else, but they carry a legacy of disadvantage that undermines self-confidence and discourages achievement.

Sources: Herrnstein & Murray (1994) and Sowell (1994, 1995).

Prejudices are *prejudgments* that can be positive or negative. Our positive prejudices exaggerate the virtues of people like ourselves, while our negative prejudices condemn those who differ from us. Negative prejudice runs along a continuum, from mild aversion to outright hostility. Because such attitudes are embedded in culture, everyone has at least some measure of prejudice.

Prejudice often takes the form of stereotypes (*stereo* is derived from Greek, meaning "hard" or "solid"), which are biased characterizations of some category of people. Many white people hold stereotypical views of minorities. But minorities, too, use stereotypes, sometimes of whites and sometimes of other minorities, including themselves. Some Koreans, for example, portray African Americans as dishonest. Some African Americans, in turn, express the same attitude toward Jewish people (Smith, 1996).

Racism

A powerful and destructive form of prejudice, **racism** refers to *the belief that one racial category is innately superior or inferior to another.* Racism has pervaded world history. The ancient Greeks, the peoples of India, and the Chinese—despite their many notable achievements—were all quick to consider people unlike themselves as inferior.

Racism has also been widespread in the United States where, for centuries, ideas about racial inferiority supported slavery. Today, overt racism in this country has subsided to some extent because our more egalitarian culture urges us to evaluate people, in Dr. Martin Luther King's words, "not by the color of their skin, but by the content of their character."

Even so, racism—in thought and deed—remains a serious social problem everywhere, as people still contend that some racial and ethnic categories are "better" than others. As the Critical Thinking box on pages 151–152 explains, however, racial differences in mental abilities are due to environment rather than to biology.

Theories of Prejudice

What are the origins of prejudice? Social scientists provide various answers to this question, including frustration, personality, culture, and social conflict.

Scapegoat Theory

Scapegoat theory holds that prejudice springs from frustration among people who are themselves disadvantaged (Dollard, 1939). Take the case of a white woman unhappy with her low pay in a textile factory. Directing hostility at the powerful people who employ her carries obvious risk; therefore, she may blame her low pay on the presence of minority co-workers. Her prejudice may not go far toward improving her situation, but it serves as a relatively safe way to vent her anger, and it may give her the comforting sense that at least she is superior to someone.

A **scapegoat,** then, is *a person or category of people, typically with little power, whom people unfairly blame for their troubles.* Because they are "safe targets," minorities are often scapegoats.

Authoritarian Personality Theory

According to T.W. Adorno (1950), extreme prejudice appears as a personality trait in certain individuals. This conclusion is supported by research, which shows that people who display strong prejudice toward one minority are usually similarly intolerant of all minorities. These *authoritarian personalities* rigidly conform to conventional cultural values, see moral issues as clear-cut matters of right and wrong, and look upon society as a naturally competitive arena where "better" people (like themselves) inevitably dominate those who are weaker.

Adorno also found that people tolerant toward one minority are likely to be accepting of all. They tend to be more flexible in their moral judgments and treat all people as equals.

Adorno thought that people with little education and those raised by cold and demanding parents tend to develop authoritarian personalities. Filled with anger and anxiety as children, they grow into hostile and aggressive adults, seeking scapegoats whom they consider inferior.

Cultural Theory

A third theory contends that while extreme prejudice is found in certain people, some prejudice is found in everyone because it is embedded in culture. Emory Bogardus (1968) studied the effects of culturally rooted prejudices for more than forty years. He developed the concept of *social distance* to gauge how close or how distant people feel towards various racial and ethnic categories. Bogardus found that most people feel closest to individuals with English, Canadian, and Scottish backgrounds, even welcoming marriage with them. Attitudes are less favorable toward the French, Germans, Swedes, and Dutch, and most negative towards people of Asian and African descent.

According to Bogardus, prejudice is so widespread that we cannot explain it as merely a trait of a handful of people with authoritarian personalities, as Adorno suggests. Rather, Bogardus believed everyone expresses some bigotry because we live in a "culture of prejudice."

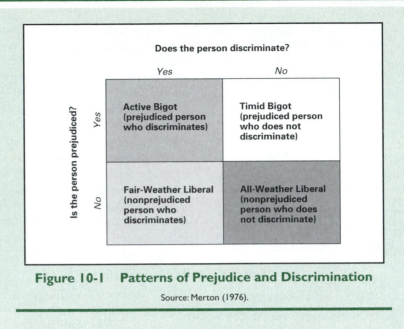

Figure 10-1   Patterns of Prejudice and Discrimination

Source: Merton (1976).

Conflict Theory

A fourth explanation states that powerful people use prejudice to justify oppressing others. To the extent that Anglos look down on Latino immigrants in the Southwest, for example, well-off people can pay the immigrants low wages for hard work. Similarly, all elites benefit when prejudice divides workers along racial and ethnic lines and discourages them from working together to advance their common interests (Geschwender, 1978; Olzak, 1989).

Another conflict-based argument, advanced by Shelby Steele (1990), is that minorities themselves cultivate a climate of *race consciousness* in order to win greater power and privileges. Because of their historic disadvantages, minorities claim that they are now victims entitled to special consideration based on their race. While this strategy may yield short-term gains, Steele cautions that such thinking is likely to spark a backlash from whites or others who oppose "special treatment" for anyone solely on the basis of race or ethnicity.

Discrimination

Closely related to prejudice is **discrimination,** *treating various categories of people unequally.* While prejudice refers to attitudes, discrimination is a matter of action. Like prejudice, discrimination can be either positive (providing special advantages) or negative (creating obstacles). Discrimination also ranges from subtle to blatant.

Prejudice and discrimination often occur together: A prejudiced personnel manager, for example, may refuse to hire minorities. Robert Merton (1976) describes such a person as an *active bigot,* as shown in Figure 10-1. But prejudice and discrimination may not occur together, as in the case of the prejudiced personnel manager who, out of fear of lawsuits, *does* hire minorities. Merton calls this person a *timid bigot.*

People who are generally tolerant of minorities yet discriminate when it is to their advantage to do so are *fair-weather liberals.* Finally, Merton's *all-weather liberal* is free of both prejudice and discrimination.

Institutional Prejudice and Discrimination

We typically think of prejudice and discrimination as the hateful ideas or actions of specific people. But thirty years ago, Stokely Carmichael and Charles Hamilton (1967) pointed out that far greater harm results from **institutional prejudice and discrimination,** which refers to *bias inherent in the operation of any of society's institutions,* including schools, hospitals, the police, and the workplace. For example, lawyers defending O. J. Simpson during his murder trial claimed that racial bias makes the U.S. criminal justice system unfair to African Americans, a conviction shared by a majority of African Americans in the United States (Smolowe, 1994).

According to Carmichael and Hamilton, people are slow to condemn or even recognize institutional prejudice and discrimination because it often involves respected public officials and long-established traditions. A case in point is the Supreme Court's 1954 *Brown* decision, described in the opening to this chapter. Before this, the principle of "separate but equal" was the law of the land, upholding institutional racism in the form of an educational caste system. Today, decades later, the law may have changed, but most U.S. students still attend schools that are overwhelmingly one race or the other. Indeed, in 1991, the courts declared that neighborhood schools will never provide equal education as long as our population is segregated, with most African Americans living in central cities and most white people (and Asian Americans) living in politically separate suburbs.

Prejudice and Discrimination: The Vicious Cycle

Prejudice and discrimination reinforce each other. The Thomas theorem, discussed in Chapter 4 ("Social Interaction in Everyday Life"), offers a simple explanation of this fact: *Situations that are defined as real become real in their consequences* (1966:301; orig. 1931).

As W. I. Thomas recognized, stereotypes become real to people who believe them, sometimes even to those victimized by them. Prejudice on the part of white people toward African Americans, for example, does not produce *innate* inferiority but it can produce *social* inferiority, consigning minorities to poverty and racially segregated housing. Then, if white people interpret social disadvantage as evidence that minorities do not measure up to their standards, they unleash a new round of prejudice and discrimination, giving rise to a vicious cycle whereby each perpetuates the other.

Majority and Minority: Patterns of Interaction

Social scientists describe four models of interaction between majority and minority members of a society: pluralism, assimilation, segregation, and genocide.

Pluralism

Pluralism is *a state in which people of all races and ethnicities, while distinct, have social parity.* In other words, people who differ in appearance or social heritage all share resources more or less equally.

The United States is pluralistic to the extent that all people have equal standing under the law. Moreover, large cities contain countless "ethnic villages," where people proudly display the traditions of their immigrant ancestors: These include New York's Spanish Harlem, Little Italy, and Chinatown; Philadelphia's Italian "South Philly"; Chicago's "Little Saigon"; and Latino East Los Angeles.

But the United States is not really pluralistic for three reasons. First, while many people appreciate their cultural heritage, only a small proportion want to live with only their "own kind" (NORC, 1999). Second, our tolerance for social diversity is limited. One reaction to the growing proportion of minorities in the United States, for example, is a social movement to make English this nation's official language. Third, as we shall see later in this chapter, people of various colors and cultures have attained unequal social positions.

Assimilation

Assimilation is *the process by which minorities gradually adopt patterns of the dominant culture.* Assimilation involves changing styles of dress, values, religion, language, and friends.

Many people think of the United States as a "melting pot," in which different nationalities blend together. But, in truth, rather than everyone "melting" into some new cultural pattern, most minorities have adopted the dominant culture established by the earliest settlers. Why? Assimilation is both the avenue to upward social mobility and a way to escape the prejudice and discrimination directed against more visible foreigners (Newman, 1973).

The amount of assimilation varies by category. For example, Germans and Irish have "melted" more than Italians, and the Japanese more than the Chinese or Koreans. Multiculturalists, however, oppose assimilation because it suggests minorities are "the problem" and defines them

(rather than majority people) as the ones who need to do all the changing.

Note, too, that assimilation involves changes in ethnicity but not in race. For example, many descendants of Japanese immigrants have discarded their traditions but retained their racial identity. For racial traits to diminish over generations requires **miscegenation,** *biological reproduction by partners of different racial categories.* Although the rate of interracial marriage is rising, it is still low; only four in one hundred births are to parents of different races.

Segregation

Segregation is *the physical and social separation of categories of people.* Sometimes minorities, especially religious orders like the Amish, voluntarily segregate themselves. Usually, however, majorities segregate minorities by excluding them. Neighborhoods, schools, occupations, hospitals, and even cemeteries can be segregated. While pluralism fosters distinctiveness without disadvantage, segregation enforces separation to the detriment of a minority.

Racial segregation has a long history in the United States, beginning with slavery and evolving into racially separate lodging, schooling, buses, and trains. Decisions such as the 1954 *Brown* case have reduced *de jure* (Latin, meaning "by law") discrimination in the United States. However, *de facto* ("in fact") segregation continues in the form of countless neighborhoods that are home to people of a single race.

Research points to modest declines in racial segregation in the United States during recent decades (Farley, 1997). Yet Douglas Massey and Nancy Denton (1989) documented the *hypersegregation* of African Americans in some inner cities. These people have little contact of any kind with people in the larger society. *Hypersegregation* affects about one-fifth of all African Americans but only a few percent of comparably poor whites (Jagarowsky & Bane, 1990).

Segregated minorities understandably object to their second-class citizenship, and sometimes the actions of even a single individual can make a difference. On December 1, 1955, Rosa Parks boarded a bus in Montgomery, Alabama, and sat in a section designated by law for African Americans. When a crowd of white passengers boarded the bus, the driver asked four black people to give up their seats to white people. Three did so, but Rosa Parks refused. The driver left the bus and returned with police, who arrested her for violating the racial segregation laws. She was later convicted in court and fined $14. Her stand (or sitting) for justice rallied the African American community of Montgomery to boycott city buses and ultimately ended this form of segregation (King, 1969).

Genocide

Genocide is *the systematic killing of one category of people by another.* Although this deadly form of racism and ethnocentrism violates nearly every recognized moral standard, it has occurred time and again in human history.

Genocide figured prominently in contact between Europeans and the original inhabitants of the Americas. From the sixteenth century on, as the Spanish, Portuguese, English, French, and Dutch forcefully colonized North and South America, they decimated native populations. Some native people fell victim to calculated killing sprees; most succumbed to diseases brought by Europeans, to which they had no natural defenses (Matthiessen, 1984; Sale, 1990).

Genocide also occurred in the twentieth century. Unimaginable horror befell European Jews in the 1930s and 1940s during Adolf Hitler's reign of terror known as the Holocaust. The Nazis murdered more than 6 million Jewish men, women, and children. Soviet dictator Josef Stalin slaughtered his country's people on an even greater scale, killing some 30 million real and imagined enemies during his violent rule. Between 1975 and 1980, Pol Pot's Communist regime in Cambodia butchered anyone linked in any way to capitalist cultural influences. Men and women able to speak a Western language and even people who wore eyeglasses, viewed as an elitist symbol, were cut down. In all, some 2 million people (one-fourth of the population) perished in the Cambodian "killing fields" (Shawcross, 1979).

Sadly, genocide continues in today's world. Recent examples include Hutus killing Tutsis in the African nation of Rwanda and Serbs killing Bosnians in Eastern Europe.

These four patterns of minority-majority contact have all been played out in the United States. We are proud to point to patterns of pluralism and assimilation, but reluctantly acknowledge the degree to which our way of life was built on segregation (of African Americans) and genocide (of Native Americans). The remainder of this chapter examines how these four patterns have shaped the past and present social standing of major racial and ethnic categories in the United States.

Race and Ethnicity in the United States

Give me your tired, your poor,
Your huddled masses yearning to breathe free,
The wretched refuse of your teeming shore,
Send these, the homeless, tempest-tossed to me:
I lift my lamp beside the golden door.

These words by Emma Lazarus, inscribed on the Statue of Liberty, express cultural ideals of human dignity, personal freedom, and opportunity. Indeed, the United States has provided more of the "good life" to more immigrants than any other nation. But as the history of this country's minorities reveals, our golden door has opened more widely for some than for others.

Native Americans

The term *Native Americans* refers to the hundreds of societies—including Aleuts, Cherokee, Zuni, Sioux, Mohawk, Aztec, and Inca—who first settled the Western Hemisphere. Some 30,000 years before Columbus "discovered" the Americas, migrating peoples crossed a land bridge from Asia to North America where the Bering Strait (off the coast of Alaska) is today. Gradually, they spread throughout North and South America.

When the first Europeans arrived late in the fifteenth century, Native Americans numbered in the millions. But by the beginning of this century, after relentless subjugation and even acts of genocide, the "vanishing Americans" numbered a mere 250,000 (Dobyns, 1966; Tyler, 1973).

It was Christopher Columbus (1446-1506) who first referred to Native Americans as *Indians,* because he thought he had reached India. Actually, he had landed in the Bahama Islands in the Caribbean. Columbus found the indigenous people passive and peaceful, a stark contrast to the materialistic and competitive Europeans (Matthiessen, 1984; Sale, 1990). Yet, even as Europeans seized the land of Native Americans, they justified their actions by calling their victims thieves and murderers (Unruh, 1979; Josephy, 1982).

After the Revolutionary War, the new U.S. government adopted a pluralist approach to Native American societies and sought to gain more land through treaties. Payment for land was far from fair, however, and when Native Americans resisted surrender of their homelands, the U.S. government simply used superior military power to evict them. By the early 1800s, few Native Americans remained east of the Mississippi River.

In 1871, the United States declared Native Americans wards of the government and adopted a strategy of forced assimilation. Now Native Americans continued to lose their land, and they were well on their way to losing their culture as well. Reservation life fostered dependency, replacing ancestral languages with English and traditional religion with Christianity. Officials took many children from their parents and handed them over to boarding schools, where they were resocialized as "Americans." Authorities gave local control of reservations to the few Native Americans who supported government policies, and distributed reservation land—traditionally held collectively—as private property to individual families (Tyler, 1973).

Not until 1924 were Native Americans entitled to U.S. citizenship. After that, many migrated from reservations, adopting mainstream cultural patterns and marrying non-Native Americans. Many large cities now contain sizable Native American populations. As shown in Table 10-2, however, the 1990 median family income for Native Americans was far below the U.S. average, and relatively few Native Americans earn a college degree.[1]

From in-depth interviews with Native Americans in a western city, Joan Albon (1971)

---

[1]In making comparisons of education and income, keep in mind that categories of the U.S. population have different median ages. The 1998 median age for all U.S. people was 35.3 years. White people have a median age of 36.4 years; for Native Americans, the figure is 27.5 years. Because people's income and schooling increase over time, this age difference accounts for some of the disparities shown in Table 10-2.

Table 10-2 The Social Standing of Native Americans, 1990

	Native Americans	Entire United States
Median family income	$21,750	$35,225
Percent in poverty	30.9%	13.1%
Completion of four or more years of college (age 25 and over)	9.3%	20.3%

Source: U.S. Bureau of the Census (1998).

concluded that their low social standing reflects cultural factors, including a noncompetitive view of life and reluctance to pursue higher education. In addition, she noted, many Native Americans have dark skin, which makes them targets of prejudice and discrimination.

Like other racial and ethnic minorities in the United States, Native Americans have recently reasserted pride in their cultural heritage. Native American organizations report a surge in new membership applications, and many children are learning to speak native tongues better than their parents (Fost, 1991; Johnson, 1991; Nagel, 1996). Moreover, the legal autonomy of reservations has turned out to be an ace-up-the-sleeve for many Native American tribes, who have built gaming casinos and now control 20 percent of all U.S. gambling. But such financial windfalls benefit relatively few native people; most endure their disadvantages with a profound sense of the injustice they have suffered at the hands of white people.

White Anglo-Saxon Protestants

White Anglo-Saxon Protestants (WASPs) were not the first people to inhabit the United States, but they came to dominate this nation once English settlement began. Most WASPs are of English ancestry, but this category also includes Scots and Welsh. With more than 50 million people of English ancestry, one in five members of our society claims some WASP background.

Historically, WASP immigrants were highly skilled and motivated toward achievement by what we now call the Protestant work ethic. Because of their numbers and power, WASPs were not subject to the prejudice and discrimination experienced by other categories of immigrants. The historical dominance of WASPs has been so great that, as noted earlier, others sought to become more like them.

WASPs were never one single group; especially during colonial times, considerable hostility separated English Anglicans, for example, from Scotch-Irish Presbyterians (Parrillo, 1994). But during the nineteenth century, most WASPs joined together to oppose the arrival of "undesirable foreigners" (including Germans in the 1840s and Italians in the 1880s). Political movements managed to get laws passed to limit the flow of immigrants. Those who could afford it sheltered themselves in exclusive suburbs and restrictive clubs. Thus the 1880s—the decade that saw the Statue of Liberty welcome immigrants to the United States—also saw the founding of the first country club, with all WASP members (Baltzell, 1964).

By the mid-twentieth century, however, WASP wealth and power had peaked, as indicated by the 1960 election of John Fitzgerald Kennedy as the first Irish-Catholic president. But the majority of people in the upper-upper class are still WASPs (Baltzell, 1964, 1976, 1979, 1988). And the WASP cultural legacy remains. English is this country's dominant language and Protestantism, the majority religion. Our legal system, too, reflects its English origins. But the historical dominance of WASPs is most evident in the widespread use of the terms "race" and "ethnicity" to describe everyone but them.

African Americans

Although African Americans accompanied Spanish explorers to the New World in the fifteenth century, most accounts mark the beginning of black history in the United States as 1619, when a Dutch trading ship brought twenty Africans to Jamestown, Virginia. Whether these people arrived as slaves or as indentured servants who paid their passage by performing labor for a specified period, being of African descent on these shores soon became virtually synonymous with being a slave. In 1661, Virginia enacted the first law recognizing slavery (Sowell, 1981).

Slavery was the foundation of the southern colonies' plantation system. White people ran plantations with slave labor and, until 1808, some were also slave traders. Traders—including North Americans, Africans, and Europeans—forcibly transported some 10 million Africans to various countries in the Americas, including 400,000 to the United States. On board small sailing ships, hundreds of slaves were chained for the several weeks it took to cross the Atlantic Ocean. Filth and disease killed many and drove others to suicide. Overall, perhaps half died en route (Tannenbaum, 1946; Franklin, 1967; Sowell, 1981).

Surviving the journey was a mixed blessing, since it brought only a life of servitude. Although some slaves worked in cities at various trades, most labored in the fields, often from daybreak until sunset, and even longer during the harvest season. The law allowed owners to impose whatever disciplinary measures they deemed necessary to ensure that slaves were obedient and productive. Even the killing of a slave by an owner rarely prompted legal action. Owners also divided slave families at public auctions, where human beings were bought and sold as pieces of property. Unschooled and dependent on their owners for all their basic needs, slaves had little control over their destinies (Franklin, 1967; Sowell, 1981).

Free persons of color lived in both the North and the South, laboring as small-scale farmers, skilled workers, and small-business owners. But the lives of most African Americans stood in glaring contradiction to the principles of freedom on which the United States was founded. The Declaration of Independence states:

> We hold these Truths to be self-evident, that all Men are created equal, that they are endowed by their Creator with certain unalienable Rights, that among these are Life, Liberty, and the Pursuit of Happiness....

Most white people did not apply these ideals to African Americans. In the Dred Scott case in 1857, the U.S. Supreme Court addressed the question, "Are blacks citizens?" by writing, "We think they are not, and that they are not included, and were not intended to be included, under the word 'citizens' in the Constitution, and can therefore claim none of the rights and privileges which that instrument provides for and secures for citizens of the United States" (quoted in Blaustein & Zangrando, 1968:160). Thus arose what Swedish sociologist Gunnar Myrdal (1944) termed the *American dilemma:* a democratic society's denial of basic rights and freedoms to an entire category of people. To resolve this dilemma, many white people simply defined African Americans as innately inferior.

In 1865, the passage of the Thirteenth Amendment to the Constitution outlawed slavery. Three years later the Fourteenth Amendment reversed the Dred Scott ruling, granting citizenship to all people born in the United States. The Fifteenth

Amendment, ratified in 1870, stated that neither race nor previous condition of servitude should deprive anyone of the right to vote. However, so-called Jim Crow laws—classic cases of institutionalized discrimination—continued to segregate U.S. society into two racial castes. Especially in the South, white people beat and lynched black people (and some white people) who challenged the racial hierarchy.

The twentieth century brought dramatic changes for African Americans. After World War I, tens of thousands of women and men fled the rural South for jobs in northern factories. While some did find more economic opportunity, few escaped the racial prejudice and discrimination that placed them lower in the social hierarchy than white immigrants arriving from Europe at the same time (Lieberson, 1980).

In the 1950s and 1960s, a national civil rights movement grew out of the landmark judicial decisions that outlawed segregated schools and overt discrimination in employment and public accommodations. In addition, the "black power" movement gave African Americans a renewed sense of pride and purpose.

Gains notwithstanding, people of African descent continue to occupy a subordinate position in the United States, as shown in Table 10-3. The median income of African American families in 1997 ($28,602) was only 61 percent of white family income ($46,754),[2] a ratio that has not changed in thirty years. African American households are more than twice as likely as white households to be poor.

---

[2]Here again, a median age difference (white people, 36.4; black people, 30.0) accounts for some of the income and educational disparities shown. Disparities also reflect a higher proportion of one-parent families among blacks than whites. Comparing only married-couple families, African Americans (median income $45,372 in 1997) earned 87 percent as much as whites ($52,098).

Table 10-3   The Social Standing of African Americans, 1997*

	African Americans	Entire United States
Median family income	$28,602	$44,568
Percent in poverty	23.6%	10.3%
Completion of four or more years of college (age 25 and over)	13.3%	23.9%

*For purposes of comparison with other tables in this chapter, 1990 data are as follows: median family income, $21,423; percent in poverty, 31.9%; completion of four or more years of college, 11.3%.

Source: U.S. Bureau of the Census (1998).

The number of African American families securely in the middle class has risen by half since 1980; four in ten families now earn more than $35,000 a year (26 percent earn $50,000 or more). But, for many African Americans, earnings have slipped during the last fifteen years as factory jobs—vital to residents of inner cities—have been lost to other countries where labor costs are lower. Thus, black unemployment is more than twice as high as white unemployment; among African American teenagers in many cities, the figure exceeds 40 percent (Jacob, 1986; Lichter, 1989; U.S. Bureau of the Census, 1998).

Since 1980, African Americans have made remarkable educational progress. The share of adults completing high school rose from half to almost three-fourths, nearly closing the gap between whites and blacks. Between 1980 and 1997, moreover, the share of African American adults with at least a bachelor's degree rose from 8 to 13 percent. But, as Table 10-3 shows, African Americans are still at half the national standard when it comes to completing four years of college.

The political clout of African Americans has also increased. As a result of both black migration to cities and white flight to the suburbs, half of this country's ten largest cities have elected African American mayors. At the national level, however, only 1 percent of elected leaders are African Americans. After the 1998 Congressional elections, 39 black men and women (of 435) were in the House of Representatives and not one of the 100 seats in the Senate was filled by an African American.

In sum, for more than 350 years, people of African ancestry in the United States have struggled for social equality. As a nation, we can certainly take pride in how far we have come in this pursuit. Overt discrimination is now illegal, and research documents a long-term decline in prejudice against African Americans (Firebaugh & Davis, 1988; J. Q. Wilson, 1992; NORC, 1999).

In 1913—fifty years after the abolition of slavery—W. E. B. Du Bois proudly noted the extent of black achievement. But Du Bois also cautioned that racial caste remained strong in the United States, and, as we enter another new century, racial hierarchy persists.

Asian Americans

Although Asian Americans share some racial traits, enormous cultural diversity marks this category of people. The 1990 census put their number at more than 7 million—approaching 3 percent of the U.S. population. The largest category of Asian Americans is people of Chinese ancestry (1.6 million), followed by Filipino (1.4 million), Japanese (850,000), Asian Indian (815,000), and Korean (800,000) background. Forty percent of Asian Americans reside in California.

Young Asian Americans have commanded attention and respect as high achievers and are disproportionately represented at our country's best colleges and universities. Many of their elders, too, have made economic and social gains; most Asian Americans now live in middle-class suburbs (O'Hare, Frey, & Fost, 1994). Yet despite (and sometimes because of) their record of achievement, Asian Americans may find others aloof or outright hostile to them.

At the same time, the "model minority" image of Asian Americans obscures the poverty found among their ranks. We will focus on the history and current standing of Chinese Americans and Japanese Americans—the longest-established Asian American minorities—and conclude with comments about the most recent arrivals.

Chinese Americans

Chinese immigration to the United States began in 1849 during the economic boom of the California Gold Rush. With new towns and businesses springing up overnight, businesses in need of cheap labor employed some 100,000 Chinese immigrants. Most Chinese workers were young, hard-working men willing to take lower-status jobs shunned by whites. But the economy soured in the 1870s, and desperate whites began to compete with the Chinese for whatever jobs could be found. Suddenly, the industriousness of the Chinese posed a threat. In short, economic hard times led to prejudice and discrimination (Ling, 1971; Boswell, 1986).

Soon, whites acted to bar the Chinese from many occupations. Courts also withdrew legal protections, unleashing vicious campaigns against the "Yellow Peril." Everyone seemed to line up against the Chinese, as expressed in the popular phrase of the time that a person "didn't have a Chinaman's chance" (Sung, 1967; Sowell, 1981).

In 1882, the U.S. government passed the first of several laws curtailing Chinese immigration.

This action created domestic hardship because, in the United States, Chinese men outnumbered women by twenty to one. This imbalance sent the Chinese population plummeting to only 60,000 by 1920. Chinese women already in the United States, however, were in high demand, and they soon became far less submissive to men (Hsu, 1971; Lai, 1980; Sowell, 1981).

Responding to racial hostility, some Chinese moved eastward; many more sought the relative safety of urban Chinatowns. There, Chinese traditions flourished, and kinship networks, called clans, offered financial assistance to individuals and represented the interests of all. At the same time, however, living in Chinatown discouraged people from learning English, and this limited their job opportunities (Wong, 1971).

A renewed need for labor during World War II prompted President Franklin Roosevelt to end the ban on Chinese immigration in 1943 and extend the rights of citizenship to Chinese Americans born abroad. Many responded by moving out of Chinatowns and pursuing cultural assimilation. In 1900, 70 percent of the Chinese people lived in Honolulu's Chinatown, for example; a century later, the figure is below 20 percent.

By 1950, many Chinese Americans had experienced upward social mobility. Today, people of Chinese ancestry are no longer restricted to self-employment in laundries and restaurants; many hold high-prestige positions, especially in fields related to science and new information technology.

As shown in Table 10-4, the median family income of Chinese Americans in 1990 ($41,316) stood above the national average ($35,225). Note, however, that the higher income of all Asian Americans reflects a larger number of family members in the labor force.[3] Chinese Americans also have an enviable record of educational achievement, with twice the national average of college graduates.

Despite their success, many Chinese Americans still grapple with subtle (and sometimes

[3]Data for 1994 place median family income of Chinese Americans at $44,456, above the national figure of $36,782. Median age for all Asian Americans in 1997 was 31.3, somewhat below the national median of 35.3 and the white median of 35.7. But specific categories vary considerably in median age: Japanese, 36.1; Chinese, 32.1; Filipino, 31.1; Korean, 29.1; Asian Indian, 28.9; Cambodian, 19.4; Hmong, 12.5 (U.S. Bureau of the Census, 1995, 1998).

Table 10-4   The Social Standing of Asian Americans, 1990

	All Asian Americans	Chinese Americans	Japanese Americans	Korean Americans	Filipino Americans	Entire United States
Median family income	$42,240	$41,316	$51,550	$33,909	$46,698	$35,225
Percent in poverty	14.0%	14.0%	7.0%	13.7%	6.4%	13.1%
Completion of four or more years of college (age 25 and over)	37.7%	40.7%	34.5%	34.5%	39.3%	20.3%

Source: U.S. Bureau of the Census (1998).

overt) prejudice and discrimination. Such hostility is one reason that poverty among Chinese Americans stands above the national average. Poverty is higher still among those who remain in the restrictive circle of Chinatowns, working in restaurants or other low-paying jobs. Thus, sociologists debate whether racial and ethnic enclaves help their residents or exploit them (Portes & Jensen, 1989; Zhou & Logan, 1989; Kinkead, 1992; Gilbertson & Gurak, 1993).

Japanese Americans

Japanese immigration to the United States began slowly in the 1860s, reaching only 3,000 by 1890. Most of these immigrants came to the Hawaiian Islands (annexed by the United States in 1898 and made a state in 1959) as a source of cheap labor. Early in this century, however, as the number of Japanese immigrants to California rose and they demanded better pay, white people responded by seeking limits to immigration (Daniels, 1971). In 1907, the United States signed an agreement with Japan curbing the entry of men—the chief economic threat—while allowing Japanese women to immigrate in order to ease the sex-ratio imbalance. In the 1920s, state laws in California and dozens of other states mandated segregation and prohibited interracial marriage, virtually ending further Japanese immigration. Not until 1952 did the United States extend citizenship to foreign-born Japanese.

Japanese and Chinese immigrants differed in three ways. First, there were fewer Japanese immigrants, so they escaped some of the hostility directed at the more numerous Chinese. Second, the Japanese knew much more about the United States than the Chinese did, which eased their assimilation (Sowell, 1981). Third, Japanese immigrants favored rural farming to clustering together in cities.

But many white people objected to Japanese ownership of farmland. California acted in 1913 to bar further purchases. Many foreign-born Japanese (called the *Issei*) subsequently operated farms legally owned by their U.S.-born children (*Nisei*), who were constitutionally entitled to citizenship.

Japanese Americans faced their greatest crisis after Japan bombed the U.S. naval fleet at Hawaii's Pearl Harbor on December 7, 1941. Rage toward Japan was directed at the Japanese living in the United States. Some feared that Japanese here would spy for Japan or commit acts of sabotage. Within a year, President Franklin Roosevelt signed Executive Order 9066, an unprecedented action intended to protect national security by detaining people of Japanese descent in military camps. Authorities soon relocated 110,000 people (90 percent of all U.S. Japanese) to remote, inland reservations.

While concern about national security always rises in times of war, Japanese internment was criticized sharply. First, it targeted an entire category of people, not one of whom was ever known to have committed a disloyal act. Second, roughly two-thirds of those imprisoned were *Nisei*—U.S. citizens by birth. Third, although the United States was also at war with Germany and Italy, no such action was taken against people of German or Italian ancestry.

Relocation meant selling homes, furnishings, and businesses on short notice for pennies on the dollar. As a result, almost the entire Japanese American population was economically devastated. In military prisons—surrounded by barbed wire and guarded by armed soldiers—families crowded into single rooms, often in buildings that had previously sheltered livestock (Fujimoto, 1971; Bloom, 1980). The internment ended in 1944, when the Supreme

Court declared the policy unconstitutional. In 1988, Congress awarded $20,000 as token compensation to each victim.

After World War II, Japanese Americans staged a dramatic recovery. Having lost their traditional businesses, many entered new occupations and, because their culture values education and hard work, Japanese Americans have enjoyed remarkable success. In 1990, the median income of Japanese American households was almost 50 percent above the national average. The rate of poverty among Japanese Americans was only half the national figure.

Upward social mobility has encouraged cultural assimilation and interracial marriage. The third and fourth generations of Japanese Americans (the *Sansei* and *Yonsei*) rarely live in residential enclaves, as many Chinese Americans still do, and a majority marry non-Japanese partners. In the process, many have abandoned their traditions and lost the ability to speak Japanese. A high proportion of Japanese Americans belong to ethnic associations as a way of maintaining their ethnic identity (Fugita & O'Brien, 1985). Still, some appear to be caught between two worlds, no longer culturally Japanese, yet not completely accepted in the larger society because of racial differences.

Recent Asian immigrants

More recent immigrants from Asia include Koreans, Filipinos, Indians, Vietnamese, Samoans, and Guamanians. When added to the existing population of Chinese and Japanese descent, Asian Americans are this country's fastest growing minority, accounting for one-third of all immigration to the United States (U.S. Immigration and Naturalization Service, 1998).

Generally speaking, the entrepreneurial spirit remains strong among Asian immigrants.

Asians are slightly more likely than white people, three times more likely than Latinos, and four times more likely than African Americans and Native Americans to own and operate small businesses (U.S. Bureau of the Census, 1995).

Among all Asian Americans, moreover, Koreans are the most likely to own small businesses. Residents of New York City, for example, know that most small grocery stores there are Korean-owned; Koreans also own a large share of liquor stores in Los Angeles. Many Koreans work long hours; even so, Korean American families earn slightly lower than average incomes, as shown in Table 10-4. Moreover, Korean Americans face limited social acceptance, even among other categories of Asian Americans.

The data in Table 10-4 show that Filipinos generally have fared well. But a closer look reveals a mixed pattern, with some Filipinos highly successful in the professions (especially in medicine), while others hold low-skill jobs (Parrillo, 1994).

For many Filipino families, the key to high income is gender. Almost three-fourths of Filipino American women are in the labor force, compared to just half of Korean American women. Moreover, 42 percent of Filipino American women have a four-year college degree, compared to 26 percent of Korean American women.

In sum, a survey of Asian Americans presents a complex picture. The Japanese come closest to having achieved social acceptance; but, especially for Koreans and Chinese Americans, economic success has not toppled historical prejudice and discrimination. Although many Asian Americans have prospered, others remain poor. One clear trend is that the exceptionally high immigration rate means that people of Asian ancestry will play a central role in U.S. society in the new century (Lee, 1994).

Hispanic Americans

In 1998, Hispanics numbered at least 30 million, about 11 percent of the U.S. population. Yet few actually describe themselves as "Hispanic" or "Latino" (the term favored on the West Coast). Like Asian Americans, Hispanics are really a cluster of distinct populations, each of which identifies with a particular country (Marín & Marín, 1991).

About two out of three Hispanics (20 million) are Mexican Americans or "Chicanos." Puerto Ricans are next in population size (3 million), followed by Cuban Americans (1.2 million). Many other societies of Latin America are represented in smaller numbers. Due to a high birth rate and heavy immigration, analysts predict that Hispanics will surpass African Americans to become this nation's largest racial or ethnic minority about the year 2010 (U.S. Bureau of the Census, 1997).

Much of the U.S. Hispanic population lives in the Southwest. One of four Californians is Latino (in greater Los Angeles, almost half the people are Latino). Median family income for all Hispanics—$28,142 in 1997—stands well below the national average.[4] As the following sections

---

[4]The 1998 median age of the U.S. Hispanic population was 26.5 years, well below the national median of 35.3 years. This difference accounts for some of the disparity in income and education.

reveal, however, some categories of Hispanics have fared better than others.

Mexican Americans

Some Chicanos are descendants of people who lived in a part of Mexico annexed by the United States after the Mexican American War (1846-1848). Most Mexican Americans, however, are recent immigrants. Today, more immigrants come to the United States from Mexico than from any other country.

Like many other immigrants, many Mexican Americans have worked as low-wage laborers, on farms or elsewhere. Table 10-5 shows the 1990 median family income for Mexican Americans was $23,240, about two-thirds the national standard. One-fourth of Chicano families are poor—almost twice the national average. Finally, despite gains since 1980, Mexican Americans still receive less schooling than U.S. adults as a whole and have a high drop-out rate.

Puerto Ricans

Puerto Rico (like the Philippines) became a possession of the United States when the Spanish American War ended in 1898. In 1917, Puerto Ricans (but not Filipinos) became U.S. citizens.

Table 10-5   The Social Standing of Hispanic Americans, 1990

	All Hispanics	Mexican Americans	Puerto Ricans	Cuban Americans	Entire United States
Median family income	$23,431	$23,240	$18,008	$31,439	$35,225
Percent in poverty	25.0%	25.0%	37.5%	13.8%	13.1%
Completion of four or more years of college (age 25 and over)	9.2%	6.2%	10.1%	18.5%	20.3%

Source: U.S. Bureau of the Census (1998).

New York City is the center of Puerto Rican life in the continental United States. Today, this city is home to about 1 million Puerto Ricans. However, one-third of this Puerto Rican community is severely disadvantaged. Adjusting to cultural patterns on the mainland—including, for many, learning English—is one major challenge; also, Puerto Ricans with darker skin encounter prejudice and discrimination. As a result, about as many people return to Puerto Rico each year as arrive.

This "revolving door" pattern hampers assimilation. About three-fourths of Puerto Rican families in the United States speak Spanish at home, compared with about half of Mexican American families (Sowell, 1981; Stevens & Swicegood, 1987). Speaking only Spanish maintains a strong ethnic identity, but it also limits economic opportunity. Puerto Ricans also have a higher incidence of women-headed households than other Hispanics, a pattern that raises a family's risk of poverty. Table 10-5 shows that in 1990 the median household income for Puerto Ricans was $18,008, about half the national average. Although long-term mainland residents have made economic gains, more recent immigrants from Puerto Rico continue to struggle to find work. Averaging out the differences, Puerto Ricans remain the most disadvantaged Hispanic minority (Rivera-Batiz & Santiago, 1994; Holmes, 1996).

Cuban Americans

Within little more than a decade after the 1959 Marxist revolution led by Fidel Castro, 400,000 Cubans had emigrated to the United States. Most settled in Miami. Many immigrants were highly educated business and professional people who wasted little time becoming as successful here as they had been in their homeland (Fallows, 1983; Krafft, 1993).

Table 10-5 shows that the median household income for Cuban Americans in 1990 was $31,439—above that of other Hispanics yet still below the national average. The 1 million Cuban Americans living in the United States today have managed a delicate balancing act—achieving success in the larger society while retaining much of their traditional culture. Of all Hispanics, Cubans are the most likely to speak Spanish in their homes; eight out of ten families do (Sowell, 1981). However, their cultural distinctiveness and their highly visible communities like Miami's Little Havana provoke hostility from some people.

White Ethnic Americans

The term *white ethnics* recognizes the ethnic heritage—and social disadvantages—of many white people. White ethnics are non-WASP people whose ancestors lived in Ireland, Poland, Germany, Italy, or other European countries. More than half of the U.S. population falls into one or another white ethnic category (Alba, 1990).

Unprecedented emigration from Europe during the nineteenth century first brought Germans and Irish and then Italians and Jews to our shores. Despite cultural differences, all shared the hope that the United States would offer greater political freedom and economic opportunity than their homelands. Most did live better in this country, but the belief that "the streets of America are paved with gold" turned out to be a far cry from reality. Many immigrants found only hard labor for low wages.

White ethnics also endured their share of prejudice and discrimination. Nativist organizations opposed the entry of non-WASP Europeans to the United States, and many newspaper ads seeking workers warned new arrivals: "None need apply but Americans" (Handlin, 1941:67).

In 1921, the nativists declared victory when Congress passed legislation that imposed a

CONTROVERSY & DEBATE

Affirmative Action: Problem or Solution?

Adarand Constructors, a white-owned Colorado company, submitted the lowest bid for a federal highway project erecting guard rails. But Adarand did not get the job. Despite having to pay a higher price, the government selected Gonzales Construction, a minority-owned firm. Adarand sued. As a bitter company manager, Randy Perch, explained: "What is prejudice? It's when government makes a decision based on something that doesn't matter, like race or gender."

Should race or ethnicity or gender matter in how we treat people? This question lies at the heart of the affirmative action debate. To begin, what, exactly, is this controversial policy and how did it start?

After World War II, the U.S. government funded higher education for veterans of all races. The G.I. Bill held special promise for African Americans, most of whom needed financial assistance to enroll in college. The program was so successful that, by 1960, some 350,000 black men and women were on college campuses with government funding.

But a problem remained: These individuals were not finding the kinds of jobs for which they were qualified. In short, *educational* opportunity was not producing *economic* opportunity.

Thus, in the early 1960s, the Kennedy administration devised a program of "affirmative action" to provide a broader "net of opportunity" for qualified minorities. Employers and educators were instructed to monitor carefully hiring, promotion, and admissions policies to eliminate discrimination—even if unintended—against minorities.

Proponents defend affirmative action as a sensible response to our nation's racial and ethnic history, especially for African Americans, who suffered under two centuries of slavery and a century of segregation under Jim Crow laws. Throughout our history, they claim, being white gave people a big advantage. Thus, minority preference today is a fair step toward just compensation for unfair majority preference in the past.

Second, given our racial history, the promise of a "color-blind" society strikes many analysts as hollow. Prejudice and discrimination are deep in the fabric of U.S. society; thus, simply endorsing the principle of color-blindness does not mean everyone will compete fairly from now on.

Third, proponents maintain that affirmative action has worked. Where would minorities be if our government had not enacted this policy three decades ago? Indeed, major employers, such as fire and police departments in large cities, began hiring minorities and women only because of affirmative action. Affirmative action has played an important part in the expansion of the African American middle class.

quota on immigration that lasted until 1968. The most severe restrictions targeted southern and eastern Europeans—people likely to have darker skin and to differ culturally from the dominant WASPs (Fallows, 1983).

In response to bigotry, many white ethnics formed supportive residential enclaves. Some also gained footholds in certain businesses and trades: Italian Americans entered the construction industry; Irish Americans worked in construction and took civil service jobs; Jews predominated in the garment industry; many Greeks (like the Chinese) worked in the retail food business (Newman, 1973).

But affirmative action has always drawn criticism and, by the mid-1990s, courts began cutbacks in such programs. Critics argue that affirmative action started out as a temporary remedy to ensure fair competition but became a system of "group preferences" and quotas. In other words, the policy did not remain true to the goal of promoting color-blindness as set out in the 1964 Civil Rights Act. Within a decade, it had become "reverse discrimination," favoring people not because of their qualifications or performance but on the basis of their race, ethnicity, or sex.

Second, critics contend that affirmative action polarizes people. If racial preferences were wrong in the past, they are wrong now. Moreover, why should whites or men today—many of whom are far from privileged—be penalized for past discrimination that was in no way their fault? Our society has undone most of the institutionalized prejudice and discrimination of earlier times, opponents continue, so that minorities can and do enjoy success when they have the talent and make the effort. Giving entire categories of people special treatment inevitably compromises standards, calls into question the real accomplishments of minorities, and provokes a hostile response from white people.

The third argument is that affirmative action benefits those who need it least. Favoring minority-owned corporations or allocating places in law school for minorities helps already-privileged people. Affirmative action has done little for the African American underclass who most needs a leg up.

In sum, there are good reasons to argue for or against affirmative action. Indeed, people who believe the ultimate goal is a society where no racial or ethnic category dominates fall on both sides of this debate. The disagreement is not over whether people of all colors should have equal opportunity, but whether a particular policy—affirmative action—is part of the solution or part of the problem.

Continue the Debate ...

1. Assuming that talent is spread throughout the population, should all minorities be represented in jobs or universities in proportion to their numbers in the larger population? Why or why not?
2. Should affirmative action include only disadvantaged categories of minorities (say, African Americans and Native Americans) and exclude more affluent categories (such as Japanese Americans)? Why or why not?
3. What about replacing race-based affirmative action with a class-based policy to help those who need it most?

Sources: Carr (1995), Cohen (1995), Curry (1997), and NORC (1999).

Many working-class people still live in traditional neighborhoods, although those who prospered gradually assimilated. Most descendants of immigrants who labored in sweatshops and lived in crowded tenements have higher incomes and lead comfortable lives, their ethnic heritage now serving as a source of pride.

Race and Ethnicity: Looking Ahead

The United States has been, and will probably remain, a land of immigrants. We are a country of striking cultural diversity with tales of success, hope, and struggle told in hundreds of tongues.

Most immigrants arrived in a great wave that peaked about 1910. The next two generations brought gradual economic gain and at least some cultural assimilation. The government also extended citizenship to Native Americans (1924), foreign-born Filipinos (1942), Chinese Americans (1943), and Japanese Americans (1952).

A second wave of immigration began after World War II and swelled as the government relaxed immigration laws in the 1960s. During the 1990s, about 1 million people came to the United States each year, more than twice the number that arrived during the "Great Immigration" a century ago (although newcomers now enter a country with five times as many people).

But now most immigrants to the United States come not from Europe but from Latin America and Asia, with Mexicans, Filipinos, and South Koreans arriving in the largest numbers. Many new arrivals face much the same prejudice and discrimination as those who came before them. Indeed, recent years have witnessed rising hostility toward foreigners (sometimes called *xenophobia,* with Greek roots meaning "fear of what is strange"). In 1994, California voters passed Proposition 187, cutting social services (including schooling) to illegal immigrants, and, more recently, voters there mandated that all children learn English in school. Moreover, as the Controversy & Debate box on pages 168–169 explains, the debate over affirmative action still rages as hotly as ever.

As in the past, many immigrants try to blend into U.S. society without completely giving up their traditional culture. Some, however, still build racial and ethnic enclaves, so that the Little Havanas and Koreatowns of today stand alongside the Little Italys and Germantowns of the past. New arrivals also share the traditional hope, like those who came before them, that their racial and ethnic diversity can be a source of pride and not a badge of inferiority.

Summary

1. Race involves a cluster of biological traits. Although, a century ago, scientists identified three broad categories—Caucasoids, Negroids, and Mongoloids—there are no pure races. Ethnicity is based not on biology but on shared cultural heritage. Minorities—including people of certain races and ethnicities—are categories of people both socially distinct and socially disadvantaged.

2. Prejudice is a rigid and biased generalization about a category of people. Racism, a destructive type of prejudice, asserts that one race is innately superior or inferior to another.

3. Discrimination is a pattern of action by which a person treats various categories of people unequally.

4. Pluralism means that racial and ethnic categories, although distinct, have equal social standing. Assimilation is a process by which minorities gradually adopt the patterns of the dominant culture. Segregation is the physical and social separation of categories of people. Genocide is the extermination of a category of people.

5. Native Americans—the original inhabitants of the Americas—have endured genocide, segregation, and forced assimilation. Today, Native Americans' social standing is well below the national average.

6. WASPs predominated among the original European settlers of the United States, and many continue to enjoy high social standing today.

7. African Americans experienced two centuries of slavery. Emancipation in 1865 gave way to segregation by law. Today, despite legal equality, African Americans are still relatively disadvantaged.

8. Chinese and Japanese Americans have suffered both racial and ethnic hostility. Although some prejudice and discrimination continues, both categories now have above-average income and schooling. Recent Asian immigration—especially of Koreans and Filipinos—makes Asian Americans the fastest-growing racial category of the U.S. population.

9. Hispanics represent many ethnicities sharing a Spanish heritage. Mexican Americans, the largest Hispanic minority, are concentrated in the Southwest. Puerto Ricans, most of whom live in New York, are poorer. Cubans, concentrated in Miami, are the most affluent category of Hispanics.

10. White ethnics are non-WASPs of European ancestry. While making gains during the last century, many white ethnics still struggle for economic security.

11. Immigration has increased in recent years. No longer primarily from Europe, most immigrants now arrive from Latin America and Asia.

prejudice (page 150) A rigid and irrational generalization about an entire category of people.

racism (page 152) The belief that one racial category is innately superior or inferior to another.

scapegoat (page 153) A person or category of people, typically with little power, whom people unfairly blame for their troubles.

discrimination (page 154) Treating various categories of people unequally.

institutional prejudice and discrimination (page 155) Bias inherent in the operation of any of society's institutions.

pluralism (page 155) A state in which people of all races and ethnicities, while distinct, have social parity.

assimilation (page 156) The process by which minorities gradually adopt patterns of the dominant culture.

miscegenation (page 156) Biological reproduction by partners of different racial categories.

segregation (page 156) The physical and social separation of categories of people.

genocide (page 157) The systematic killing of one category of people by another.

Key Concepts

race (page 147) A category of men and women who share biologically transmitted traits that members of a society deem socially significant.

ethnicity (page 148) A shared cultural heritage.

Critical-Thinking Questions

1. Differentiate between race and ethnicity. Do you think all non-white people should be considered minorities, even if they have above-average incomes?

2. In what ways do prejudice and discrimination reinforce each other?

3. Are *all* generalizations about minorities wrong? What distinguishes a fair generalization from an unfair stereotype?

4. Do you think U.S. society is becoming more, or less, color-blind? Is color-blindness a goal worth striving for? Why or why not?

Learning Exercises

1. Does your college or university take account of race and ethnicity in its admissions policies? Ask to speak with an admissions officer and see what you can learn about your school's policies and the reasons for them. Ask, too, if there is a "legacy" policy that favors children of parents who attended the school.

2. Give several of your friends or family members a quick quiz, asking them what share of the U.S. population is white, Hispanic, African American, and Asian (see Table 10-1). If they are like most people, they will exaggerate the share of all minorities and

understate the white proportion (Labovitz, 1996). What do you make of the results?

3. There are probably immigrants on your campus or in your local community. Have you ever thought about asking them to tell you about their homeland and their experiences since arriving in the United States? Most immigrants would be pleased to be asked, and you can learn a great deal.

4. If you have Internet access, visit the Web site of an organization working to improve the social standing of a U.S. minority: the National Association for the Advancement of Colored People (http://www.naacp.org); the Jewish Defense League (http://www.jdl.org), or the Institute for Puerto Rican Policy (http://www.iprnet.org/IPR/). What are the organization's strategies and goals?

5. Install the CD-ROM, packaged inside the back cover of your text, to view videos, read additional text, use the animated maps, visit Web destinations, and take the practice tests for this chapter.

VOCABULARY LESSON

The purpose of this vocabulary lesson is to help you review and deepen your knowledge of the ten general vocabulary words you worked with at the beginning of this chapter.

A. Structural Analysis—Affixes and Root Words
    1. Circle the suffixes of the following words:
        a. Succumbed
        b. Plummeting
    2. Find the dictionary definitions of the root words of the words above and write the definitions by the words.
B. Use of Context
    1. Read the sentence in which the word *continuum* is used on page 152 and in your own words write a definition for *continuum*:

        _____

    2. Read the sentence in which the word *detriment* is used on page 156 and in your own words write a definition for *detriment*:

        _____

    3. Read the sentence in which the word *plummeting* is used on page 163 and in your own words write a definition for *plummeting*:

        _____

C. Multiple Meanings of Words
    1. Circle the definition below of the word *succumbed* that fits the way it is used on page 157, "most *succumbed* to diseases."
        a. Give way under pressure, yield
        b. Die
D. Synonyms and Antonyms
    1. List one synonym (same meaning) and one antonym (opposite meaning) for each of the following words:

Word	**Synonym**	**Antonym**
Overt		
Detriment		

E. Generate Your Own Language
    1. When has a friend given you a *subtle* hint that you either appreciated or resented?
    2. Has your home life *fostered* your independence of or dependence on family?
    3. When have you observed *blatant* discrimination?
    4. Do any of your friends suffer from *xenophobia*? Explain.

F.   Textbook Preview: The following words that appear in this chapter will
     be some of your vocabulary words for Part II of this textbook. How well
     do you already know them? Which ones do you use in your written and
     oral language?
     1.   Aborigines (aboriginal)
     2.   Virtually
     3.   Egalitarian
     4.   Bigotry
     5.   Traditions
     6.   Decimated
     7.   Obscures
     8.   Assimilation

VOCABULARY EXTENSION

The purpose of this vocabulary exercise is to help you see to what degree you know
the ten general vocabulary words in this chapter. Matching a word with its definition is the beginning of knowing a word. Using the word in your speaking and writing is full knowledge.

See if you have increased your vocabulary by following the directions below:

A.   List the vocabulary words from this lesson that you can now use in
     both your speaking and writing.
B.   List the vocabulary words from this lesson that you can now use in
     writing but are still not comfortable using in speaking.
C.   List the vocabulary words from this lesson that you cannot use yet but
     will recognize in reading.
D.   List general vocabulary words from this lesson that are still difficult to
     understand.
E.   Use *five* vocabulary words from this lesson in a five-sentence para-
     graph on the topic of this lesson.
F.   Illustrate the meaning of *one* of the vocabulary words from this lesson
     through some form of artwork or a cartoon. (This exercise is for right-
     brain students who enjoy drawing better than writing!)

EXTENDED READING ACTIVITIES

The purpose of this section is to give you a variety of options for independent study
or investigation of the chapter topic. Reading is a skill that must be practiced each
day if progress is to take place. These activities are designed to give you a variety
of reading experiences through which you can improve your general vocabulary
and increase your higher-level comprehension skills.

Your instructor may wish to (a) assign one or more activities to the class as a whole, (b) assign various activities to small groups, (c) assign one or more activities to individual students, or (d) let students choose to do the activities or not.

A. Weekly Reading Report: If it is helpful, continue to keep a Weekly Reading Report. A form is in Appendix C.

B. Attend a Reading Lab: If you have access to a reading lab and find the work helpful, continue attending for at least thirty minutes at a time.

C. Read a fiction book. Use the novel report form in Appendix C if you wish.
   1. Adult
      a. David Guterson, *Snow Falling on Cedars*
      b. Amy Tan, *The Joy Luck Club, The Kitchen God's Wife, The Hundred Secret Senses,* or *The Bonesetter's Daughter*
   2. Young Adult: Young Adult novels are written for middle and high school students. The ones recommended in this textbook are listed for recreational reading and contain interesting characters and serious themes. Their appeal is ageless and the reading is easy.
      a. Jeanne Wakatsuke Houston and James D. Houston, *Farewell to Manzanar*
      b. Kyoto Mori, *Shizuko's Daughter, One Bird*
      c. Alice Childress, *Rainbow Jordan*
      d. Pleasant DeSpain, *The Emerald Lizard* (a collection of Latin American tales in English and Spanish)
   3. Children: The children's books listed here are written for middle school students but contain mature themes such as prejudice and death. The narrators are young people.
      a. Christopher Paul Curtis, *The Watsons Go to Birmingham—1963* and *Bud, Not Buddy*
      b. Mildred D. Taylor, *Let the Circle Be Unbroken*
      c. Robert Newton Peck, *A Day No Pigs Would Die*

D. Reading/Writing Connection: Write an entry in your beginning college experience journal on one of the topics below:
   1. Review the section "Critical Thinking: Does Race Affect Intelligence?" What are the arguments for and against race affecting intelligence? What makes the most sense to you? Did you think of other arguments not discussed in this section?
   2. Review "Controversy & Debate: Affirmative Action: Problem or Solution?" How do you feel about affirmation action? What do you know about it from your family and community experiences?
   3. Is your family interested in its genealogy? What do you know about your racial or ethnic roots? What would you like to know?

E. Use the Internet
   1. Use the Internet to research one of the following broad topics: race, ethnicity, prejudice, discrimination, pluralism, segregation, genocide,

or immigration. Narrow the broad topic to one part that you find interesting and continue your research. You may also want to research the Japanese internment during World War II and the restitution made in 1988, or California's Proposition 187 (1994).

2. Use the Internet to research one of the following groups of people: WASPs, African Americans, Chinese or Japanese Americans, Mexicans, Puerto Ricans, Cubans, or white ethnics. Again, narrow your search to one or two aspects.

3. Look up the United States Bureau of the Census site for "Interracial Married Couples: 1960 to the Present" (MS-3) at <http://www.census.gov/population/socdemo/ms-la/tabms-3>.

F. Keep a Vocabulary Journal: You were introduced to the Vocabulary Journal in the previous chapter. If you find keeping this journal helpful for this class or lab or for one of your content area classes, continue by using the Vocabulary Journal form in Appendix C.

G. Magazine/Journal/Newspaper Reading: Find magazines and/or journals in your public or school library that would appeal to various races and ethnic groups. Also find ones that appeal to people in your region of the country or in your state. For example, I live in Appalachia and enjoy reading about the area. Read articles in major city newspapers about race and ethnicity. Use the form at the end of this chapter to record what you read.

H. Major Journal Reading: Read magazines and/or journals in your major as an alternative to the above. If you are fairly sure of your major, browse through your campus library to find what people in that major read about. Use the form provided at the end of this chapter if you wish.

I. Research: Of the more than sixty studies cited throughout the chapter, I have chosen a representative sampling so that, if you wish, you may read the original information used by the author. They are listed in order of appearance in the chapter.

1. Sowell, Thomas. *Ethnic America*. New York: Basic Books, 1981.

2. Geschwender, James A. *Racial Stratification in America*. Dubuque, IA: Wm. C. Brown, 1978.

3. Steele, Shelby. *The Content of Our Character: A New Vision of Race in America*. New York: St. Martin's Press, 1990.

4. Newman, William M. *American Pluralism: A Study of Minority Groups and Social Theory*. New York: Harper & Row, 1973.

5. Matthiessen, Peter. *Indian Country*. New York: Viking Press, 1984.

6. Jagarowsky, Paul A., and Mary Jo Bane. *Neighborhood Poverty: Basic Questions*. Discussion paper series H-90-3. John F. Kennedy School of Government. Cambridge, MA: Harvard University Press, 1990.

7. Sale, Kirkpatrick. *The Conquest of Paradise: Christopher Columbus and the Columbian Legacy*. New York: Alfred A. Knopf, 1990.

8. Tyler, S. Lyman. *A History of Indian Policy*. Washington, D.C.: U.S. Department of the Interior, Bureau of Indian Affairs, 1973.

9. Fost, Dan. "American Indians in the 1990s." *American Demographics*. Vol. 13, No. 12 (December 1991): 26–34.

10. Ling, Pyau. "Causes of Chinese Emigration." In Amy Tachiki et al., eds. *Roots: An Asian American Reader*. Los Angeles: UCLA Asian American Studies Center, 1971: 134–138.

11. Zhou, Min, and John R. Logan. "Returns of Human Capital in Ethnic Enclaves: New York City's Chinatown." *American Sociological Review*. Vol. 54, No. 5 (October 1989): 809–820.

12. Kinkead, Gwen. *Chinatown: A Portrait of a Closed Society*. New York: HarperCollins, 1992.

13. Rivera-Batiz, Francisco L., and Carlos Santiago, cited in Sam Roberts, "Puerto Ricans on Mainland Making Gains, Study Finds." *New York Times* (October 19, 1994): A20.

14. Holmes, Steven A. "For Hispanic Poor, No Silver Lining." *New York Times* (October 13, 1996): section 4, p. 5.

15. Fallows, James. "Immigration: How It's Affecting Us." *The Atlantic Monthly*. Vol. 252 (November 1983): 45–52, 55–62, 66–68, 85–90, 94, 96, 99–106.

REFLECTION

MIND REVOLUTION

The Mind Revolution grew out of my awareness that too many times students do not incorporate what they learn in class into their personal lives. Learning remains compartmentalized and sometimes wasted. This is an attempt to get you to see how the chapter information can be personally important. Hopefully, you will encounter a new idea in each chapter that you can incorporate into your own life, or at least have something new to think about as you go about your daily routine. Life should never be boring!

The large number of racial and ethnic groups of people and the number of languages they speak, as discussed in this chapter, reminds us that we live in a complex society. If you live in an area of the country that is dominated by one racial and/or ethnic group as I presently do, it would be easy not to see the significance of issues important to groups not represented in your area.

VOCABULARY

If most of the specialized vocabulary words discussed in the first sections of the chapter are new to you, then you probably have a beginner's understanding. In other words, you can probably match these words to their definitions, and you have some idea of their importance. Meanings of such words as *race, ethnicity, prejudice, discrimination, pluralism, assimilation, miscegenation, segregation,* and *genocide* will hopefully deepen and broaden as you take history, sociology, psychology, and anthropology courses.

COMPREHENSION

Your background knowledge and experience played an important part in your understanding what you read. If you strongly disagreed with information in the chapter, your emotions could have interfered with your comprehension. For example, if you began reading the chapter with the notion that everyone in the country should speak English, you may have been surprised to learn how many languages other than English are spoken here. Reading about people living in ethnic villages and continuing their languages and culture may have surprised you if you have never visited a large city. It is important to be aware of our emotions as well as our intellect when we read.

Density of concepts was probably not a major problem for you in this chapter. If you did not have a vast amount of academic knowledge about the topics, you probably had strong opinions about many of them.

Weekly Magazines/Journals/Newspapers Reading Report

Your Name _____

Directions: Read thirty minutes a day for this class. You may spend one hour a week reading from magazines, journals, and newspapers. Try to read articles from sources that cover national interest topics. Most of them can be found in your campus library, hometown public library, or on-line.

A. List the names of magazines and/or journals you have read.

_____

_____

B. List the titles of articles that you have read.

_____

_____

C. Summarize the most interesting article you read this week.

_____

_____

D. Give your opinion about the article you summarized.

_____

_____

E. List two new vocabulary words you found in the articles you read and write their dictionary definitions.

1. Word _____

Definition _____

2. Word _____

Definition _____

Reading in Your Major Journal Report

Your Name _____

Your Major _____

Directions: Choose journals in your major and read as many articles as you have time. Report on one of them below by providing the information indicated. Some journals in your major may be too difficult for you at this time. You may need advanced knowledge in the field to understand the articles. Browsing through them can still be fun just to see what you will be able to talk about in a year or two. If everything you encounter is too boring to read, you may want to consider another major.

A. Bibliographical information:
   1. Article title _____
   2. Author(s) _____
   3. Journal's name _____
   4. Date of journal _____
   5. Page numbers of article _____
B. Topic (subject) of the article:

   _____

   _____

C. I learned the following about this topic (state main ideas):

   _____

   _____

D. The information above related to what I already knew about the topic in the following way:

   _____

   _____

E. I would rate my level of interest in this topic as
   high___   average___   low___
   because:

   _____

   _____

F. This topic is important to my major in the following way:

   _____

   _____

G. I have changed my ideas about my major in the following ways as a result of reading this article:

   _____

   _____

Environmental Geology:
Philosophy and Fundamental Concepts

Overview

Extended Reading Activities
Reflection
   Mind Revolution
   Vocabulary
   Comprehension

VOCABULARY/METACOGNITION

The purpose of this exercise is to help you become aware of when you know the meaning of a word and to help you know when you do not know the meaning of a word. This is metacognition awareness.

On a scale of 1–5 (see below), rate your knowledge of the following vocabulary words from "Philosophy and Fundamental Concepts." After matching words with definitions on page 182, check your answers and then check your number *ones* and *fives* below. Did you know when you really knew a word and when you really did not know the word?

Scale

1. I absolutely do not know.
2. I do not think I know.
3. There's a 50/50 chance I have seen or heard it.
4. I think I know it.
5. I know the word and can use it.

Words

_____ 1. Devastate
_____ 2. Adverse
_____ 3. Degrade
_____ 4. Resilient
_____ 5. Finite
_____ 6. Replenish (replenished)
_____ 7. Sustain (sustainability)
_____ 8. Viable
_____ 9. Propensity
_____10. Confluence

Go to page 182. See if you can match the right definition with the word and then write sentences for any three words in the list.

Words   **Definitions**

_____ 1. Devastate   A. (1) Contrary in purpose or effect; opposite;
                                       (2) harmful to one's interests; unfortunate
_____ 2. Adverse
                                   B. (1) Springing back; rebounding; (2) buoyant;
_____ 3. Degrade   not readily discouraged

_____ 4. Resilient   C. Fill again

_____ 5. Finite   D. (1) Capable of living, esp. able to live outside
                                      the womb; (2) (Informal) workable; practical
_____ 6. Replenish (replenished)
                                   E. (1) A flowing together as of streams; their place
_____ 7. Sustain (sustainability)   of meeting; (2) the coming together of people;
                                      a crowd
_____ 8. Viable
                                   F. A natural tendency; bent
_____ 9. Propensity
                                   G. (1) Maintain; support; keep alive; (2) assist;
_____10. Confluence   (3) endure; undergo; (4) corroborate; affirm;
                                      (5) of a tone, prolong

                                   H. Having limits; restricted

                                   I. (1) Reduce in rank or degree; (2) demean;
                                      debase; (3) decompose chemically

                                   J. (1) Lay waste; pillage; (2) (Informal)
                                      overwhelm by disappointment, grief, etc.

Write three words from the list and your own sentences that show you know how
to use the words. Choose words that you marked a *five* if possible.

1. Word _____

   Sentence _____

2. Word _____

   Sentence _____

3. Word _____

   Sentence _____

PRE-READING THE TEXTBOOK CHAPTER

The purpose of this *first* of three steps in your reading plan is to suggest things
to do *before* you read. First, as part of your pre-reading, read the Prior Knowledge section beginning on page 183, the Academic Study Skills section's
overview on page 191, and the first part of the Textbook Study Aids Plan (Pre-
Reading) on pages 191–192. When you finish, return to this section and continue your pre-reading.

Tapping Prior Knowledge

Tap your experience and prior knowledge about the title of this selection by writing words and phrases that come to your mind. You are pulling up your file on the topic and focusing on what you will read. What do you already know about the subject? Do not look at your textbook at this time, as these answers will vary from person to person and won't be found in the textbook. There are no wrong answers for this part of the lesson.

Predicting

Predict in one sentence what you will read. Try to predict in some detail. Don't write, "I predict that I will read about the philosophy and fundamental concepts of environmental geology." What behavior, action, and/or information do you expect to read about? Predicting helps you identify your expectations of what you will read. Not reading what you have predicted will serve as a warning that you have misjudged the topic of the article and will help you adapt to what is in the chapter.

Overviewing

Overview the chapter by turning to the Textbook Study Aids Plan in the Academic Study Skills section of this chapter on page 191 and following the directions for Pre-Reading. Note that you have six major sections with several subheadings under each one, especially the last one. Add the new information you learn to what you learned in the Prior Knowledge section of this lesson.

Prior Knowledge

This section presents a model to show you what will help you comprehend this chapter by using your own background knowledge. If you know much of the information listed below, you have a better background for reading this chapter. This section will suggest helpful kinds of background information and help you activate what you know; do not try to look up or learn everything listed. Ask yourself what you need to know before you read and what you already know that will help you to understand this chapter.

Writing Pattern Overview

The natural sciences include biology, botany, chemistry, physics, and geology. Generally, when reading in these disciplines, look for the writing to be organized in a step-by-step sequence writing pattern and organized by process. If you have ever written out your favorite recipe for a friend or directions to your favorite shopping mall, then you have experience with this type of writing. In this type of writing you will find lists or categories, comparison/contrast, and cause/effect. The writing reflects the scientific method itself. If you have written scientific research papers or lab reports, you already recognize the difference between this type of writing and ordinary prose. This writing is usually plain, unadorned, and objective. See the Prior Knowledge sections of the reading section for an analysis of the various sections' writing patterns.

Reading skills required for scientific writing include (1) classifying or grouping information under headings that show relationships, and (2) the ability to generalize, such as seeing broad concepts that apply to an entire group of objects or ideas. Generalizing is part of the inferential level of comprehension and present in the text-implicit questions in the reading lessons.

Directions for Reading This Section

First, notice the categories of information: (a) vocabulary, (b) writing patterns, and (c) concepts and background knowledge and experience. Next, skim the sections, noting what is familiar and what is not. If a great amount is familiar and/or interesting to you, you should find reading the chapter easier than if you do not recognize anything and find the information boring.

Chapter Sections

I. Case History: Ducktown, Tennessee (pages 202–203)
    A. Vocabulary
        1. General
            a. Devastation
            b. Adverse
            c. Optimistic
            d. Restoration
            e. Developing (countries)
        2. Specialized
            a. Hardwood forest
            b. Noxious gas
            c. Sulfur dioxide
            d. Particulates
            e. Acid rain
            f. Erosion
    B. Recognition of Writing Patterns or Arrangement of Ideas and Devices
        1. Narration
        2. Cause/effect
        3. Use of reference for support
    C. Concepts and Background Knowledge and Experience
        1. Personal Knowledge
            a. Seeing the area of Copper Basin
            b. Experience soil erosion
        2. Academic Knowledge
            a. Acid rain and acid dust—what it is and what it harms

        b.   Significance of soil erosion (use of prior knowledge of Dust Bowl documentaries and novel/movie *Grapes of Wrath*; read Karen Hesse's *Out of the Dust*)

II.   Introduction to Environmental Geology
- A.   Vocabulary
  - 1.   General
    - a.   Degradation (environmental)
  - 2.   Specialized
    - a.   Definitions in context and/or listed in Key Terms
      - (1) Geology
      - (2) Environmental geology
    - b.   Other specialized vocabulary
      - (1) Solar nebula (definition in text)
      - (2) Fossils
      - (3) *Homo sapiens*
      - (4) Protostars
      - (5) Hydrologic processes
- B.   Recognition of Writing Patterns or Arrangement of Ideas and Devices
  - 1.   Explanation
  - 2.   Broad to specific
  - 3.   Definitions in context
  - 4.   List
- C.   Concepts and Background Knowledge and Experience
  - 1.   Personal
    - a.   Interests/hobbies in use of rocks, minerals, and soils; geologic processes such as mountain formation
    - b.   Experience with study or importance of water resources in personal life; interest in environmental issues
    - c.   Nature lover, mountain climber, backpacker, mountain biker, water sports enthusiast
  - 2.   Academic
    - a.   Broad concept of time and perspective
    - b.   How the earth was physically formed
    - c.   Geology course or interest in topics

III. How Geologists Work: The Scientific Method
- A.   Vocabulary
  - 1.   General
    - a.   Qualitatively (understand)
  - 2.   Specialized
    - a.   Hypothesis
    - b.   Scientific Method
    - c.   Theory
    - d.   Greenhouse Effect

    e. Carbon dioxide

    f. Time Periods: Pleistocene, Holocene (page 204)

  B. Recognition of Writing Patterns or Arrangement of Ideas and Devices

   1. Expository

   2. General to specific

   3. Step-by-step sequence with brief explanation

   4. Definition in context

   5. Statement with example

   6. Ends with transitional paragraph

  C. Concepts and Background Knowledge and Experience

   1. Personal

    a. Curious about how things work

    b. Worked in a lab or did field study for a hobby

    c. A rock hounder

   2. Academic

    a. Study and use of scientific method

    b. Made observations, took notes on a project

    c. Knowledge of geologic time and its significance

IV. Culture and Environmental Awareness

  A. Vocabulary

   1. General

    a. Comparable (page 205)

  B. Recognition of Writing Patterns or Arrangement of Ideas and Devices

   1. Expository

   2. Statement (no support)

   3. Comparison

  C. Concepts and Background Knowledge and Experience

   1. Personal

    a. Worked for environmental causes through cultural or social institutions

   2. Academic

    a. The broad way the phrase *environmental awareness* is used (page 205)

    b. Understand the need for inclusion of our cultural and social institutions in the solution to environmental problems

V. Environmental Ethics

  A. Vocabulary

   1. Specialized

    a. *Land ethic* defined in context and listed in Key Terms section

  B. Recognition of Writing Patterns or Arrangement of Ideas and Devices

   1. Expository

2. Statement
3. Comparison (historical)
4. Definition in context
5. Use of reference for support

C. Concepts and Background Knowledge and Experience
1. Personal
    a. Personal experience in losing social or individual freedom
    b. Ability to be flexible in thought and action in facing environmental stress; ability to sacrifice the personal for a greater cause
2. Academic
    a. Understanding of old idea and new idea that people cannot be held as property
    b. Understanding significance of people no longer having the right to dispose of physical property as they wish
    c. Understanding the difference between conquering and protecting the land

VI. The Environmental Crisis
A. Vocabulary
    None
B. Recognition of Writing Patterns or Arrangement of Ideas and Devices
1. Expository
2. Cause/effect
3. Listing
4. Statement with support
5. Use of reference for support
C. Concepts and Background Knowledge and Experience
1. Personal
    a. Live in or visited an overpopulated area
    b. Live in an area with a severe pollution problem
    c. Live in or visited a place where the forest has not been properly used, where an area has been overmined, or where clean water is a problem
    d. Drink bottled water instead of tap water
2. Academic
    a. Ability to see significance of several causes working together to create the environmental crisis; to see the complexity of the problem

VII. Fundamental Concepts of Environmental Science
A. Vocabulary
1. General
    a. Pessimistic
    b. Optimistic
    c. Replenished

        d.   Sustainability

        e.   Viable

        f.   Propensity

        g.   Coalition

        h.   Confluence

        i.   Input

        j.   Output

        k.   Infer

        l.   Inferences

  2. Specialized

        a.   Exponential growth (defined in context)

        b.   Principle of environmental unity

        c.   Open system

        d.   Closed system

        e.   Average residence time

        f.   Uniformitarianism

B. Recognition of Writing Patterns or Arrangement of Ideas and Devices

  1. Concept One: Population Growth

        a.   Expository

        b.   Several statements supported by an authority, a figure, and numbers

        c.   Definition in context with example

        d.   Use of reference for support

  2. Concept Two: Sustainability

        a.   Expository

        b.   Statement with documentation and source

        c.   Use of reference

  3. Concept Three: Systems

        a.   Expository

        b.   Statements and examples

        c.   Definitions in context and examples

        d.   Transitional word *however*—to move from open to closed systems

        e.   Use of a figure to help clarify

        f.   Cause/effect (input-output analysis)

  4. Concept Four: Limitation of Resources

        a.   Expository

        b.   Statements and examples and rewording of statement; note use of "in other words," page 214

        c.   Use of reference for support

  5. Concept Five: Uniformitarianism

        a.   Expository

        b.   Definition in context

        c.   Quote authority in field

        d.   Rewording of statement "as the name suggests" (page 215)

        e.   States limitations of idea (pages 215–216); note transition words *furthermore* and *however*

        f.   Statements and examples

   6.   Concept Six: Hazardous Earth Processes

        a.   Expository writing

        b.   Historical view of struggle with nature

        c.   Basically statement of problem with no examples

   7.   Concept Seven: Geology as a Basic Environmental Science

        a.   Expository writing

        b.   Listing with brief description of disciplines

        c.   Additional listing of disciplines contributing research

        d.   Statement

C.   Concepts and Background Knowledge and Experience

   1.   Personal

        a.   Live in or visited an area affected by overpopulation that reduces the quality of life

        b.   Involved in causes such as Zero Population Growth

        c.   Experience with gasoline shortages or soaring gas prices

        d.   Experience with blackouts and brownouts or soaring electricity prices

        e.   Lived in areas where tornadoes, hurricanes, earthquakes, and/or flooding were a serious threat

   2.   Academic

        a.   Understand what having too many people on earth does to the social and physical environment

        b.   See relationships with broad perspective—how the earth cannot sustain an excessive number of people

        c.   See need for understanding how the earth's systems are interconnected in order to protect them

        d.   Recognize that the earth is our only habitat for now and we must protect it

        e.   Overview of environmental changes through time

        f.   Understanding of complexity of the field of geology and all that it encompasses

VIII. A Closer Look: Earth's Place in Space

   A.   Vocabulary

      1.   General

         a.   Resilient

         b.   Finite

      2.   Specialized

         a.   Crustal

         b.   Biosphere

           c.   Supernova

           d.   Accretionary processes

           e.   Photosynthesis

           f.   Stratospheric ozone layer

           g.   Fossils

           h.   Law of faunal assemblages

           i.   Biodiversity

    B.   Recognition of Writing Patterns or Arrangement of Ideas and Devices

        1.   Expository; presents overview; condensed

        2.   Use of nonscientific writing in quotes

        3.   Quotes authority; use of reference

        4.   Definitions in context

        5.   Quote and explanation

        6.   Symbol for ozone = O^3

        7.   Definitions in context with examples

    C.   Concepts and Background Knowledge and Experiences

        1.   Personal

           a.   Sense of being a part of the earth

           b.   Hunted fossils; interested in dinosaurs

        2.   Academic

           a.   Understanding the difference in scientific writing and ordinary prose

           b.   Previous study of earth's beginnings and geologic time

           c.   Knowledge of mass extinction, such as of the dinosaurs and theories as to why they disappeared

  IX.   Case History, page 211

    A.   Vocabulary

       None

    B.   Recognition of Writing Patterns or Arrangement of Ideas and Devices

        1.   Descriptive and expository

        2.   Symbols

        3.   Statement and examples

        4.   Reference for support

  X.   A Closer Look: The Gaia Hypothesis

    A.   Vocabulary

        1.   General

           a.   Metaphor

    B.   Recognition of Writing Patterns or Arrangement of Ideas and Devices

        1.   Expository

        2.   Listing

        3.   Statement and examples

        4.   Transitional phrase "on the other hand"

C. Concepts and Background Knowledge and Experience
   1. Personal
       a. Curiosity, pleasure reading and documentary viewing on various ideas of how our planet works and how scientists in various disciplines work together toward new knowledge
   2. Academic
       a. Knowledge of the Gaia hypothesis

ACADEMIC STUDY SKILLS

OVERVIEW

The textbook supplies an abundance of study aids for this chapter, which include (1) learning objectives, (2) chapter numbering of sections, (3) figures, (4) a Summary, (5) a list of Key Terms, and (6) Review and Critical Thinking Questions. The question becomes one of deciding how to use them and how they are helpful. Which are essential to your learning? Which are supplementary, providing different explanations and examples? Which help extend your interest in the subject beyond the information in the chapter?

TEXTBOOK STUDY AIDS PLAN

For this last chapter in Part I, textbook study aids continue to be the focus of attention. By the time you reach Part II, you should be familiar with which parts of a textbook to overview, such as the learning objectives, outlines, summaries, and questions. You are also aware of format and the use of various kinds of visuals as aids to understanding.

Following is one plan of action in using the textbook aids provided for this chapter. If it does not meet your needs or approach to studying, modify it.

Pre-Reading   In previous chapters the figures were saved until last. Try something different for this chapter. Work easily into the chapter, especially if you have little interest or background information in the subject. Warm up to the subject by first looking at the figures (especially if you are a visual learner). Think about what is familiar and/or interesting to you. What do the figures make you think about as you view them?

Continue overviewing the chapter as a pre-reading activity. Now that you have done your warm-up exercise, move to a moderate level of effort in using the aids by reading the summary and the two sets of questions at the end of the chapter. The summary provides you with an overview of the chapter and its main ideas. The first set of questions asks about important ideas in the chapter and the second set asks you to use or extend the information you have learned. These questions provide a good preview for what you will be able to do after studying the chapter, how you will be able to think about the material and incorporate it into your own life.

Full steam ahead! At the beginning of the chapter, learning objectives are listed. As part of your pre-reading activities, look at them carefully because they, with the section numbering system, provide you with an outline and guide to reading the chapter. You may want to come back to the objectives and self-test yourself about each.

Reading   During the reading part of your Active Questioning reading plan, use extra aids if you need them. For example, if the exponential growth idea is still fuzzy, take time to look at Figure 1.2 on page 210, with its two examples. Remember that looking at information presented in a different way can help you better understand what you need to learn.

Contemporary textbook authors and publishers are sensitive to students' needs for aids in reading textbooks. They try to clarify and enliven the reading of text. Sometimes, especially when you do not know very much about the subject at hand, the book or an especially difficult chapter may take on a cluttered look. You may be overwhelmed by too much help. If this happens to you as you read this chapter, try "reading by the numbers," that is, look at the section numbering system and read each of the numbered parts, 1.1 through 1.6. Part 1.6 contains seven concepts, so be sure to read all of those. Reading by the numbers means that you are skipping the supplementary material at this point. Once you have the main reading done, then you can read the other sections. Use the Learning Objectives and the Chapter Summary to check that you have read the major parts of the chapter.

Post-Reading   As a part of your post-reading activities, relax and look at the textbook aids that are there to extend your interest or add background knowledge to the subject. For example, "A Closer Look: Earth's Place in Space," on pages 207–208, gives you an historic view of earth's beginnings. It could provide you with a better understanding of long periods of time; after all, twelve billion years is a lot of time to contemplate. You may also simply enjoy and identify with some of the quotes at the beginning of this supplementary section.

The second supplementary section provided for you, "A Closer Look: The Gaia Hypothesis," page 215, can again expand and deepen your interest in the earth, and, hopefully, give you something new to think about. For example, the term *living earth* may take on new significance for you.

ACTIVE QUESTIONING

OVERVIEW

Your first step of the three-part reading plan was pre-reading in which you activated your prior knowledge and experience, predicted what you would read, and overviewed the chapter before reading.

As the second step in this three-part reading plan, you will read the selected chapter by using the Active Questioning reading plan as explained below. An alternative plan, Reciprocal Teaching, is in Appendix A. In both plans you break up the chapter in sections and read and think about each as you read. The purpose of both plans is to keep you reading actively.

GENERAL DIRECTIONS

A. The purpose for writing questions on three levels of comprehension is to first get the facts and basic information to understand the chapter on a literal level.

B. From there you move to combining this information in the chapter with your own prior knowledge to synthesize information, draw conclusions, and make judgments.

C. The last level of comprehension gives you the opportunity to incorporate the information you have learned into your own life. The lowest level, literal, is easier because you can copy the answer from the text. Many times you can get this answer right without really understanding what you are reading. Answers to questions on the last two higher levels of comprehension, inferential and critical/creative, take more time to process and sometimes you may feel insecure about your answers, but it is important to do something with the literal level information to see its significance; therefore, it is important to work on the two higher levels.

ASSIGNMENT

Before beginning this assignment, read the "Reading" section of your Textbook Study Aids Plan in the Academic Study Skills section on page 192.

When independently using active questioning, you write questions on the literal, inferential, and creative/critical levels. In Chapter 2, the introductory chapter to using Active Questioning, you answered teacher-made questions on all three levels. In this second chapter using Active Questioning, you will move to writing literal level questions and answering the teacher-made questions on the inferential and creative/critical levels. You are combining teacher modeling with guided practice in the process of becoming independent readers.

A. Read "Case History: Ducktown, Tennessee" and follow the directions below to write and respond to questions about the reading.

1. Text-explicit: A literal level question requires the reader to read the line. The answer will come from one line of print. Model text-explicit question: When does the story of Ducktown begin? Answer: 1843. Write one text-explicit, literal-level question.

Your text-explicit question _____

Answer _____

2. Text-implicit (inferential level): A question that requires the reader to read between the lines. The answer will come from more than one line of print. You will need to make judgments and draw conclusions. Answer this text-implicit question: What were the steps in the destruction of vegetation in Copper Basin?

Answer _____

3. Experience-based (critical/creative level): A question that requires the reader to read beyond the lines. Apply what you have learned to your world. Question what you have read. Answer this experience-based question: Describe any destruction of the landscape that you know about. Who profits? For example, do you know about any gold mining in other countries that destroyed the land?

Answer _____

B. Read "1.1 Introduction."

1. Model text-explicit, literal-level question: When did life on earth begin? Answer: 3.5 billion years. Write one text-explicit, literal-level question and answer the inferential and creative/critical questions below.

Your text-explicit question _____

Answer _____

2. Answer this text-implicit question: What three problems do geologists deal with and what do they have to study to do so? In your state which problem is most important?

Answer _____

3. Answer this experience-based question: Rank the three problems listed in this section in terms of our nation as a whole and then of the world—according to your own knowledge and value system. Justify your choice.

Answer _____

C. Read "1.2 The Scientific Method."

1. Model text-explicit question: What is the important variable that distinguishes geology from most of the other sciences? Answer: consideration of time. Write one text-explicit, literal-level question and answer the inferential and creative/critical questions below.

Your text-explicit question _____

Answer _____

2. Answer this text-implicit question: List the steps in the scientific method. Which step would be the most difficult for you?

Answer _____

3. Answer one of these three experience-based questions:

a. In what courses were you taught the scientific method in high school? Did you write a scientific report based on the scientific method? Describe it.

    b. What hypothesis would you like to test? How would you test it? What results would you hope for?

    c. Look at the example of designing a hypothesis on global warming and then identify another environmental issue for study; if you have time, design a hypothesis for it.

Answer _____

D. Read "1.3 Culture and Environmental Awareness."

    1. Model text-explicit question: List the cultural and social institutions that affect the way we perceive and respond to our physical environment. Answer: political, economic, ethical, religious, aesthetic. Write one text-explicit, literal-level question.

Your text-explicit question _____

Answer _____

    2. Answer this text-implicit question: Which two of the following cultural and social institutions, political, economic, ethical, religious, and aesthetic, have the most power to affect the way we perceive and respond to our physical environment? Justify your choices.

Answer _____

    3. Answer this experience-based question: What personal changes have you made to help solve environmental problems?

Answer _____

E. Read "1.4 Environmental Ethics."

    1. Example of a text-explicit question: What does a *land ethic* assume? Answer: that we are responsible not only to other individuals and society, but also to the total environment, that larger community consisting of plants, animals, soil, atmosphere and so forth. Write one text-explicit, literal-level question.

Your text-explicit question _____

Answer _____

    2. Answer this text-implicit question: What issues emerge when people and land are held as property?

Answer _____

    3. Answer one of these three experience-based questions:

        a. Explain the difference in protecting and conquering the land

        b. How does your community respond to its land? What evidence is there that the community reveres, loves, and protects its land rather than allowing economics to determine land use?

        c. How does the present national administration show that it protects the land?

Answer _____

F. Read "1.5 The Environmental Crisis."

    1. Model text-explicit question: What has created the environmental crisis? Answer: See first sentence of this section. Write one text-explicit, literal-level question.

Your text-explicit question _____

Answer _____

2. Answer this text-implicit question: List the three causes of the environmental crisis in order of importance to you personally and justify your listing.

Answer _____

3. Answer this experience-based question: Are you pessimistic or optimistic about solving the problems of our environmental crisis? Support your response.

Answer _____

G. Read "1.6 Concepts"

Concept One: Population Growth

1. Model text-explicit question: What is the number one environmental problem? Answer: human population. Write one text-explicit, literal-level question.

Your text-explicit question _____

Answer _____

2. Answer one of the three text-implicit questions:
   a. How does the author support his statement that overpopulation is becoming a global problem?
   b. Review the definition of exponential growth and then explain why a constant percentage of the current population is important.
   c. According to Figure 1.1, which country or continent seems to have the largest population? Draw conclusions about the reasons for this large number.

Answer _____

3. Answer one of the three experience-based questions:
   a. What social and cultural factors can help with the population bomb? How?
   b. What is your solution? What obstacles do you see?
   c. Why does education make a difference?

Answer _____

Concept Two: Sustainability

4. Model text-explicit question: With what are geologists and environmentalists concerned? Answer: human environment. Write one text-explicit, literal-level question.

Your text-explicit question _____

Answer _____

5. Answer this text-implicit question: Review the two definitions of sustainability and choose one that is closer to your environmental position. Explain.

Answer _____

6. Answer this experience-based question: How does the statement that the earth will survive us make you feel? What do you envision as happening when humans become extinct?

Answer _____

Concept Three: Systems

7. Model text-explicit question: What is a system? Answer: any defined part of the universe that we select for study. Write one text-explicit, literal-level question.

Your text-explicit question _____

Answer _____

8. Answer this text-implicit question: In this section, you are given an example of how knowing the average residence time for an oil spill in a river and in groundwater is important. How could it also be important to know the average residence time for chemical fertilizers in the soil?

Answer _____

9. Answer this experience-based question: Why is it important to understand the connectedness of all systems in order to guard the human environment? Give an example.

Answer _____

Concept Four: Limitation of Resources

10. Model text-explicit question: What are the two fundamental truths included in this concept? Answer: First, earth is the only place to live that is now accessible to us, and second, our resources are limited. Write one text-explicit, literal-level question.

Your text-explicit question _____

Answer _____

11. Answer this text-implicit question: Which of the two resources discussed for recycling, (1) solid and liquid waste and (2) land, would be more complicated to recycle? Why?

Answer _____

12. Answer this experience-based question: How can we recycle resources on a large scale without harming the environment? What problems are involved? Give an example.

Answer _____

Concept Five: Uniformitarianism

13. Model text-explicit question: What is uniformitarianism? Answer: The idea that the present is the key to the past. Write one text-explicit, literal-level question.

Your text-explicit question _____

Answer _____

14. Answer one of the two text-implicit questions:

a. Why is it important to recognize that processes we observe today also operated in the past?

b. Why must we consider the effects of human activity on natural earth processes? Give an example when this was done or not done. Look at the textbook example for guidance.

Answer _____

15. Answer one of the two experience-based questions:
    a. Have you experienced floods or landslides in your state? Describe what happened. Has human activity been involved in the cause?
    b. Have you seen or read about worldwide flooding or landslides on the world news? Has human activity been involved in the cause? Do you belong to any organizations that help with disaster relief?

Answer _____

Concept Six: Hazardous Earth Processes

16. Model text-explicit question: After earth scientists have identified potentially hazardous processes, what obligation do they have? Answer: to make the information available to planners and decision makers. Write one text-explicit, literal-level question.

Your text-explicit question _____

Answer _____

17. Answer this text-implicit question: In our early history we probably struggled with natural processes on a day-to-day basis. Compare and contrast that period in our history with modern times. What has changed?

Answer _____

18. Answer this experience-based question: Why do people knowingly live in high-risk areas of the United States?

Answer _____

Concept Seven: Geology as a Basic Environmental Science

19. Model text-explicit question: What is geomorphology? Answer: the study of landforms and surface processes. Write one text-explicit, literal-level question.

Your text-explicit question _____

Answer _____

20. Answer this text-implicit question: List two geology disciplines that would be important to your area of the country and explain their importance.

Answer _____

21. Answer this experience-based question: Identify an environmental problem and list disciplines that could contribute to its solution. Justify your choices.

Answer _____

Optional Section on Supplementary Material

H.   Read "A Closer Look: Earth's Place in Space"

1.   Model text-explicit question: What is the law of faunal assemblages? Answer: Rocks with similar fossils suggest a similar geologic age of the rocks. Write one text-explicit, literal-level question.

Your text-explicit question _____

Answer   _____

2.   Answer this text-implicit question: The author gives two possible causes of the extinction of dinosaurs. What are they? What else do you know? Which seems more plausible to you? Why?

Answer   _____

3.   Answer this experience-based question: What words in the Preston Cloud quote would you consider non-scientific? Possible choices: "wreckage of stars," "clothed in its filmy garments ..." and "hot breath of volcanoes." Where would you expect to find them? What kind of writing do they represent? What course?

Answer   _____

I.   Read "A Closer Look: The Gaia Hypothesis"

1.   Model text-explicit question: For whom is the hypothesis named? Answer: Gaia, the Greek goddess Mother Earth. Write one text-explicit, literal-level question.

Your text-explicit question _____

Answer   _____

2.   Answer the text-implicit questions:

a.   State the last hypothesis listed in the series of hypotheses.

b.   What is your response to this hypothesis? Have you ever thought about such things before? Can you connect your response to other pieces of information you already know or to your feelings or intuition about the idea?

Answer   _____

3.   Answer this experience-based question: The Gaia hypothesis revives the idea of a living earth. How do you view the earth and your relationship to it?

Answer   _____

J.   Read "A Case History," on page 211.

1.   Model text-explicit question: What has nearly eliminated the Aral Sea in a period of only thirty years? Answer: water diversion for agriculture. Write one text-explicit, literal-level question.

Your text-explicit question _____

Answer   _____

2.   Answer this text-implicit question: List changes that have occurred in the region of the Aral Sea and then choose the one that seems the most serious and justify your choice.

Answer   _____

3. Answer this experience-based question: Discuss other regional changes that you know about that are caused by environmental damage. For example, at the writing of his textbook, some southern West Virginia residents, according to a television news program, blame strip mining and deforestation for the excessive damage done by a summer thunderstorm. Do you know of other bodies of water like the Aral Sea that are damaged? Marshlands?

Answer _____

POST-READING THE TEXTBOOK CHAPTER

OVERVIEW

In the second part of your three-part reading plan, you practiced reading your textbook chapter section by section, wrote literal-level questions, and answered inferential and creative/critical comprehension questions.

In this third part of the three-part reading plan, you will find suggestions for what to do after you read. Your task is to compare what you predicted with what you actually read as an aid to comprehension, to add what you have learned to your file of information on the topic, and to think about it.

ASSIGNMENT

Before following the directions below, follow the directions in the Post-Reading section of your Textbook Study Aids Plan in the Academic Study Skills section on page 192.

A. Compare what you predicted you would read with what you actually read. Did anything you predicted cause you a problem with comprehension? What? How?

B. What did you learn from the reading that you did not know about before working on this lesson?

C. Look at the words and phrases that you listed as your prior knowledge in the Pre-Reading section of this lesson. Group them (on page 201) with relevant information in "B" above. This is your new file of information on environmental geology. (The ability to group ideas and to see relationships requires more complex comprehension than merely memorizing isolated facts.)

D. What have you learned from this chapter that is important?

E. What do you already know that you can relate to it?

F. What do you see differently as a result of reading this chapter?

Your Headings	Words and Phrases from Pre-Reading	Relevant Information from "B"

Philosophy and Fundamental Concepts

FROM EDWARD A. KELLER, *INTRODUCTION TO ENVIRONMENTAL GEOLOGY**

Learning Objectives

In this chapter we discuss and define geology and environmental geology, focusing on aspects of culture and society that are particularly significant to environmental awareness. We present some basic concepts of environmental science that provide the philosophical framework of this book. After reading this chapter, you should be prepared to discuss the following:

- Geology and environmental geology as a discipline
- Geologic time and its significance
- The scientific method
- Important factors related to the "environmental crisis"
- Increasing human population as the number one environmental problem
- The concept of sustainability
- Systems theory and changes in systems
- The concepts of environmental unity and uniformitarianism and why they are important to environmental geology

Case History: Ducktown, Tennessee

The land surrounding Ducktown once looked more like the Painted Desert of Arizona than the lush vegetation of the Blue Ridge Mountains

of the southeastern United States (1). The story starts in 1843 with what was thought to be a gold rush that turned out to be a rush for copper. By 1855, 30 companies were transporting copper ore by mule over the mountains to a site called "Copper Basin" and to Ducktown. Huge ovens—open pits 200 m long and 30 m deep—were constructed to separate the copper from zinc, iron, and sulfur. The local hardwood forest was cut to fuel these ovens, and the tree stumps were pulled to be turned into charcoal. Eventually, every tree over an area of about 130 km^2 (an area about four times that of Manhattan Island) was removed. The ovens produced great clouds of noxious gas that were reportedly so thick that mules wore bells to keep from colliding with people and each other. The sulfur dioxide gas and particulates produced acid rain and acid dust that killed what vegetation remained. Loss of vegetation led to extensive soil erosion, leaving behind a hard mineralized rock cover resembling a desert. The scarred landscape is so large that it is one of the few human landmarks visible from space.

The devastation resulting from the Ducktown mining activity produced adverse economic and social change. Nevertheless, people in Ducktown in the 1980s remained optimistic. A sign at the entry to the town states, "Copper

*From *Introduction to Environmental Geology* by Edward A. Keller. © 1999 by Prentice-Hall, Inc. Reprinted by permission of Pearson Education, Inc. Upper Saddle River, NJ.

made us famous. Our people made us great." Revegetation started in the 1930s, and by 1970 approximately two-thirds of the area was covered with some vegetation. However, it will probably take hundreds of years for the land to completely recover. What is learned from the restoration of the Copper Basin will provide useful information for other areas in the world where humanmade deserts occur, such as the area around the smelters in Sudbury, Ontario. Finally, there is still worry for mining areas, particularly in developing countries, where landscape destruction similar to that at Copper Basin is still happening (1).

1.1 Introduction to Environmental Geology

Everything has a beginning and an end. Our Earth began about 4.5 billion years ago when a cloud of interstellar gas known as a *solar nebula* collapsed, forming protostars and planetary systems (see *A Closer Look: Earth's Place in Space*). Life on Earth began about 3.5 billion years ago, and since then multitudes of diverse organisms have emerged, prospered, and died out, leaving only their fossils to mark their place in Earth's history. Just a few million years ago, our ancestors set the stage for the present dominance of the human species. As certainly as our Sun will die, we too will eventually disappear. Viewed in terms of billions of years, our role in Earth's history may be insignificant, but for those of us now living and for our children and theirs, our impact on the environment is significant indeed.

Geologically speaking, we have been here for a very short time. Dinosaurs, for example, ruled the land for more than 100 million years. We do not know how long our own reign will

be, but the fossil record suggests that all species eventually become extinct. How will the history of our own species unfold, and who will write it? We can hope that we will leave something more than some fossils that mark a brief time when *Homo sapiens* flourished. Hopefully, as we evolve we will be more environmentally aware and find ways to live in harmony with our planet.

Geology is the science of processes related to the composition, structure, and history of Earth and its life. **Environmental geology** is applied geology. Specifically, it is the use of geologic information to help us solve conflicts in land use, to minimize environmental degradation, and to maximize the beneficial results of using our natural and modified environments. The application of geology to these problems includes the study of the following:

- *Earth materials* (such as minerals, rocks, and soils) to determine how they form, their potential use as resources or waste disposal sites, and their effects on human health
- *Natural hazards* (such as floods, landslides, earthquakes, and volcanic activity) in order to minimize loss of life and property
- *Land* for site selection, land-use planning, and *environmental impact analysis*
- *Hydrologic processes* of groundwater and surface water to evaluate water resources and water pollution problems
- *Geologic processes* (such as deposition of sediment on the ocean floor, the formation of mountains and the movement of water on and below the surface of Earth) to evaluate local, regional, and global change

Considering the breadth of its applications, we can define environmental geology as the branch of Earth science that studies the entire spectrum of human interactions with the physical environment.

1.2 How Geologists Work: The Scientific Method

Most scientists are motivated by a basic curiosity of how things work. Geologists are excited by the thrill of discovering something previously unknown about how the world works. This drives them to continue their work. The creativity and insight that may result from scientific breakthroughs often starts with asking the right question. Given that we know so little about how our world works, how do we go about studying it? Most studies start with identification of some problem of interest to the investigator. If little is known about the topic or process being studied, the first step is to try to qualitatively understand what is going on. This involves making careful observations in the field or, perhaps, a laboratory. Based upon his or her observations, the scientist may then develop a question or series of questions about those observations. Next the investigator suggests an answer or several possible answers to the question or questions. These are **hypotheses** to be tested. The best hypotheses can be tested by designing an experiment that involves data collection, organization, and analysis. Following collection and analysis of the data, the scientist interprets the data and draws a conclusion. The conclusion is then compared with the hypothesis and the hypothesis may be rejected or tentatively accepted. Often a series of questions or multiple hypotheses are developed and tested. If all hypotheses suggested to answer a particular question are rejected, then a new set of hypotheses must be developed. This method is sometimes referred to as the **scientific method**. If a hypothesis withstands a sufficient number of experiments to test it, it may be accepted as a **theory**. A theory is a strong scientific statement that the hypothesis behind the theory is likely to be true but has not been proven conclusively. New evidence often disproves existing hypotheses or scientific theory; absolute proof of scientific theory is not possible. Thus, much of the work of science is to develop and test hypotheses, striving to reject current hypotheses and develop better ones.

Geologists often begin their observations in the field or in the laboratory by taking careful notes. In field studies geologists may identify and describe the earth materials present and make maps to show how these materials are distributed at the surface of Earth.

The important variable that distinguishes geology from most of the other sciences is the consideration of time. Geologists are interested in Earth history over time periods that are nearly incomprehensible to most people. Humans evolved during the Pleistocene epoch (the last two million years), which is less than 0.05 percent of the age of Earth. In answering environmental geology questions, we are often interested in the latest Pleistocene (last 18,000 years), but we are most interested in the last few thousand or few hundred years of the Holocene, which started approximately 10,000 years ago. Thus, in geologic study, it is often the task of the geologist to design hypotheses to answer questions integrated through time. For example, we may wish to test the hypothesis that burning fossil fuels such as coal and oil, which we know releases carbon dioxide into the atmosphere, is causing global warming by trapping heat in the lower atmosphere. We term this the "Greenhouse Effect" (discussed in Chapter 13). One way to test this would be to show that prior to the Industrial Revolution, when we started burning a lot of coal and, later, oil, the mean global temperature was significantly lower than it is now. We might be particularly interested in the last few hundred to few thousand years before temperature measurements were recorded at various spots around the planet as they are today. To test the hypothesis that global warming is occurring, the investigator could examine prehistoric earth materials that might provide indicators of global temperature. This might involve studying glacial ice or sediments from the bottoms of the oceans or lakes to estimate past levels of carbon dioxide in the atmosphere. Properly completed, studies can provide conclusions to test the hypothesis that global warming is occurring or to reject the hypothesis.

With our increased understanding of what environmental geology is and how geologists work, we will now consider some of the philosophical underpinnings of studying the environment and introduce fundamental concepts of environmental geology.

1.3 Culture and Environmental Awareness

Environmental awareness involves the entire way of life that we have transmitted from one generation to another. To uncover the roots of our present condition, we must look to the past, to see how our culture and our social institutions—political, economic, ethical, religious, and aesthetic—affect the way we perceive and respond to our physical environment.

To solve environmental problems such as overpopulation, disposal of hazardous waste, global warming, and resource depletion, we must look to the future. If our social institutions are to contribute to the solutions, fundamental changes in how society works at both the personal and institutional level will be necessary. The magnitude of this adjustment may

be comparable to that of the Industrial Revolution, which changed the relationship between people and the environment by producing ever-increasing demands on resources and releasing ever-increasing quantities of toxic waste into the surroundings.

1.4 Environmental Ethics

An ethical approach to the environment is the most recent development in the long history of human ethical evolution, which has included changes in our concept of property rights. In earlier times human beings were often held as property, and their masters had the unquestioned right to dispose of them as they pleased. Slaveholding societies certainly had codes of ethics, but these codes did not include the modern idea that people cannot be property. Similarly, until very recently, few people in the industrialized world have questioned the right of landowners to dispose of land as they please. Only within this century has the relationship between civilization and its physical environment begun to emerge as a relationship involving ethical considerations.

Environmental (including ecological and land) ethics involve limitations on social as well as individual freedom of action in the struggle for existence in our stressed environment. A **land ethic** assumes that we are responsible not only to other individuals and society, but also to the total environment, that larger community consisting of plants, animals, soil, atmosphere, and so forth. According to this ethic, we are the land's citizens and protectors, not its conquerors. This role change requires us to revere, love, and protect our land rather than allow economics to determine land use (5).

1.5 The Environmental Crisis

The demands made on diminishing resources by a growing human population, along with the ever-increasing production of human waste, has produced what is popularly referred to as the **environmental crisis**. This crisis in America and the world is a result of overpopulation, urbanization, and industrialization, combined with too little ethical regard for our land and inadequate institutions to cope with environmental stress (6). Today the raid on resources continues on a global scale:

- Deforestation and accompanying soil erosion and water and air pollution occur on many continents.
- Mining of resources such as metals, coal, and petroleum wherever they occur produces a variety of environmental problems.
- Development of both ground and surface water resources results in loss and damage to many environments on a global scale (see *Case History: Aral Sea*).

On a positive note, we have learned a great deal from the environmental crisis. We know a lot about the relationship of environmental degradation to resource utilization, and many innovative plans have been and are being developed to lessen or eliminate environmental problems.

1.6 Fundamental Concepts of Environmental Science

In the rest of this chapter we discuss some fundamental concepts of environmental science that are particularly relevant to environmental geology. The seven concepts presented here do not constitute a list of everything that is important to environmental geologists, and they are not meant to be memorized. However, understanding the general thesis of each concept will help you to understand and evaluate the philosophical and technical material presented in the rest of the text.

Concept One: Population Growth

The number-one environmental problem is the increase in human population.

The number-one environmental problem is the ever-growing human population. Well-known human ecologist Garrett Hardin has stated that the total environmental impact of population is equal to the product of the impact per person times the population. Therefore, as population increases, the total impact must also increase. As population increases, more resources are needed and, given our present technology, greater environmental disruption results.

Overpopulation has been a problem in some areas for at least several hundred years, but it is now apparent that it is becoming a global problem. From 1830 to 1930, the world's population doubled from 1 to 2 billion people. By 1970 it had nearly doubled again, and by the year 2000, it is expected that there will be more than 6.3 billion people on Earth. By the middle of the next century, there will probably be 10 to 15 billion people on Earth! The problem is sometimes called the *population bomb*, because the **exponential growth** of the human population results in the explosive increase shown in Figure 1.1 (on page 209). Exponential growth means that the number of people added to the population each year is not constant; rather, it is a constant *percentage* of the current population.

A CLOSER LOOK

Earth's Place in Space

The famous geologist Preston Cloud, who was one of my first mentors in environmental geology, wrote (2):

> Born from the wreckage of stars, compressed to a solid state by the force of its own gravity, mobilized by the heat of gravity and radioactivity, clothed in its filmy garments of air and water by the hot breath of volcanoes, shaped and mineralized by four and a half billion years of crustal evolution, warmed and peopled by the Sun, this resilient but finite globe is all our species has to sustain it forever.

In this short, eloquent statement, Cloud takes us from the origin of Earth to the concept of sustainability that today is at the forefront of thinking about the environment and our future.

The place of humanity in the universe is stated well in the *Desiderata* (3): "You are a child of the universe, no less than the trees and the stars; you have the right to be here. And whether or not it is clear to you, no doubt the universe is unfolding as it should." To some this might sound a little out of place in science but, as emphasized further by Cloud, people can never escape the fact that we are one piece of the biosphere, and although we stand high in it, we are not above it (2).

Scientists studying the stars and the origin of the universe believe that about 12 billion years ago, there was a giant explosion known as the "big bang." This explosion produced the atomic particles that later formed galaxies, stars, and planets. It is believed that about 7 billion years ago, one of the first generations of giant stars experienced a tremendous explosion known as a **supernova**. This released huge amounts of energy, producing a solar nebula that is thought to be a spinning cloud of dust and gas. The solar nebula condensed as a result of gravitational processes, and our Sun formed at the center, but some of the particles are thought to have been trapped in solar orbits as rings, similar to those we observe around the planet Saturn. The density of particles in individual rings was evidently not constant and so gravitational attraction from the largest density of particles in the rings attracted others until they collapsed into the planetary system we have today. Thus, the early history of planet Earth, as with the other planets in our solar system, was characterized by intense bombardment of meteorites associated with the accretionary processes (particles of various sizes, from dust to meteorites many kilometers in diameter coming together) that resulted in Earth about 4.5 billion years ago (2, 4). This is the part of Earth's history that Cloud refers to when he states that Earth was born from the wreckage of stars and compressed to a solid state by the force of its own gravity. Heat generated deep within Earth, along with gravitational settling of heavier elements such as iron, helps differentiate the planet into its layered structure we see today (see Chapter 2). Outgassing from volcanoes and other processes produced Earth's early atmosphere and water. About 3.5 billion years ago the first primitive life forms appeared on Earth in an oxygen-deficient environment. Some of these primitive organisms began producing oxygen through photosynthesis, which profoundly affected Earth's atmosphere. Early, primitive, oxygen-producing life probably lived in the ocean, protected from the Sun's ultraviolet radiation. However, as the atmosphere evolved and oxygen increased, a stratospheric ozone (O_3) layer was produced that shielded Earth from harmful radiation and allowed the planet to green: Plants evolved that colonized the land surface, producing forests, meadows, fields, and other environments that made the evolution of animal life on the land possible (2).

The spiral of life highlights evolution as life changed from simple to complex over several billion years of Earth's history. The names of the eras, periods, and epochs that geologists use to divide **geologic time** are labeled with their range in millions or billions of years from the present. If you go on to study geology, they will become as familiar to you as the months of the year. The boundaries between eras, periods, and epochs are based on both the study of what was living and on important global geologic events in Earth's history. Relative ages of rocks are based on the assemblage of **fossils** (evidence for past life such as shells, bones, teeth, leaves, seeds, etc., found in rocks or sediments). It's a general principle of geology, known as the **law of faunal assemblages**, that rocks with similar fossils suggest a similar geologic age of the rocks. For example, if we find bones of dinosaurs in a rock, we know the rocks are Mesozoic in age, 245–65 million years old. Fossils provide relative ages of rocks; numerical (or absolute) dates depend upon a variety of sophisticated chemical age-dating techniques. Using such techniques with the fossils, geologists can often pin down the geologic age of rocks containing fossils to within a few million years or better.

The evolutionary process as deduced from the fossil record has not been a smooth continuous one but instead has been punctuated by explosions of new species at some times and extinction of many species at other times. Evolution and extinction of species are natural processes, but for those times when many species became extinct at approximately the same time, we use the term "mass extinction." For example, approximately 65 million years ago the dinosaurs became extinct. Some geologists believe this resulted from climatic and environmental changes that naturally occurred on Earth; others believe the planet was struck by a "death star," an asteroid of about 10 km in diameter that landed in what is today the Yucatan Peninsula in Mexico. It is believed that such an impact could produce fire storms and huge dust clouds that would circle Earth in the atmosphere for a prolonged period of time, blocking out sunlight, which would greatly reduce or stop photosynthesis, eventually leading to mass extinction of those species that eat plants as well as the predators who feed on the plant eaters (4).

It is speculated that asteroids of the size that may have caused the dinosaurs to become extinct are not unique and such catastrophic impacts have occurred at other times during Earth history. Such an event is the ultimate geologic hazard, the effects of which might result in another mass extinction, perhaps including humans! Fortunately, the probability of such an occurrence is very small during the next few thousand years. In addition, we are developing the technology to identify and deflect such unwelcome visitors. The history of our solar system and Earth, briefly outlined here, is an incredible story of planetary and biologic evolution. What will the future bring? We don't know this, of course, but certainly it will be punctuated by a change, and as the evolutionary processes continue, we too will evolve, perhaps to a new species. Through the processes of pollution, agriculture, urbanization, industrialization, and the land clearing of tropical forest, humans appear to be causing an acceleration of the rate of extinction of plant and animal species. This is significantly reducing Earth's biodiversity, the number and variability of species over time and space (area), and is thought to be a major environmental problem. This is because many living things (including humans) on Earth depend on the existence of an environment with a diversity of life forms.

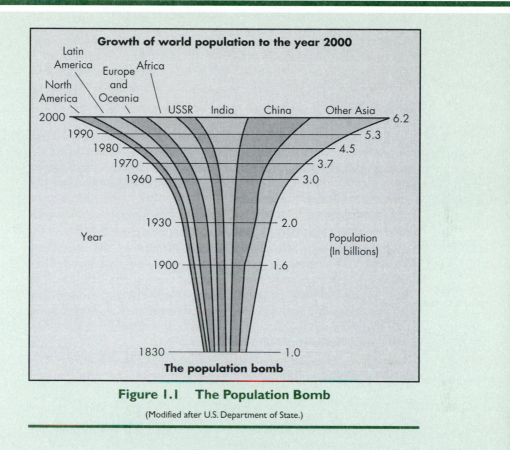

Figure 1.1   The Population Bomb

(Modified after U.S. Department of State.)

As an extreme example of exponential growth (see Figure 1.2a on page 210), consider the student who, after taking a job for 1 month, requests from the employer a payment of 1 cent for the first day of work, 2 cents for the second day, 4 for the third day, and so on. In other words, the payment would double each day. What would be the total? It would take the student 8 days to earn a wage of more than $1 per day, and by the eleventh day, earnings would be more than $10 per day. Payment for the sixteenth day of the month would be more than $300, and on the last day of the 31-day month, the student's earnings for that 1 day would be more than $10 million! This is an extreme case because the constant rate of increase is 100 percent per day, but it shows that exponential growth is a very dynamic process. The human population increases at a much lower rate—1.7 percent per year today—but even this slower exponential growth eventually results in a dramatic increase in numbers (see Figure 1.2b on page 210). Exponential growth will be discussed further under Concept Three, in which we consider systems and change.

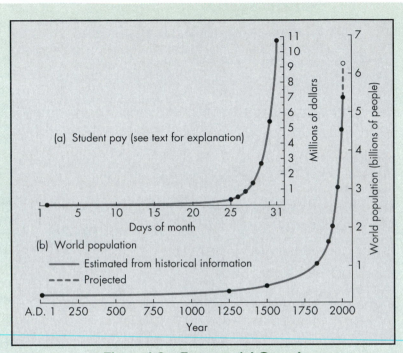

Figure 1.2   Exponential Growth

(a) Example of a student's pay, beginning at 1 cent for the first day of work and doubling daily for 31 days. (b) World population. Notice both curves have the characteristic J shape, with a slow initial increase followed by a rapid increase. The actual shape of the curve depends on the scale at which the data are plotted. It often looks like the tip of a skateboard.

(Population data from U.S. Department of State.)

Because Earth's population is increasing exponentially, many scientists are concerned that in the twenty-first century it will be impossible to supply resources and a high-quality environment for the billions of people who may be added to the world population. Increasing population at local, regional, and global levels compounds nearly all environmental geology problems, including pollution of ground and surface waters; production and management of hazardous waste; and exposure of people and human structures to natural processes (hazards), such as floods, landslides, volcanic eruptions, and earthquakes.

There is no easy answer to the population problem. In the future we may be able to mass produce enough food from a nearly landless agriculture to support our ever-growing numbers. However, this does not solve the problems of the space available to people and the quality of their lives. Some studies suggest that the present population is already above a comfortable

CASE HISTORY

Aral Sea

Water diversion for agriculture in the southern region of what was the Union of Soviet Socialist Republics (USSR) has nearly eliminated the Aral Sea in a period of only 30 years. A tourist vacation spot in 1960, it is now a dying sea surrounded by thousands of square kilometers of salt flats, and the change is permanently damaging the economic base of the region.

In 1960, the area of the Aral Sea was about 67,000 km^2. Diversion of the two main rivers that fed the sea has resulted in a drop in surface elevation of more than 20 m and loss of about 28,000 km^2 of surface area. Towns that were once fishing centers on the shore of the lake are today about 30 km inland. Loss of the sea's moderating effect is changing the regional climate: the winters are now colder and the summers warmer. Windstorms pick up salty dust and spread it over a vast area, damaging the land and polluting the air.

The lesson of the Aral Sea is how quickly environmental damage can bring about regional change. Many worry that what people have done to the Aral region is symptomatic of what we are doing on many fronts on a global scale (7).

variety of cultures, values, and norms in the world today, it appears that our greatest hope for population control is, in fact, through education (8).

When resource and other environmental data are combined with population growth data, the conclusion is clear: it is impossible, in the long run, to support exponential population growth with a finite resource base. Therefore, one of the primary goals of environmental work is to ensure that we can defuse the population bomb. Pessimistic scientists believe that population growth will take care of itself through disease and other catastrophes, such as famine. Optimistic scientists hope that we will find better ways to control the population of the world within the limits of our available resources, space, and other environmental needs.

Concept Two: Sustainability

Sustainability is the environmental objective.

There is little doubt that we are using living environmental resources such as forests, fish, and wildlife faster than they can be naturally replenished. We have extracted minerals, oil, and groundwater without concern for their limits or for the need to recycle them. As a result there are shortages of some resources. We must learn how to *sustain* our environmental resources so that they continue to provide benefits for people and other living things on the planet. **Sustainability** is something that we are still struggling to define. Some would define it as ensuring that future generations have equal access to the resources that our planet offers. Others would argue that sustainability refers to types of development that are economically viable, do not harm the environment, and are socially just (8).

carrying capacity (the maximum number of people Earth can hold without causing environmental degradation that reduces the ability of the planet to support the population) for the planet. *The role of education is paramount in the population problem.* As people (particularly women) become more educated, the population growth rate tends to decrease. As the rate of literacy increases, population growth is reduced. Given the

The environmental statement of the 1990s is "save our planet." Is Earth's very survival really in danger? In the long view of planetary evolution, it seems highly likely that Earth will survive us. Our Sun is likely to last another several billion years at least, and if all humans became extinct in the next few years, life would still flourish on our planet. The changes we have made in the landscape, the atmosphere, and the waters might last for a few hundreds or thousands of years, but they would eventually be cleansed by natural processes. What we are concerned with, as environmentalists, is the quality of the *human* environment on Earth.

Concept Three: Systems

Understanding Earth's systems and their changes is critical to solving environmental problems. Earth itself is an open system with respect to energy, but it is essentially a closed system with respect to materials.

A **system** is any defined part of the universe that we select for study. Examples of systems are a planet, a volcano, an ocean basin, or a river. Most systems contain component parts that mutually adjust, so changes in one part brings about changes in the others.

The propensity for change in the various parts of the environment is known as the **principle of environmental unity**. Put more simply, this principle says that everything affects everything else. For example, an increase in the magnitude of the processes that uplift mountains may affect the atmosphere by causing regional changes in precipitation patterns as a new rain shadow is produced. This in turn affects the local hydrology as more or less runoff of water reaches the ocean basins. Biospheric changes as a result of changes in the environment (such as

change in types of plants and animals present) also can be expected. Eventually, the steeper slopes will also affect the soil and rock at the surface of Earth: increased erosion will change types of sediments produced, as well as the shapes of hillslopes, valleys, gullies, and ridges.

The dynamic nature of Earth is that of an **open system**, that is, one that exchanges energy or material with its surroundings. This is certainly true with respect to energy, since Earth receives energy from the Sun and radiates energy back into space. There is also some exchange of matter between Earth and its surroundings: meteors fall to Earth, and a small amount of earth material escapes into space as gas. However, most of Earth's material is continuously recycled within the system. When we consider natural cycles, such as the water and rock cycles, we can best think of Earth as a **closed system** or, more accurately, a coalition of many closed systems (9). The rain that falls today will eventually return to the atmosphere, and the sediment deposited yesterday will be transformed into solid rock.

Growth Rates

Since growth is an important change in many systems, we must understand something about **growth rates**. Exponential growth, described under Concept One, is particularly significant to the systems we are concerned with. Consider again Figure 1.2, which illustrates two examples of exponential growth. In each case, the thing being considered (student pay or world population) grows quite slowly at first, then begins to increase more rapidly, and then *very* rapidly.

There are two important measures of exponential growth:

- The **growth rate** measured as a percentage
- The **doubling time**

As already stated, exponential growth is characterized by a constant percent increase; for example, a population might be increasing at a rate of 2 percent per year, so that the number of individuals added each year is greater than the number added the year before. Doubling time is the time necessary for the quantity of whatever is being measured to double. A rule of thumb is that doubling time is roughly equal to 70 divided by the growth rate. Using this approximation, we find that a population with a 2 percent annual growth rate would double in about 35 years. The rule works well for growth rates under about 10 percent, but for higher rates the error becomes quite large.

Many systems in nature display exponential growth some of the time, so it is important that we be able to recognize such growth. For example, we are having a very difficult time controlling (stopping) the growth of the human population on Earth.

Input-Output Analysis

This is an important method for analyzing change in *open* systems, that is, in systems with an input and output of materials or energy. There are three types of change in a pool or stock of materials; in each case the net change depends on the relative rates of the input and output. Where the input into the system is equal to the output, a rough steady state is established and no net change occurs. The example shown is a university in which students enter as freshmen and graduate 4 years later at a constant rate. Thus, the pool of university students remains a constant size. Our planet is a roughly steady-state system with respect to energy: incoming solar radiation is roughly balanced by outgoing radiation from Earth. In the second type of change, the input into the system is less than the output. Examples include the use of resources such as fossil fuels or groundwater, or the harvest of certain plants or animals. If the input is much less than the output, then the fuel or water source may be completely used up, or the plants or animals may become extinct. In a system in which input exceeds output, the stock of whatever is being measured will increase. Examples are the buildup of heavy metals in lakes or the pollution of soil and water.

By evaluating rates of change or the input and output of a system, we can derive an **average residence time** for a particular material, such as a resource. The residence time is a measure of the time it takes for the total stock or supply of the material to be cycled through a system. To compute the average residence time (assuming constant size of the system and constant rate of transfer), we take the total size of the stock and divide it by the average rate of transfer through the system. For example, if a reservoir holds 100 million cubic meters (m^3) of water, and both the average input from streams entering the reservoir and the average output over the spillway are 1 m^3/sec, then the average residence time for a cubic meter of water in the reservoir is 100 million seconds, or about 3.2 yrs. We can also calculate average residence time for systems that vary in size and rates of transfer, but the mathematics is more difficult. It is often possible to compute a residence time for a particular resource and, knowing this, apply the information to developing sound management principles. For example, the average residence time of water in rivers is about 2 weeks compared to thousands of years for some groundwater. Thus, strategies to treat a one-time pollution event of oil spilled in a river will be much different than removing oil floating on groundwater that resulted from a rupture of an underground pipeline. The oil in the river is a relatively accessible, straightforward, short-term problem with which to deal, whereas polluted groundwater is a more difficult problem that may take many years to remediate or solve.

Earth Systems Science

This is an emerging field of study that attempts to understand the entire planet Earth as a system in terms of its component systems (see *A Closer Look: The Gaia Hypothesis*). It asks how components such as the atmosphere (air), hydrosphere (water), biosphere (life), and lithosphere (rocks) are linked and have formed, evolved, and been maintained; how these components function; and how they will continue to evolve over periods ranging from a decade to a century and longer (10). The challenge is to learn to predict changes likely to be important to society, and then to develop management strategies to minimize adverse environmental impacts. For example, study of atmospheric chemistry suggests that our atmosphere has changed. Trace gases such as carbon dioxide have increased by about 100 percent since 1850. Chlorofluorocarbons (CFCs) released at the surface have migrated to the stratosphere, where they react with energy from the Sun, causing ozone depletion. The important topics of global change and Earth systems science will be discussed in Chapter 13, following topics such as Earth materials, natural hazards, and energy resources.

Concept Four:
Limitation of Resources

Earth is the only suitable habitat we have, and its resources are limited.

Concept Four includes two fundamental truths: first, that Earth is indeed the only place to live that is now accessible to us; and second, that

our resources are limited, and while some resources are renewable, many are not. To meet future resource demands, we will eventually need large-scale recycling of many materials. Almost everything can theoretically be recycled. The challenge is to find ways to do it that do not harm the environment and are economically viable.

A large part of our solid and liquid waste-disposal problems could be alleviated if these wastes were reused or recycled. In other words, many wastes that are now considered pollutants can be considered resources out of place. Land is also an important resource. Due in part to human population increase that demands more land for urban and agricultural purposes, human-induced change to Earth is increasing at a rapid rate. A recent study of human activity and ability to move soil and rock concluded that human activity (agriculture, urbanization, etc.) moves as much or more soil and rock on an annual basis than any other earth process, including mountain building or river transport of sediment. This, combined with the visual changes to Earth (leveling hills, etc.), suggests that human activity is the most significant process shaping the surface of Earth (12). Land use planning is discussed in Chapter 14.

Concept Five: Uniformitarianism

The physical processes that are modifying our landscape today have operated throughout much of geologic time. However, the magnitude and frequency of these processes are subject to natural and artificially induced change.

Understanding the natural processes that are now forming and modifying our landscapes helps us make inferences about a landscape's geologic

A CLOSER LOOK

The Gaia Hypothesis

In 1785 at a meeting of the prestigious Royal Society of Edinburgh, James Hutton, the "father of geology," said he believed that planet Earth is a super organism. He compared the circulation of Earth's water, with its contained sediments and nutrients, to the circulation of blood in an animal. In Hutton's metaphor, the oceans are the heart of Earth and the forest the lungs (11). Two hundred years later, British scientist and professor James Lovelock introduced the **Gaia hypothesis**, reviving the idea of a living Earth. The hypothesis is named for Gaia, the Greek goddess Mother Earth.

The Gaia hypothesis is best stated as a series of hypotheses:

- Life significantly affects the planetary environment. Very few scientists would disagree with this concept.
- Life affects the environment for the betterment of life. This hypothesis has some support from studies that have shown that life on Earth plays an important role in regulating planetary climate so that it is neither too hot nor too cold for life to survive. For example, it is believed that single-cell plants floating near the surface of the ocean partially control carbon dioxide content of the atmosphere and thereby global climate (11).
- Life deliberately (consciously) controls the global environment. There are very few scientists who accept this third hypothesis. Interactions and linking of processes that operate in the atmosphere, on the surface of Earth, and in the oceans are probably sufficient to explain most of the mechanisms by which life affects the environment. On the other hand, humans are beginning to make decisions concerning the global environment, so the idea that *humans* can consciously influence the future of Earth is not an extreme view. Some people have interpreted this idea as support for the broader Gaia hypothesis.

The real value of the Gaia hypothesis is that it has stimulated a lot of interdisciplinary research to understand how our planet works. As interpreted by most scientists, the hypothesis does not suggest foresight or planning on the part of life but rather that automatic processes of some sort are operating. From a geologic perspective, this means that throughout much of Earth's history, life has affected the physical and chemical systems of Earth, just as these systems affect life.

history. The idea that "the present is the key to the past," called **uniformitarianism**, was first suggested by James Hutton (referred to by some as "the father of geology") in 1785 and is heralded today as a fundamental concept of Earth sciences. As the name suggests, uniformitarianism holds that the processes we observe today also operated in the past.

Uniformitarianism does not demand or even suggest that the magnitude and frequency of natural processes remain constant with time. Furthermore, we now know that the principle cannot be extended back to include all of geologic time: the processes operating in the oxygen-free environment of Earth's first 2 billion years were quite different from those operating today. However, for as long as Earth has had an atmosphere, oceans, and continents similar to those of today, we can infer that the present processes were operating.

In making inferences about geologic events, we must consider the effects of human activity on natural earth processes. For example, rivers flood regardless of human activities, but such activities can greatly increase or decrease the magnitude and frequency of flooding. Therefore, to predict the long-range effects of a natural process, we must be able to determine how our future activities will change its magnitude and rate. In this case, *the present is the key to the future.* For example, when environmental geologists examine recent landslide deposits in an area designated to become a housing development, they must use uniformitarianism to infer where there will be future landslides, as well as to predict what effects urbanization will have on the magnitude and frequency of future landslides.

Concept Six:
Hazardous Earth Processes

There have always been earth processes that are hazardous to people. These natural hazards must be recognized and avoided where possible and their threat to human life and property minimized.

Because the geologic processes we know today were operating long before humans made their appearance, we have always been obligated to contend with processes that make our lives more difficult. Interestingly, we humans apparently are a product of the Pleistocene Ice Ages (last 1.65 million years), a time characterized by rapid climatic changes from relatively cold, harsh glacial conditions as recently as a few thousand years ago, to relatively warm interglacial conditions we enjoy today.

Early in the history of our species, our struggle with natural earth processes was probably a day-to-day experience. However, our numbers were neither great nor concentrated, so losses from hazardous earth processes were not very significant. As people learned to produce and maintain a constant food supply, the population increased and became more concentrated locally. The concentration of population and resources also increased the impact of periodic earthquakes, floods, and other natural disasters. This trend has continued, so that many people today live in areas likely to be damaged by hazardous earth processes or susceptible to the adverse impact of such processes in adjacent areas.

We can recognize many natural processes and predict their effects by considering climatic, biologic, and geologic conditions. After Earth scientists have identified potentially hazardous processes, they have the obligation to make the information available to planners and decision makers, who can then consider ways of avoiding or minimizing the threat to human life or property.

Concept Seven: Geology
as a Basic Environmental Science

The fundamental component of every person's environment is the geologic component, and understanding our environment requires a broad-based comprehension and appreciation of Earth sciences and related disciplines.

All geology can be considered environmental. An understanding of our complex environment requires considerable knowledge of such disciples as **geomorphology**, the study of landforms and surface processes; **mineralogy-petrology**, the study of minerals and rocks; **sedimentology**, the study of environments of deposition of sediments; **tectonics**, the study of processes that produce continents, ocean basins, mountains, and other large structural features; **hydrogeology**, the study of surface and subsurface water; **pedology**, the study of soils; **economic geology**, the application of geology to locating and evaluating mineral materials; and **engineering geology**, the application of geologic information to engineering problems. Beyond this, the serious Earth scientist should also be aware of the contributions to environmental research from such areas as biology, conservation, atmospheric science, chemistry, environmental law, architecture, and engineering, as well as physical, cultural, economic, and urban geography.

Environmental geology, then, is the domain of the generalist with a strong interdisciplinary interest. This in no way denies the significant contributions of specialists in various aspects of environmental studies, or the importance of focusing on specific problems or areas of research. It merely suggests that, although our research interests may be specialized, we should always be aware of other disciplines and their contribution to environmental geology. Also, many projects may be studied best by an interdisciplinary team of scientists.

Summary

The immediate causes of the environmental crisis are overpopulation, urbanization, and industrialization, which have occurred with too little ethical regard for our land and inadequate institutions to cope with environmental stress. Solving environmental problems involves both scientific understanding and the fostering of social, economic, and ethical behavior that allow solutions to be implemented.

Seven fundamental concepts establish a philosophical framework for our investigation of environmental geology:

1. The increasing world population is the number-one environmental problem.
2. Sustainability is the environmental objective.
3. Earth is essentially a closed system with respect to materials, and an understanding of systems and rates of change in systems is critical to solving environmental problems.
4. Earth is the only suitable habitat we have, and its resources are limited.
5. Today's physical processes are modifying our landscape and have operated throughout much of geologic time, but the magnitude and frequency of these processes are subject to natural and artificially induced change.
6. Earth processes that are hazardous to people have always existed. These natural hazards must be recognized and avoided where possible, and their threat to human life and property must be minimized.
7. The fundamental component of every person's environment is the geologic one, and understanding our environment requires an understanding of Earth sciences and related disciplines.

References

1. Barnhardt, W. 1987. The death of Ducktown. *Discover*, October, 35–43.
2. Cloud, P. 1978. *Cosmos, Earth and man.* New Haven: Yale University Press.
3. Ermann, M. 1927. *Desiderata.* Terre Haute, IN.

4. Davidson, J. P., Reed, W. E., and Davis, P. M. 1997. *Exploring Earth*. Upper Saddle River, NJ: Prentice Hall.

5. Leopold, A. 1949. *A Sand County almanac*. New York: Oxford University Press.

6. Moncrief, L. W. 1970. The cultural basis for our environmental crisis. *Science* 170: 508–12.

7. Ellis, W. S. 1990. A Soviet sea lies dying. *National Geographic* 177 (2): 73–92.

8. Brown, L. R., Flavin, C., and Postel, S. 1991. *Saving the planet*. New York: W. W. Norton & Co.

9. National Research Council. 1971. *The Earth and human affairs*. San Francisco: Canfield Press.

10. Earth Systems Science Committee. 1988. *Earth systems science*. Washington, DC: National Aeronautics and Space Administration.

11. Lovelock, J. 1988. *The ages of Gaia*. New York: W. W. Norton & Co.

12. Hooke, LeB. 1994. On the efficiency of humans as geomorphic agents. *GSA Today* 4(9):217, 224–25.

Key Terms

average residence time (p. 213)
Earth systems science (p. 214)
environmental crisis (p. 206)
environmental geology (p. 203)
environmental unity (p. 212)
exponential growth (p. 206)
fossil (p. 208)
Gaia hypothesis (p. 215)
geologic time (p. 208)
geology (p. 203)
hypothesis (p. 204)

input-output analysis (p. 213)
land ethic (p. 205)
law of faunal assemblages (p. 208)
scientific method (p. 204)
sustainability (p. 211)
system (p. 212)
theory (p. 204)
uniformitarianism (p. 215)

Review Questions

1. What is environmental geology? (p. 203)
2. Define the components of the scientific method. (p. 204)
3. What are the roots of the so-called "environmental crisis"? (p. 206)
4. Why are we so concerned about the increase in human population? (pp. 206, 209–211)
5. What is sustainability? (p. 211)
6. Define the principle of environmental unity and provide a good example. (p. 212)
7. What is the difference between an open and closed system? (p. 212)
8. What is exponential growth? (pp. 206, 212-213)
9. What do we mean by average residence time? (p. 213)
10. How can the principle of uniformitarianism be applied to environmental geology? (p. 215)

Critical Thinking Questions

1. Assuming that there is an environmental crisis today, what possible solutions are available to alleviate the crisis? How will solutions in developing countries differ

from those in highly industrialized societies? Will the role of religion or a political system have a bearing on potential solutions? If so, how?

2. It has been argued that we must control human population because otherwise we won't be able to feed everyone. Assuming that we could feed 10 to 15 billion people on Earth, would we still want to have a smaller population than that? Why?

3. We state that sustainability is the environmental objective. Construct an argument to support this statement. Is the idea of sustainability and building a sustainable

economy different in developing, poor countries from those countries that are affluent, with a high standard of living? How and why?

4. The concept of environmental unity is an important one today. Consider some major development being planned for your region and outline how the principle of environmental unity could help in determining potential environmental impact. In other words, consider a development and then a series of resulting consequences. In your estimation, which of the impacts may be positive or negative?

VOCABULARY LESSON

The purpose of this vocabulary lesson is to help you review and deepen your knowledge of the ten general vocabulary words you worked with at the beginning of this chapter.

A. Structural Analysis—Affixes and Root Words
    1. Identify the root (or base) word by underlining it: Sustainability
    2. Circle the suffix of the following word: Replenished
B. Use of Context: Read the following sentence in which the word *degradation* is used and in your own words write a definition for it below: "Specifically, it is the use of geologic information to help us solve conflicts in land use, to minimize environmental *degradation*, and to maximize the beneficial results of using our natural and modified environments." (page 203)

    _____

C. Synonyms and Antonyms: List one synonym (same meaning) and one antonym (opposite meaning) for each of the following words:

Word	Synonym	Antonym
Devastate		
Adverse		
Finite		

D. Generate Your Own Language
    1. Which friends or family members show the most *resilience* in their lives? Why would you say so?
    2. What *viable* options do you have for surviving this quarter or semester and making good grades?
    3. Who do you know who has a *propensity* for making delicious pasta? For what do you have a *propensity*?
E. Word Confusion
    1. Do not confuse *adverse* with *averse*. The dictionary definition for *averse* is "disposed against." Review the dictionary definition for *adverse* and then write a sentence below that shows you know the two words.

    _____

    2. *Sustain* has five definitions listed in your vocabulary words. It is the root word of *sustainability*. Look at the two textbook definitions of *sustainability* on page 211 and see if you can match them with one of those for *sustain*. You do not have to write an answer.
F. Textbook Preview: The following words that appear in this chapter will be some of your vocabulary words for Part II of this textbook. How well

do you already know them? Which ones do you use in your written and oral language?

1. Tentatively
2. Paramount
3. Diversity
4. Complex
5. Emerge
6. Essentially
7. Principle
8. Speculate
9. Urban

VOCABULARY EXTENSION

The purpose of this vocabulary exercise is to help you see to what degree you know the ten general vocabulary words in this chapter. Matching a word with its definition is the beginning of knowing a word. Using the word in your speaking and writing is full knowledge. See if you have increased your vocabulary by following the directions below:

A. List the vocabulary words from this lesson that you can now use in both your speaking and writing.
B. List the vocabulary words from this lesson that you can now use in writing but are still not comfortable using in speaking.
C. List the vocabulary words from this lesson that you cannot use yet but will recognize in reading.
D. List general vocabulary words from this lesson that are still difficult to understand.
E. Use *five* vocabulary words from this lesson in a five-sentence paragraph on the topic of this lesson.
F. Illustrate the meaning of *one* of the vocabulary words from this lesson through some form of artwork or a cartoon. (This exercise is for right-brain students who enjoy drawing better than writing!)

EXTENDED READING ACTIVITIES

The purpose of this section is to give you a variety of options for independent study or investigation of the chapter topic. Reading is a skill that must be practiced each day if progress is to take place. These activities are designed to give you a variety of reading experiences through which you can improve your general vocabulary and increase your higher-level comprehension skills.

Your instructor may wish to (a) assign one or more activities to the class as a whole, (b) assign various activities to small groups, (c) assign one or more activities to individual students, or (d) let students choose to do the activities or not.

A. Weekly Reading Report: Begin or continue keeping a Weekly Reading Report. Use the form in Appendix C if you wish.

B. Attend a Reading Lab on Campus: Begin or continue attending a reading lab.

C. Read a non-fiction book.
    1. Rachel Carson, *Silent Spring*
    2. Lee R. Kump, James F. Kasting, Robert G. Crane, *The Earth System*
    3. Kristiina A. Vogt (ed.), *Ecosystems: Balancing Science with Management*
    4. Roger Rosenlatt (ed.), *Consuming Desires: Consumption, Culture, and the Pursuit of Happiness*
    5. Roger Gottlieb, *The Sacred Earth: Religion, Nature, Environment*

D. Read with/to your children: These three books can be read to pre-school children or read with first to third graders.
    1. Gerald McDermott, *Papagayo*
    2. C. Vance Cast, *Pollution: Where Does It Come From?* (a Clever Calvin book)
    3. Dr. Seuss, *The Lorax*

E. Reading/Writing Connection: Use one of the following topics for an entry in your college experience journal.
    1. United States' political parties usually claim concern about the environment. Choose an environmental concern that at least the major political parties claim concern for and then show what they consider the causes and the solutions. How do they differ? How are they alike?
    2. Is the earth approaching critical environmental thresholds that may be irreversible? Research this topic and then take a stand and defend it.
    3. Choose one of the chapter critical thinking questions and respond to it.
    4. Become an observer. Keep a journal of your daily or weekly observations about the environment. Narrow the topic to your own interest; for example, you may be most interested in natural hazards. Later see if you can make long-term predictions based on what you have personally observed. You may also want to keep a scrapbook or computer file of information you have found on the topic.

F. Use the Internet.
    1. Look up <http://pbs.org/earthonedge> and<www.millennium assessment.org> for information on "Bill Moyers Reports Earth on Edge" which was shown on PBS in June 2001. Topics of interest that relate to this environmental geology chapter include: (a) agricultural ecosystems, (b) freshwater ecosystems, and (c) forest ecosystems.

You may also wish to look up those topics as each has several sites listed. "Earth on Edge" also has resources, including web sites, environmental information sites, environmental news sources, books and periodicals, and environmental organizations.

2. Pbs.org/frontline's "Fooling with Nature," "What's Up with the Weather?" and "To the Last Fish" also may relate to topics of interest to you.

3. The site <http://earthtrends.wri.org> is an on-line environmental information database you may find useful.

4. Chapter words that might lead to interesting material include *deforestation, environmental degradation, hydrologic processes,* and *geologic processes*. Each has several sites listed. If you are interested in population growth, try <pbs.org/kqed/population_bomb>, <irs.aber.ac.uk>, and/or <pbs.org/sixbillion>. For natural disasters try <pbs.org/wgbh/amex> or <pbs.org/wnet/savageearth/ earthquakes> and <pbs.org/wnet/savageearth/volcanoes>. For water issues, try <pbs.org/cadillacdesert>. Another site of interest is pbs.org/weta/planet.

5. Research the organizations involved in working on environmental issues. See the list provided at the web site <http://pbs.org/ earthonedge> or use other sources. Investigate and join an organization if you wish. A few of the organizations listed at this web site that are the largest and that seem to be related to textbook information are Environmental Defense, Sierra Club, Wilderness Society, and World Wildlife Fund.

6. Scientists mentioned include Preston Cloud, page 207, Garrett Harden, a human ecologist, page 206, and James Hutton, father of geology, page 215. Find out more about them.

G. Vocabulary Journal: Begin keeping or continue keeping a Vocabulary Journal. Use the form in Appendix C if you wish.

H. Magazine/Journal/Newspaper Reading: Begin or continue reading magazines, journals, and newspapers on topics you are reading about in class. Find articles on environmental issues. Use the form in Appendix C if you wish. You may also want to continue reading journals in your major. That form is also in Appendix C if you wish to use it.

REFLECTION

MIND REVOLUTION

The Mind Revolution grew out of my awareness that too many times students do not incorporate what they learn in class into their personal lives. Learning remains compartmentalized and some times wasted. This is an attempt to get you to see how the chapter information can be personally important. Hopefully, you will encounter a new idea in each chapter that you can incorporate into your own life, or at least have something new to think about as you go about your daily routine. Life should never be boring!

Environmental problems beyond our control may be affecting our everyday quality of life. According to some of the experts on "Earth on Edge," we may have thirty years to turn things around. According to our textbook chapter, human population must be reduced. Can we afford not to be interested in environmental concerns or not to try to understand the complexity and interrelatedness of environmental issues?

VOCABULARY

Specialized vocabulary is the most important vocabulary issue in this chapter. Review the number of specialized words in the Prior Knowledge section of the chapter. How many were familiar to you before you read the chapter? Did any that you did not know interfere with your comprehension of chapter material? How many do you now know that are new?

COMPREHENSION

Life would be easier if we could reduce everything down to a simple formula or two-step process. How many magazine articles have you read that contain ten steps to happiness, weight reduction, material success, or enlightenment? Do they ever work? This chapter is a good example of how we must embrace the complexity of our lives, the interconnectedness among ecosystems, humans and other forms of life, and our joint responsibility for trying to care for the earth and each other. It would be great if picking up and recycling aluminum cans would take care of the environment, but it is not enough. We need complicated solutions to a complicated problem, so we cannot afford to be ignorant or simple-minded. The complexity of the problem of dealing with our environment is reflected in the number of disciplines involved in trying to reach solutions. In the textbook chapter, concept seven emphasizes an interdisciplinary approach. Review this section and think about the amount of knowledge about the environment contained in the disciplines, much more than one popular magazine article's worth.

Comprehending this chapter is a challenge because understanding on a literal level is not enough. We might memorize the list of terms at the end of the chapter and successfully match them with definitions on an objective test, but that would not mean that we understood the significance of what we had read. We must combine the pieces of information and make sense of them. We must understand how things work together. One such piece of information is understanding the processes taking place on earth and the time spans involved. In our media world of sound bytes, M-TV, and advertisement banners on our computers, in our world of multiple flashing images, we must pause to contemplate what billions of years means, what time is involved in processes that take millions of years to occur or become evident. We might wonder if we are capable of focusing long and deep enough to begin to understand our world. Your textbook chapter defines geology as "the science of processes related to the composition, structure, and history of Earth and its life." How do you understand *processes*?

Part II

Introduction

ORGANIZATIONAL PATTERN FOR PART II

The same organizational pattern as found in Part I is used in Part II. Vocabulary and metacognitive vocabulary exercises begin each chapter and are followed by pre-reading instructions with prior knowledge information and academic study skills exercises as part of the pre-reading. Next comes the second part of the three-part reading plan, either Reciprocal Teaching or Active Questioning with some model teacher-made questions or responses. Alternative reading plans for each chapter are in Appendix B. Post-reading activities follow the Reciprocal Teaching/Active Questioning lesson. The featured "textbook chapter" follows the three-part reading plan. The last two vocabulary exercises, Vocabulary Lesson and Vocabulary Extension, are placed after the featured "textbook chapter." Two sections for extending interest in the chapter topics, the Extended Reading Activities and Reflection, are placed at the end of the chapter.

VOCABULARY

Metacognitive vocabulary exercises at the beginning of each chapter help readers know when they know and when they do not know a word. This exercise is part of the help provided students so that they can see what they need to learn. By monitoring their own thought processes, they improve their reading and become successful in the academic environment.

In Part I students were asked to choose three vocabulary words and write sentences with them in the beginning vocabulary exercises. In Part II they are asked to choose five words. Hopefully, by working on vocabulary in the first four chapters of Part I, including previewing many of the Part II words and by doing the outside vocabulary exercises and reading suggested in the Extended Reading Activities, they will be able to recognize five words and to write sentences using them.

COMPREHENSION

The featured "textbook chapters" in this part of the book are all original and specifically written for this book by J. L. Dillard, Ph.D. Dr. Dillard has written "textbook chapters" on a variety of subjects that readers will encounter in higher education, chapters that are written on the college level. It is important that the featured chapters in this book represent college-level work because many students in a reading course or lab are taking college-level courses at the same time and must be able to cope with all course reading or possibly fail. The lessons based on these chapters will help the readers cope with difficult reading. As seen in Part I, difficulty comes from vocabulary, writing style, patterns of organization, density of concepts, required background knowledge and experience of a subject, and interest.

Part I contained reproduced content-area chapters that were quite long. Obviously, a reading textbook could end up being twice as long as any content-area text if the whole reading textbook contained such chapters. Part II contains shorter chapters on a variety of subjects but the writing presents all the problems seen in Part I. Short does not mean simple in Part II. Hopefully, by working with a reading plan that attacks those problems, students will continue to improve their reading of difficult material.

STUDY SKILLS

One of the biggest differences in the two parts of this book is the approach to using study skills. In Part I, using the textbook study aids was emphasized, and all the textbook aids provided in those four chapters were used. In Part II each new chapter not only introduces a new study skill but also integrates it into the three-part lesson. One of the big concerns for years in developmental reading has been the transfer of skills. Will a study skill taught in isolation transfer to other chapters and courses? In an effort to receive a positive response to that question, I am providing guided practice in the use of these skills with specific content-area reading. I have also provided follow-up guided practice for later chapters once a skill is introduced. These lessons are in Appendix D.

The study skills introduced in Part II help improve (a) comprehension monitoring strategies, or metacognitive strategies, through SQ4R and its modified version, (b) the management of internal factors such as memory, (c) various levels of textbook strategies such as the complex rehearsal strategies of underlining and highlighting and the complex elaboration strategy of notetaking from textbooks through annotation, (d) effective notetaking methods for lectures, and the complex organizational strategies of outlining and mapping (visuals). Many of these study skills appear simple on the surface but require much of the reader; for example, many depend on the reader's ability to find the main ideas and separate them from supporting details.

The study skills can be used in a variety of ways, according to the student's needs. If, for example, SQ4R works well and aids comprehension, then the remaining chapters can be used for practice in this skill by following the lessons in Appendix D. If the study plan is too time consuming, then the introductory part of the chapter may be all students wish to do. Continuing to use the skills in later chapters could be by assignment or by choice. Students may also choose not to do the study skills sections of the chapters.

INTRODUCTION TO PART II "TEXTBOOK CHAPTERS"

In Chapter 5, the featured chapter "The Study of Our Own Language" was written for me when I became aware that many of my first-generation students were too self-conscious about what they termed "bad" speech. Sometimes this resulted in their not feeling free to talk or enter discussions in my classes or, along with other problems, in their dropping out. I was fully aware that they will have to use Standard English to compete in the job market, but I needed a way to help them through a transition period. The basic message in this chapter is that the students should keep their nonstandard language, if that is what they have grown up speaking, but learn where to use it. While not being ashamed of their first language and using it where it is appropriate, they acquire a second language, Standard English. (After all, we do not ask our international students to give up their first language in order to learn English.) Sometimes, in our enthusiasm to help our students, teachers forget what they are asking of a student when they insist on Standard English only. In my area, using only Standard English could cause a student to lose family and culture. I find it best not to ask students to give up anything, but to add to what they bring to the classroom. I am reminded of the time I went off to college and after a few months returned home and visited a favorite aunt. At the end of the visit, in her special Savannah, Georgia accent, she said that I was the same as I had always been. From her that was as high a compliment as I could wish for that day, and we remained close friends until her death at almost ninety-six. I did not want to lose her respect and at the same time I knew I needed to grow and change, so I continued to communicate in both worlds. Many of my students are also experiencing these feelings and changes.

In Chapter 6, "Travel and Language" shows the author's problems in foreign countries when he did not know the cultural assumptions he should. He knew the languages, but that was not enough. I especially love talking about the Kola Nut ceremony when I teach this chapter. This is the most informal featured chapter in the book and is based on true experiences. My secret wish for my students is that after reading this chapter they will accept their *faux pas* with grace. Chapter 3 provides background knowledge for this chapter.

In Chapter 7, "Some Problems with Columbus's 'Discovery' of America" presents a more complicated picture of the discovery of America than some students may have. It also shows issues probably new to students, such as the importance of primary sources in research. For students who grew up with perfect pictures of heroes, the picture of Columbus as one with faults will be different. The chapter grew out of a great deal of research by the author during the 1992 celebration.

In Chapter 8, "Two Views of the Study of Society and Culture" presents two different approaches, that of anthropology and sociology, to the study of different societies and cultures. Field work on the part of graduate students, the use of informants for insights into other cultures, and generally, what a researcher does when studying another society or culture may all present new reading experiences. Chapters 2 and 3 provide background knowledge for this chapter.

In Chapter 9, "The Fiction of Chinua Achebe" presents an overview of the author's works and shows the connections among the main novels. The novels present culture clash and the toll it takes on the people involved. The novels present complicated characters; no one is totally good or bad. The reader is left with questions about the good of imposing one culture on another.

In Chapter 10, "The Blues" gives a historical look at this type of music and will probably be new information for the reader. Hopefully, after reading the selection, a reader will be able to see the influence of the blues on other types of music. When I lived in Louisiana, traditional blues was still played in clubs like Tabby's Blues Box in Baton Rouge.

In Chapter 11, "American English: Does It Have a History?" presents an overview of the development of American English. For those instructors who took a graduate course in the history of English that stopped with language development in the early modern period, this chapter may present a different approach. Yes, there is a history, an interesting one. The author has written a book on the subject. Contact language theory is alive and well!

In Chapter 12, "Sociolinguistics and the Crucifixion Narrative" is an example of how to use text to help substantiate a theory. Many students will have no prior knowledge or experience with such an idea. In an age of computer research, primary research tools are often neglected. Introducing such research techniques will plant the idea that such approaches exist. In a way, this chapter circles back to differences in language use in Chapter 5. Instead of informal or non-Standard English, we treat the vernacular differently in this chapter.

In Chapter 13, "Ethnicity and the National Pastime," written out of a lifetime love of baseball, presents the sport as a way for new minorities to enter mainstream society. The author shows parallels in immigration patterns and baseball. This chapter is also used for a different reading plan, one that provides an opportunity for independence in the reading process.

METHOD

The method used in Part II is the same as in Part I. The plan is to move readers from teacher dependency to independence. Guided practice is used throughout the chapters and teacher-made models are given in the Reciprocal Teaching and Active Questioning sections. If students do not need the models, the alternative plans, found in Appendix B, may be used.

Linguistics:
The Study of Your Own Language

Reflection
    Mind Revolution
    Vocabulary
    Comprehension

VOCABULARY/METACOGNITION

The purpose of this exercise is to help you become aware of when you know the meaning of a word and to help you know when you do not know the meaning of a word. This is metacognition awareness.

    On a scale of 1–5 (see below), rate your knowledge of the following vocabulary words from "The Study of Your Own Language." After matching words with definitions on page 231, check your answers and then check your number *ones* and *fives* below. Did you know when you really knew a word and when you really did not know the word?

Scale

1. I absolutely do not know.
2. I do not think I know.
3. There's a 50/50 chance I have seen or heard it.
4. I think I know it.
5. I know the word and can use it.

Words

_____ 1. Revoke (irrevocably)
_____ 2. Exemplary
_____ 3. Inculcate (inculcated)
_____ 4. Principle (principles)
_____ 5. Essential (essentially)
_____ 6. Formal
_____ 7. Repertory
_____ 8. Detests
_____ 9. Err (unerringly)
_____10. Analogy (analogous)

Go to page 231. See if you can match the right definition with the word and then write sentences for any five words in the list.

Words	Definitions
_____ 1. Revoke (irrevocably)	A. A fundamental truth or doctrine on which others are based
_____ 2. Exemplary	B. Annul by taking back; repeat; cancel
_____ 3. Inculcate (inculcated)	C. An inventory, a stock
_____ 4. Principle (principles)	D. Serving as a model or example
_____ 5. Essential (essentially)	E. Dislike intensely; abhor
_____ 6. Formal	F. Similarity or agreement between one thing and another; resemblance; comparison
_____ 7. Repertory	G. Impress on the mind, as by admonition
_____ 8. Detest (detests)	H. Absolutely necessary; indispensable
_____ 9. Err (unerringly)	I. Go astray; be mistaken; blunder
_____ 10. Analogy (analogous)	J. Adhering to established form or mode; conventional

Write five words from the list and your own sentences that show you know how to use the words. Choose words that you marked a *five* if possible.

1. Word _____

   Sentence _____

2. Word _____

   Sentence _____

3. Word _____

   Sentence _____

4. Word _____

   Sentence _____

5. Word _____

   Sentence _____

PRE-READING THE TEXTBOOK CHAPTER

The purpose of this *first* of three steps in your reading plan is to suggest things to do *before* you read. First, as part of your pre-reading, skim the Prior Knowledge section beginning on page 232. When you finish, return to this page and continue your pre-reading.

TAPPING PRIOR KNOWLEDGE

Tap your experience and prior knowledge about the title of this selection by writing words and phrases that come to your mind. You are pulling up your file on the topic and focusing on what you will read. What do you already know about the subject? Do not look at your textbook at this time, as these answers will vary from person to person and won't be found in the textbook. There are no wrong answers for this part of the lesson.

PREDICTING

Predict in one sentence what you will read. Try to predict in some detail. Don't write, "I predict that I will read about the study of English." What behavior, action, and/or information do you expect to read about? Predicting helps you identify your expectations of what you will read. Not reading what you have predicted will serve as a warning that you have misjudged the topic of the article and will help you adapt to what is in the chapter.

OVERVIEWING

Overview the chapter by following the Survey section of the SQ4R plan in the Academic Study Skills section on page 235. During the second part of the Reciprocal Teaching Reading Plan, you will work with the rest of SQ4R.

PRIOR KNOWLEDGE

This section, part of your pre-reading, presents a model to show you what will help you comprehend this chapter by using your own background knowledge. If you know much of the information listed below, you have a better background for reading this chapter. This section will suggest helpful kinds of background information and help you activate what you know; do not try to look up or learn everything listed. Ask yourself what you need to know before you read and what you already know that will help you to understand this chapter. Your instructor may want to use this section for a whole-class or small group discussion or have you read it silently.

CHAPTER SECTIONS

I. Differences about Language in the Academic World
    A. Vocabulary (general and specialized, multiple meanings, denotation and connotation, and figurative language)
        1. Paragraph One
            a. Irrevocably (use affixes) [general vocabulary]
            b. Monolingual (use affixes) [specialized vocabulary]
        2. Paragraph Two
            a. Linguistics [s.v.]
            b. Naturalist hypothesis (definition in context) [s.v.]
            c. Exemplary [g.v.]
            d. Discipline (m.m.)
            e. Explicating
        3. Paragraph Three
            a. Proficiency [g.v.]

        b.   Methodology [s.v.]

        c.   Inculcated [g.v.]

  B. Recognition of Writing Patterns or Arrangement of Ideas and Devices

      1. Introduction

      2. General-to-specific pattern

      3. Contrast pattern

      4. Use of mechanical devices for special effect/meaning

  C. Concepts and Background Knowledge and Experience

      1. People discuss and often disagree about language.

      2. There is more than one way to talk about language.

      3. The public school system is not necessarily the final authority on language (requires the critical ability to question authority).

      4. It is possible to talk about language in more ways than by the terms "good" and "bad."

II. A Simple Illustration of the Differences

  A. Vocabulary

      1. (Latin) prose [s.v.]

      2. Syntax [s.v.]

      3. Derivations (multiple meanings) [s.v.]

      4. Puristic

      5. Pedantry (pedantic) (use affixes) [g.v.]

      6. Locution [s.v.]

  B. Recognition of Writing Patterns or Arrangement of Ideas and Devices

      1. Complex illustration

  C. Concepts

      1. Traditional grammar vs. other systems

      2. Problems with traditional grammatical rules/usage

      3. Ability to see problems (grammatical rules)

      4. Much English grammar based on Latin rules

      5. You can compare English language structure to languages other than Latin

  D. Background Knowledge

      1. Grammar

         a.   Identification of parts of speech

         b.   Traditional grammatical rules for prepositions

      2. Latin grammatical rules/Turkish

      3. Ability to play with language/operate above the literal level of comprehension

      4. High level of language knowledge in order to see why Churchill's quote is funny ("sophisticated humor")

III. A Third View: Sociolinguistics

  A. Vocabulary

      1. Sociolinguistics [s.v.]

 2. Internalize [g.v.]
 3. Latinate [s.v.]
 4. Greekified [s.v.]
 5. Repertory (multiple meanings) [s.v.]
 6. Detests [g.v.]
 7. Empirical [s.v.]
 8. Unerringly (use affixes) [g.v.]
 9. Decried [g.v.]
 10. Error analysis [s.v.]
 11. Homey [g.v.]
 12. Vast [g.v.]
 13. Analogous [g.v.]
B. Recognition of Writing Patterns or Arrangement of Ideas and Devices
 1. Illustration (continued)
C. Concepts
 1. *Formal/informal* used as terms to describe language
IV. Chapter Summary
A. Vocabulary
 1. Manifestation
B. Pattern
 1. Contrast
V. Chapter Questions
A. Pattern
 1. Question and Answer
B. Concepts
 1. Inferential and critical/creative levels of comprehension

ACADEMIC STUDY SKILLS

DIRECTIONS FOR SQ4R

In the pre-reading section of the Reciprocal Teaching lesson and the Active Questioning lesson, you have an opportunity to overview the featured chapter by reading the summary and questions first and then briefly looking at the titles of the major headings. In both lessons you work with one section of the chapter at a time, thus breaking up the lesson into manageable parts. In both lessons you ask your own questions and answer them, and in the Reciprocal Teaching lesson you summarize the main ideas. All of these methods are important to various study plans, such as the one you will now learn, SQ4R. In following this study plan, you survey, question, read, record information, recite information, and review. Follow the directions for "Survey" (page 235) as part of your pre-reading. Follow the directions for "Reading" (page 235) as part of your reading and "Post-Reading" (page 236) as part of your post-reading.

A. Pre-Reading
1. Survey
a. Read the title of this chapter and write it below.
b. Read the first paragraph of the chapter and list the two points of view about the study of your own language.

_____

_____

_____

c. List the major headings of this chapter.

_____

_____

_____

d. Read the author's questions at the end of the chapter.

B. Reading
1. Question
a. Read the questions you have already written and answered for the lesson you completed for this selection. Add new ones you now find significant.

_____

_____

_____

2. Read
a. Reread each section, one at a time, and then read the questions you wrote and answered for each section. Can you now think of better answers to your old questions? Answer the new questions you wrote in number one above.

_____

_____

_____

3. Record
a. Record any relevant information that will help you to remember the main ideas of this chapter. Then answer the questions that follow.
(1) Have you recorded all important ideas? Where and how did you record them? You may want to underline in the chapter, write notes in the margins, use flashcards, and/or create visual maps.
(2) Do you have sufficient examples?
(3) Are definitions in context marked or noted in some way?
(4) Do you know how all of these pieces of information connect?

    C. Post-Reading
       1. Recite
          a. With a partner, recite relevant information, especially the ideas in the Reciprocal Teaching lesson.
       2. Review: Review important information with your partner. Read the author's summary and questions. Ask each other the questions you wrote. Talk through important ideas. Discuss why the material is important.

RECIPROCAL TEACHING

OVERVIEW

Your first step of the three-part reading plan was pre-reading. In pre-reading, you activated your prior knowledge, predicted what you would read, and overviewed the chapter before reading.

As the second step in this three-part reading plan, you will read the chapter "The Study of Your Own Language" by using the Reciprocal Teaching reading plan as explained below. An alternative plan, Active Questioning, is in Appendix B. In both plans you break up the chapter in sections and read and think about each as you read. The purpose of both plans is to keep you reading actively.

GENERAL DIRECTIONS

The concept of Reciprocal Teaching outlined here is adapted from Palinscar and Brown, 1986.

    A. Both partners read a section under a subheading at a time. Take turns summarizing the section in as few sentences as possible. In summaries, give the main ideas; do not give your opinion.
    B. Take turns asking a high level question or two on each section (inferential or critical/creative).
    C. Explain or clarify difficult parts to each other. Practice repeating main ideas and supporting details in your own words.
    D. Read the next subheading and predict what the section will be about. Discuss (exchange) ideas.

ASSIGNMENT

You practiced using two versions of the Reciprocal Teaching reading plan in Chapter 1 and Chapter 3 in Part I of this textbook. Both versions provided teacher-made models and opportunities for guided practice. The following version of the Reciprocal Teaching reading plan also provides models and guided practice. Especially note the inclusion of leading questions that help you find the main ideas for your summaries. You may substitute the second version from Part I for this lesson if you wish. In the second version the steps are predict, question, clarify, and summarize.

A. Read the first section, "Differences about Language in the Academic World" and follow the directions below.

   1. Summarize the first section in your own words: Leading questions: Paragraph One: When you enter the English classroom, what will you be told? Paragraph Two: When you enter the linguistics classroom, what will you be told? Paragraph Three: What is the split among academics? Model summary: "Many students in English classes will find that they are expected to learn new strategies and usages in order to communicate whereas students in linguistics will learn that all physically normal people are quite proficient. Therefore, there is a real split in point of view about language in the academic world." What can you add to, delete from, or change about this summary?

Your summary _____

_____

_____

   2. Write one high-level question on this section and then answer your own question. Model question: What are the differences of opinion about language in the academic world? Answer: Traditionalists feel that language is corrupt whereas linguists do not.

Your question _____

Your answer _____

   3. Identify one difficult idea from this section and then orally explain or clarify it in your own words to your partner. Model idea: Natural hypothesis. Even though this term is defined in context, it is still a difficult concept to understand if the reader has no background knowledge.

Your idea _____

   4. Predict in one sentence what you will read in the next section, "A Simple Illustration of the Differences." Model prediction: The author will give examples of the differences in point of view about language.

Your prediction _____

B. Read "A Simple Illustration of the Differences."

   1. Summarize the section in your own words. Leading question: What is the importance of rules governing prepositions to the study of our language? Model summary: "Through the illustration of rules governing the use of prepositions in English and the use of prepositions and postpositions in other languages, one can see that a more flexible (tolerant, open-minded) approach has to be taken in the study of language." What can you add, delete, change?

Your summary _____

_____

_____

2. Write one high-level question on this section and then answer your own question. Model question: Why is Churchill's objection to a correction of usage humorous? ["up with which I will not put"]

Your question _____

Your answer _____

3. Identify one difficult idea from this section and then orally explain or clarify it in your own words to your partner. Model idea: The use of prepositions and how in traditional English classes you are taught that you may not end a sentence with one.

Your idea _____

4. Predict in one sentence what you believe you will read about in the third section, "A Third View: Sociolinguistics." Model prediction: The author will show how sociolinguists view language.

Your prediction _____

C. Read "A Third View: Sociolinguistics."

1. Summarize the section in your own words. Model summary: One way sociolinguists describe language is in terms of formal and informal. A child's informal speech is complex, not crude or simple. Both naturalist linguists and academically oriented teachers have a place in the classroom because all need both formal and informal language. We should not be ashamed of our language, but at the same time, we should take advantage of learning all we can about language. Don't be limited by knowing only your own language. Enjoy both worlds. What can you add, delete, change?

Your summary _____

_____

_____

2. Write a high-level question on this section and then answer your own question. Model question: In your own language, when do you use formal English and informal English? Has anyone ever "corrected" your language [written or oral]? How did you feel?

Your question _____

Your answer _____

3. Identify one difficult idea from this section and then orally explain or clarify it in your own words to your partner. Model idea: *Correct* and *incorrect* are inappropriate terms to use in discussing language.

Your idea _____

Now that you have completed the second part of the Reciprocal Teaching reading plan, return to the SQ4R plan in the Academic Study Skills section and complete the Question, Read, and Record steps under "Reading" (page 235). When you finish these steps in the SQ4R plan, complete the three-part reading plan by doing the post-reading activities on page 239.

POST-READING THE TEXTBOOK CHAPTER

OVERVIEW

In the second part of your three-part reading plan, you practiced reading a textbook chapter section by section, wrote section summaries, asked and answered questions, explained or clarified important ideas, and made predictions for what you read in the next section. You also used the first four steps of the SQ4R study plan as part of your pre-reading and reading activities. Now complete SQ4R by doing the Recite and Review steps under "Post-Reading" on page 236.

ASSIGNMENT

In the third part of the three-part reading plan, you will find suggestions for what to do after you read. Your task is to compare what you predicted with what you actually read as an aid to comprehension, to add what you have learned to your file of information on the topic, and to think about what you have read.

A. Look at your prediction of what you would read in the Pre-Reading section of this lesson. What did you correctly predict that you would read?

B. What did you learn from the reading that you did not know about before working on this lesson?

C. Look at the words and phrases that you listed as your prior knowledge on page 231. Group them in the table at the bottom of the page with relevant information from "B" above. This is your new file of information on linguistics. (The ability to group ideas and to see relationships requires more complex comprehension than merely memorizing isolated facts.)

D. What have you learned from this chapter that is important?

E. What do you already know that you can relate to it?

F. What do you see differently as a result of reading this chapter?

Learning/Feelings/ Experience	Words and Phrases from Pre-Reading	Relevant Information from "B"

THE STUDY OF YOUR OWN LANGUAGE

Differences about Language in the Academic World

It is established, probably irrevocably, that almost all students in American educational institutions will study "English." Most of them speak that language, or some variety of it, as a native language; and very many, like Hispanics or recent immigrants from Asia, have spoken it from childhood and manage it with native-speaker fluency. Yet even monolingual speakers of American English will probably be told, if they enter college classes, that they must learn many new strategies and usages in order to read, write, and in general communicate effectively in their own language.

The few who enter upper division undergraduate or graduate courses in the relatively new and still little-known discipline of linguistics will hear a different story. The prevailing theory in that field is what is called a naturalist hypothesis, which says that mastery of the complexities of a language is a species-specific trait; that is, that every physiologically normal member of the species *homo sapiens* manages a language with exemplary skill. In fact, the entire discipline of linguistics is given over to the explicating of just how the normal human being manages to do all the things he does with his language, and no one in the field considers the task anything like completely done.

The student who bothers to look into the matter extensively will find, then, that there is a real split among academics as to what he does and what he should do with his native language or with the one which he manages with a high degree of proficiency. Better known popularly, represented in newspaper columns aggressively commanding one to "Get It Right!" is the viewpoint that ordinary, everyday language is somehow corrupt and greatly in need of correction. Despite some modifications in the later 1960s, when National Defense Institute seminars inculcated some of the principles of linguistics into classroom teachers, the public school system generally sponsors this point of view. On the other side are the professionals of language study, who tend to hold that "corruption"—at least, in a non-technical sense—is meaningless when applied to the language of a native speaker. An army of teachers of English as a Second Language, now spread over most parts of the world, utilizes a methodology based upon this second point of view. These teachers hold that to teach a nonspeaker of English to use even "mistakes" (like *ain't*) naturally is a major accomplishment. But the student who stays at home in the United States and has to fulfill his school's requirements in English still has to cope with teachers and professors who are dedicated essentially to the first viewpoint.

A Simple Illustration of the Differences

Perhaps the difference in viewpoint can be illustrated from the use of a troublesome class of little words like

in, on, out, about, of, from, by, to, over, under, with, without, against, like, at, around, beside, upon, along …

These are called *prepositions* in school grammars and even in some professional treatments. Based upon the Latin components *pre-* meaning "before" and *posit-* meaning "placed," the proposition has developed that these words must always come before something—specifically a noun.

On that premise, a "preposition" at the end of a sentence constitutes an "error"—as it perhaps would have been in Latin prose. A typical "correction" would be to change

the town I live in,

to

the town in which I live,

which more nearly represents the order in which a Latin prose sentence would have been constructed.

Linguists, on the other hand, have studied other languages besides Latin and the languages influenced by it, especially in the last two centuries. They have studied languages like Turkish in which the typical structure is:

adam	lar	dan
man	plural marker	to

and in which the phrase means, in English, 'to the men.' No one, presumably, would say that Turkish "has it wrong" because its syntax is not identical to that of Latin. If, on the other hand, one is conscious of word derivations, one finds it confusing at best to describe the Turkish words as *prepositions*. In fact, the term *postpositions* is in general use in the field of linguistics.

While English is historically closer to Latin than to Turkish, still mightn't we have developed "postpositions" of our own? There are famous examples of objections to corrections of usage, including the one attributed to Churchill that puristic alteration was pedantry:

up with which I will not put.

Realistically speaking, the most pedantic English teacher would not recommend such an artificial locution, but some will "correct":

which I will not put up with.

A probable compromise would be:

which I will not tolerate

where *tolerate* is more formal, and more academic, than *put up with*. Whether it is more "precise" or more "expressive" is still an arguable point.

A Third View: Sociolinguistics

Here the discipline of sociolinguistics might be permitted to enter the picture. The sociolinguist might point out that while both "prepositions" (which might better be called "postpositions" anyway in certain functions) in compounds with verbs (*put*) and unitary, Latin-derived verbs (*tolerate*) have a respectable function in the English language, their function is not entirely the same. Attitudinal research can be performed to show that there is a kind of correlation between

put up with—less formal

and

tolerate—more nearly formal

and that both are "right"—provided the situation in which they are used is appropriate. It is easily observable that small children, whose ability to internalize the very complex structure of a native language or languages is a subject of wondering inquiry for linguists, tend to use the less formal words and combinations. Older people, in positions of greater responsibility, tend toward the more Latinate (or Greekified) repertory, although that tendency can easily be carried too far.

There is a standard example to show that the child's domain of language use, that called "less formal" above, is not in any sense crude or simple. Take the example of a little boy whose parent always reads to him at bedtime, the boy's bedroom being upstairs. There are two books, one of which the little boy likes and another which he detests, from which the parent is accustomed to read. One night the little boy spots the parent coming upstairs with the wrong book and complains,

> What are you bringing that book that I don't like to be read to out of up for?

Here we have no less than five "pre-" (or "post-") positions at the end of the sentence, yet the boy's objection is perfectly clear. To "correct" it to

> Why are you bringing upstairs that book out of which I do not like for you to read to me?

is not to gain much. (Here the teacher oriented toward correcting everyday usages would be likely to point out that business and technical reports—and English themes—seldom contain complaints from little boys whose parents are bringing up the wrong book.)

From a hard-headed, empirical view, on the other hand, it is impossible to call the sentence unstructured. Look at the five "pre"positions:

to	out	of	up	for
1	2	3	4	5

Now try putting them in different order, say 5 4 3 2 1:

for	up	of	out	to

or

2	1	4	3	5
out	to	up	of	for

In fact, there are about 120 possible orders for these five position-words, and the small boy in the story unerringly chose the one which would work and (at least subconsciously) rejected the other 119. This is a (quite simple) example of what linguists mean when they say that children by the time they are five or six years old are in command of an amazingly complex, completely systematic language structure. Or try:

put	up	with
	1	2

in its only alternative sequence:

put	with	up
	2	1

and you will see why many linguists have decried the use of terms like "error" for the usages which happen to have been associated with a lesser degree of formality.

But the work of the world, the academically oriented teacher might rejoin, is not accomplished by daddies and mommies coming up the stairs with books to read to the kiddies. In the privacy of the home, *put up with* has a striking appropriateness, as does *What ... for?* But few of us can remain at home always. Before hundreds of strangers (perhaps thousands in a public speech or millions on a television program) we would do well to resort to *tolerate* and *Why …?* And, because of the very complexity of language which calls the "error" analysis of the less formal usages into question, few of us are really ready to face a public confrontation with strangers without extensive instruction in how to talk to them.

It would seem, then, that both the "naturalist" linguist and the academically oriented teacher have a place in our educational process. Certainly, we don't want to be limited to language which is appropriate to the home and the family, any more than we would want to limit our wardrobe to the pajamas which the parent may have been wearing when he or she carried the book up to read to the child. We want to be able to speak—and to dress—formally when the occasion demands it. But we don't want to go to the other extreme; we don't want to wear top hat, white tie, and tails upstairs to read the children to sleep. We want to be able to be relaxed and informal in situations in which formality would produce unnecessary tension.

There would seem to be two inescapable conclusions. First, we should never be ashamed of our language—even at its most homey and informal. People who talk to us about our "bad" language show their lack of linguistic sophistication more than anything else. Second, we want to avail ourselves of all the vast resources of the language, or languages, with which we come into contact (or which we come in contact with). We want to be able to wear both night clothes and formal dress (or, at least, business suits) and we want to be in command of the language forms which are analogous to each. And we might be happier with instruction which put its goals in those terms rather than in terms of "correct" or "incorrect" usage.

Summary

Professional linguists and school teachers often differ as to the nature of language, but sociolinguistics can explain the differences. Linguists stress that the physiologically normal member of genus *homo sapiens* has full competence in a language. Schoolteachers stress the need for learning usages appropriate to more formal situations. When they look at both situations, sociolinguists emphasize respect for the great complexity of anyone's language, even in its least formal manifestation, and recognize that special forms are needed for public and more formal occasions.

Questions on Your Own Language

1. Why are knowing English and making a good grade in an English class somewhat different things?

2. Why do linguists not always agree with English teachers on every point?

3. Why should one not condemn any native speaker's use of English?

4. How can the demands of formal public usage be reconciled with respect for less-formal language?

Vocabulary Lesson

The purpose of this vocabulary lesson is to help you review and deepen your knowledge of the ten general vocabulary words you worked with at the beginning of this chapter.

A. Structural Analysis—Affixes and Root Words
  1. Circle the prefixes and underline the suffixes of the words below.
  2. Find the dictionary definition of the root word of each and write it by the word:
     a. Unerringly
     b. Irrevocably
  3. Now look at the prefixes and suffixes of the above words. By using the prefixes, suffixes, and root words, write what you think each word means:
     a. Unerringly
     b. Irrevocably
B. Definition in Paragraph: Find and write the definition of the following phrase as it is defined in the second paragraph of the chapter: *Naturalistic hypothesis*

_____

C. Use of Context: Read the paragraphs in which the following words appear, and in your own words write a definition for each:
     a. Analogous (section 3, last paragraph)
     b. Repertory (section 3, first paragraph)

_____

_____

D. Multiple Meanings of Words: Circle the definition below of the word *formal* as it is used in the study of language
  1. adhering to established form or mode; conventional; ceremonious; precise
  2. not familiar or friendly in manner; stiff
  3. perfunctory
  4. a formal occasion
  5. an evening dress
E. Synonyms and Antonyms: List one synonym (same meaning) and one antonym (opposite meaning) for each of the following words:

Word	Synonym	Antonym
Detests		
Essentially		
Formal		

   F. Generate Your Own Language

1. Name five *essential* items you would need if you were stranded on a desert island.
2. If your behavior were *exemplary,* would you be rewarded or punished?
3. What basic truths have your parents *inculcated* in you?
4. What foods do you *detest?*
5. Describe your own *language.* When do you use *formal* English?

   G. Word Confusion: Write a sentence that shows you know the difference between *principles* and *principals.*

   H. Additional Vocabulary Study Exercise (Optional)

1. Specialized Vocabulary: Write one dictionary definition for each of the following words:
   a. syntax
   b. linguistics
   c. sociolinguistics
   d. (Latin) prose
   e. locution
   f. empirical
   g. error analysis
   h. methodology

VOCABULARY EXTENSION

The purpose of this exercise is to help you see to what degree you know the ten general vocabulary words in this chapter. Matching a word with its definition is the beginning of knowing a word. Using the word in your speaking and writing is full knowledge. See if you have increased your vocabulary by following the directions below:

   A. List the vocabulary words from this lesson that you can now use in both your speaking and writing.

   B. List the vocabulary words from this lesson that you can now use in writing but are still not comfortable using in speaking.

   C. List the vocabulary words from this lesson that you cannot use yet but will recognize in reading.

   D. List general vocabulary words from this lesson that are still difficult to understand.

   E. Use *five* vocabulary words from this lesson in a five-sentence paragraph on the topic of this lesson.

   F. Illustrate the meaning of *one* of the vocabulary words from this lesson through some form of artwork or a cartoon. (This exercise is for right-brain students who enjoy drawing better than writing!)

EXTENDED READING ACTIVITIES

The purpose of this section is to give you a variety of options for independent study or investigation of the chapter topic. Reading is a skill that must be practiced each day if progress is to take place. These activities are designed to give you a variety of reading experiences through which you can improve your general vocabulary and increase your higher-level comprehension skills.

Your instructor may wish to (a) assign one or more activities to the class as a whole, (b) assign various activities to small groups, (c) assign one or more activities to individual students, or (d) let students choose to do the activities or not.

A. Weekly Reading Report: Begin or continue keeping a weekly report of your reading. Record what you read each day for your courses and what you read for fun. Use the form in Appendix C if you wish.

B. Attend a Reading Lab on Campus: If your school has a reading lab, continue or begin to attend it for at least thirty minutes at a time. Work on exercises that are slightly difficult for you. If you make more than seventy percent on a comprehension exercise, go to a higher level. If you make below seventy percent on several exercises, go to a lower level. Work on skills exercises that you know are helping you, not on skills exercises at which you are already proficient.

C. Read a Novel: Find a novel to read, one that you will enjoy. Ask a friend for a suggestion. Choose a skinny paperback, a science fiction, romance, comedy, or fantasy. Two quick reads with a female narrator are Sharon Creech's *Walk Two Moons* and Elizabeth George Speare's *The Witch of Blackbird Pond*. Two quick reads with a male narrator are Ernest Hemingway's *The Old Man and the Sea* and Robert Peck's *A Day No Pigs Would Die*. (*A Day No Pigs Would Die* was also suggested in the Chapter 3 list.) Use the Fiction Report form provided at the end of this chapter to turn in to your instructor.

D. Reading/Writing Connection: Continue keeping a personal journal about your beginning college experience. Observe differences in the use of formal and informal language on your campus and write about your observations. Does the use of either formal or informal English make you comfortable or uncomfortable with the speakers? Does a person's speech influence your choice of a friend? What else is important or unimportant in new friendships on campus? Write your responses in your journal. Use a new vocabulary word in your response.

E. Use the Internet: If you are interested in the use of English and its many forms, search the Internet for additional information. In the continuing argument over the use of standard and nonstandard English, political issues have surfaced. California has been a hot spot in issues like Ebonics and language diversity. English Only movements have also occurred in other places. I found 1,740,095 web sites listed for "language diversity," 3,454,715 for "Standard

English," 2,426,845 for "English Only movement," and 3,090 for "Ebonics." Our historical background as to language preference is also interesting. I found 6,992,750 web sites for "English Language History." See what you can find that is interesting to you.

F. Content Area Report: Try another content area report for another class. Use the form in Appendix C.

REFLECTION

MIND REVOLUTION

The Mind Revolution grew out of my awareness that too many times students do not incorporate what they learn in class into their personal lives. Learning remains compartmentalized and some times wasted. This is an attempt to get you to see how the chapter information can be personally important. Hopefully, you will encounter a new idea in each chapter that you can incorporate into your own life, or at least have something new to think about as you go about your daily routine. Life should never be boring!

You need never give up or be ashamed of your first language if it is non-standard. However, if you want to compete for good jobs, you will probably need to add standard or formal English as a tool.

VOCABULARY

Review the "Vocabulary Extension" for this chapter and see if you are using the words that are most familiar to you. Have you used them in your speech? In your writing? Were you comfortable with them? Review the words that were the most difficult for you. You might want to re-read them in context for help in using them correctly. Choose one of the words to work on and, when you are comfortable, use the word in something you are writing—a paper for a course or an e-mail to a friend. Ask the friend to comment on your use of the word.

COMPREHENSION

Lack of background knowledge and experience in thinking about the study of English probably caused you the most problems in comprehension for this chapter. For example, have you ever questioned the way English is taught? Have you always accepted the use of terms like *good* and *bad* or *proper* and *improper* as descriptive of the way people talk? If your answer to both questions is yes, then you may have had difficulty in accepting the linguist's approach. If part of your judgment of others has been based on their speech, then again, you may have had difficulty in being open to the linguist's approach. Lack of participation in discussions of divergent views of language study could cause difficulty in comprehension.

Another area that could have caused you difficulty in comprehension is having a weak or rusty background in grammar terminology. The section on prepositions and postpositions could have been meaningless to you. If you also have no knowledge of other languages, that lack of knowledge combined with no grammar terminology could sink you. With these insights into comprehension failure, you can help yourself. For example, what could you do if you had a test on this information and you wanted to pass it? First, find an English handbook (borrow one from a friend) and look up prepositions. Practice writing standard sentences with the prepositions and then write the same sentences using the prepositions at the end of the sentences. Next, review the section in the chapter, especially the examples.

A last barrier to your comprehension may be your interest in the subject. You will read much and listen to many lectures in the next four years that are boring to you. How can you learn to increase your interest in subjects that initially do not appeal to you? Trying to connect the information to your personal life may be a good beginning. For example, begin listening to your family and friends and compare and contrast their formal or informal English with that of your instructors. What are the differences? What are the similarities? Pretend that you are going for a job interview and your speech and writing are critical to your getting the job. What changes could you make to give yourself a better chance of being hired? Pretend you are running for office in a campus organization and that you must make a campaign speech. Should you use formal or informal English? Who is your audience?

Listen on campus to people around you and make observations (not judgments) about them. Is anyone saying any of the following phrases?

I'll see *you'uns* tomorrow!
What time *it is*?
She don't drive to school.
They *come* in late last night.
It *ain't* too late.
You *might could* do it.
I *shall* be your waitress.
The box *in which it came in* is on the table.
You can go with him and *I*.
This is *he*.
He not coming to class *cause he sick*.

If you hear any of these phrases, notice who the speakers are and make any other observation about their language that you can. Are the speakers basically using formal or informal English and to whom are they speaking? Where are they?

Fiction Report

Your Name _____

A. Title of Novel _____

   Author _____

B. Check the appropriate major conflict or theme:

___ Person vs. Person (e.g., two people battling for the same position)

___ Person vs. Nature (e.g., a person surviving in a forest)

___ Person vs. God (e.g., a person fighting against fate or Divine Will)

___ Person vs. Himself/Herself (e.g., a person's greatest enemy is within.)

C. Plot (Choose C1 or C2 below).

1. What happened in the work?

   a. What was the normal situation at the beginning?

   b. How was the status quo upset? What changed? Did someone move? Lose his/her job? Was someone killed or attacked? Did someone fall in or out of love? Get divorced? Did someone begin an adventure?

   c. What adventures or experiences occurred?

   d. How did the work end?

   _____

   _____

2. Plot the action. Let the content dictate the form. (See examples a–g.)

   a. Boy meets Girl.

   b. Boy falls in love with Girl.

   c. Boy and Girl are engaged.

   d. Boy goes out with Girl's best friend.

   e. Girl finds out and breaks engagement.

   f. Boy regrets his decision. He performs unselfish act to redeem himself, such as saving a child from a fire at great personal risk.

   g. Boy and Girl are reconciled and marry.

   _____

   _____

D. Characters.

1. List the name(s) of the major character(s).

   _____

   _____

2. Do these characters change by the end of the story? Yes___ No___ How do they change? How do you know? What do they do? How does the author describe their change?

   _____

   _____

3. Are any of these characters types of people you recognize in any work of fiction or movie?   Yes___   No___
    What do you recognize about them? Are they courageous like John Wayne, the underdog like Woody Allen, tough and ruthless like Clint Eastwood, alienated like Holden Caulfield, dependent on the physical like Rambo?

    _____

    _____

E. Setting.
    1. Physical Setting. The main place the work takes place is (circle the appropriate response):
        a. city
        b. country
        c. fantasy world
        d. science fiction world
        e. other _____
    2. Psychological Setting: The place is not really identified and would be unimportant to the story.   Yes___   No___
    3. Time Setting. Circle the appropriate response:
        a. Present (modern, post-twentieth century) How is it identified? _____
        b. Past. What century? _____
            How is it identified?   _____
        c. Future. How is it identified? _____

F. Mood. Circle the response that reflects the predominant mood of the work:
    1. dark and gloomy
    2. fearful and terrifying
    3. light-hearted and comical
    4. serious
    5. everyday atmosphere
    6. other _____

G. Narrator and Point of View.
    1. Who is telling the story? Circle the appropriate response:
        a. a person in the story
        b. a person outside of the story
    2. What is the point of view? Circle the appropriate response:
        a. First person narrator (Uses "I")
        b. Third person narrator (Uses "They")

H. Style. How would you describe the author's style? Circle the appropriate response:
    1. lots of description
    2. long sentences

    3.   digressions

    4.   direct, straightforward

    5.   other _____

I.   In twenty-five words or less, describe the most memorable scene in the story:

_____

_____

_____

_____

_____

J.   Reflection.

    1.   Look at the title of this work. Look back at your identification of the theme of the story on the first page of this report. Now answer these questions:

        a.   What did you think the story would be about, based on the title?

        _____

        b.   What was different from what you expected?

        _____

        c.   How does the story fit the theme you chose?

        _____

        d.   What experiences—real or vicarious—have you had that you can relate to this theme?

        _____

    2.   What did you already know about the setting? Have you been there? Have you seen pictures? Do you know someone who lived or visited there?

        _____

        _____

    3.   How was the setting different from anything you knew about? How did the author help you to visualize it? At what point did you accept it as familiar?

        _____

        _____

    4.   What "real" people or characters that you have seen in movies or on television behave very much like the characters in the story? How are they alike? What do they do? Are they also different in a significant way?

        _____

        _____

5. Review your answers on setting, style, mood, and characters. Did recognition of the theme, setting, style, mood, and/or characters help you understand what you read? Yes___ No___
Did such recognition help keep you interested in what you read? Yes___ No___

K. Response
   1. If you were bored by the work, identify the reason(s):
      a. Reading too difficult
         (1) couldn't figure out what was happening
         (2) didn't make sense
         (3) too many difficult words
         (4) too many complicated sentences
         (5) couldn't tell when something was happening; time jumped around
         (6) other (please identify) _____
      b. Genre, theme, plot, setting, characters were uninteresting
         (1) ideas not easy to relate to my values, life style, culture
         (2) didn't like what happened
         (3) didn't like the characters
         (4) didn't like this type of story
         (5) didn't like this type of setting
         (6) didn't like the writing style
         (7) took too long to get to the point
         (8) other (please identify) _____
   2. If you enjoyed the selection, identify reason(s):
      a. easy to read
      b. could personally relate to the theme and/or character
      c. discovered something new
         (1) new way of "seeing" situations/new solutions
         (2) interesting characters
         (3) interesting style
         (4) interesting "different world"
         (5) other (please identify) _____

L. Rating
   1. On a scale of 1–10, with 10 as the highest, how would you rate this work? ___
   2. Review your answers to the above questions. Based on your responses, give one specific reason for your rating:

   _____
   _____
   _____

Cultural Studies:
Travel and Language in Its Cultural Context

Overview

Reflection
    Mind Revolution
    Vocabulary
    Comprehension

VOCABULARY/METACOGNITION

The purpose of this exercise is to help you become aware of when you know the meaning of a word and to help you know when you do not know the meaning of a word. This is metacognition awareness.

On a scale of 1–5 (see below), rate your knowledge of the following vocabulary words from "Travel and Language in Its Cultural Context." After matching words with definitions on page 255, check your answers and then check your number *ones* and *fives* below. Did you know when you really knew a word and when you really did not know the word?

Scale

1. I absolutely do not know.
2. I do not think I know.
3. There's a 50/50 chance I have seen or heard it.
4. I think I know it.
5. I know the word and can use it.

Words

_____ 1. *Faux pas*
_____ 2. Redundant
_____ 3. *Persona non grata*
_____ 4. Miff (miffed)
_____ 5. Terminate (terminated)
_____ 6. Prosperity
_____ 7. Inadvertent (inadvertently)
_____ 8. Militate
_____ 9. Ubiquitous
_____10. Assumption (assumptions)

Go to page 255. See if you can match the right definition with the word and then write sentences for any five words in the list.

Words	Definitions
_____ 1. *Faux pas*	A. Superfluous, especially using more words than are needed
_____ 2. Redundant	B. From Latin, literally a "person not pleasing" or welcome. Originally, in diplomatic usage, it designated a representative of a foreign country who would not be allowed to remain within the host nation. Figuratively, it has been extended to mean any person who is not acceptable or welcome in a given group. (Definition by J. L. Dillard)
_____ 3. *Persona non grata*	
_____ 4. Miff (miffed)	
_____ 5. Terminate (terminated)	
_____ 6. Prosperity	
_____ 7. Inadvertent (inadvertently)	
_____ 8. Militate	
_____ 9. Ubiquitous	
_____10. Assumption (assumptions)	C. A social error; mistake
	D. (1) Act of assuming; (2) a supposition or hypothesis
	E. Offend
	F. Existing everywhere; inescapable
	G. Bring to an end; finish; conclude
	H. Thriving; successful
	I. Unintentional; accidental
	J. To have weight or force against or for

Write five words from the list and your own sentences that show you know how to use the words. Choose words that you marked a *five* if possible.

1. Word _____

   Sentence _____

2. Word _____

   Sentence _____

3. Word _____

   Sentence _____

4. Word _____

   Sentence _____

5. Word _____

   Sentence _____

PRE-READING THE TEXTBOOK CHAPTER

The purpose of this *first* of three steps in your reading plan is to suggest things to do *before* you read. First, as part of your pre-reading, read the Prior Knowledge section beginning on page 256. When you finish, return to this section and continue your pre-reading. You will use the Academic Study Skills section as a post-reading activity but you may want to skim it at this time so that you will know what to expect.

Tapping Prior Knowledge

Tap your experience and prior knowledge about the title of this selection by writing words and phrases that come to your mind. You are pulling up your file on the topic and focusing on what you will read. What do you already know about the subject? Do not look at your textbook at this time, as these answers will vary from person to person and won't be found in the textbook. There are no wrong answers for this part of the lesson.

Predicting

Predict in one sentence what you will read. Try to predict in some detail. Don't write, "I predict that I will read about travel and language in its cultural context." What behavior, action, and/or information do you expect to read about? Predicting helps you identify your expectations of what you will read. Not reading what you have predicted will serve as a warning that you have misjudged the topic of the article and will help you adapt to what is in the chapter.

Overviewing

Overview the chapter by reading the summary and questions on pages 268–269 and by outlining the chapter below.

Travel and Language in its Cultural Context

I. _____

II. _____

III. _____

IV. _____

Prior Knowledge

This section, part of your pre-reading, presents a model to show you what will help you comprehend this chapter by using your own background knowledge. If you know much of the following information, you have a better background for reading this chapter. This section will suggest helpful kinds of background information and help you activate what you know; do not try to look up or learn everything listed. Ask yourself what you need to know before you read and what you already know that will help you to understand this chapter. Your instructor may want to use this section for a whole-class or small group discussion or have you read it silently.

Chapter Sections

I. The Special Problem of Food in Ecuador
   A. Vocabulary
      1. *Faux pas*
      2. Redundant
      3. Comestibles
      4. *Persona non grata*
   B. Recognition of Writing Patterns or Arrangement of Ideas and Devices
      1. Informal style
      2. Personal essay
      3. Chronological order
      4. Use of examples and specific details
   C. Concepts and Background Knowledge and Experience
      1. Personal travel
      2. Knowledge of Spanish
      3. Sensitivity to cultural differences
      4. Lived in a different culture
      5. Knowledge of Ecuador
      6. Fulbright Scholarships
      7. Ability to relate to someone who is to blame or made an innocent mistake
II. A *Faux pas* in the Cameroun
   A. Vocabulary
      1. Skeptical
      2. Ubiquitous
      3. Terminated
      4. Customary
      5. Prosperity
      6. Apportioning
      7. Inadvertently
   B. Recognition of Writing Patterns or Arrangement of Ideas and Devices
      1. See above
   C. Concepts and Background Knowledge and Experience
      1. Knowledge of world geography
      2. Knowledge of French
      3. Knowledge of Africa
      4. Knowledge of the Cameroun (Yaoundé, capital)
      5. Knowledge of the Ewondo tribe
      6. Sophisticated view of social customs—broad perspective
III. Eating Problems in Burundi
   A. Vocabulary
      1. Rapport
      2. Miffed

  B. Recognition of Writing Patterns or Arrangement of Ideas and Devices
    1. See above
  C. Concepts and Background Knowledge and Experience
    1. Knowledge of concept of lingua franca
    2. Knowledge of French
    3. Knowledge of Africa
    4. Knowledge of Burundi
    5. ESL background
    6. Knowledge of social taboos

IV. Problems in Traveling, Even Close to Home
  A. Vocabulary
    1. Ludicrous
    2. Militate
    3. Interlocutor
  B. Recognition of Writing Patterns or Arrangement of Ideas and Devices
    1. See above
  C. Concepts and Background Knowledge and Experience
    1. Experience in misreading someone from another culture—speech or body language
    2. Experience of being insulted or made fun of by others in a different cultural or geographical setting
    3. Experience of being abused by a New Yorker
    4. Knowledge of the Southern code of conduct
    5. Experience of someone standing too close to you during a conversation
    6. Good experiences in contacts with others who are different
    7. Ability to accept those who are different and to learn from them
    8. Desire to grow through exchanges with those who are different or desire to understand the customs and values of those who are different

V. Summary
  A. Concepts and Background Knowledge and Experience
    1. Concept of communication difficulties based on unshared cultural assumptions
    2. Understanding of the necessity of speaking another language and understanding the customs of a country you plan to visit in order to learn and grow from the experience
    3. Knowledge of the "Ugly American" concept—the perception by foreigners that American tourists are indifferent toward their language and customs

VI. Questions
  A. Vocabulary
    1. Assumptions
    2. Presuppositions

B.   Recognition of Writing Patterns or Arrangement of Ideas and Devices
1.   All three questions are experience-based (critical/creative). You must "read beyond the lines" in order to answer the questions adequately. Use your own background knowledge and experiences—those real and vicarious—in your responses.
C.   Concepts and Background Knowledge and Experience
1.   Understand your responsibility as a tourist in a foreign land in matters of communication

ACADEMIC STUDY SKILLS

DIRECTIONS FOR MODIFIED SQ4R

For this chapter we will adapt the format of the textbook reading lessons to the SQ4R approach. Review the information on the SQ4R study plan in Chapter 5 of this textbook. Would such a plan be necessary for this chapter?

Yes__   No__   Maybe__

Does this chapter look like it will be easier or more difficult than the previous chapters? Support your response. Give specific reasons for its being easier or more difficult.

_____

_____

_____

A.   Pre-Reading—Survey: You have already surveyed this chapter by skimming the section on Prior Knowledge, by tapping into your prior knowledge and experience, by predicting what you will read, and by overviewing the chapter. From your overview write below what was difficult to understand.

The following was difficult:
1.   _____
2.   _____
3.   _____
4.   _____
5.   _____

B.   Reading—Question/Read/Record: You have already read this chapter by the Reciprocal Teaching lesson or by the Active Questioning lesson. In both lessons you have read the chapter section by section. In both lessons you asked questions about the material and answered them. Go back and reread the chapter section by section and answer the questions on page 260.

1. What are the most important ideas in each section?
   a. "The Special Problem of Food in Ecuador"
   b. "A *Faux pas* in the Cameroun"
   c. "Eating Problems in Burundi"
   d. "Problems in Traveling, Even Close to Home"

2. Significant Support for Most Important Ideas: What supports these ideas in each section? Your summaries (Reciprocal Teaching lesson) and your questions from either the Reciprocal Teaching or Active Questioning lesson should help you find the support.
   a. "The Special Problem of Food in Ecuador"
   b. "A *Faux pas* in the Cameroun"
   c. "Eating Problems in Burundi"
   d. "Problems in Traveling, Even Close to Home"

C. Post-Reading—Recite/Review

1. With a partner recite the information you have learned. Use the summary and questions at the end of the chapter, your Active Questioning lesson questions and answers, and the work you have done for this academic study skills lesson for guidance about the significance of the information you are discussing.

2. Review the work that you have already completed for the chapter, including the questions you have written. Below, write and answer questions that better reflect the important information in the chapter.

   Questions
   a. "The Special Problem of Food in Ecuador"

   Question: _____

   Answer: _____

   b. "A *Faux pas* in the Cameroun"

   Question: _____

   Answer: _____

   c. "Eating Problems in Burundi"

   Question: _____

   Answer: _____

   d. "Problems in Traveling, Even Close to Home"

   Question: _____

   Answer: _____

3. Ask yourself what you know and what you do not know. Monitor your own learning much like you have done on the vocabulary exercises for the textbook chapters. Reflect on what you have learned, especially on how you connected information in the chapter to your life. Add new thoughts to the post-reading section of either the Reciprocal Teaching or Active Questioning lesson you completed.

ACTIVE QUESTIONING

OVERVIEW

Your first step of the three-part reading plan was pre-reading. In pre-reading, you activated your prior knowledge, predicted what you would read, and overviewed the chapter before reading.

As the second step in this three-part reading plan, you will read the chapter "Travel and Language in its Cultural Context" by using the Active Questioning reading plan as explained below. An alternative plan, Reciprocal Teaching, is in Appendix B. In both plans you break up the chapter in sections and read and think about each as you read. The purpose of both plans is to keep you reading actively.

GENERAL DIRECTIONS

When using active questioning, write questions on the literal, inferential, and creative/critical levels. In Part I of this textbook, you answered the teacher-made questions in Chapter 2 then wrote literal-level questions and answered teacher-made questions on the inferential and critical/creative levels of comprehension in Chapter 4. Teacher-made questions are provided as models in all sections of this chapter. If you still are not comfortable writing your own higher-level comprehension questions at this time, then answer the model questions. Students often find the inferential level questions more difficult to write. If this is true for you, try writing the literal and the experience-based questions and answer the model questions on the inferential level. Remember that you are gradually moving from teacher modeling through guided practice to independence.

ASSIGNMENT

A. Read section one, "The Special Problem of Food in Ecuador," and ask one text-explicit question (literal), one text-implicit question (inferential), and one experience-based question (critical/creative) each on this section. Please answer all three questions. Do not ask a question that you cannot answer.

1. Text-explicit (literal level): A question that requires the reader to read the line. The answer will come from one line of print. Model text-explicit question: In what year did the author go to Quito?

Your text-explicit question _____

Answer _____

2. Text-implicit (inferential level): A question that requires the reader to read between the lines. The answer will come from more than one line of print. You will need to make judgments and draw conclusions. Model text-implicit question: Give three examples that show that the author did not do well in economic situations in Quito and tell what you think the local people must have thought of him.

Your text-implicit question _____

Answer _____

3. Experience-based (critical/creative level): A question that requires the reader to read beyond the lines. Apply what you have learned to your world. Question what you have read. Model experience-based question: Do Americans take advantage of foreigners when they use their labor and services at a cheaper rate than they would pay in the United States? Support your response.

Your experience-based question _____

Answer _____

B. Read the second section, "A *Faux pas* in the Cameroun," and ask one text-explicit question, one text-implicit question, and one experience-based question each on this section. Please answer all three questions. Do not ask a question that you cannot answer.

1. Model text-explicit question: What European language was spoken in Yaounde?

Your text-explicit question _____

Answer _____

2. Model text-implicit question: Retell in your own words the kola nut ceremony. What went wrong with the author's visit? What could have prevented the sad ending?

Your text-implicit question _____

Answer _____

3. Model experience-based question: What customs do people in your area of the country have that are strange to foreigners? How do they react? How do you show hospitality to visitors? What do you do that could be misunderstood?

Your experience-based question _____

Answer _____

C. Read the third section, "Eating Problems in Burundi," and ask one text-explicit question, one text-implicit question, and one experience-based question each on this section. Please answer all three questions. Do not ask a question that you cannot answer.

1. Model text-explicit question: In what years did the author go to Bujumbura?

Your text-explicit question _____

Answer _____

2. Model text-implicit question: What is the purpose of the example of the ESL lesson that asks, "Is the secretary at home"?

Your text-implicit question _____

Answer _____

3. Model experience-based question: What do Americans consider taboo? What kinds of things are not done in public that might be acceptable in another culture or time?

Your experience-based question _____

Answer _____

D. Read the fourth section, "Problems in Traveling, Even Close to Home," and ask one text-explicit question, one text-implicit question, and one experience-based question each on this section. Please answer all three questions. Do not ask a question that you cannot answer.

1. Model text-explicit question: How do out-of-towners characterize New Yorkers?

Your text-explicit question _____

Answer _____

2. Model text-implicit question: What are some techniques that are important in communication other than language? What can go wrong if you are not aware of these differences?

Your text-implicit question _____

Answer _____

3. Model experience-based question: Have you ever judged a stranger as rude and later found out differences between you were the problem?

Your experience-based question _____

Answer _____

POST-READING THE TEXTBOOK CHAPTER

OVERVIEW

In the second part of your three-part reading plan, you practiced reading your textbook chapter section by section and asked and answered questions.

In this third part of the three-part reading plan, you will find suggestions for what to do after you read. Your task is to compare what you predicted with what you actually read as an aid to comprehension, to add what you have learned to your file of information on the topic, and to think about what you have read.

ASSIGNMENT

As part of your post-reading activity, follow the directions for the modified SQ4R plan in the Academic Study Skills section on page 259. When you finish, return to this section and follow the directions on page 264.

A.   Compare what you predicted you would read with what you actually read. Did anything you predicted cause you a problem with comprehension? What? How?

B.   Look at your prediction of what you would read in the pre-reading section of this lesson on page 256. What did you correctly predict that you would read?

C.   What did you learn from the reading that you did not know about before working on this lesson?

D.   Look at the words and phrases that you listed as your prior knowledge in the pre-reading section of this lesson on page 256. Group them below with relevant information in "B" above. This is your new file of information on cultural studies. (The ability to group ideas and to see relationships requires more complex comprehension than merely memorizing isolated facts.) Headings are provided, but you may select your own if these do not fit.

E.   What have you learned from this chapter that is important?

F.   What do you already know that you can relate to it?

G.   What do you see differently as a result of reading this chapter?

	Travel	Language	Cultural Knowledge	Personal/ Vicarious Experience
Personal				
Vicarious				

TRAVEL AND LANGUAGE IN ITS CULTURAL CONTEXT

Before embarking on this particular account of experiences, it is necessary to say something about my language background. With little experience in actually transacting business in those languages, I had a fairly good *academic* background in Spanish, French, and German (as well as Latin, a year of Greek, and older stages of the Germanic languages like Old and Middle English, Gothic and Old Norse). Misunderstandings based on imperfect language learning were undoubtedly part of the total experience, but there were some misunderstandings in which the language component was fairly well under control. In those cases, it was primarily assumptions and preconceptions which led to misunderstandings and outright *faux pas*.

The Special Problem of Food in Ecuador

Going to Quito on a Fulbright in English as a Second Language in 1958, I felt moderately secure about Spanish. Classroom activity would be in ESL, so that use of Spanish would be concerned only with personal affairs like shopping. Volunteer interpreters were usually to be found around airline offices and in many stores; often their services seemed to be redundant.

Forced to do the shopping for meat and some other comestibles as the only one in the household qualified to do so, I soon found that the system was different from that of the United States but not so different as to make any great deal of difference. I do not remember who first told me about *lomo fino*, a fine cut of beef

available at the butcher shops (there were no supermarkets worthy of the name, so that shopping for meat was done at the butcher shop, for bread at the bakery, etc.—a system which I still think of as a good one). I do not remember, either, at which shop I first purchased *lomo fino*. I do vaguely remember the question "¿Algo mas?" ("Something else?") or perhaps even the direct question "¿No quiere huesos?" ("Don't you want some bones?") I remember also that the *second* time I went back to buy *lomo fino* I typically got the answer "No tenemos lomo fino" ("We don't have lomo fino.")

It is probable that Ema, my Ecuadorian maid, tried to explain to me what was going wrong. At least, she mentioned something about *huesos* (bones). I asked her whether she wanted some bones for the cooking, and her answer was an unreserved no. Therefore, I decided that buying *huesos* was out of the question.

Economics had a great deal to do with the misunderstanding involved. Goods, except for some manufactured goods like typewriters and electronic equipment, were cheap in Quito in 1958–9. Ema, our Ecuadorian maid who was paid less than $20 a month (plus, of course, her room and board) always thought I was paying too much for things. I, on the other hand, fancied my own bargaining power. I will not soon forget when I bought a mat for the front porch for only five sucres (less than thirty cents at the exchange rate). I bragged to Ema about it, only to be told "O, señor, le roban la plata" ("Oh, señor, they're stealing your money.")

Ema, in other words, felt that *lomo fino*—which in my memory cost something like forty cents a pound, 1958-9 currency—was too expensive for our household. By her standards, it probably was. She was capable of taking the equivalent of three or four dollars down to the native market once a week and coming back with enough vegetables for us for the entire week. She refused, however, to do the meat shopping. It was basically her decision that we should do without the "expensive" *lomo fino*—and the *huesos*.

Not until becoming *persona non grata* in all the accessible butcher shops of Quito did I find out that the assumption was that anyone who bought *lomo fino* would also buy *huesos*. Breaking that (apparently) unwritten (and virtually unspoken) rule, I became unwittingly offensive to the butchers of the city. Only after that realization did it become understandable to me why butchers who had been extremely courteous on my first visit to their store turned grim and sour on the second. It was a lesson in language and culture, but it came too late for us to have *lomo fino*.

A *Faux Pas* in the Cameroun

The trip to the Cameroun in 1963–4 was preceded by a fairly adequate preparation in French. In Yaoundé, people, including a houseboy whom I hired early in my stay there, regularly spoke French to me and there were no major communication barriers. When the houseboy invited me to the native quarter to meet his *prince*, I felt quite well prepared for the experience— although I had learned to be skeptical as to whether he meant the same thing by *prince* as others might.

The meeting with the *prince* went fairly well for a time. We were ushered into a sitting room, decent and fairly well furnished by Camerounian standards. We conversed for a short time ("How long have you been here?") in French

until, with a seemingly friendly tone of voice, the host asked, "Vous prenez kola?"

Now, so far as I knew he was offering me a Coca Cola—an ubiquitous drink overseas, especially for those who were unwilling to trust the local water supply. It seemed like the friendly thing to accept, I did, and the host gave an order to a servant in an African language (probably Bamoun).

Shortly the servant returned with a metal tray containing a small, rather ugly green thing. Never having seen a kola nut before, I did not recognize it; but the servant held the tray before me in such a manner as to indicate that I was supposed to do something about it. On the principle of the lesser of two evils, I took the small nut and popped it into my mouth. It tasted quite bitter, and I fear I grimaced at the taste of it. The remainder of the visit was quite stiff and formal. Not knowing quite what, I realized that something had gone wrong as we terminated the visit.

It was some time later that I learned of the West African kola nut ceremony. One can read about it in the novels of Chinua Achebe, but I had read very little West African literature at the time. It is customary for the host to offer kola to an honored guest; not to offer kola is to express either lack of prosperity on the part of the host or lack of respect for the guest—or both. The nut is offered to the guest, along with the honor of dividing it and apportioning sections to the host and to himself. (The pronoun can stand; I have never read about the partaking of kola by West African women.) The guest declines the honor, saying that it belongs rather to the host. This can go on for some time, until one participant accepts the *honor* and divides it. It is probable that the apportioning of relative sizes of kola indicates something about the assumed social status of the participants. By hogging both the breaking and the kola, I had inadvertently said to my host, "You have no status at all so far as I am concerned." Of course, sometimes people will make the excuse, "Oh, well, he's just an ignorant foreigner." For the sake of Camerounian–American relations, it would be well if the prince finally came to that conclusion.

Eating Problems in Burundi

My trip to Bujumbura, Burundi, on another Fulbright ESL grant, in 1967–8 also involved the use of French as the lingua franca in a territory where there were African languages (chiefly Kirundi and Kinyarwanda) in use. Practice in the Cameroun and on French-speaking islands of the Caribbean like Guadeloupe and Martinique made me feel rather secure in the use of French. It turned out, of course, that understanding of French as such was not the only problem.

For my ESL classes at the *Université Officiele de Bujumbura*, the text by Wright and MacGillvray, *Let's Learn English*, was in use. As *Aprendamos inglés*, this text had proved to be a satisfactory one in Latin America. It was a good work by textbook standards, dealing with practice in everyday situations which the student might be expected to know about. It was, in short, culturally well adapted—for Latin America.

Soon my class was into *Let's Learn English*, doing rather well. Then we came to one of those "culturally neutral" sections, dealing with meals and eating. My class clammed up. They seemed unwilling to answer questions like "What do you have for breakfast?" although they had seemed to be able to deal with even more complex material earlier. Whatever rapport with the class had been enjoyed seemed to disappear.

The solution came in a barroom—or in a hotel dining room which dealt as much in drinks as in food. Since I had no cooking facilities at the residence supplied for me, I ate regularly at one of the four such facilities in Bujumburi—along with most of the foreign population and some of the locals. Barundi (natives of Burundi) would sit drinking then one by one disappear and stay away for quite a while—longer than would be required to go to the restrooms.

A now-forgotten informant finally enlightened me. The Barundi did not like to eat in public, although drinking in public was quite all right. (The reverse situation, one would think, applied in certain establishments during Prohibition in the United States). They were going into the back rooms to *eat*!

The problem soon solved itself for the ESL classes. Skipping over the mealtime lessons, I went on to other everyday activities. The class picked up again, and altogether it was one of my more successful classes.

Of course, there was an occasional slip, such as the question:

"Is the secretary at home?"

where the woman is sitting at a typewriter and the expected answer is

"No, she is at work."

The actual response was

"No, she is in labor."

But, then, one expects such things in second language environments.

The *chargé d'affairs* in the embassy at Bujumbura (our ambassador had been kicked out of the country some time before) had perhaps greater difficulty with the Barundi's attitude toward eating in public. As the chief of the U. S. diplomatic mission in the country, he tended to depend heavily upon the diplomatic staple of the buffet dinner. He was openly miffed that the leading Barundi did not participate enthusiastically in those buffets. A Bostonian with a good education, he seemed to me to speak quite elegant French, although he apparently paid no attention to Kirundi, the native language of the Barundi.

Some time later, when the problems in Cambodia were at their height, I happened to read of the *chargé d'affairs* in that country. You might guess: It was the same man.

Problems in Traveling, Even Close to Home

We all have our troubles in traveling, whether we know the language of the country or not. A gesture which we think of as innocent may be regarded as threatening, insulting—or ludicrous. It takes a long time to get to know the assumptions and presuppositions of a culture, and orientation courses have traditionally not dealt in such matters. But it is not only when traveling abroad that we run such risks.

I am now convinced of the truth of an observation which I did not make until the end of my four-year stay in New York City. Out-of-towners tend to think of New Yorkers as rude, although any concept of uniformity of populations would militate against that being true in any absolute sense. It occurred to me, after four years, that a cashier in a drugstore where I had long had coffee was not really rude after all. The courtesies—and this may be true of many New Yorkers—were rather reserved for the end of the transaction. In the

beginning stages, such people seem to be strictly business. As a Southerner by birth, I had tended to internalize the opposite distribution: elaborate courtesies at the beginning, then abrupt termination once the business was finished. The upshot of all this is that both of us, the cashier and I, may have come away from a routine transaction each thinking of the other as rude and unfriendly whereas in truth no such intention existed at all. I only wish I had thought of that before I moved away from New York.

How close one person in a conversation stands to another, how loud they talk, and what gestures they use may be extremely important to the communication. It is doubtful that such factors outweigh a basic knowledge of the language involved, but they should never be overlooked. In such cases, a foreign accent—something that most language classes are aimed at eliminating—may be a positive advantage. It's probably better to have your interlocutor think, "He's just a stupid foreigner; listen to his accent" than "He has a wonderful accent, but he's a very rude person."

Summary

Even a person who goes to a foreign country fairly well versed in the language of that country can have communication difficulties based on unshared cultural assumptions. In Quito, I was unable to maintain a supply of fine, inexpensive meat that was available because of my lack of understanding that the butchers expected to sell soup bones with the meat. In the Cameroun, my failure to understand the meaning of the kola ceremony ruined one potential relationship with a citizen of that country. In Burundi, a near disaster in teaching was averted when I found out, barely in time, that the people there (including my students) did not like to eat or discuss food in public. Even in New York City, a southerner may have suffered less pleasant relationships than were possible because of expecting courtesies to be at the beginning rather than at the end of transactions. A traveler to another area needs to study the language of that area, but he also needs to be aware of the customs.

Questions

1. Why is it important to know the language of a country to which one is traveling?

2. What problems may one encounter—even if one knows the language—that have to do with non-linguistic matters?

3. How widespread are the matters of cultural assumptions and presuppositions in total communication?

VOCABULARY LESSON

The purpose of this exercise is to help you review and deepen your knowledge of the ten general vocabulary words you worked with at the beginning of this chapter.

A. Structural Analysis—Affixes and Root Words
   1. Underline the suffix of the following word: *Miffed*
   2. Find the dictionary definition of the root word for *miffed* and write it below:

   _____

   3. How has the suffix changed the word?
   4. Write an original sentence with *miffed* and then one with just the root word.

      a. _____

      b. _____

B. Use of Context
   1. Read the paragraph (section four, second paragraph) in which the word *militate* appears, and in your own words write a definition for it.

   _____

   2. Read the paragraph (section two, paragraph five) in which the word *inadvertently* appears, and in your own words write a definition for it.

   _____

C. Multiple Meanings of Words
   1. Circle the definition below of the word *redundant* that fits its use in this chapter:
      a. superfluous, especially using more words than are needed
      b. serving as a backup for a system

D. Synonyms and Antonyms: List one synonym (same meaning) and one antonym (opposite meaning) for the words below:

Word	**Synonym**	**Antonym**
Ubiquitous		
Prosperity		

E. Generate Your Own Language
   1. Briefly describe your most embarrassing *faux pas.*
   2. When have you found yourself *persona non grata*?
   3. What brand of pop or soda is *ubiquitous* on your campus?
   4. On what basis would you *terminate* a relationship?
   5. What circumstances would *militate* against your leaving college?
   6. What *assumptions* did you make about college life before you arrived on campus?

VOCABULARY EXTENSION

The purpose of this exercise is to help you see to what degree you know the ten general vocabulary words in this chapter. Matching a word with its definition is the beginning of knowing a word. Using the word in your speaking and writing is full knowledge. See if you have increased your vocabulary by following the directions below.

A.   List the vocabulary words from this lesson that you can now use in both your speaking and writing.

B.   List the vocabulary words from this lesson that you can now use in writing but are still not comfortable using in speaking.

C.   List the vocabulary words from this lesson that you cannot use yet but will recognize in reading.

D.   List general vocabulary words from this lesson that are still difficult to understand.

E.   Use *five* vocabulary words from this lesson in a five-sentence paragraph on the topic of this lesson.

F.   Illustrate the meaning of *one* of the vocabulary words from this lesson through some form of artwork or a cartoon. (This exercise is for right-brain students who enjoy drawing better than writing!)

EXTENDED READING ACTIVITIES

The purpose of this section is to give you a variety of options for independent study or investigation of the chapter topic. Reading is a skill that must be practiced each day if progress is to take place. These activities are designed to give you a variety of reading experiences through which you can improve your general vocabulary and increase your higher-level comprehension skills.

Your instructor may wish to (a) assign one or more activities to the class as a whole, (b) assign various activities to small groups, (c) assign one or more activities to individual students, or (d) let students choose to do the activities or not.

A.   Weekly Reading Report: Continue keeping a weekly report of your reading. Is your reading time increasing? How much time does your academic reading take each day? Do you have to think deeply about your pleasure reading? Are you reading more than the local sports page, advice columns, your horoscope, and the comics? (Use the form in Appendix C if you wish.)

B.   Attend a Reading Lab on Campus: Continue using the reading lab at your school. Find exercises that help you improve your general vocabulary and your higher comprehension skills. Making judgments and drawing conclusions would be good exercises for the inferential level of comprehension.

C.   Read a Novel: If you decided to read a novel for pleasure as suggested, continue reading it at least thirty minutes a day. If you cannot get interested in the novel you chose, change to one more interesting. If you like rites of passage novels as well as reading about different cultures, try Gary Paulsen's *Dogsong* or Jean George's *Julie of the Wolves*.

D. Reading/Writing Connection: Continue keeping a personal journal about your beginning college experience. Write about any misconceptions you have had about people from other cultures. Reflect on past travel to different places and your response to the local people. What did you like and dislike about their customs? If you could travel to any place in the world, where would you go? Why? Write your insights in your journal. Use a new vocabulary word in your response.

E. Use the Internet: Search the Internet under the topic *travel*. Are there any good deals on travel to exotic places? If you are interested in environmental issues, find environmentally concerned organizations, such as the Audubon Society, and look for special trips organized by them. Could you go to Africa and shoot (with a camera) big game? Look up *Cameroun*, *Ecuador*, *Burundi*, or *New York*.

F. Vocabulary Journal: Begin or continue keeping a vocabulary journal by recording five words a week, which you know but not completely. Record the word, its source, a sentence or phrase in which it was used, what you think the word means, and then a dictionary definition that shows its meaning as it is used in the sentence. The words can come from academic or pleasure reading. Use the form in Appendix C if you wish.

G. Journal/Magazine/Newspaper Reading: Begin or continue to read a journal or magazine in your major. Find one that matches your level of information about the field. Some magazines and journals in your school library may be intended for college seniors and contain technical or higher-level information for which you have little background at this time. Find several articles of interest to you. Record the names of the magazines or journals, dates, titles of articles and authors if listed. Write a one-paragraph summary of one article and then in another paragraph give your opinion about the topic and support it. Use the form provided in Appendix C if you wish. If you are undecided as to your major, read from the following list of health science and engineering magazines and journals that follows. Some may be too difficult for you at this time.

1. Health Sciences: *American Journal of Nursing, Psychosocial Nursing, Clinical Nursing Research, Nursing Education, American Journal of Public Health, Annals of Emergency Medicine, Journal of Emergency Services, Emergency Medicine, Applied Radiology, The Canadian Journal of Medical Radiation Technology, Journal of Dental Education, Journal of Dental Hygiene, Hospital and Health Networks, Cardiopulmonary Physical Therapy Journal, Canadian Journal of Medical Laboratory Science, CHEST. The Cardiopulmonary and Critical Care Journal, Clinical Chemistry, Clinical Laboratory Science, The Occupational Therapy Journal of Research, Modern Healthcare, Laboratory Medicine, The Journal of Infectious Diseases, Journal of Immunology, Journal of Clinical Microbiology, Critical Care Medicine, Heart and Lung, Home Healthcare Nurse, Hospitals and Health Networks, Inside Ambulatory Care, Journal of Allied Health*

2. Engineering: *3D Design, Tech Trends, Chemical Engineering, Plastics News, Modern Plastics, Plastics Technology, Automotive Plastics, Mechanical Engineering, Popular Mechanics, Popular Science, Machine Design, Industry Week, Electronics Now, Technology Review, Environmental Science and Engineering Magazine, Molding Systems, Cadalyst, Cadence, Design News, Hydraulics and Pneumatics, Hydrocarbon Processing, Engineering Technology, Power*

REFLECTION

MIND REVOLUTION

The Mind Revolution grew out of my awareness that too many times students do not incorporate what they learn in class into their personal lives. Learning remains compartmentalized and some times wasted. This is an attempt to get you to see how the chapter information can be personally important. Hopefully, you will encounter a new idea in each chapter that you can incorporate into your own life, or at least have something new to think about as you go about your daily routine. Life should never be boring!

Knowing another language or taking a language dictionary to another country may not be enough to help you have a pleasant experience. Not understanding the culture could cause you to return home with unpleasant thoughts about the people you visited.

VOCABULARY

Review the "Vocabulary Extension" for this chapter and see if you are using the words that are most familiar to you. Review the words that were the most difficult for you. Do you understand the connotation of the words? What about the foreign-sounding words, *persona non grata* and *faux pas*? Now wouldn't it be fun to mysteriously walk up to friends and ask them if they felt like *persona non grata* at a party? What about telling your roommates about your *faux pas* at the party the night before? Be adventurous!

COMPREHENSION

For a monolingual speaker or for a person who has not traveled very far or often, this selection would be more difficult to read. Readers who speak more than one language and/or have traveled broadly could probably relate to the ideas. Readers who have difficulty admitting mistakes, especially out loud, may find it difficult to read about someone else who has certainly embarrassed himself and who is left with regrets, especially when it comes to kola nuts. Lack of background knowledge and experience can interfere with our comprehension. Sometimes emotionally charged subjects can also cause us to miss information in a reading selection; for example, a discussion of taboo subjects could make readers so uncomfortable that comprehension is lost. To build our background knowledge and experience, we do not always have to learn about other cultures from direct experience. We can learn vicariously through the adventures of friends and relatives, movies, documentaries, and, of course, reading.

Another barrier to comprehension may be your interest in languages and cultures. If you are attending college to get a job, not an education, your attitude and single-minded goal could interfere with your understanding in many of your classes. You may be shutting out information that you do not see as directly related to your future job. Many fields employ well-rounded, knowledgeable people who can relate to a variety of people in a variety of ways. Career promotions may also include moving to new places where knowing the languages and culture will help you be successful. One of the keys to reading improvement is to read on a variety of subjects. You may not want to go to South America or Africa after reading this chapter, but where would you enjoy traveling that requires you to know another language and to understand the culture of its people? What would help you prepare for such a journey? The journey can be real or vicarious.

American History: Some Problems with Columbus's "Discovery" of America

Overview

Extended Reading Activities
Reflection
  Mind Revolution
  Vocabulary
  Comprehension

VOCABULARY/METACOGNITION

The purpose of this exercise is to help you become aware of when you know the meaning of a word and to help you know when you do not know the meaning of a word. This is metacognition awareness.

On a scale of 1–5 (see below), rate your knowledge of the following vocabulary words from "Some Problems with Columbus's 'Discovery' of America." After matching words with definitions on page 277, check your answers and then check your number *ones* and *fives* below. Did you know when you really knew a word and when you really did not know the word?

Scale

1. I absolutely do not know.
2. I do not think I know.
3. There's a 50/50 chance I have seen or heard it.
4. I think I know it.
5. I know the word and can use it.

Words

_____ 1. Misconceive (misconception)

_____ 2. Prominent (prominence)

_____ 3. Cosmopolitan

_____ 4. Archetype (archetypical)

_____ 5. Notorious (notoriously)

_____ 6. Presumptuous

_____ 7. Speculate (speculations)

_____ 8. Aboriginal

_____ 9. Ambivalence

_____10. Decimate (decimated)

Go to page 277. See if you can match the right definition with the word and then write sentences for any five words in the list.

Words	Definitions
_____ 1. Misconceive (misconception)	A. (1) Familiar with all the world; at home anywhere; (2) peopled from all the world, as a city
_____ 2. Prominent (prominence)	
_____ 3. Cosmopolitan	
_____ 4. Archetype (archetypical)	B. Destroy a great number of, literally one-tenth
_____ 5. Notorious (notoriously)	C. Arrogant; overbold
_____ 6. Presumptuous	D. Misunderstand
_____ 7. Speculate (speculations)	E. Mixed or conflicting feelings
_____ 8. Aboriginal	F. An original model; prototype
_____ 9. Ambivalence	G. (1) Meditate or ponder; reflect; (2) theorize; conjecture; (3) make a risky investment
_____ 10. Decimate (decimated)	H. (1) Standing out; jutting; (2) conspicuous; distinguished
	I. Widely but not favorably known
	J. (1) Pertaining to earliest times or conditions; primitive; (2) indigenous

Write five words from the list and your own sentences that show you know how to use the words. Choose words that you marked a *five* if possible.

1. Word _____

   Sentence _____

2. Word _____

   Sentence _____

3. Word _____

   Sentence _____

4. Word _____

   Sentence _____

5. Word _____

   Sentence _____

PRE-READING THE TEXTBOOK CHAPTER

The purpose of this *first* of three steps in your reading plan is to suggest things to do *before* you read. First, as part of your pre-reading, read the Prior Knowledge section beginning on page 278. When you finish, return to this section and continue your pre-reading. You will use the Academic Study Skills section as a post-reading activity but you may want to skim the lesson at this time so that you will know what to expect.

TAPPING PRIOR KNOWLEDGE

Tap your experience and prior knowledge about the title of this selection by writing words and phrases that come to your mind. You are pulling up your file on the topic and focusing on what you will read. What do you already know about the subject? Do not look at your textbook at this time, as these answers will vary from person to person and won't be found in the textbook. There are no wrong answers for this part of the lesson.

PREDICTING

Predict in one sentence what you will read. Try to predict in some detail. Don't write, "I predict that I will read about some of Columbus's problems." What behavior, action, and/or information do you expect to read about? Predicting helps you identify your expectations of what you will read. Not reading what you have predicted will serve as a warning that you have misjudged the topic of the article and will help you adapt to what is in the chapter.

OVERVIEWING

Overview the chapter by outlining it on page 287 under the Post-Reading section of this lesson (major sections only) and by reading the Summary and the Questions at the end of the chapter.

PRIOR KNOWLEDGE

This section, part of your pre-reading, presents a model to show you what will help you comprehend this chapter by using your own background knowledge. If you know much of the information listed below, you have a better background for reading this chapter. This section will suggest helpful kinds of background information and help you activate what you know; do not try to look up or learn everything listed. Ask yourself what you need to know before you read and what you already know that will help you to understand this chapter. Your instructor may want to use this section for a whole-class or small group discussion or have you read it silently.

CHAPTER SECTIONS

I. Introduction and Section One: Cosmopolitan Nature of Columbus and the Crew of His First Voyage
    A. Vocabulary
        1. Quincentennial
        2. Misconception
        3. Reservations
        4. Prominence
        5. Unanimously

      6. Archetypical

      7. Maritime

      8. Notoriously

      9. Prestige

      10. Fluent

      11. Courtier

  B. Recognition of Writing Patterns or Arrangement of Ideas and Devices

      1. Introduction: Statement of problem; use of quotation marks

      2. Section One: Explanation

  C. Concepts and Background Knowledge and Experience

      1. Specific information on Columbus and his voyages

      2. Names of Columbus's ships

      3. Knowledge of Basques

      4. Knowledge of Cervantes and his novel *Don Quixote*

      5. Awareness of the 1992 celebration of the discovery

II. Problems in Documenting Columbus's First Voyage

  A. Vocabulary

      1. Philologists

      2. Reflected

      3. Faithfully

      4. Monarch

      5. Presumptuous

  B. Recognition of Writing Patterns or Arrangement of Ideas and Devices

      1. Explanation

  C. Concepts and Background Knowledge and Experience

      1. Understanding the significance of Columbus's journal not being the original

      2. Ability to question popular information on Columbus's first voyage

III. Certain and Possible Pre-Columbian Voyages to the Americas

  A. Vocabulary

      1. Facility

      2. Prominently

      3. Speculations

      4. Garrison

      5. Contrived

      6. Aboriginal

      7. Embittered

  B. Recognition of Writing Patterns or Arrangement of Ideas and Devices

      1. Explanation

  C. Concepts and Background Knowledge and Experience

      1. Ability to process the knowledge that Columbus was not the first European to "discover" the Americas

      2. Entertain other ideas on who "discovered" the Americas

      3. See that Columbus was human, not perfect

      4. Understand that Columbus was not happy with his rewards for his discoveries

IV. The Effects of Columbus's Voyages

    A. Vocabulary

      1. Ambivalence

      2. Syphilis

      3. Decimated

      4. Expansionism

      5. Colonialism

    B. Recognition of Writing Patterns or Arrangement of Ideas and Devices

      1. Explanation

    C. Concepts and Background Knowledge and Experience

      1. Many results of Columbus's "discovery" are regrettable.

      2. Many results of Columbus's "discovery" are good.

      3. We can learn from our history and try not to repeat our mistakes.

ACADEMIC STUDY SKILLS

DIRECTIONS

If you found the modified SQ4R study plan helpful and would like to use it for this chapter, follow the directions found in Appendix D, Chapter 7. The new study skills lesson below will be used as part of the post-reading lesson. You may want to skim it as part of your pre-reading so that you will know what to expect.

STUDY SKILL: MEMORY

The following exercise is intended to help you improve your memory and ability to place material in your long-term memory. Please follow the steps below:

    A. Review the reading lesson that you just completed, the Reciprocal Teaching lesson, or the Active Questioning lesson.

    B. What will you remember? Select what you think will be important for you to remember. Choose one important idea from each of the four sections of the chapter that you believe is important to remember. For example, from the first section, would you want to remember that the Basques were a minority group in Columbus's time or some information about Columbus himself? Try to choose information that is broad in scope and something you can talk about rather than choosing isolated facts.

      1. "Cosmopolitan Nature of Columbus and the Crew of His First Voyage"

      2. "Problems in Documenting Columbus's First Voyage"

      3.   "Certain and Possible Pre-Columbian Voyages to the Americas"

      4.   "The Effects of Columbus's Voyages"

C. Why will you remember the four pieces of material you have listed? If you cannot think of a reason, consider changing the material you have selected. For example, if I choose to remember the material about the Basques, my reason might be a general interest in minority groups, a specific interest in Basques because they still fight for independence from Spain, or because I know that in my history course we will study about them in greater detail. I also might plan to do a research paper on Columbus from the angle of his use of Basque sailors.

Why you will remember the four pieces of material you have listed:

_____

_____

_____

_____

D. How are the four pieces of material you have chosen to remember connected? For example, if I chose to remember material about Columbus in section one, and the question of his intent to travel to the Far East in section two, the fact that he was not a good administrator or a happy man in section three, and that good and bad resulted from his voyages in section four, I might ask myself a question about Columbus that would include all the above information in order to find the connection. I might ask, "How was Columbus a complex and mysterious man?"

How are the four pieces of material you have chosen to remember connected?

_____

_____

_____

_____

E. How can you self-check at this point to be sure that you know what you think you know? The following questions are good for reflection at this point:

      1.   Do you understand the material you have chosen? Could you talk about it? Could you write an essay on it? Do you have a sense of "depth of information" or merely superficial knowledge?

      2.   Do you see the significance of the material? Do you understand why it is important or where it is important?

      3.   Do all four parts connect to each other?

F. Ask yourself: What experience with and prior knowledge about the material I have selected do I have to remember that will expand my file on Columbus? Does any of my experience or prior knowledge conflict with my new knowledge? Review the Prior Knowledge section beginning on page 278 to jolt your memory. For example, I knew before I read the first section what the names of Columbus's ships were. I probably had to learn them in elementary school. I had read *Don Quixote* but had not connected the reference to Basques in it to Columbus's sailors. I also attended the 1992 celebration in Columbus, Ohio, and read articles on the controversy over the celebration. Section three of this reading selection brought conflicts between old and new knowledge for me. Elementary school biographies pretty much convinced me that great men and women were perfect human beings. I was surprised that Columbus was not perfect or satisfied with his rewards. He became a little more human for me as I read section three. I was a mature adult before I questioned the results of Columbus's voyages. Awareness of unjust treatment of other minority groups helped me to see the complexity of such adventures.

Your prior knowledge:

_____

_____

_____

Conflicts between your prior knowledge and what you read:

_____

_____

_____

G. How will you connect your prior knowledge and new information and then store it in your long-term memory? For example, if you enjoy talking more than writing, you can discuss your new information with a friend. If you enjoy writing, try connecting the information in a personal journal entry. Record your information and your thoughts and feelings about it. If you are creative, write an outline for a play, or a poem. Draw a computer graphic that symbolizes the essence of the information and your attitude about it. Visualize segments of the information and then relate it to your life. If you had been on one of the voyages, what would you have learned, felt, or experienced? If you have a tendency to be a perfectionist who is never satisfied with your achievements, what could you learn from Columbus?

You will connect your prior knowledge and the new information you read and then store it in your long-term memory by doing the following things:

_____

_____

_____

H. How can you be sure that you can retrieve this new file of information on Columbus at a later date? One way that should help you to retrieve this file at a later date is to think of several categories under which you can store the file. For example, words that have significance for me would be *Columbus, voyages, risk taking, complex people, complex outcomes,* and *minorities.*

You will use the following categories to store the file:

_____

_____

_____

I. What rewards can you expect? From my file, my greatest reward is a new way of seeing people that will help me in my everyday encounters. Instead of thinking of successful people as perfect human beings, I will look for complexity and conflict in their lives that did not keep them from great achievements. I will remember that people who have weaknesses and character faults can achieve. Human beings can overcome all kinds of barriers. In my own life, I will look for ways to overcome barriers, not to make excuses. Other rewards might include passing a history test on Columbus or winning an argument with a friend over minority rights.

Your rewards for learning and remembering this new information and connecting it with what you already knew will be:

_____

_____

_____

RECIPROCAL TEACHING

OVERVIEW

Your first step of the three-part reading plan was pre-reading. In pre-reading, you activated your prior knowledge, predicted what you would read, and overviewed the chapter before reading.

As the second step in this three-part reading plan, you will read the chapter "Some Problems with Columbus's 'Discovery' of America" by using the Reciprocal Teaching reading plan as explained below. An alternative plan, Active Questioning, is in Appendix B. In both plans you break up the chapter in sections and read and think about each as you read. The purpose of both plans is to keep you reading actively.

GENERAL DIRECTIONS

The concept of Reciprocal Teaching outlined here is adapted from Palinscar and Brown, 1986.

A. Both partners read a section under a subheading at a time. Take turns summarizing the section in as few sentences as possible.
B. Take turns asking a high level question or two on each section (inferential or critical/creative).
C. Explain or clarify difficult parts to each other. Practice repeating main ideas and supporting details in your own words.

    D.   Read the next subheading and predict what the section will be about. Discuss (exchange) ideas.

ASSIGNMENT

In this fourth Reciprocal Teaching reading plan you are given models for guided practice. If you are still not comfortable generating your own answers, try modifying the models rather than just answering them. You may use the Reciprocal Teaching model in Chapter 3 if you wish; the steps are predict, question, clarify, and summarize.

    A.   Read the introduction and the first section, "The Cosmopolitan Nature of Columbus and the Crew of His First Voyage," and follow the directions below.

        1.   Write a summary of the first major section. Model summary: Columbus's crew consisted of, among others, a minority group of people, the Basques. In many respects, Columbus as a person remains a mystery, but we do know that he went to Portugal, wrote in Portuguese-influenced Spanish, and read and wrote Latin. It is also assumed that he spoke Italian. What can you add, delete, and/or change?

Your summary _____

_____

_____

        2.   Write one question on this section. Try to write an inferential or a critical/creative question. If you can't, write a literal level question. Model question: Give support for calling Columbus "cosmopolitan."

Your question _____

        3.   Orally explain or clarify an important idea. (Model idea: Relate the information about the Basques to the problem stated in the introduction of this chapter.

Your idea _____

        4.   Predict what you will read in the second major section, "Problems in Documenting Columbus's First Voyage." Model prediction: I will read about specific problems that historians have in writing about what really happened on the first voyage.

Your prediction_____

    B.   Read the second section, "Problems in Documenting Columbus's First Voyage."

        1.   Summarize this second major section. Model summary: Columbus kept a journal but the original is lost. We do not know what changes were made in copies of the original. Historians are not sure that Columbus intended to go to the Far East. What can you add, delete, and/or change?

Your summary _____

_____

_____

2. Write one question on this section. Try to write an inferential or a critical/creative question. If you can't, write a literal level question. Model question: What are some of the problems associated with Columbus's journal?

Your question _____

3. Orally explain or clarify an important idea in this section. Model idea: What is the significance of the concern over Columbus's journal?

Your idea _____

4. Predict what you will read in the third major section of the chapter, "Certain and Possible Pre-Columbian Voyages to the Americas." Model prediction: I predict that Columbus may not have been the first explorer to reach the Americas.

Your prediction _____

C. Read the third section, "Certain and Possible Pre-Columbian Voyages to the Americas."

1. Summarize this third major section. Model summary: Many other explorers, such as the Basques, Atlantic fishermen, Leif Ericson, and Africans, may have reached the Americas before Columbus. Columbus was not a good administrator and he was not happy at the end of his life with his rewards. What can you add, delete, and/or change?

Your summary _____

_____

_____

2. Write one question on this section. Try to write an inferential or a critical/creative question. If you can't, write a literal level question. Model question: What evidence can you find of Columbus 's not being a good administrator?

Your question _____

3. Orally explain or clarify an important idea in this section. Model idea: What is the significance to history of there being early explorers to the Americas?

Your idea _____

4. Predict what you will read in the fourth major section of the chapter, "The Effects of Columbus's Voyages." Model prediction: I predict that I will read about the importance of Columbus's voyages to contemporary life.

Your prediction _____

    D. Read the fourth section, "The Effects of Columbus's Voyages."

        1. Summarize this fourth major section. Model summary: Various products were exchanged between the Americas and Europe. The population of the Americas was reduced whereas European expansionism grew. Colonialism and enslavement were two sad results. What can you add, delete, and/or change?

Your summary _____

_____

_____

        2. Write one question on this section. Try to write an inferential or a critical/creative question. If you can't, write a literal level question. Model question: Compare/contrast the good and bad results of Columbus's voyages and then answer whether or not the good outweighed the bad. Support your position.

Your question   _____

        3. Orally explain or clarify an important idea in this section. Model idea: Why the bad results of the voyages were bad.

Your idea   _____

        4. Prediction. There is no prediction because you have just read the last section of the chapter.

POST-READING THE TEXTBOOK CHAPTER

OVERVIEW

In the second part of your three-part reading plan, you practiced reading your textbook chapter section by section, wrote section summaries, asked and answered questions, explained or clarified important ideas, and made predictions for what you would read in the next section.

    In this third part of the three-part reading plan, you will find suggestions for what to do after you read. Your task is to compare what you predicted with what you actually read as an aid to comprehension, to add what you have learned to your file of information on the topic, and to think about what you have read.

ASSIGNMENT

As part of your post-reading activity, follow the directions for the memory exercise in the Academic Study Skills section on page 280. When you finish, return to this page and follow the directions below.

    A. Compare what you predicted you would read with what you actually read. Did anything you predicted cause you a problem with comprehension? What? How?

B. What did you learn about some problems of Columbus's discovery of America that you did not know?

C. Look at the words and phrases that you listed as your prior knowledge in the pre-reading section of this lesson on page 278. Group them below with relevant information in "B" above under the headings provided. Create your own headings if these do not work for you. This is your new file of information on American history. (The ability to group ideas and to see relationships requires more complex comprehension than merely memorizing isolated facts.)

D. In your pre-reading assignment, you recorded the major headings below. Now make up your own subheadings for the major headings on your outline of the chapter. Make up at least two subheadings for each of the four sections.

Some Problems with Columbus's "Discovery" of America

I. _____

    A. _____

    B. _____

II. _____

    A. _____

    B. _____

III. _____

    A. _____

    B. _____

IV. _____

    A. _____

    B. _____

E. What have you learned from this chapter that is important?

F. What do you already know that you can relate to it?

G. What do you see differently as a result of reading the chapter?

Columbus	Protests	Importance	Disadvantages	Other Explorers

SOME PROBLEMS WITH COLUMBUS'S "DISCOVERY" OF AMERICA

The quincentennial celebration of Christopher Columbus's discovery of the Americas in 1992 turned out to be, for many people, something less than a celebration. In fact, the mood of many who observed the anniversary seemed rather mournful than celebratory. It was pointed out that Native Americans, who had "discovered" the continents many centuries before, suffered diseases and enslavement from Columbus's coming, and that by many standards they were better off before the Europeans arrived. Native Americans, who generally rejected the term "Indians" which had been applied to them because of the famous misconception as to where Columbus had actually landed, made the quincentennial an occasion for voicing their reservations, almost their resentments that the Pinta, the Niña, and the Santa María had made the trip across the ocean. It was also pointed out that Africans were brought as slaves not long after Columbus discovered this "New World"; minority groups, with a recently developed prominence and power in American society in general, had a long list of complaints rather than a celebration of what had formerly been considered one of the world's great discoveries.

The Cosmopolitan Nature of Columbus and the Crew of His First Voyage

Hardly noticed in the general disturbance about the great discoverer and his no longer unanimously approved discovery was that at least one minority group complicated the usual picture of Columbus's group being pure Spaniards coming to extend the domain of the monarchs of Castile and Aragon over a new territory. These were Basques, members of perhaps the archetypal minority group in Europe. Speaking a language not related to any of the European, Asiatic, or other world languages, the Basques had been subject to Spain for some centuries but had retained their distinctness culturally as well as linguistically. Cervantes in *Don Quixote* makes a Basque an object of fun for his dialect of Spanish. A little more than a century before this Golden Age attention, say some of their American descendants, Basques had outfitted the Santa María, Columbus's flagship on the first voyage, and comprised a significant portion of the crew of that ship as well as of the Niña. Other authorities merely report that a significant number of the sailors on the Santa María were northerners—Galicians and Basques. Even stronger Basque participation could apparently be claimed for Columbus's third voyage.

No one can know how many of these matters were on Columbus's mind when he sailed from Palos, Spain, on August 2, 1492. In fact, not too much is known about his life before the sailing. His family is said to have been Genoan wool merchants, and Columbus himself—perhaps in that connection—was from an early age active in the Mediterranean maritime trade. At one time or another he went to Portugal and associated himself with the Portuguese; some think that, some time in the early 1480s, he may have accompanied Portuguese sailors who were already traveling along the West African coast. His journals are written in a notoriously Portuguese-influenced Spanish, but there is evidence that such Spanish was a prestige language among the Portuguese in that period and it is not certain that Columbus was necessarily fluent in Portuguese. (It is assumed that he spoke Italian, although direct evidence is slight.) There is evidence that he read and even wrote in Latin, a version of which was useful as a trade language in the Mediterranean. He had been reading and annotating Biblical and other texts concerning the existence of other lands. And, being able to persuade Ferdinand and Isabella to support him—although of course not without a great deal of difficulty—he had presumably acquired the polish of a courtier.

Problems in Documenting Columbus's First Voyage

At first glance, Columbus's activities after sailing would seem to be extremely well documented. He kept a journal in which he recorded the activities of the first of his four voyages in great detail. This would seem to be the best possible kind of evidence. But philologists have raised questions. The manuscript is not the autograph (that produced in the hand of the original writer) but a copy made by Las Casas. The fact that Columbus's Portuguese-accented Spanish is reflected in the copy is one argument that Las Casas made few changes, but the possibility remains that changes were made. And even if Columbus's manuscript is faithfully represented in what we now have, we have no other accounts to check against it to insure its accuracy.

Everyone knows that Columbus had not arrived in the "Indies" when he landed on a small island in the Bahamas, possibly what is today called San Salvador or Watling Island. It is generally assumed that he *intended* to travel to the Far East, but even that is not completely certain. If his mission was indeed to establish trading relationships with the Great Khan, would he have dared to enslave the subjects of that monarch whom he encountered in the outlying islands? Would he have been so presumptuous as to claim the island for their Catholic majesties? Or was "sailing to the Far East" merely a kind of smoke screen for an entirely different intention?

Certain and Possible Pre-Columbian Voyages to the Americas

Return briefly to consider that minority group which was represented on the Santa Maria, the Basques. As fishers and whalers, Basques had long operated out into the Atlantic, probably at least as far as Iceland. Geographically, there was no such barrier as the Pillars of Hercules for Mediterranean sailors, but the Basques had many of the same advantages of international contact which Greeks, Italians, and others would have had. Later, Basques were credited with a special facility in communicating with Native Americans, although there is no relationship between the Basque language and any Amerindian language.

It has long been suggested that Atlantic fishermen (the Bretons had figured prominently in speculations) had been operating on the banks of Newfoundland and that their knowledge of a continent to the West had become fairly general among Mediterranean sailors. The earlier explorations of Leif Ericson are of course well known, and other suggestions have been made concerning early "discovery" of the Americas by others than the Asians who migrated across Bering Strait and strangely came to be labeled "Indians." The shortest distance between the Old World and the New is that between West Africa and Brazil, and there has been speculation that Africans could have made the trip and perhaps have passed the knowledge on to Portuguese who were "exploring" the west coast of their continent.

Whether he was a blunderer on an oceanic scale or a great navigator, Columbus does not seem to have been an especially good administrator. Alonso Pinzón, captain of the Pinta, had an early disagreement with Columbus and sailed off on his own; there is considerable disagreement as to the conditions under which they were reunited. The garrison Columbus left behind on Hispanola when returning from the first trip contrived apparently to offend even the mild-mannered Arawak Indians aboriginal to the islands and was destroyed by them. Columbus was accorded the title Admiral of the Ocean Seas, with all the honor attendant thereupon, but it never seems to have been made clear how much of the income derived from his explorations was rightfully his. It is commonplace that he ended his life embittered because of not receiving all that he felt was coming to him.

The Effects of Columbus's Voyages

What happened a little over five hundred years ago? In spite of all the uncertainties, in spite of ambivalence toward the results, it is certain that the influences from what happened were far-reaching. The "Columbian Exchange" meant that products like potatoes, tomatoes, corn, and tobacco were brought into Europe. (Some think that syphilis was still another "gift" of the New World to the Old.) Cattle, horses, and wheat from Europe were only part of the culture-transforming importations to the Americas. If the population of the Americas was decimated, that of Europe had breathing room and more; European expansionism got a huge boost from the geographic discoveries. Colonialism, the feeling that Europeans were entitled to dominate and to exploit non-Europeans, soon expanded all the way across the globe; enslavement, or its practical equivalent, of the non-European populations resulted and lasted over a period of centuries.

Summary

The expected celebration of the Columbus quincentennial in 1992 turned out to be something more like a protest demonstration in some respects. Those who refused to celebrate the "discovery" pointed out the high incidence of suffering and death which the coming of the Europeans brought to Native Americans, reducing them to a "disadvantaged" minority. It is ironic that perhaps the most typical European minority, the Basques, may have played an important role in Columbus's voyages. In fact, there are many theories as to how other groups, less prominent than the Spanish, may have come earlier than Columbus. Even the true purpose of Columbus's first voyage is subject to question. However this may be, the wholesale mixing of European and Native American cultures began with Columbus's voyages; neither Europe nor the "New World" would ever be the same again.

Questions

1. What groups have been the leaders in questioning the assumption that Columbus's trip to the Americas was a great deed by a great man?

2. Why has it been those groups rather than others that raised the questions?

3. What would be the implications if it proved true that the Basques were prominent in the fleets of Columbus's first and third voyages?

4. Even if Columbus was not the first to come from the "Old World" to the "New World," what undeniable significance do his explorations have?

VOCABULARY LESSON

The purpose of this exercise is to help you review and deepen your knowledge of the ten general vocabulary words you worked with at the beginning of this chapter.

A. Structural Analysis—Affixes and Root Words
1. Circle the prefix and underline the suffix of the following word: *Misconception*
    a. Write a sentence in which you show you know the word.

       _____

    b. Write a sentence in which you show you know the root word.

       _____

2. Underline the suffix of the following word: *Archetypical*
    a. Circle the two root words in the word above.
    b. Write a sentence in which you show you know the last root word.

       _____

B. Use of Context
1. Read the sentence in the third section, third paragraph of the chapter in which the word *aboriginal* appears and in your own words write a definition for the word.

       _____

2. Read the sentence in section two, second paragraph of the chapter in which the word *presumptuous* appears and in your own words write a definition for the word.

       _____

C. Multiple Meanings of Words
1. Circle the definition of the word *prominence* that shows how it is used in this chapter.
    a. Standing out; jutting
    b. Conspicuous; distinguished
2. Circle the definition of the word *speculation* that shows how it is used in this chapter.
    a. meditate or ponder; reflect
    b. theorize; conjecture
    c. make a risky investment
D. Synonyms and Antonyms: List one synonym (same meaning) and one antonym (opposite meaning) for each of the following words:

Word	Synonym	Antonym
Cosmopolitan		
Notorious(ly)		

E.   Generate Your Own Language
1.   What *misconceptions* did you have about college before becoming a student?
2.   What *speculations* have you made about your life four years from now?
3.   Describe your *ambivalence* about the Significant Other in your life or your pet.
4.   What recent wars have *decimated* targeted groups of people?
5.   Would it be *presumptuous* on the part of a man to ask his date to pay for her dinner on their first date?

VOCABULARY EXTENSION

The purpose of this exercise is to help you see to what degree you know the ten general vocabulary words you worked with at the beginning of this chapter. Matching a word with its definition is the beginning of knowing a word. Using the word in your speaking and writing is full knowledge.

A.   List the vocabulary words from this lesson that you can now use in both your speaking and writing.
B.   List the vocabulary words from this lesson that you can now use in writing but are still not comfortable using in speaking.
C.   List the vocabulary words from this lesson that you cannot use yet but will recognize in reading.
D.   List general vocabulary words from this lesson that are still difficult to understand.
E.   Use *five* vocabulary words from this lesson in a five-sentence paragraph on the topic of this lesson.
F.   Illustrate the meaning of *one* of the vocabulary words from this lesson through some form of artwork or a cartoon. (This exercise is for right-brain students who enjoy drawing better than writing!)

EXTENDED READING ACTIVITIES

The purpose of this section is to give you a variety of options for independent study or investigation of the chapter topic. Reading is a skill that must be practiced each day if progress is to take place. These activities are designed to give you a variety of reading experiences through which you can improve your general vocabulary and increase your higher-level comprehension skills.

Your instructor may wish to (a) assign one or more activities to the class as a whole, (b) assign various activities to small groups, (c) assign one or more activities to individual students, or (d) let students choose to do the activities or not.

A.   Weekly Reading Report: Continue keeping a weekly report of your reading. Use the form in Appendix C if you wish. Are you increasing your interest in a variety of topics? What is something new that you read and thought about? Have you read something that took some time to understand but was worth it? How have you changed as a result of something you read? What do you read on the Internet?

B. Attend a Reading Lab: Continue to attend the reading lab on your campus if you have one. Practice on timed readings to increase your reading rate. You read faster when you know something about the subject and are interested in it. Vocabulary, writing style, patterns of organization, density of concepts, and required background can slow you down.

C. Read Your Novel: Continue reading your novel. If it has become boring, quit reading and choose another. Try a different genre. For example, if you are reading a romance, try a science fiction novel. If you are reading a boring fictionalized historical biography, try a biography about a different person, historical period, or type of work for which the person is famous. Pleasure reading should not be boring after the first fifty pages. If you are not offended by a little profanity, try Chris Crutcher's *Staying Fat for Sarah Byrnes* or Robert Cormier's *The Chocolate War*. If social class clash is interesting to you, try S. E. Hinton's *The Outsiders*. If you choose *The Outsiders*, you may enjoy watching the video of *Westside Story* and comparing it to the novel since both deal with the problems related to gang membership.

D. Read with your children
   1. Jean Fritz, *Where Do You Think You're Going, Christopher Columbus?*
   2. Philippa Wingate & Struan Reid, *Who Were the First North Americans?*

E. Reading/Writing Connection: Continue your college journal. What is your school's history? Have other members of your family attended or graduated from your school? Are there historical buildings on campus? Are they an important part of the school's image? What kind of sense of history have you developed since beginning school there? Does the presence or absence of a sense of history on campus influence your perception of yourself as a student? How? Are traditions important on your campus? What are they? Do you buy into them? Do they enrich your life? How? Write your insights in your journal. Use a new vocabulary word in your response.

F. Use the Internet: Look up Columbus, Basques, *Santa Maria, Niña*, and *Pinta* or *quincentennial*.

G. Vocabulary Journal: Continue keeping a vocabulary journal. Use the form in Appendix C if you wish. Try to find general vocabulary words, words that appear in mainstream magazines and in textbooks. If you are taking a course filled with technical vocabulary that is difficult for you, you might want to keep a separate vocabulary journal for it. Such a journal should help you with the course.

H. Magazine/Journal/Newspaper Reading: Read a magazine or journal about minorities. Use the form in Appendix C if you wish. Some titles about African Americans that might interest you are *African American Review, Black Enterprise, Ebony, Journal of Black Studies, Jet, Black Issues Book Review*, and *Negro History Bulletin*. What else can you find? What other minorities interest you? You may also be interested in the magazines and journals in education. If so, read *Phi Delta Kappan, Academe (Bulletin of the American Association of University Professors)*,

Educational Researcher, Educational Studies, Educational Technology, Journal of Adolescent & Adult Literacy, Journal of Learning Disabilities, The Journal of Special Education, Reading Today.

REFLECTION

MIND REVOLUTION

Not all high achievers or heroes are perfect. What have you not attempted because of your fear of failure? What mixed results (both good and bad) have you had from something you did try? Did you let the bad stop you from trying something else?

VOCABULARY

What feelings do you have about the vocabulary word *cosmopolitan*? Many times we can add a dictionary definition to a word and think we understand it but we do not. *Cosmopolitan* could be one of those words. If you are from a rural area that is economically hard-pressed and losing its young people, you may have negative feelings about the word. It may make you think of the nearest large city where some of your friends are going to find jobs. The idea of living a sophisticated life style in a large city may make you feel the loss of your friends, your environment, and your culture. The values in your culture may clash with a cosmopolitan life style. The things you do, the things you talk about, the places you enjoy going may differ. The feelings that words evoke are called *connotations* and influence your use and understanding of words, especially where there are emotional attachments involved. What positive connotations do you have for the word *cosmopolitan*? Can you think of other words whose connotations influence your understanding and use of them?

COMPREHENSION

Build your background knowledge and interest in history. When you were in high school, did you enjoy history classes or did you sleep through them? Were you one of those students who could not see the significance of having to learn about things in the past? What was your reaction when your history teacher said that we need to know about the past in order to learn from our mistakes and not repeat them? Do you see evidence of our having not learned from our past now? What are the results? For example, what feelings do you have about neo-Nazis? What do you know about Germany's ability to deal with such groups today? Why do such groups exist in the United States? What do you know about World War II and the Nazis? What you know (and do not know) probably influences what you think about these groups. During the writing of this textbook, a movie came out about Pearl Harbor and with it a few television shows about World War II. Have you seen any of these?

What do you know about the Civil Rights Movement of the 1960s in the United States? What present political issues derive from legislation from that period? What do you know about the Women's Movement? What issues have been important to women for the last thirty years? Can you imagine a time in which African–Americans and women could not vote? It happened.

Anthropology and Sociology: Two Views of the Study of Society and Culture

Overview

VOCABULARY/METACOGNITION

The purpose of this exercise is to help you become aware of when you know the meaning of a word and to help you know when you do not know the meaning of a word. This is metacognition awareness.

On a scale of 1–5 (see below), rate your knowledge of the following vocabulary words from "Two Views of the Study of Society and Culture." After matching words with definitions on page 298, check your answers and then check your number *ones* and *fives* below. Did you know when you really knew a word and when you really did not know the word?

Scale

1. I absolutely do not know.
2. I do not think I know.
3. There's a 50/50 chance I have seen or heard it.
4. I think I know it.
5. I know the word and can use it.

Words

_____ 1. Naive

_____ 2. Bizarre

_____ 3. Verisimilitude

_____ 4. Expedient

_____ 5. Elicit (eliciting))

_____ 6. Egalitarian

_____ 7. Compensate (compensatory)

_____ 8. Staple

_____ 9. Intuition

_____10. Caste

Go to page 298. See if you can match the right definition with the word and then write sentences for any five words in the list.

Words	Definitions
_____ 1. Naive	A. Draw out; bring forth; evoke
_____ 2. Bizarre	B. Unsophisticated; artless
_____ 3. Verisimilitude	C. A social class
_____ 4. Expedient	D. Odd; whimsical; grotesque
_____ 5. Elicit (eliciting)	E. Comprehension without effort of reasoning; instinctive knowledge
_____ 6. Egalitarian	F. An appearance of truth
_____ 7. Compensate (compensatory)	G. (1) A loop of wire driven as a nail or fastener; (2) a principal commodity; (3) a raw material
_____ 8. Staple	H. (1) Serving to promote a desired object; advisable; (2) conducive to present advantage or self-interest
_____ 9. Intuition	I. (1) Make up (for); offset; (2) pay (for); recompense
_____10. Caste	J. Advocating equal rights for all

Write five words from the list and your own sentences that show you know how to use the words. Choose words that you marked a *five* if possible.

1. Word _____

    Sentence _____

2. Word _____

    Sentence _____

3. Word _____

    Sentence _____

4. Word _____

    Sentence _____

5. Word _____

    Sentence _____

Pre-Reading the Textbook Chapter

The purpose of this *first* of three steps in your reading plan is to suggest things to do *before* you read. First, as part of your pre-reading, read the Prior Knowledge section beginning on page 299. When you finish, return to this section and continue your pre-reading. You will use the Academic Study Skills section as a post-reading activity but you may want to skim it at this time so that you will know what to expect.

Tapping Prior Knowledge

Tap your experience and prior knowledge about the title of this selection by writing words and phrases that come to your mind. You are pulling up your file on the topic and focusing on what you will read. What do you already know about the subject? Do not look at your textbook at this time, as these answers will vary from person to person and won't be found in the textbook. There are no wrong answers for this part of the lesson.

Predicting

Predict in one sentence what you will read. Try to predict in some detail. Don't write, "I predict that I will read about two views of the study of society and culture." What behavior, action, and/or information do you expect to read about? Predicting helps you identify your expectations of what you will read. Not reading what you have predicted will serve as a warning that you have misjudged the topic of the article and will help you adapt to what is in the chapter.

Overviewing

Overview the chapter by outlining it on page 307 under the post-reading section of this lesson (major sections only) and by reading the summary and the questions at the end of the chapter.

Prior Knowledge

This section, part of your pre-reading, presents a model to show you what will help you comprehend this chapter by using your own background knowledge. If you know much of the following information, you have a better background for reading this chapter. This section will suggest helpful kinds of background information and help you activate what you know; do not try to look up or learn everything listed. Ask yourself what you need to know before you read and what you already know that will help you to understand this chapter. Your instructor may want to use this section for a whole-class or small group discussion or have you read it silently.

Chapter Sections

I. The Nature of Anthropological Research
    A. Vocabulary
        1. Discipline
        2. Exotic
        3. Advantageous
        4. Naive
        5. Bizarre
        6. Exaggerate
        7. Polygynous
        8. Polyandrous

9. Ethnography
10. Scandalizes
11. Verisimilitude
12. Neo-classical
13. Universalist (universality)
14. Romanticism
15. Particularity
16. Expedient
17. Appreciable
18. Specialized (specialization)
19. Informants
20. Eliciting

B. Recognition of Writing Patterns or Arrangement of Ideas and Devices
   1. Comparison/Contrast
     a. Introduction
     b. Difference between amateurs and professionals
   2. Explanation
   3. Use of examples to support thesis statement (paragraph 3)

C. Concepts and Background Knowledge and Experience
   1. Interest in differences between anthropology and sociology
   2. Awareness of one's own cultural pattern
   3. Ability to accept cultural differences
   4. Experience of others judging one's own culture
   5. Experience enough with cultural differences to see that there is more than one way to see or do things
   6. Literary background
     a. Have read or at least know who Melville is
     b. Literary periods—Neo-classical and Romantic
   7. Watch Discovery and PBS television channels that show documentaries on unusual places and people
   8. Experienced being cut off from one's own culture or first language
   9. Aware of significance of time spent in a different culture in order to understand it
   10. Have an intense, long-lasting interest in something—hobby, subject, etc.
   11. Knowledge of or experience with survey sampling techniques and questionnaires
   12. Interest in or curiosity about other languages

II. Cultural and Linguistic Relativism
  A. Vocabulary
    1. Egalitarian
    2. Compensatory
    3. Staple

    B. Recognition of Writing Patterns or Arrangement of Ideas and Devices
       1. Contrast (naive observer vs. cultural relativist)
       2. Transitional paragraph
       3. Comparison/contrast
    C. Concepts and Background Knowledge and Experience
       1. Relativism vs. deficit theory
       2. Respect for different cultures
III. The Nature of Sociological Research
    A. Vocabulary
       1. Intuition
       2. Statistical significance
       3. Dialectology
       4. Caste
       5. Stratificational (factors)
       6. Complementary
       7. Contradictory
    B. Recognition of Writing Patterns or Arrangement of Ideas and Devices
       1. Contrast continued
       2. Conclusion
    C. Concepts and Background Knowledge and Experience
       1. Background in sociology, such as a course
       2. Familiar with sociology methodology, such as use of questionnaires and sampling procedures, statistics
       3. Awareness of the connection between language and social class
       4. Awareness of the varieties of American English

ACADEMIC STUDY SKILLS

DIRECTIONS

If you found the modified SQ4R plan and the exercise on memory helpful and would like to use them for this chapter, follow the directions found in Appendix D, Chapter 8.

The new study skills lesson below will be used as part of the post-reading lesson. You may want to skim it as part of your pre-reading so that you will know what to expect.

STUDY SKILL: ANNOTATION

Another useful study skill is annotation. Annotation is making notes in the margin of your textbook that can be useful when you have a difficult reading assignment or are facing a big test on the material. If you had no background knowledge or experience about anthropologists and sociologists, you may have found this material difficult; therefore, the following exercise is offered to help you see if you really know the material and to see if you can now identify the most important information in the chapter.

A. We will begin by planning to write one main idea, significant examples, and any definitions for each paragraph.

B. In the introduction, the author tells the reader how the two fields of anthropology and sociology are alike and different. In the margin of your textbook write these two pieces of information in your own words. Do not use the words of the author.

C. The author begins the first paragraph of the first section, "The Nature of Anthropological Research," with a statement about anthropology and amateur effort. Write that statement in your own words in the margin of your textbook by that paragraph. Now find one example of such amateurs and write that one word in the same margin and mark it "example."

D. The second paragraph of this section deals with the "bizarreness reaction" of untrained observers or amateurs. In the margin by this paragraph of your textbook write what this reaction is in your own words. Find two examples of it and write one word for each in the margin, marking them as examples.

E. The third paragraph of this section discusses the use of fiction in the description of cultures. Write this information in your own words in the margin by this paragraph. Next find one example and write it in the same margin.

F. In the fourth paragraph of this section, the history of literature's connection to the development of anthropology is discussed. What neo-classical ideas and Romantic ideas influenced the study of strange cultures? Write the answers to these questions in your own words in the margin of your textbook by this paragraph. What literary work is listed as an example of the neo-classical type of literature discussed? Write the name and author in the margin as an example.

G. After listing the influences on anthropology in the above paragraphs, the author shifts ground in the fifth paragraph. Instead of depending on novelists and amateurs, what must the anthropologist do? What is this called? Write the answers to these questions in your own words in the margin of your textbook by this paragraph.

H. In the sixth paragraph the author discusses a problem the field worker faces. What is it? Briefly write it in your own words in the margin of your textbook by this paragraph.

I. In the seventh paragraph the author discusses problems field workers face in questioning members of a culture. What are the problems? Briefly list them in your own words in the margin of your textbook by this paragraph.

J. In the eighth and last paragraph of this section, the author discusses the importance of the anthropologists who learn exotic languages around the world and share information about them. What information do they share? What do they stress? Are anthropologists more or less important to the field of linguistics in contemporary times? Answer these questions in your own words and write the information in the margin of your textbook by this paragraph.

K. Another kind of information that can be written in annotations is questions you may have about the material. For example, you may notice at this point that the author has written eight paragraphs that basically deal with anthropologists, but he has only written three paragraphs each for the second and third sections of the chapter. Does he consider anthropology more important than sociology? Is he simply more interested in the field of anthropology? Take time to go back and write in the margins any questions you may have for this first section of the chapter.

L. In the first and second paragraphs of the second section, "Cultural and Linguistic Relativism," the author discusses cultural relativism and how cultural relativists perceive strange cultures in a different way from amateurs or naive observers. Briefly write the difference in your own words by the two paragraphs. The naive observer's perception is given in the first paragraph and the cultural relativist's perception is given in the second. Now find two examples of how cultural relativists see the poor and rich in a culture. Write a word for each by the second paragraph and mark them as examples.

M. The third and last paragraph of this section is a transitional paragraph that moves the reader from anthropology to a focus on sociology. What is the different angle that sociology uses? Make a list of the differences in the margin of your textbook by this paragraph. Note that you are building on the information you learned in the first section of this chapter.

N. What questions do you have about this section? Did you get lost in the technical vocabulary or strange ideas about language? Write any questions you have in the margins in this section.

O. In the first paragraph of the third section, "The Nature of Sociological Research" the author discusses the use of questionnaires and some of the problems sociologists encounter. What are the problems and how do the sociologists deal with them? Answer this question in your own words and write the answer in the margin of your textbook by this paragraph.

P. In the second paragraph, the author discusses sociological procedures and language. Do the procedures work better on dialects or on exotic languages? The author further states that dialect behavior correlates with social class and has influenced the study of dialects and the study of social classes. With what have sociological studies of language tended to deal? List them in the margin of your textbook by this paragraph.

Q. In the third and last paragraph, the author closes the chapter by stating that both anthropologists and sociologists have the same aim. What is it? How are the two alike? Do research projects need both? Put the information in your own words and write it in the margin of your textbook by this paragraph.

R. What questions do you have about this section? Did you get lost in the technical vocabulary or strange ideas about language? Write any questions you have in the margins in this section.

   S.   Review the information you have learned from the reading lesson and from your annotation of the text. Write a formal outline of this information. You wrote the major headings for the outline as part of your pre-reading lesson. The outline is located in your post-reading section of this chapter on page 307.

Active Questioning

Overview

Your first step of the three-part reading plan was pre-reading. In pre-reading, you activated your prior knowledge, predicted what you would read, and overviewed the chapter before reading.

   As the second step in this three-part reading plan, you will read this chapter by using the Active Questioning reading plan as explained below. An alternative plan, Reciprocal Teaching, is in Appendix B. In both plans you break up the chapter in sections and read and think about each as you read. The purpose of both plans is to keep you reading actively. This will be the fourth time you have used this plan. Teacher-made questions are given for guidance. You have answered teacher-made questions and written some questions on your own. You are somewhere between guided practice and independence in using this plan. When you have difficulty generating your own questions, modify and then answer the models.

General Directions

When using active questioning, write questions on the literal, inferential, and creative/critical levels.

Assignment

   A.   Read section one, "The Nature of Anthropological Research," and ask one text-explicit question (literal), one text-implicit question (inferential), and one experienced-based question (critical/creative) each on this section. Please answer all three questions. Do not ask a question that you cannot answer.

      1.   Text-explicit (literal level): A question that requires the reader to read the line. The answer will come from one line of print. Model text-explicit question: Who provided some of the information available about exotic cultures before university training in the discipline was available?

Your text-explicit question _____

Answer _____

      2.   Text-implicit (inferential level): A question that requires the reader to read between the lines. The answer will come from more than one line of print. You will need to make judgments and draw

conclusions. Model text-implicit questions: (1) What are three sources for information on other cultures? (2) What four things must anthropologists know and do as they study a different culture?

Your text-implicit question _____

Answer _____

   3.   Experience-based (critical/creative level): A question that requires the reader to read beyond the lines. Apply what you have learned to your world. Question what you have read. Model experience-based question: If you were an anthropologist, what culture would you study? What would be your strengths and weaknesses? What would be fun? Difficult?

Your experience-based question _____

Answer _____

B.   Read the second section, "Cultural and Linguistic Relativism," and ask one text-explicit question, one text-implicit question, and one experienced-based question each on this section. Please answer all three questions. Do not ask a question that you cannot answer.

   1.   Model text-explicit question: What is the naive observer likely to see in a different culture?

Your text-explicit question _____

Answer _____

   2.   Model text-implicit questions: (1) Can you list some differences in point of view of the naive observers who see deficiencies in a strange culture and the cultural relativists who see both poor and rich elements in the culture? (2) What are some of the differences in how sociologists study societal behavior?

Your text-implicit question _____

Answer _____

   3.   Model experience-based questions: (1) Would your observations of a different culture be that of a naive observer or a cultural relativist? Explain. (2) What kind of kinship system do you have in the culture in which you were raised? What are its strengths and weaknesses?

Your experience-based question _____

Answer _____

C.   Read the third section, "The Nature of Sociological Research," and ask one text-explicit question, one text-implicit question, and one experienced-based question each on this section. Please answer all three questions. Do not ask a question that you cannot answer.

   1.   Model text-explicit question: Does the sociologist or the anthropologist depend the most on the self-report of the society being studied?

Your text-explicit question _____

Answer _____

2. Model text-implicit questions: (1) How do sociologists and anthropologists differ in the way they handle informants' information? (2) How are they alike?

Your text-implicit question _____

Answer _____

3. Model experience-based question: To what social class do you belong? How is your dialect a reflection of that class? If you wanted to rise socially, how would your language change?

Your experience-based question _____

Answer _____

POST-READING THE TEXTBOOK CHAPTER

OVERVIEW

In the second part of your three-part reading plan, you practiced reading your textbook chapter section by section and asked and answered questions.

In this third part of the three-part reading plan, you will find suggestions for what to do after you read. Your task is to compare what you predicted with what you actually read as an aid to comprehension, to add what you have learned to your file of information on the topic, and to think about it.

ASSIGNMENT

As part of your post-reading activity, follow the directions for the annotation exercise in the Academic Study Skills section beginning on page 301. When you finish, return to this page and follow the directions below.

A. Compare what you predicted you would read with what you actually read. Did anything you predicted cause you a problem with comprehension? What? How?

B. What did you learn from the reading that you did not know about before working on this lesson?

C. Look at the words and phrases that you listed as your prior knowledge in the pre-reading section of this lesson on page 299. Group them below with relevant information in "B" above. This is your new file of information on anthropology and sociology. (The ability to group ideas and to see relationships requires more complex comprehension than merely memorizing isolated facts.) Use the headings on page 307 or create your own.

	Alike	Different
Anthropologists		
Sociologists		

D. Make up your own subheadings for the major headings on your outline of the chapter. Make up at least two subheadings for each of the four sections. You were told to write a formal outline in the annotation exercise, so use that information to help you create subheadings. When you finish, turn the outline into a map (see Chapter 1, Extended Reading Activities, Content Area Report, page 63, for map directions).

Two Views of the Study of Society and Culture

I. _____

    A. _____

    B. _____

II. _____

    A. _____

    B. _____

III. _____

    A. _____

    B. _____

E. What have you learned from this chapter that is important?
F. What do you already know that you can relate to it?
G. What do you see differently as a result of reading this chapter?

TWO VIEWS OF THE STUDY OF SOCIETY AND CULTURE

Anthropology and sociology are closely related fields, both of them dealing with human society and behavior patterns. Especially at small colleges, the same person may teach in both fields. There are, however, some rather important differences in the way they approach the topic of human social structure and behavior. In anthropology, the key word is perhaps *culture*; in sociology, *society*. Although neither word is excluded from either discipline, the vocabulary difference gives a rough idea of the difference in emphasis. Furthermore, there are rather great methodological differences.

The Nature of Anthropological Research

Although a good anthropologist needs extensive training, anthropology is often considered to lend itself more nearly to amateur effort than sociology. In the past, before university training in the discipline was available, travelers and even tourists provided some of the information available about "exotic" cultures. Missionaries often found that knowledge not only of the religion but of the culture of another group was advantageous to the spread of Christianity. To some degree, these people provided the earliest records we have of foreign cultures. Although such information from the past needs to be checked by the requirements of good anthropological method, in many cases such records are all there is available insofar as culture history is concerned.

Part of what makes the information provided by untrained observers usable to some degree has to do with recognition of a kind of reaction which anthropologically naive observers tend to exhibit. This can be called the "bizarreness reaction." What an untrained observer labels—whether overtly or simply in his general attitude—as "bizarre" can, with some confidence, be said to contrast with his own cultural practice. Thus, if an anthropologist had nothing to go on but tourist reports which might be expected to exaggerate the "exotic" and overlook the commonplace, he could still assume that the things considered reportable were outside the ordinary experience of the reporter in his home environment. A naive observer might, for example, expect people in all parts of the world to dress as he, his family, and his friends dressed; observation of different attitudes toward clothing would be likely to be expressed in terms of wonder or even disapproval. Or he might expect all societies to have the marriage patterns of Europe and America, where only one legal mate is possible at a time, rather than the polygynous ("many wives") patterns which exist in many other societies and the polyandrous ("many husbands") pattern which exists in a few.

Even fiction may serve some purpose in the description of culture, although of course professional students of ethnography prefer to gather information from other sources wherever possible. In the first chapter of *Typee*, for example, Herman Melville, no anthropologist by any stretch of the imagination but an intelligent observer, has a scene in which a lady of high rank from the South Seas scandalizes some Europeans by lifting her skirt (which she is wearing perhaps to please those Europeans) above her head to show her tattoos to a common sailor whose tattoos she admires. While we cannot be sure that Melville, in his stay in the South Pacific, ever saw such an event—or reported it on the basis of reliable communication—the scene has a certain verisimilitude in light of the fact that non-Europeanized populations have different attitudes toward covering parts of the body from the Europeans.

To some degree it could even be said that the history of literature anticipates the development of anthropology. In the eighteenth century, with its neo-classical ideas of the perfection of society, there was at first little interest in lands outside Europe. Gradually, however, the universalist concerns of prominent writers led them to show how underlying patterns manifested themselves in seemingly exotic cultures. A fairly representative work of this type might be Oliver Goldsmith's *A Citizen of the World*. When nineteenth-century Romanticism turned to interest in particularity rather than in universality, there was already in place the beginning of a mechanism for looking at "strange" behavior patterns in other lands with other peoples.

But the interests of societal disciplines became greatly different from those of literary men, particularly since amateurs cannot be depended upon for precise observation. To keep from depending upon novelists and tourists, the anthropologist usually finds that there is only one expedient: Go there himself or herself. Thus, ethnography frequently involves a great deal of what is called field work. The anthropologist, often but not necessarily a graduate student at work on a dissertation, actually goes to where the culture to be studied exists in as pure a form as possible, stays there for an appreciable time, and tries to live within the culture. This is called *participant observation*. It means, of course, that the field worker should be willing not only to enter into another culture but to cut himself off from his own culture.

No matter how talented, the field worker can seldom if ever achieve his or her goal of being identical to members of the culture being studied. To have the equivalent of a lifetime in the society being studied, he or she would need to live a lifetime there, and duties and responsibilities remain at home, especially for the researcher who must exist in an American or European university environment. It is seldom possible to spend more than a year or two in the field, although the specialized worker returns to his region of specialization as often as he or she can.

To make up for the lack of time, the researcher must sooner or later resort to questioning members of the culture being studied. Full-time members of the culture are treated as *informants* (although the term *consultant* is coming to be preferred) and are usually paid for their information. Even so, eliciting information is not an uncomplicated process. It is an axiom of field work that "the unusual informant responds." The twin pitfalls are undercooperation (the informant simply will withhold information) and overcooperation (the informant will tell the researcher what the latter seems to want to hear). Overcooperation is as great a danger as undercooperation; Caribbean writer Derek Walcott has written amusingly of a ritual his people performed "to please an anthropologist." Crosschecking of informants, as well as a feel for what is real and what is fictitious, is usually necessary. Some knowledge of sampling procedure and questionnaire techniques may be required, although such procedures and techniques are difficult to utilize in the interior of Africa or in the Amazon basin.

Usually, the field worker will be leaving behind his or her native language—or any language with which he is familiar through study in school. Learning the culture of an "exotic" group also means learning the language. In the past, anthropologists have made significant contributions to linguistics, especially in the sense of providing information as to how words, expressions, and grammatical and phonological systems may differ from those of the familiar European languages of the schools. Anthropological linguistics tended to stress the differences between languages, to suggest that communicative strategies foreign to the well-studied languages were to be found among American Indians, in Africa, in parts of Asia, or in other relatively unexplored places. More recent linguistic theory stresses the universality of human language structure, especially insofar as basic design features go; anthropologists are perhaps not so important to linguistics in the twenty-first century as they were in the early decades. But much of the attention which has been given to the relatively unstudied languages of the world might never have been given had it not been for anthropologists learning "exotic" languages as part of "exotic" cultures and reporting what they had learned to the academic world at large.

Cultural and Linguistic Relativism

An important principle which came out of ethnographic field work is that of cultural—and linguistic—relativism. The naive observer whom we discussed above—the tourist away from home on a brief trip—is likely to see difference as deficiency. His descriptions of a culture are likely to concentrate on the things that are missing. If he learns a little bit about the language, he may observe that speakers of "exotic" languages may not have, for example, the same kind of article system as exists in English or most of the European languages. He is likely to report that the language "lacks articles." There are books which purport to be grammars of little-studied languages which spend a lot of time and space on what is "missing" from that language.

The cultural relativist has to be a kind of egalitarian. He likes to point out that a culture which seems "poor" in some areas may be extremely "rich" in another. A fairly good example has to do with technology and kinship systems. In "under-developed" countries, the technology which is found in the United States or in western Europe may well be missing. In an African village or even in a city, there may be many adults who are not able to drive automobiles. It is fairly safe, however, to assume that they have compensatory abilities; the ability to carry a few stalks of bananas on their heads is one which is likely to be lacking from the repertory of a European or American for whom driving a car is the simplest kind of everyday activity. Kinship terminology is another area where the relativist can point out compensatory complexity. Highly mobile Americans and western Europeans may lose their family roots and not know distant relatives at all. They may even lack terminology for certain relationships. An "exotic" language may not have as many terms for automobile parts or computer terminology as English, Spanish, or German; but it may well have a much more complex terminology for kinship relations. In fact, study of kinship systems is a staple of anthropological field work.

While not lacking in any of the characteristics discussed above for anthropology, sociology tends to approach the study of societal behavior from a different angle. Questionnaires and sampling procedures are a kind of beginning point rather than an ultimate goal for the sociologist. To some degree, sociological studies have a narrower scope but a more precise result than anthropological field work. There is no objection to the sociologist's being, or becoming, a full-fledged member of the society being studied, but he or she does not typically indulge in participant observation. The relationship of sociology to literary history is not so clear as is that of anthropology, but some of the novels written in the United States in the 1930s, when writers were preoccupied with the effect of the society on the individual, have been referred to as "sociological" novels. A prominent sociological work of the past illustrated its points about the class system of the United States by reference to a work by Sinclair Lewis. Other writers, like Upton Sinclair and John Steinbeck, dealt with similar matters of social conflict.

The Nature of Sociological Research

The sociologist depends to a greater degree than the anthropologist on the self-report of members of the society, something that follows naturally from the greater use of questionnaires. This does not mean that the sociologist naively believes everything an informant says about his or her own culture. Rather than using one's own intuition, experience, and talent as a cross-check, however, sociological procedure seems to rely upon careful design of the questionnaire and knowledge of sampling procedure. It is not that the undercooperative or overcooperative informant is assumed not to exist but rather that

such informants are assumed to constitute a certain proportion of the population sampled; it is assumed that statistical procedures can compensate for such "natural" tendencies. Statements about the statistical degree of significance are, then, rather basic to the sociologist's study of a group.

Applied to language, sociological procedures seem to work better on dialects than on "exotic" languages discovered or first examined carefully in the field. Correlations of dialect behavior with social class have, for example, influenced dialectology in that some variation patterns once assumed to be matters of geographical residence or origin are now seen to involve complex class/caste relationships. Even the favored notion that density of communication is the dominant factor in determining dialect or language variety can be called into question. In a caste society, a member of a lower caste may communicate to an overwhelmingly greater degree with upper caste members than with his caste peers without coming to use the upper caste dialect features. (In popular terms, we might say they don't *dare*.) In general, sociological studies of language have tended to deal with stratificational factors; studies of class varieties in American English, for example, have tended to follow the observations of sociologists who dispelled the myth of a classless United States.

Although their methods differ slightly, sociologists and anthropologists still have the same aim: to provide objective information about a society or culture. Anthropologists may write more about the need for relativism, but sociologists seemingly must proceed on something like the same assumptions. In the long run, the two disciplines are complementary rather than contradictory, cooperative rather than conflicting. Research projects dealing with language or culture often will do well to have at least one sociologist and at least one anthropologist on the staff.

Summary

Anthropology and sociology are closely related disciplines dealing with culture and society, but they tend to have different emphases and methods. The anthropologist is often a participant observer, trying to live as a member of the culture which he is studying and to communicate in its language. Cultural and linguistic relativism are indispensable attitudes for this researcher. The sociologist needs those attitudes, also, but members of this discipline are less likely to engage in participant observation. Historically, sociology has depended more than anthropology on the formal questionnaire and on statistical analysis. The two disciplines are complementary, and adherents of both often work together.

Questions

1. Why is an anthropologist often a participant observer?
2. Why does an anthropologist need to learn the language of the group he is studying?
3. What is the basic difference in emphasis between anthropology and sociology?

VOCABULARY LESSON

The purpose of this exercise is to help you review and deepen your knowledge of the ten general vocabulary words you worked with at the beginning of this chapter.

A. Structural Analysis—Affixes and Root Words
   1. Underline the suffix of the following word: *Eliciting*
   2. Find the dictionary definition of the *root word* of the word above and write it below.

   _____

B. Use of Context
   1. Read the paragraph (second paragraph of section two) in which the following words appear, and in your own words write a definition:
       a. Egalitarian_____
       b. Compensatory _____
   2. Read the first section, third paragraph in which the following word appears, and in your own words write a definition: *Verisimilitude*

   _____

C. Multiple Meanings of Words
   1. Circle the definition below of the word *staple* (on page 310) that fits the way it is used in this chapter:
       a. A loop of wire driven as a nail or fastener
       b. A principal commodity
       c. A raw material

D. Synonyms and Antonyms: List one synonym (same meaning) and one antonym (opposite meaning) for each of the following words:

Word	Synonym	Antonym
Naive		
Bizarre		

E. Generate Your Own Language
   1. Describe the most *bizarre* behavior you have witnessed.
   2. Since it is *expedient* for you to do your homework in this class, what will you do before coming to the next class meeting?
   3. When have you acted on your own *intuition* and were right to do so?
   4. If a big snowstorm were coming to your area, what *staples* would you buy?

F. Word Confusion: What is the difference in meaning between *cast* and *caste*? Illustrate the difference in a sentence.

   _____

VOCABULARY EXTENSION

The purpose of this exercise is to help you see to what degree you know the ten general vocabulary words you worked with at the beginning of this chapter. Matching a word with its definition is the beginning of knowing a word. Using the word in your speaking and writing is full knowledge.

A. List the vocabulary words from this lesson that you can now use in both your speaking and writing:

B. List the vocabulary words from this lesson that you can now use in writing but are still not comfortable using in speaking:

C. List the vocabulary words from this lesson that you cannot use yet but will recognize in reading:

D. List general vocabulary words from this lesson that are still difficult to understand:

E. Use *five* vocabulary words from this lesson in a five-sentence paragraph on the topic of this lesson:

F. Illustrate the meaning of *one* of the vocabulary words from this lesson through some form of artwork or a cartoon. (This exercise is for right-brain students who enjoy drawing better than writing!)

EXTENDED READING ACTIVITIES

The purpose of this section is to give you a variety of options for independent study or investigation of the chapter topic. Reading is a skill that must be practiced each day if progress is to take place. These activities are designed to give you a variety of reading experiences through which you can improve your general vocabulary and increase your higher-level comprehension skills.

Your instructor may wish to (a) assign one or more activities to the class as a whole, (b) assign various activities to small groups, (c) assign one or more activities to individual students, or (d) let students choose to do the activities or not.

PROGRESS CHECK

In the seven previous chapters, you chose reading activities that would help you increase your vocabulary and your higher-level comprehension skills. The following questions are designed to help you see your progress.

A. Have you read every day for at least thirty minutes at a time?
Yes___ No___

B. Have you included difficult reading along with the easy stuff?
Yes___ No___ I'm Trying___

C. Are you using ideas from this reading textbook to help you with difficult material in your other courses? For example, are you trying to increase your interest in the courses you are taking? How? If material is difficult, are you investigating what you need to know in order to understand the material? What should you already know before reading a difficult chapter?

Your Response _____

Activities

A. Weekly Reading Report: Continue or begin keeping a weekly report of your reading. Use the form in Appendix C if you wish.

B. Attend a Reading Lab: Continue or begin attending your reading lab. Are you better at synthesizing information? Are you better at drawing conclusions based on the text? What background information do you draw on to answer questions?

C. Read Your Novel: Continue reading a novel that is interesting to you. If you enjoy reading about other cultures, you might enjoy Kyoko Mori's *Shizko's Daughter*, a novel about a Japanese teenager whose life is turned upside down with her mother's suicide and her father's remarriage. (Two of Mori's novels, *Shizko's Daughter* and *One Bird* were on your Chapter 3 list.) If you like survival stories, you might enjoy Robb White's *Deathwatch*. An extra novel report form is in Appendix C if you wish to use it.

D. Read with your child
    1. Gerald McDermott, *Raven: A Trickster Tale from the Pacific Northwest*
    2. Gerald McDermott, *Arrow to the Sun: A Pueblo Indian Tale*
    3. Byrd Baylor, *Hawk, I'm Your Brother*
    4. Byrd Baylor, *Amigo*
    5. Paul Goble, *The Girl Who Loved Wild Horses*
    6. Paul Goble, *Star Boy*
    7. William Morgan (collector), *Navajo Coyote Tales*
    8. Virginia Grossman & Sylvia Long, *Ten Little Rabbits*
    9. Mary Regina Ulmer Galloway (ed.), *Aunt Mary, Tell Me a Story: A Collection of Cherokee Legends and Tales as told by Mary Ulmer Chiltoskey*
    10. Arthur Dorros, *Abuela*

E. Reading/Writing Connection: Continue your college journal. Go to the campus bookstore and browse through the table of contents of textbooks used in anthropology and sociology. Are any topics especially interesting? List topics that you would like to know more about. In your journal write about why they are interesting to you. Would you want to major in either of these fields? If so, what would you want to do in that field? If not, why have you chosen your present major? Write about your interest in your major and why it is more satisfying to you than anthropology or sociology. Use a new vocabulary word in your responses.

F. Use the Internet: Are you interested in other cultures? What can you find to read about them? Have you looked them up on the Internet? What about Hispanic, Irish, Japanese, Chinese, Vietnamese, Haitian cultures? Are you curious about anthropology and/or sociology? Have you had a class in either subject? Look them up on the Internet and find something interesting about them.

G. Vocabulary Journal: Continue or begin keeping a vocabulary journal. Use the form in Appendix C if you wish.

H. Magazine/Journal/Newspaper Reading: Read magazine and journal articles about cultures that are different from yours. For example, have you heard of Appalachia where I live? Three journals that may be in your school library are *Appalachia*, *Appalachian Heritage*, and *Appalachian Journal*. Did you see the movie *Coal Miner's Daughter*? Some of the background information for the movie came from the library at Alice Lloyd College in Pippa Passes, Kentucky, a part of Appalachia. Are you interested in dulcimer music? Jack Tales? Bluegrass music? Have you read poems by Al Stewart? Poems and fiction by James Still? All of these interests are a part of Appalachia in some way. For a more general read about culture, you may enjoy *Multicultural Review*. For general interest reading you may enjoy *American Heritage*, *The Atlantic Monthly*, *The New York Review of Books*, *Newsweek*, *Tech Trends*, *Time*, *U.S. News & World Report*. Use the form in Appendix C for reporting on your magazine, journal, and newspaper reading if you wish.

REFLECTION

MIND REVOLUTION

Your attitude about different behavior or customs you encounter may reveal that you are a naive observer or a cultural relativist. When you observe the way other people express themselves in communication style, dress, or taste, you may react with shock and consider them bizarre, or you may see them as interesting and different. Think about your reactions to other students on campus.

VOCABULARY

Some of the specialized vocabulary, such as *ethnography, neo-classical, universalist, Romanticism, anthropology, sociology, dialectology,* and *linguistics* may cause trouble with comprehension. Foggy notions of terms like *culture* and *society* can do the same.

You can easily find definitions of *caste* and *class*; *consultant* and *informant*. What about the connotations of each pair? Do you have more positive feelings toward the word *class* than you do *caste*? Would you rather be part of a social *class* or part of a *caste* system? Would you rather be a *consultant* or an *informant*? How do they differ?

COMPREHENSION

This chapter is difficult because of (1) lack of background knowledge and experience, (2) assumptions of the reader's knowledge by the author, and (3) density of concepts.

If you have always assumed that the way you and the significant others around you do things is the right or only way to do things, you may have trouble understanding the importance of being nonjudgmental when encountering different cultures. If you have traveled extensively but stayed with your companions instead of "going native," then you may also lack experience necessary to understand. For example, if you have been to Mexico, have you been to places where other tourists do not go? Did you try to learn a little Spanish? Did you eat in a real Mexican restaurant where the locals eat or did you hunt for a McDonald's? If you have ever had the experience of being the minority somewhere, your experience will help you understand the material in this chapter.

Another kind of knowledge and experience that you may lack is being widely read, especially in literary periods. If you had a traditional high school English or American literature course as part of your college preparation, you probably have at least heard of the neo-classical or Romantic periods in literature. If you had a nontraditional literature course, you may not have approached literature by historical periods or studied their characteristics.

Still another kind of knowledge and experience that you may lack is knowledge and experience of the academic environment. If you are attending a community college, a junior college, or a four-year college, you may not know what a graduate student does and may wonder why on earth a student is off studying exotic cultures instead of attending classes. Not understanding the university's emphasis on research and therefore the necessity for research trips and field work may interfere with your understanding of the section on participant observation.

You may have more experience dealing with the sociology material in the section on questionnaires, sampling procedures, and statistical degrees of significance because our present environment seems to be teeming with telemarketers, direct-mail questionnaires and surveys, and endless polls over television news programs telling us what people, ideas, and things we love and hate. We get frequent opinions on everything. At the end of such reports, the margin of error is usually given so that we can judge the reliability of the poll. If you have this kind of knowledge, it is important to transfer it to the reading of this difficult material. It helps you to help yourself.

An author does not always know his intended audience. Textbook authors are usually writing for either introductory courses or upper-division courses for majors in their field. The level of difficulty and the assumption of reader knowledge are important to both. If the textbook is for an introductory course, the author may assume that the reader went to a very good high school, took college prep courses, and had one or more courses in his or her field. Several assumptions were made about reader background by the author of this chapter.

First, the author assumes that the reader has background knowledge of overcooperation and undercooperation on the part of informants. He also assumes that the reader understands the statement that the "unusual informant responds." Where would a freshman student pick up such knowledge? Television documentaries about different cultures could provide such information. Sociology and anthropology courses, films, or lectures would be other sources. To self-check to find out if you really understand this idea, see if you can talk to a classmate or to yourself about the role of informants and elaborate on the idea. If you have difficulty, you could find an introductory anthropology textbook and build your background knowledge.

Second, the author assumes that the reader knows about the 1930s sociological novels and about Sinclair Lewis. If you had an American literature course in high school that included modern times, you may have encountered such novels and writers. If you are an avid old-movie addict, you may have seen a movie based on Sinclair Lewis's *Elmer Gantry*. If you have ever questioned how much free will you have in your own life or how much of your life is governed by forces outside yourself, you may be interested in the sociological novels. If you have strong feelings about underclass people being victims of the social system, you also might be interested in these novels.

Along with the author's assumptions about the reader's background comes density of concepts. The author assumes certain information on the reader's part and then builds on that assumption. The best example in this chapter is the last section's discussion of the connection of sociology and language study, especially the reference to dialectology. The author, a sociolinguist, assumes that the reader has background information and ideas about the study of language. He uses some unknown terms and then briefly refers to the "universality of human language structure" as part of an example. If the readers have not had at least a good course in the study of grammar or an introduction to language study, or seen one of the good television documentaries on language, then they are probably lost at that point. Luckily, in this chapter that information is not the main idea, only support, so the reader can ask for clarification in class on the subject. In connection with the density of concepts dealing with language, anthropological linguists stressing the differences in language is also difficult. On the surface, the reader could pass a literal-level test on it, but what deep knowledge does the reader have? Why is the statement important? What is its opposite? Again, a lack of coursework in the study of language probably means that the reader has few concepts to build on.

Another concept not elaborated upon by the author states that people's language differs not only by where they live but also by social relationships. The reader needs to know that the language one speaks and its acquisition is a complicated subject. For example, there are dialect geographers in the field of linguistics and then there are the sociolinguists. How do they differ? Where do the sociologists come in? Have you ever identified someone's speech by national region?

Another concept referred to in the discussion of language is "density of communication." Again, it was used as part of an example and was not a main idea, but the example would be unclear to a reader with no knowledge or concept of this phrase as it applies to language study.

What information do you have about caste systems? If you have seen a documentary, a television movie, or a travel program on India, then you have some idea and the example given would be meaningful to you. The word *caste* would be easy to look up.

One last concept is easier to follow. *Stratificational factors* is a term used in the last section of the chapter. Its meaning becomes fairly clear because of context clues. In addition, context clues help the reader understand the term *compensatory complexity*.

West African Literature: The Fiction of Chinua Achebe

Overview

Progress Check

Activities

Reflection

Mind Revolution

Vocabulary

Comprehension

Vocabulary/Metacognition

The purpose of this exercise is to help you become aware of when you know the meaning of a word and to help you know when you do not know the meaning of a word. This is metacognition awareness.

On a scale of 1–5 (see below), rate your knowledge of the following vocabulary words from "The Fiction of Chinua Achebe." After matching words with definitions on page 321, check your answers and then check your number *ones* and *fives* below. Did you know when you really knew a word and when you really did not know the word?

Scale

1. I absolutely do not know.
2. I do not think I know.
3. There's a 50/50 chance I have seen or heard it.
4. I think I know it.
5. I know the word and can use it.

Words

_____ 1. Adherent

_____ 2. Taboo

_____ 3. Intractable

_____ 4. Bigot (bigoted)

_____ 5. Scrupulous (unscrupulousness)

_____ 6. Complicity

_____ 7. Altruism

_____ 8. Retaliate (retaliation)

_____ 9. Decadence

_____10. Transparent (transparently)

Go to page 321. See if you can match the right definition with the word and then write sentences for any five words in the list.

Words	Definitions

Words

_____ 1. Adherent
_____ 2. Taboo
_____ 3. Intractable
_____ 4. Bigot (bigoted)
_____ 5. Scrupulous (unscrupulousness)
_____ 6. Complicity
_____ 7. Altruism
_____ 8. Retaliate (retaliation)
_____ 9. Decadence
_____10. Transparent (transparently)

Definitions

A. Stubborn; hard to control
B. Return like for like, especially evil for evil
C. (1) Upright; moral; (2) exact; punctilious
D. (1) Permitting distinct vision through a solid substance; (2) easily understood; manifest
E. One who follows a teacher or supports a cause
F. A person intolerant of creeds, opinions, etc. other than his or her own
G. Regard for the welfare of others; benevolent practices
H. A process or state of decay or deterioration
I. A ban or prohibition (noun); prohibited; ostracized (adjective)
J. The state of being an accomplice

Write five words from the list and your own sentences that show you know how to use the words. Choose words that you marked a *five* if possible.

1. Word _____
   Sentence _____
2. Word _____
   Sentence _____
3. Word _____
   Sentence _____
4. Word _____
   Sentence _____
5. Word _____
   Sentence _____

PRE-READING THE TEXTBOOK CHAPTER

OVERVIEW

The purpose of this *first* of three steps in your reading plan is to suggest things to do *before* you read. First, as part of your pre-reading, read the Prior Knowledge section beginning on page 322. When you finish, return to this section and continue your pre-reading. The Academic Study Skills section will be used as a part of your post-reading assignment. You may want to skim it as a part of your pre-reading.

ACTIVITIES

The directions below are simplified; if you are not sure what to do, look at the more detailed directions in earlier chapters.

A. Tap experience and prior knowledge about the title of this selection.
B. Predict what you will read.
C. Overview by reading the summary and the questions at the end of the selection. Write the main headings of the selection below.

The Fiction of Chinua Achebe

I.   _____

II.   _____

III. _____

PRIOR KNOWLEDGE

This section, part of your pre-reading, presents a model to show you what will help you comprehend this chapter by using your own background knowledge. If you know much of the following information, you have a better background for reading this chapter. This section will suggest helpful kinds of background information and help you activate what you know; do not try to look up or learn everything listed. Ask yourself what you need to know before you read and what you already know that will help you to understand this chapter. Your instructor may want to use this section for a whole-class or small group discussion or have you read it silently.

CHAPTER SECTIONS

I.   Introduction and the Initial Period of Nigerian-British Contact
  A. Vocabulary
    1. Polygynous
    2. Doctrinaire
    3. Adherent
    4. Machete
    5. Thwarted
    6. Taboo
    7. Intractable
    8. Bigoted
    9. Afoul

    B.   Recognition of Writing Patterns or Arrangement of Ideas and Devices
        1.   Introduction: thesis statement
        2.   Section One: Support #1, narrative and explanation
    C.   Concepts and Background Knowledge and Experience
        1.   Know story pattern
        2.   Understand culture clash
        3.   Know that all countries do not have the same values and ways of seeing
        4.   Have historical knowledge of European rule of African countries
        5.   Be open-minded to different types of names or naming systems
        6.   Read William Butler Yeats's poetry or at least be familiar with it
        7.   See complexity in relationships, see that all is not black and white, that there are grey areas

II.   Novels Dealing with the More Recent Situation in Nigeria
    A.   Vocabulary
        1.   Assimilation
        2.   Cognizant
        3.   Unscrupulousness
        4.   Lured
        5.   Complicity
        6.   Venial
        7.   Quixotic
        8.   Hedonistic
        9.   Altruism
        10. Idealism
        11. Contingency
        12. Ennobling
        13. Degraded (world)
        14. Pathetic
        15. Tragic (character)
        16. Retaliation
        17. Pervading
        18. Decadence
    B.   Recognition of Writing Patterns or Arrangement of Ideas and Devices
        1.   Support #2, explanation, narrative, comparison/contrast
    C.   Concepts and Background Knowledge and Experience
        1.   Familiarity with Achebe's novels
        2.   Know something about Nigeria, its people and history
        3.   Knowledge of multilingual societies
        4.   Knowledge of political corruption and greed
        5.   Ability to work with complicated themes
        6.   Knowledge of the 1960s Biafran war

III. The Style of Achebe's Fiction
    A. Vocabulary
        1. *Avant garde*
        2. Reportorial
        3. Sarcastically
        4. Sentimentality
    B. Recognition of Writing Patterns or Arrangement of Ideas and Devices
        1. Support #3, explanation
        2. Conclusion (comes full circle by tying back in to the introduction)
    C. Concepts and Background Knowledge and Experience
        1. Knowledge of literary styles, especially differences in the nineteenth and the twentieth centuries and in European and African styles
        2. Knowledge of literary prizes and standards
IV. Chapter Summary
    A. Vocabulary
        1. Transparently
    B. Recognition of Writing Patterns or Arrangement of Ideas and Devices
        1. Thesis statement and support
    C. Concepts and Background Knowledge and Experience
        1. Recognition of synthesis of information

ACADEMIC STUDY SKILLS

DIRECTIONS

Review the study skills you have practiced in previous lessons and decide if you wish to use one with this lesson. Consider the difficulty of the material, your purpose for learning the material, and your interest in the subject.

If you found the modified SQ4R plan and the exercises on memory and annotation helpful and would like to use them for this chapter, follow the directions found in Appendix D, Chapter 9. They provide guided practice.

The study skills lesson below will be used as part of the post-reading lesson. You may want to skim it as part of your pre-reading so that you will know what to expect.

STUDY SKILL: UNDERLINING/HIGHLIGHTING

A new study skill that you have probably already used is underlining or highlighting. It can be a useful study strategy for students who can sort out main ideas from supporting details. If such a task is still difficult, then it could be a waste of your study time. Use the "Goldilocks test" to help you decide whether or not to highlight. Find some previous work that you highlighted and ask yourself if you highlighted too much or too little. If the highlighting was not "just right," then this exercise should be beneficial. The following provides guided practice in finding the most important information and highlighting that information. Obviously, you will need a colored highlighting pen. If you do not have one, you can underline the information if you wish.

A. Introduction: The first sentence states a fact. The second sentence tells you that Achebe loves his tribe but also sees its flaws. The third sentence tells you that Achebe's novels represent something very like a history of West African–European culture clash. Since the title of this chapter is "The Fiction of Chinua Achebe," let's assume the third sentence is the most important and highlight it. Before continuing, let's make sure that we understand the term *culture clash*. Two examples with which you may be familiar are (1) Anglo culture clashing with Native American tribes with results that include the lost of tribal traditions and (2) rural young people moving to the large cities and losing their roots, their sense of family, and their value systems. Documentaries on Appalachian culture have shown the loss of independence by Appalachians when coal-mining operations have entered and left their homeland.

B. Section One: The Initial Period of Nigerian–British Contact: The first two paragraphs summarize the plot and introduce major characters of Achebe's first novel, *Things Fall Apart*. The second paragraph includes the culture clash between the Africans and Europeans. Note that by the title of this section we have reduced *West African* to *Nigerian* and *European* to *British*. Highlight the sentence in paragraph one that tells you the name of the novel and its major character. Highlight the sentence in the second paragraph that tells you that Okonkwo scorns the Europeans' ways.

In the third paragraph of this section, Dillard states in the first sentence that "Achebe does not see the relationship between the Ibo and the European in simple terms." Highlight this sentence and then look for examples of characters and their actions that support this statement and highlight them. You may want to highlight words, phrases, and parts of sentences here. In helping you to decide what is important to highlight, ask yourself if Okonkwo and the Christian missionaries are all good or all bad.

Paragraph four briefly summarizes the plot of *Arrow of God*. To help you find the main ideas, keep focused on the Nigerian–British culture clash. Ask yourself why there is not much information on this novel. Now highlight two pieces of information on the novel that will help you answer the question. Remember that you do not have to highlight whole sentences if all parts of them do not contain what you consider important.

C. Section Two: Novels Dealing with the More Recent Situation in Nigeria: In this section we skip ahead in time and find Nigerians familiar with British ways and read about three later works that show changes in the lives of Nigerians. Ask yourself how the culture clash will manifest itself after generations have passed in the novels.

In the first paragraph the reader is told how the later writings differ from the earlier ones. Highlight these differences. In paragraphs two through five, the focus is on the novel *A Man of the People*. Paragraph two centers on Chief Nanga. Again, stay focused on the results of the culture clash. Highlight the sentence that tells you something about this clash in Chief Nanga's life.

Paragraphs three through five center on the British-educated young Ibo Odili Samalu from the same novel and gives a plot summary. Ask yourself how his life is different by being British educated. How does he clash with Chief Nanga? Are either noble characters? Has the British influence been a mixed blessing? Highlight parts of sentences that help you answer these questions.

In paragraph six keep focused on culture clash. What is the theme of these three novels? Highlight the sentence that answers this question. *Anthills of the Savannah* treats this theme best. Highlight the names of the two young men whose lives express the theme. Highlight the sentence that tells you they were the good guys.

In paragraph seven the reader meets another character in one of the other three novels being discussed who also represents the theme stated in paragraph six of this section. Highlight the sentence that gives you this information. Obi Okonkwo is not a noble character like the two in paragraph six. Highlight the sentence that tells you his crime. Highlight the sentence that tells you Obi is not in the category of good characters as those are in paragraph six.

In paragraph eight the first sentence tells you what to expect with independence from British rule in these three novels. Highlight the sentence and then look for examples to support the statement. When a nation gains independence, do you expect conditions to be better? Highlight the sentence or part of it that tells you what happened after independence.

After a discussion of Nigerian–British culture clash through the fiction of Chinua Achebe, paragraph nine ends the section with an update of Nigerian affairs that seems to leave the Europeans out of the picture. The clash discussed seems to occur among the Africans. Highlight parts of sentences that support this statement.

D.   Section Three: The Style of Achebe's Fiction: In the first paragraph Dillard states in the first sentence that Achebe's style is traditional and like the nineteenth century English novel. Highlight that part of the sentence. Next look for examples of "African flavor" in *A Man of the People* and highlight words and phrases that are examples. Do you find it interesting that Achebe writes of the Nigerian–British culture clash and also writes under the influence and with the knowledge of both?

In the second and last paragraph, ask yourself as you search for the important ideas how Achebe's work has been recognized. Why is his work special? What is his concern and how does he express it? Highlight this information. What else has he written? Highlight categories or types of work he has written besides novels.

Congratulations! You have just completed the task of highlighting the most important information in this chapter. After this, your task will be to frequently review what you have highlighted, especially if you are to be tested on it.

You may want to write a formal outline as a further aid to understanding and remembering important information. Below is one way to outline this information.

The Fiction of Chinua Achebe

I.   Introduction: Achebe's novels provide a history of West African–European culture clash

II.   The Initial Period of Nigerian-British Contact

    A. *Things Fall Apart,* Achebe's first novel, is the story of Okonkwo.

    B. Okonkwo scorns the Europeans' ways.

    C. Okonkwo kills a colonial government messenger and himself.

    D. Suicide is an Ibo taboo.

    E. Achebe sees the relationship between Africans and Europeans as complex.

        1. Okonkwo has flaws.

        2. Christian missionaries are not all alike.

        3. None of them can compromise enough to adapt to each other.

    F. *Arrow of God*

        1. Europeans play a smaller part in this novel.

        2. The primary focus is on intra-tribal conflict.

III. Novels Dealing with the More Recent Situation in Nigeria.

    A. The later writings differ from the earlier ones.

        1. European culture is familiar to the Nigerians.

        2. The setting is the city.

        3. A variety of people interact on a daily basis.

    B. *A Man of the People*

        1. Chief Nanga represents a superficial success story in the process of adapting to British ways.

        2. Odili Samalu, British educated, is lured into misconduct through greed.

        3. Odili Samalu undergoes major changes.

            a. Develops a genuine concern for his new party.

            b. Genuinely loves Edna.

        4. Odili and Chief Nanga lose political power.

            a. Chief Nanga tries to escape and is caught.

            b. Odili realizes that love is an ennobling factor in a degraded world.

    C. *A Man of the People, No Longer at Ease,* and *Anthills of the Savannah*

        1. Theme: the educated young man and his partial maladjustment to his own native country.

        2. Chris Oriko and Ikem Osodi's lives express the theme.

        3.   They were ennobled in death.

        4.   The value of their ideals is restated through their tragedy.

  D.   *No Longer at Ease*

        1.   Obi Okonkwo, the main character, accepts bribes.

        2.   He is caught but does not mature.

        3.   He is pathetic without ennobling qualities.

  E.   The African nation of these novels is independent of the British.

        1.   Liberty brings pain.

        2.   Unscrupulous men have power.

        3.   The nation is neither better nor worse after independence.

  F.   Update on Nigeria

        1.   Europeans are out of the picture.

        2.   Biafran war

        3.   *Girls at War and Other Stories* expresses personal decadence.

IV. The Style of Achebe's Fiction

  A.   Achebe writes in a rather traditional style.

  B.   Comparable to the nineteenth century English novel

  C.   African flavor in *A Man of the People*

        1.   African conversations

        2.   Pidgin English

        3.   Occasional Ibo word

  D.   Recognition of work

        1.   Nominated for the Nobel Prize

        2.   Awards from other countries

  E.   Achebe is concerned for Nigerians and their problems.

  F.   He expresses his concern with objectivity.

  G.   Uses sympathy, not sentimentality.

  H.   He has also written poetry and children's literature.

RECIPROCAL TEACHING

OVERVIEW

Your first step of the three-part reading plan was pre-reading. In pre-reading, you activated your prior knowledge, predicted what you would read, and overviewed the chapter before reading.

As the second step in this three-part reading plan, you will read "The Fiction of Chinua Achebe" by using the Reciprocal Teaching reading plan as explained below. An alternative plan, Active Questioning, is in Appendix B. In both plans you break up the chapter in sections and read and think about each as you read. The purpose of both plans is to keep you reading actively. You may use the Reciprocal

Teaching model in Chapter 3 if you wish; the steps are predict, question, clarify, and summarize. The first section contains models of responses to get you started. After that you become independent.

General Directions

The concept of Reciprocal Teaching outlined here is adapted from Palinscar and Brown, 1986.

A. Both partners read a section under a subheading at a time. Take turns summarizing the section in as few sentences as possible.
B. Take turns asking a high level question or two on each section (inferential or critical/creative).
C. Explain or clarify difficult parts to each other. Practice repeating main ideas and supporting details in your own words.
D. Read the next subheading and predict what the section will be about. Discuss (exchange) ideas.

Assignment

Begin reading "The Fiction of Chinua Achebe" by following the directions below:

A. Read the introduction and the first section, "The Initial Period of Nigerian–British Contact."

    1. Write a summary of the first major section. Model summary: The novels of Chinua Achebe represent something very like a history of West African–European culture clash. In his first novel, *Things Fall Apart*, this clash dominates the novel and shows the complexity of the clash.

Your summary _____

_____

_____

    2. Write one question on this section. Try to write an inferential or a critical/creative question. If you can't, write a literal level question. Model question: Although there are cultural differences between Nigerians and Americans, how could Okonkwo be a type of American father as far as his attitude toward his children is concerned?

Your question _____

Answer _____

    3. Orally explain or clarify an important idea. Model idea: People in all cultures are complex because of their unique gifts, abilities, and weaknesses as human beings.

Your idea _____

4. Predict what you will read in the second major section, "Novels Dealing with the More Recent Situation in Nigeria." Model prediction: I will read about more of Achebe's novels and how they will portray contemporary Nigerian problems.

Your prediction _____

B. Read "Novels Dealing with the More Recent Situation in Nigeria."
    1. Summarize this second major section.

Your summary _____

_____

_____

2. Write one question on this section. Try to write an inferential or a critical/creative question. If you can't, write a literal level question.

Your question _____

Answer _____

3. Orally explain or clarify an important idea in this section.

Your idea _____

4. Predict what you will read in the third major section of the chapter, "The Style of Achebe's Fiction."

Your prediction _____

C. Read "The Style of Achebe's Fiction."
    1. Summarize this third major section.

Your summary _____

_____

_____

2. Write one question on this section. Try to write an inferential or a critical/creative question. If you can't, write a literal level question.

Your question _____

Answer _____

3. Orally explain or clarify an important idea in this section.

Your idea _____

POST-READING THE TEXTBOOK CHAPTER

OVERVIEW

In the second part of your three-part reading plan, you practiced reading your textbook chapter section by section, wrote section summaries, asked and answered questions, explained or clarified important ideas, and made predictions for what you would read in the next section.

In this third part of the three-part reading plan, you will find suggestions for what to do after you read. Your task is to compare what you predicted with what you actually read as an aid to comprehension, to add what you have learned to your file of information on the topic, and to think about what you have read.

ASSIGNMENT

Before completing the work below, do the exercise in the Academic Study Skills section on underlining/highlighting beginning on page 324.

A. Compare what you predicted you would read with what you actually read. Did anything you predicted cause you a problem with comprehension? What? How?

B. What did you learn from the reading that you did not know about before working on this lesson?

C. Look at the words and phrases that you listed as your prior knowledge in the pre-reading section of this lesson on page 322. Group them below with relevant information in "B" above. Create your own headings. This is your new file of information on West African literature. (The ability to group ideas and to see relationships requires more complex comprehension than merely memorizing isolated facts.)

D. What have you learned from this chapter that is important?

E. What do you already know that you can relate to it?

F. What do you see differently as a result of reading this chapter?

Your Headings	Words and Phrases from Pre-Reading	Relevant Information from "B"

THE FICTION OF CHINUA ACHEBE

The modern Nigerian author Chinua Achebe was born into the Ibo tribe in 1930. He writes of his country and his tribe with obvious affection but with a clear vision which enables him to see the flaws of the tribe and the nation as well as the potential of its people. Together, his novels represent something very like a history of West African–European culture clash.

The Initial Period of Nigerian–British Contact

Achebe's first novel, *Things Fall Apart*, is the story of Okonkwo, an almost ideal Ibo warrior who has achieved all the honors which the father he has come to scorn never managed. Beginning with no inheritance—not even the young wife which a man in that polygynous society might hope to inherit from his father—Okonkwo has made himself, through strength and yam-farming techniques, one of the principal men of the Ibo clan of Umuofia. He has three wives—a status marker in a polygynous society—and all but the highest of the titles which his clan bestows. His children are a disappointment to him, since he does not have a son who appears to have his own character, but he still hopes to acquire at least one more wife and more children.

Things begin to "fall apart" (the allusion is to "The Second Coming" by William Butler Yeats) when Ibo culture clashes with that of the Englishmen who are now moving into the interior of Nigeria after having confined their activities more or less to the coastal area for some centuries. As a devoted, doctrinaire adherent of his own culture and his own religion, Okonkwo

scorns the Europeans' ways. (He is not even very good with guns, although he is perhaps the best around with a machete.) Returning from a temporary exile because of a ritual offense, Okonkwo is thwarted in his attempts to reestablish himself because the white man has moved in. When his oldest son becomes a convert to Christianity, Okonkwo enters into a period of furious resistance to the changes which he sees as falling apart. When his fellow villagers fail to live up to what he sees as their glorious tradition by armed resistance, Okonkwo slays a messenger of the colonial government and hangs himself. Because self-destruction is a taboo of Ibo culture, Okonkwo has fallen from the heights of prestige to the very depths. It is even forbidden for his fellow villagers to touch his body, and the despised foreigners must dispose of him.

Achebe does not see the relationship between the Ibo and the European in simple terms. Okonkwo, although close to being the ideal of an Ibo warrior in his bravery and power, has flaws: He is hot-headed and inflexible, and he is perhaps the slowest of the inhabitants of Umuofia to adapt to changing culture. The Christian missionaries who come to Umuofia are not made of one pattern. Mr. Brown, the first, is a broad-minded man who tries to point up as many resemblances as possible between his beliefs and those of the traditional Ibo religion. His successor, Mr. Smith, is an intractable, rather bigoted person who will make no compromises. Neither Okonkwo nor Mr. Smith, Achebe seems to be saying, is capable of the kind of compromise which will enable members of the two cultures to adapt to each other. The differences between these two are greater than the rather superficial one which occurs when a new convert from Umuofia, bound for communion, takes his drinking horn along.

Even though the setting of *Arrow of God* is a couple of decades later than that of *Things Fall Apart*, the Europeans play a smaller part. By this time they and their government are an established fact, not something to be the subject of long and fearful debate among the villagers. Ezeulu, a priest of his pagan cult, falls afoul of the customs of his people because of the actions of the British, but the primary focus of the novel is on the intra-tribal conflict. Ezeulu becomes mad but he does not hang himself, and one is tempted to say that he is no such tragic hero as Okonkwo.

Novels Dealing with the More Recent Situation in Nigeria

Things Fall Apart deals with the very earliest stages of African–European contact and *Arrow of God* with a slightly later time. Achebe's later writings (*A Man of the People, No Longer at Ease, Anthills of the Savannah*) tend to skip a couple of generations, to start from the time when the white man and his ways are familiar to the Nigerian scene and many of the old customs appear to be in decline. Although full assimilation to the European ways has obviously not taken place, almost everyone among the Nigerians is strongly cognizant of British culture. These novels are set not exclusively in the villages but primarily in cities, where not only the Europeans and an occasional American but members of other Nigerian tribes interact on a daily basis. Instead of communicating in Ibo (or Yoruba), the characters tend to vary between English and Pidgin English, although an African language may also be used between members of the same tribe. *A Man of the People* presents a superficial success story in the process of adapting to British ways. Chief Nanga, the Minister of Culture in what is transparently

the Nigerian government although it does not go by that name, has advanced quickly from the position of village schoolteacher and scoutmaster to a cabinet post. His striking physical appearance, his self-confidence, and his unscrupulousness have contributed more than his intellect or his talent to his rapid advance. Chief Nanga has big houses and big cars and all the trappings of success, even though many of those around him are capable of recognizing his limitations.

The status of Chief Nanga is perceived through the eyes of Odili Samalu, a British-educated young Ibo who is now teaching at the school from which Nanga began his rise. Although not fooled by Nanga's pretensions, Odili allows himself to be lured into temporary complicity with the minister because of a venial desire to share some of the luxuries which the older man can provide. When Nanga seduces a girlfriend whom Odili regards as his own, the younger man sets out on a course of revenge, determined to oppose the minister in the upcoming election and even to win away Edna, the convent-educated young girl whom Chief Nanga intends to make his second wife.

In the process of somewhat quixotic opposition to Nanga, Odili undergoes some major changes. Although his entrance into politics was motivated by the hardly admirable desire for revenge, he comes to have a genuine concern for what the new party which his educated young friends have created might be able to do for the country. And, in the process of wooing Edna in order to take her away from Nanga, he comes to feel a genuine love for her. From a purely hedonistic young man, Odili matures in the direction of altruism.

Yet the total picture is far from one of idealism. Odili is not able to win the election from Nanga, although a kind of historical contingency forces the latter's People's Organization Party out of power. It is purely greed on the part of other factions in the country which makes the people rise up and throw out the ruling POP, not any concern with political justice. Nanga attempts to escape disguised as a simple fisherman and is caught; Odili does not suffer as he might if Nanga had remained in power. Without any special illusions about what has happened, Odili comes to see love as the one ennobling factor in a degraded world.

The theme of the educated young man and his partial maladjustment to his own native country occurs in *A Man of the People*, *No Longer at Ease*, and *Anthills of the Savannah*. The last is perhaps the outstanding treatment of the theme. As Minister of Information, Chris Oriko holds the highest position of all these somewhat Europeanized young men. His friend the newspaper editor Ikem Osodi is also an educated man in a prominent position whose intelligence has brought about his rapid rise but whose independence of thought leads to his murder. Both of these men could be said to be ennobled in death, and the value of their ideals is restated through their tragedy.

The novel *No Longer at Ease* deals with a character much like Odili, Chris, and Ikem Osodi but in a much more disillusioned fashion. Obi Okonkwo, whose name is strongly reminiscent of the protagonist of *Things Fall Apart*, finding himself able to advance because of his British education, soon finds that increase in income is not necessarily an unmixed blessing. Finding himself always in need of more money because of a rising standard of living, the young man turns to dishonest activity—accepting bribes. Finally he is caught. Whereas Odili, in *A Man of the People*, came to see the value of his father's traditional ways as part of the maturing process, Obi simply does not mature. His downfall is without any ennobling qualities, and he is a pathetic but not a tragic character.

The African nation of these later novels is independent of British rule, but liberty brings pain along with it. Unscrupulous men like the ignorant Minister of Culture Chief Nanga or the power-grabbing army officer in *Anthills of the Savannah*, whose failure to be elected President for Life leads him to retaliation on men whom he can only suspect to be responsible, find it easy to operate under the political conditions which result. The downfalls of Nanga's party and of the President ("His Excellency" in ironic reference) occur almost as coincidences, and the nation appears to be neither the better nor the worse off for the change.

The most destructive event of recent Nigerian history was certainly the Biafran war, in which the two large tribes of the Ibo and the Yoruba fought and the Ibo was beaten. Achebe's most cynical production is probably *Girls at War and Other Stories*, which presents no large political outlook but which shows a pervading personal decadence.

The Style of Achebe's Fiction

Achebe's fiction is written in a rather traditional style, comparable to that of the nineteenth-century English novel rather than to the more experimental techniques which have characterized *avant garde* twentieth-century fiction. *A Man of the People*, especially, depends upon factors of coincidence which caused one student to compare Achebe to Thomas Hardy.

In addition to the Victorian reportorial style, however, there is a definite African flavor especially to the conversations his characters engage in. The use of Pidgin English, of which Achebe is an obvious master, is one factor—and something of an indicator of progressive cultural change. There is no pidgin in *Things Fall Apart*, a little in *Arrow of God*, and an abundance in *No Longer at Ease*, *A Man of the People*, and *Anthills of the Savannah*. Although he uses only an occasional word from Ibo, suggestions of African conversation are produced especially through the effective use of proverbial expressions. A favorite is "A child on its mother's back does not know that the way is long," used sarcastically against a nonparticipant who does not see the difficulty of a task and for a completely different purpose to encourage someone who sees a task as too difficult. "Since men have learned to shoot without missing, Eneke the bird has learned to fly without perching" is another which is frequently repeated.

Achebe has been nominated several times for the Nobel Prize for Literature. The body of his work is probably worthy of that high award. His obvious concern for Nigerians and their problems is presented with an impressive objectivity so that sympathy does not become sentimentality. Only an extended stay in Lagos (Bori of *A Man of the People*, Bassa of *The Anthills of the Savannah*) could give an understanding of the country equivalent to what a reader can gain from Achebe's novels. He has written poetry and children's literature as well. *The Flute, A Children's Story*, illustrated by Tayo Adenaike, appears in slightly different form as a folk tale in *Arrow of God*; frequent reference to those tales, especially to their being told by mothers to children, is made in Achebe's work. Achebe has received many awards in other countries as well as in Nigeria and is regarded by some as Africa's outstanding novelist.

unable to adapt to the loss of the old system of which he has been an outstanding example and defender. *A Man of the People*, *Anthills of the Savannah*, and *No Longer at Ease* deal with urban life, in a capital that is transparently Lagos, and problems in dealing with a political system reflecting that kind of state imposed upon tribal societies by colonialist England. Three young men of advanced educational status are the protagonists; whereas Chris Orika of *Anthills of the Savannah* and Obi Okonkwo of *No Longer at Ease* are destroyed, the latter through his own giving in to the temptation to bribery, Odili Samalu of *A Man of the People* undergoes a notable maturation through a new appreciation of the values of the traditional society. Achebe presents the problems of Nigerians in assimilating European values and the conflicts that arise sympathetically but without sentimentality. A book of short stories, *Girls at War and Other Stories*, deals rather cynically with the Ibo–Yoruba conflict in the Biafran War. These novels, along with his poetry and children's literature, have brought many honors to Achebe and make him not only an outstanding African author but one of the contemporary world's most important writers.

Questions

1. What factors are considered by those who regard Chinua Achebe as an important man of letters?

2. What different ways are there of reacting to the kind of clash which results when a colonial power imposes its government and culture upon a very different nation?

3. Why does Achebe use characters like Okonkwo and Odili Samalu to represent different stages of Nigerian assimilation to British culture rather than statistics or abstractions?

Summary

Novelist Chinua Achebe has written books dealing with the changing culture of Nigeria, particularly of the Ibo tribe, as European customs supplant more traditional folkways. *Things Fall Apart* and *Arrow of God* deal with Ibo village life at an early stage of British influence on Nigerians. Okonkwo of the former novel is tragically

VOCABULARY LESSON

The purpose of this exercise is to help you review and deepen your knowledge of the ten general vocabulary words you worked with at the beginning of this chapter.

A. Structural Analysis—Affixes and Root Words
1. Circle the prefix and underline the suffix of the following word: *Unscrupulousness*
2. Find the dictionary definition of the root word of the word above and write it:

    _____

3. Circle the prefix and underline the suffix of the following word: *Intractable*

B. Use of Context: Read the last sentence on page 334 of "Novels Dealing with the More Recent Situation in Nigeria," and in your own words write a definition for the word *decadence* below:

    _____

C. Multiple Meanings of Words: Circle the appropriate meaning below for the word *transparent (ly)* as it is used in the Summary on page 335:
1. permitting distinct vision through a solid substance
2. easily understood; manifest

D. Synonyms and Antonyms: List one synonym (same meaning) and one antonym (opposite meaning) for each of the following words:

Word	Synonym	Antonym
Taboo		
Bigot(ed)		
Decadence		
Scrupulous		

E. Generate Your Own Language
1. To what rule of life are you strictly *adherent*?
2. Give an example of your or someone else's *altruism*.
3. What subject of discussion is *taboo* with your parents?
4. When did your *complicity* in a friend's scheme get you in trouble?
5. When someone hurts your feelings, should you *retaliate*?

VOCABULARY EXTENSION

The purpose of this exercise is to help you see to what degree you know the ten general vocabulary words you worked with at the beginning of this chapter. Matching a word with its definition is the beginning of knowing a word. Using the word in your speaking and writing is full knowledge.

A. List the vocabulary words from this lesson that you can now use in both your speaking and writing.

B. List the vocabulary words from this lesson that you can now use in writing but are still not comfortable using in speaking.

C. List the vocabulary words from this lesson that you cannot use yet but will recognize in reading.

D. List general vocabulary words from this lesson that are still difficult to understand.

E. Use *five* vocabulary words from this lesson in a five-sentence paragraph on the topic of this lesson.

F. Illustrate the meaning of *one* of the vocabulary words from this lesson through some form of artwork or a cartoon. (This exercise is for right-brain students who enjoy drawing better than writing.)

EXTENDED READING ACTIVITIES

The purpose of this section is to give you a variety of options for independent study or investigation of the chapter topic. Reading is a skill that must be practiced each day if progress is to take place. These activities are designed to give you a variety of reading experiences through which you can improve your general vocabulary and increase your higher-level comprehension skills.

Your instructor may wish to (a) assign one or more activities to the class as a whole, (b) assign various activities to small groups, (c) assign one or more activities to individual students, or (d) let students choose to do the activities or not.

PROGRESS CHECK

A. Are you reading every day for at least thirty minutes at a time?
Yes____ No____

B. List the kind of difficult material you are reading:

_____

_____

C. How are you using the ideas and strategies you are learning in this book to help you in your difficult courses?
1. Using pre-reading activities such as:

_____

_____

2. Reading text by a reading plan, Reciprocal Teaching or Active Questioning: Yes____ No____ Parts of One____
3. Using post-reading activities, such as:

_____

_____

4. Using academic study skills such as:

_____

_____

ACTIVITIES

A. Weekly Reading Report: Continue keeping a weekly report of your daily reading. Use the form in Appendix C if you wish.

B. Attend a Reading Lab: Attend your reading lab. When you are reading and answering comprehension questions, can you tell the difference in types of questions? Do you find it easier to answer text-explicit questions than text-implicit ones?

C. Read your Novel: Read your novel. If you have finished reading your novel, you might want to try Virginia Hamilton's *The House of Dies Drear*, a mystery about a really spooky house with secret passages and mysterious characters. Trudy Krisher's *Spite Fences* is a good read about racial relationships. Best of all, try one of Achebe's, like *Things Fall Apart*.

D. Read with your child:
   1. Chinua Achebe, *The Flute*
   2. Harold Courlander & George Herzog, *The Cow-Tail Switch and Other West African Stories*
   3. Gerald McDermott, *Anansi the Spider: A Tale from the Ashanti*
   4. Tololwa M. Mollel, *The Princess Who Lost her Hair*
   5. Gail E. Haley, *A Story A Story*
   6. Marcia Brown, *Shadow* (trans. from the French of Blaise Cendrars)
   7. Sharon Bell Mathis, *The Hundred Penny Box*
   8. Angela Shelf Medearis, *Picking Peas for a Penny*
   9. Molly Bang, *Ten, Nine, Eight*
   10. Ezra Jack Keats, *Whistle for Willie*
   11. Eve Bunting, *Smoky Night*

E. Reading/Writing Connection: Continue keeping your beginning year college journal. Are you experiencing any conflicts between old and new values since coming to college? What are they and how are you resolving the conflicts? Do your college friends have different values from those of your hometown friends? How are the two sets of friends different? Alike? What are you looking for in your new friends? Write your responses in your journal. Use a new vocabulary word in your response.

F. Use the Internet: Look up Chinua Achebe and Nigeria on the Internet.

G. Vocabulary Journal: Continue keeping a vocabulary journal. Use the form in Appendix C if you wish.

H. Magazine/Journal/Newspaper Reading: Use the form in Appendix C if you wish for reporting on this reading. (See suggestions on page 339.)

1.   Read some of the big-city newspapers and compare their reporting of national events to your local paper. Try some of the following papers: *Cincinnati Enquirer*, *The New York Times*, *Wall Street Journal*, *The Plain Dealer* (Cleveland, Ohio), *The Christian Science Monitor*, *The Washington Post*, *Akron Beacon* (Ohio). What other big-city newspapers do you read? San Francisco? Atlanta? Boston? Be sure to read the front page and the editorial page. What events are discussed in these papers that are not in your local papers? What about coverage? Is there more depth of information or are there more supplemental articles? What appears in your local paper that could be of national interest?

2.   You may also want to read magazines and journals in the social sciences. Read from the following: *The American Journal of Psychology*, *American Psychologist*, *Psychology Today*, *Journal of Educational Psychology*, *The Journal of Social Psychology*, *American Journal of Sociology*, *American Sociological Review*, *The British Journal of Sociology*, *Journal of Sociology and Social Welfare*, *Contemporary Sociology*, *Brookings Review*, *American Political Science Review*, *Political Theory*, *Political Science and Politics*, *International Social Science Journal*, *The Journal of Politics*, *Challenge: The Magazine of Economic Affair*, *Economic Perspectives*, *Economic Quarterly*, *Economic Review*, *The Economist*, *International Journal of Middle East Studies*, *The Middle East Journal*, *Current History*, *The Journal of American History*, *Diplomatic History*, *Foreign Policy*, The American Geographical Society's *Focus*, *Geographical Review*, *Current Anthropology*.

REFLECTION

MIND REVOLUTION

You can get a sense of a people and their culture through the writings of a novelist that will give you insights that a brief visit would not. In fact, reading literature about a culture would enrich a visit to another country. What countries would you like to visit? How do you know about them? Reading, documentaries, and travel shows could have increased your knowledge and interest in them. Have sporting events, such as the Olympics, taken place in your countries of interest? What did you learn about the countries that made them interesting to you? Do you have a sense of that country's history? Would such knowledge be important to you?

VOCABULARY

The most difficult vocabulary words are proper names. Luckily, even if you have to guess at pronunciation, they do not interfere with comprehension. Since they begin with capital letters, you can guess that they are names. Context also helps you to make this distinction.

COMPREHENSION

Areas of comprehension difficulty include (1) fact overload, (2) lack of background knowledge and experience, and (3) lack of interest in the subject. Interestingly, this chapter may have been difficult for you because of so many facts. The facts make it easy to write text-explicit questions for each section. You have to keep them in focus and remember the purpose of the chapter is to investigate the culture clash between Nigerians and the British.

Your background knowledge and experience about West Africa also influence your understanding of the material. You may begin with asking yourself why you should be interested in this area. For one thing, we know that many African Americans are descended from West Africans, so knowing something about the history of the region gives you depth of knowledge and a broader perspective about African American history also. In the chapter you read about culture clash between Nigerians and the British. Understanding some of the conflicts that happened there could keep you as a tourist from being insensitive if you were to visit the area.

Another area of background knowledge that may be inadequate for the reading of this chapter is knowledge of literary analysis. The last section discusses the literary style of Achebe. If you do not know what nineteenth-century English novels are like, or who Thomas Hardy is, you may have trouble with the first paragraph. If you want to start building your literary background, read *Things Fall Apart*.

If you are not especially interested in Achebe, read a Thomas Hardy novel and think about the writing style. If you prefer, rent a movie based on one of Hardy's novels.

Your interest in the fiction of Achebe and of West Africa may be nil. If you are not specifically interested in those topics, your broader interest in the treatment of any group of people by conquerors and in what happens to the people's belief systems, values, culture, and language may be increased through seeing how the kind of information about a specific culture clash can influence your perception of culture clash in other parts of the world. Do we have the right to investigate isolated tribes in the Amazon basin? How do you feel about the loss of tribal rituals and knowledge by Native Americans? In the past or present, do we go to developing countries to try to bring them into the twenty-first century and in the process destroy part of who they are? The information in this chapter may have broadened your interest in these kinds of issues.

Music:
The Blues

Reflection
> Mind Revolution
> Vocabulary
> Comprehension

VOCABULARY/METACOGNITION

The purpose of this exercise is to help you become aware of when you know the meaning of a word and to help you know when you do not know the meaning of a word. This is metacognition awareness.

On a scale of 1–5 (see below), rate your knowledge of the following vocabulary words from "The Blues." After matching words with definitions on page 343, check your answers and then check your number *ones* and *fives* below. Did you know when you really knew a word and when you really did not know the word?

Scale

1. I absolutely do not know.
2. I do not think I know.
3. There's a 50/50 chance I have seen or heard it.
4. I think I know it.
5. I know the word and can use it.

Words

_____ 1. Consolation
_____ 2. Content
_____ 3. Tradition (traditional)
_____ 4. Complex
_____ 5. Familiar (familiarity)
_____ 6. Urban
_____ 7. Contradict (contradiction)
_____ 8. Unanimous
_____ 9. Consistent
_____10. Distinction

Go to page 343. See if you can match the right definition with the word and then write sentences for any five words in the list.

Words	Definitions
_____ 1. Consolation	A. Act or effect of consoling; solace
_____ 2. Content	B. (1) Composed of many parts; (2) involved; complicated; perplexing
_____ 3. Tradition (traditional)	C. (1) Act of distinguishing; (2) a distinguishing quality or characteristic; difference in general; (3) an honor; eminence; superiority
_____ 4. Complex	
_____ 5. Familiar (familiarity)	
_____ 6. Urban	D. Subject matter, as of a book
_____ 7. Contradict (contradiction)	E. (1) Assert the contrary; (2) deny the words of
_____ 8. Unanimous	F. (1) Congruous; in accord; (2) conforming regularly to the same pattern, habits, principles, etc.
_____ 9. Consistent	
_____10. Distinction	
	G. (1) Closely intimate; (2) well versed or acquainted; (3) well known and remembered; common
	H. Being of one mind; all agreeing, without exception
	I. The handing down of customs, practices, doctrines, etc; something so handed down
	J. Pertaining to, comprising, living in, or characteristic of a city

Write five words from the list and your own sentences that show you know how to use the words. Choose words that you marked a *five* if possible.

1. Word _____

   Sentence _____

2. Word _____

   Sentence _____

3. Word _____

   Sentence _____

4. Word _____

   Sentence _____

5. Word _____

   Sentence _____

PRE-READING THE TEXTBOOK CHAPTER

OVERVIEW

The purpose of this *first* of three steps in your reading plan is to suggest things to do *before* you read. First, as part of your pre-reading, read the Prior Knowledge section beginning on page 344. When you finish, return to this section and continue your pre-reading. The Academic Study Skills section will be used as a part of your post-reading assignment. You may want to skim it as a part of your pre-reading.

ACTIVITIES

    A. Tap experience and prior knowledge about the title of this selection.

    B. Predict what you will read.

    C. Overview by reading the summary and the questions at the end of the selection. Write the main headings of the selection below.

The Blues

I.   _____

II. _____

III. _____

PRIOR KNOWLEDGE

This section, part of your pre-reading, presents a model to show you what will help you comprehend this chapter by using your own background knowledge. If you know much of the following information, you have a better background for reading this chapter. This section will suggest helpful kinds of background information and help you activate what you know; do not try to look up or learn everything listed. Ask yourself what you need to know before you read and what you already know that will help you to understand this chapter. Your instructor may want to use this section for a whole-class or small group discussion or have you read it silently.

CHAPTER SECTIONS

I.   Defining the Blues

    A. Vocabulary

        1. Paragraph One

           a. Indigo

           b. Lyrics

           c. Proclaimed

           d. Achievement

           e. Indications

           f. Encompasses

        2. Paragraph Two

           a. Commonplace

           b. Heptatonic

       c.   Pentatonic

       d.   Eurocentric

       e.   Octave

       f.   Approximate

       g.   Correspondences

       h.   Scales

       i.   Articulate

       j.   Subtle

       k.   Perceptible

       l.   Melancholy

      m.   Accustomed

       n.   Harmonic

       o.   Relationships

  B.   Recognition of Writing Patterns or Arrangement of Ideas and Devices

     1.   General to specific

     2.   Contrast

  C.   Concepts and Background Knowledge and Experience

     1.   To be able to read or play music

     2.   To recognize "blue" notes

     3.   To understand musical scales

II.   Some Historical Background of the Blues

  A.   Vocabulary

     1.   Paragraph One

       a.   Transmitted

       b.   Holds

       c.   Sophisticated

     2.   Paragraph Two

       a.   Utilize

       b.   Voodoo

       c.   Chants

       d.   Apparently

       e.   Reflected

       f.   Consolation

       g.   Propitious

       h.   Circumstances

       i.   Improvised

       j.   Percussion

       k.   Fifes

     3.   Paragraph Three

       a.   Lined

       b.   Content

       c.   Assonance (defined in text)

    B. Recognition of Writing Patterns or Arrangement of Ideas and Devices
       1. Examples and supporting details
    C. Concepts/Background Knowledge and Experience
       1. Technical knowledge: rhyme scheme, stanza form, assonance
       2. Knowledge of slavery
       3. Knowledge of black culture in seventeenth–twentieth centuries
       4. Musical instruments
       5. Folk music—songs and musicians
       6. Some knowledge of the history and geography of West Africa and the Caribbean

III. More Modern Manifestations of the Blues
    A. Vocabulary
       1. Title
          a. Manifestations
       2. Paragraph One
          a. Utilizing
       3. Paragraph Two
          a. Improvise
          b. Complex
          c. Stanza
          d. Repetitive
          e. Pattern
       4. Paragraph Three
          a. Emancipation
          b. Acquire
          c. Mobile
          d. Stationary
          e. Raspy
       5. Paragraph Four
          a. Comparatively
          b. Facility
          c. Familiarity
       6. Paragraph Five
          a. Associated
          b. Metropolitan
          c. Urban
          d. Epitome
          e. Notion
          f. Virtual
          g. Outright
          h. Contradiction

   i. Tracing

   j. Descended

   k. Abusive

   l. Citified

   m. Unanimous

  7. Paragraph Six

   a. Anecdote

   b. Astonishment

   c. Improvisatory

  8. Paragraph Seven

   a. Improvised

   b. Portability

   c. Purists

   d. Acoustic

   e. Realized

  9. Paragraph Eight

   a. Derived

   b. Inevitable

   c. Consistent

  10. Paragraph Nine

   a. Theme

   b. Distinction

 B. Recognition of Writing Patterns or Arrangement of Ideas and Devices

  1. Recognition of specific details (as opposed to main ideas)

 C. Concepts/Background Knowledge and Experience

  1. Knowledge of the specific music and musicians mentioned as examples

  2. Technical information: repetitions, improvisation, refrain, harmony

  3. Knowledge of popular music

ACADEMIC STUDY SKILLS

DIRECTIONS

Review the study skills you have practiced in previous lessons and decide if you wish to use one with this lesson. If you need guided practice, see Appendix D for help with the SQ4R plan, memory, annotation, and underlining/highlighting. Consider the difficulty of the material, your purpose for learning the material, and your interest in the subject. The following study skill will be used as part of your post-reading.

STUDY SKILL: VISUAL MAPPING

The next study skill we will use is visual mapping. Instead of producing a formal outline as you often do in an English composition class and as you have done in previous chapters of this textbook, you will create a visual map of the material. Some learners find it more helpful than outlining. Again, the important first step is finding the most important information and its support in the chapter. Facts, explanations, and examples can provide the support. As in highlighting, you do not want to write too much. Your task is to identify the most important information and put it in a visual form. Any form you create is a good form, as long as it has meaning for you. You must maintain the hierarchies of information in your map as shown below in the directions.

A. Preparation
   1. Practice your new or improved skill of highlighting the most important ideas in this chapter. Do not highlight the whole chapter at once; work on one section at the time. Highlight the most important information in all three sections.
   2. When you have highlighted all three sections, go back and skim the material for support. How does the author support his ideas? For example, he seems to depend on many examples for support. How do they help clarify the material?
   3. In the first section, "Defining the Blues," how does the author define the blues? He never gives a straightforward definition; instead, he tells the reader that there are many ways to define them. In the second paragraph he goes to great lengths to explain the difference in the pentatonic and heptatonic scales. Why is this important information? This information explains the blue notes and becomes the basis of later information in the chapter.
   4. In the second section of the chapter, "Some Historical Background of the Blues," we find that blue notes came to America through enslaved West Africans and that slaves on plantations and farms used vocal music for consolation and for religious expression. We also find that house servants probably introduced European music and instruments to the general slave population. We end the section with an example of one type of blues, the work song and how it was sung. The classical form, *aab*, will continue to be important to the rest of the chapter.
   5. In the third and last section of the chapter, "Some Modern Manifestations of the Blues Tradition," we are told that the wording of the *aa* lines is often traditional and then are given examples of variations in hymns and variations by blues singers. Variations in work songs occur also. Next, we jump in time past emancipation and are told that musicians can now buy instruments and are given examples of instruments played. Changes in the music are next examined and we find that the *aab* stanza is retained but the repetition of *aa* is now used also. From that change we move to the blues and popular songs that came from musicians moving into

metropolitan areas. Both the refrain form and the general popular song type were associated with feeling blue. We are given examples of singers who sang the blues and popular songs. Next, we move to jazz and find that the blues is a base for jazz and that the blues is adaptable to types of songs and the variety of instruments that can be used to play it. The blues lyrics are mixed with popular songs but remain blues because of the blue notes. Another example, the torch song, is like the blues. One difference was that the torch song repeated the singer's sad feelings whereas the blues was a way of doing something about them.

6. Compare what you have highlighted with the information in A (1–5) above.

B. Draw your visual map

1. Use the title of this chapter (The Blues) as the top level of your map. It contains the broadest and most general information for this chapter.

2. Use the three main headings of the chapter on a second level under the title. These three headings must be on the same level to show they are of equal importance. These headings represent the second level of important information.

The Blues

Defining the Blues	*Some Historical Background of the Blues*	*Some Modern Manifestations of the Blues Tradition*

3. Now comes the hard part. In your own words, under each of the three main headings and on the same level, add the important ideas you have highlighted for each section of the chapter. Obviously, you must reduce the information to make it manageable and useful. This is your third level of information.

The Blues

Defining the Blues	*Some Historical Background of the Blues*	*Some Modern Manifestations of the Blues Tradition*
Variety of definitions. Heptatonic and pentatonic scales show differences and how blue notes are produced.	West African slaves brought their musical traditions. House servants introduced European music. Introduced to other slaves. aab refrain.	Variations on traditional wording. Emancipation—many instruments. aab stanza and aa refrain used. Metropolitan move and mix of blues with popular songs. Blues basis for Jazz; adaptable to types of music and variety of instruments.

4. Optional: Under the third level, the most important ideas, add a fourth level that shows support for the ideas on level three. The fourth level is your most narrow one, a list of information, more dealing with details, and the least important in this hierarchy. This level provides information for literal-level questions if you are expecting a test of that level of comprehension.

The Blues

Defining the Blues	*Some Historical Background of the Blues*	*Some Modern Manifestations of the Blues Tradition*
Variety of definitions. Heptatonic and pentatonic scales show differences and how blue notes are produced.	West African slaves brought their musical traditions. House servants introduced European music. Introduced to other slaves. aab refrain.	Variations on traditional wording. Emancipation—many instruments. aab stanza and aa refrain used. Metropolitan move and mix of blues with popular songs. Blues basis for Jazz; adaptable to types of music and variety of instruments.
	Lining a work song. aab form rhyme scheme. Different—aaa.	*Aaron Walker, Sam Hopkins. End of a line-hoe. Harmonicas, guitars, pianos. Vocal devices. Bessie Smith, Billy Holiday, Charlie Parker, Dizzy Gillespie. Torch songs.*

C. Remember to use your map to self-test and review.

RECIPROCAL TEACHING

OVERVIEW

Your first step of the three-part reading plan was pre-reading. In pre-reading, you activated your prior knowledge, predicted what you would read, and overviewed the chapter before reading.

As the *second* step in this three-part reading plan, you will read this chapter by using the Reciprocal Teaching reading plan as explained below. An alternative plan, Active Questioning, is in Appendix B. In both plans you break up the chapter in sections and read and think about each as you read. The purpose of both plans is to keep you reading actively. The Reciprocal Teaching lesson used below is the older model. You may use the newer one if you wish (predict, question, clarify, and summarize). Review Chapter 3.

ASSIGNMENT

A. Read section one, "Defining the Blues."

1. Write a summary of this first major section. Model summary: Although there are many definitions of the blues, it is better to approach an understanding through looking at so-called "blue notes" which are based on a pentatonic, rather than heptatonic, scale. How can you improve this summary?

Your summary _____

_____

_____

2. Write one question on this section. Try to write an inferential or a critical/creative question. If you can't, write a literal level question. Model experience-based question: What types of music are your favorites? How are the types musically different? Have you ever carefully listened to music you could not follow or did not like? What was the result?

Your question _____

Answer _____

3. Orally explain or clarify an important idea. Model idea: Explain the difference in the heptatonic and pentatonic scales.

Your idea _____

4. Predict what you will read in the second major section, "Some Historical Background of the Blues." Model prediction: I predict I will read about early blues and the people who created the music.

Your prediction_____

B. Read "Some Historical Background of the Blues."

1. Summarize this second major section. Model summary: Enslaved West Africans brought knowledge about how to make music and to perform on musical instruments to the United States plantations. Work songs there gave the classical *aab* form to the blues. How can you improve this summary?

Your summary _____

_____

_____

2. Write one question on this section. Try to write an inferential or a critical/creative question. If you can't, write a literal level question. Model text-implicit question: What is the historical background of the blues?

Your question _____

Answer _____

3. Orally explain or clarify an important idea in this section. Model idea: Explain "lining" a song or the *aab* form.

Your idea _____

4. Predict what you will read in the third major section of the chapter, "More Modern Manifestations of the Blues Tradition." Model prediction: I predict that I will read about the influence of the blues on modern music.

Your prediction _____

C. Read "More Modern Manifestations of the Blues Tradition."
1. Summarize this third major section. Model summary: Even though the wording of the *aa* lines of blues is often traditional, there are variations and repetitions that are not always exact. With emancipation and better economic times, many singers acquired and used instruments. Blues musicians also moved to urban centers where themes changed from those of the older work songs. Blues remained a base for jazz and influenced popular music, especially the torch song. How can you improve this summary?

Your summary _____

_____

_____

2. Write one question on this section. Try to write an inferential or a critical/creative question. If you can't, write a literal level question. Model experience-based question: What kind of music do you listen to that expresses sad feelings? When and why do you listen to it?

Your question _____

Answer _____

3. Orally explain or clarify an important idea in this section. Model idea: Explain the connection of the more general popular song and the blues, or explain how the blues has adapted to various technical conditions.

Your idea _____

POST-READING THE TEXTBOOK CHAPTER

OVERVIEW

In the second part of your three-part reading plan, you practiced reading your textbook chapter section by section, wrote section summaries, asked and answered questions, explained or clarified important ideas, and made predictions for what you would read in the next section. As part of your post-reading activity, follow the directions for visual mapping in the Academic Study Skills section beginning on page 348.

ASSIGNMENT

In this third part of the three-part reading plan, you will find suggestions for what to do after you read. Your task is to compare what you predicted with what you actually read as an aid to comprehension, to add what you have learned to your file of information on the topic, and to think about what you have read.

A. Look at your prediction of what you would read in the pre-reading section of this lesson. What did you correctly predict that you would read?

B. What did you learn from the reading that you did not know about before working on this lesson?

C. Look at the words and phrases that you listed as your prior knowledge in the pre-reading section of this lesson. Group them below with relevant information in "B" above and make up your own headings. This is your new file of information on the blues. (The ability to group ideas and to see relationships requires more complex comprehension than merely memorizing isolated facts.)

D. What have you learned from this chapter that is important?

E. What do you already know that you can relate to it?

F. What do you see differently as a result of reading this chapter?

Your Headings	Words and Phrases from Pre-Reading	Relevant Information from "B"

THE BLUES

Defining the Blues

There are many definitions of *blues*. Some relate the term to the expression *feeling blue*, and there is a strong association of the musical form with the mood called "the blues." From "Got Dem Blues" to Ellington's *Mood Indigo*, the lyrics have proclaimed that the blues is a way of feeling "low." But outstanding bluesman Sam "Lightning" Hopkins wrote a "Happy Blues for John Glenn," celebrating the astronaut's achievement; and there are other indications that the (musical) blues encompasses more than a depressed feeling.

Perhaps it might be better to approach the matter musically, through the so-called "blue notes." It is commonplace that, whereas European music (in the modern period, at any rate) is heptatonic, a lot of West African music is pentatonic. If we divide up what the Eurocentric viewpoint calls the *octave* in two ways, we can see the relationship:

8E	1
7D	5
6C	4
5B	
4A	3
3G	2
2F	
1E	1

It will be seen that there are approximate but not exact correspondences between **g** (note 3 on the left) and note 2 on the right; between **b** (5 on the left) and 3 on the right. If a musician who can play both scales plays for a while by the rules of the left side but occasionally, when coming to a **g** or a **b**, produces rather the 2nd or 3rd on the right, listeners used to the heptatonic scale (most of us) will notice a difference—whether they're able to articulate it in these or similar terms or not—but will notice the relationship to **b** or **g** (again, without being necessarily conscious of it). If it was not **b**-natural but **b**-flat that was in the original tune, an even more subtle—but perceptible—change will be noted. These, roughly speaking, are what came to be known as "blue notes." They may suggest a melancholy mood, especially to ears accustomed to different harmonic relationships.

Some Historical Background of the Blues

It would have been impossible for these blue notes to have come about if some West African culture had not been transmitted to the New World. Enslaved West Africans could hardly have brought musical instruments with them in the horrible, crowded holds of slave ships, but they could and did bring with them knowledge about how to make music and to perform on musical instruments. In fact, some authorities think they brought far more sophisticated knowledge than was possessed by their enslavers and masters.

On the plantations and farms of the Americas, especially the Caribbean, there was abundant opportunity for slaves to utilize what they remembered of vocal music. Some of it, as in Haitian voodoo chants, apparently reflected religious use of music in West Africa. Otherwise, the music of home gave a kind of consolation to the field hand who worked cutting cane or at some other back-breaking job from dawn to dusk almost every day. House servants, who were never completely separated from the field hands—under propitious circumstances a field hand could become a house servant, or *vice versa*—may have been instrumental in introducing the European music and musical instruments to the general slave community. Roughly improvised percussion and stringed instruments or fifes made of cane, in the hands of really talented performers, could produce a music almost on a par with that heard back home in Africa.

The plantation work song, sung by a highly regarded leader and a chorus of those who happened to be working with him, gave the classical **aab** form to the blues. The leader "lined" the first verse (in something of the same way that it was being done in some religious groups) and the others repeated it with him. Recognizing the pattern, the others joined with the leader in the last line of the stanza:

> **a**   (Leader) I'm gonna get up in the mornin',' do like
> Buddy Brown
> **a**   (Leader and others) I'm gonna get up in the morning, do like
> Buddy Brown
> **b**   (Leader and others) I'm gonna eat my breakfast, then lay back
> down

In this case, the letter **a** represents the content of a line rather than rhyme; actually, all three lines rhyme—more or less—and the *rhyme scheme* (not the stanza form) for the traditional blues would be **aaa**. Often assonance (the repetition of a vowel sound, whether or not the consonants match) replaces rhyme; Hopkins, in

"Goin' to Dallas, See My Pony Run," makes *time* at the end of **aa** and *retire* at the end of **b** seem perfectly natural.

Some Modern Manifestations of the Blues Tradition

The wording of the **aa** lines is often traditional, even formulaic:

> **a**   Sometimes I sing the blues, when I know I should be praying
> **a**   (Repeat)
> **b**   …

Slight variations on lines from sources like hymns are not uncommon, as in Aaron "T. Bone" Walker's semi-quotation of a line from "Amazing Grace":

> Once I was blind but now I can see

Individual blues singers, especially when utilizing this traditional stanza form, often are not fully aware whether they are inventing or remembering. On the other hand, combination of the same stanzas to make identical songs is rare indeed. There is also a great deal of variation in the traditional lines, sometimes as simple as

> Sometimes I sing the blues when, you know, I should be praying

In the work song versions also, repetitions are not always exact; the leader, having already transmitted the wording to his fellow singers, may improvise on the second **a**:

> Man, I'm gonna get up in the morning, do like
> Buddy Brown

As in Sam Hopkins's "Black Gal," parts of each **a** could be repeated and varied in order to make a very complex stanza still clearly based upon this simple scheme. Singers, nevertheless, realized that a repetitive pattern was present. As John Dee Holeman put it (interview in the Columbus, Ohio, *Dispatch*, for November 4, 1992, p. 10F), the blues are about feeling so much that "we sing some lines twice."

The end of any line might be punctuated by a stroke of the hoe or other agricultural instrument with which the workers might be doing their field duties. Those who have heard early bluesman Huddie ("Leadbelly") Ledbetter's recordings may remember the *sotto voce* "Bam!" with which he punctuated his lines, apparently recalling the falling of the hoe or ax in the work songs which were the source of his blues.

With emancipation and better economic times, many of the singers were able to acquire instruments. Harmonicas and guitars for the mobile singers and pianos for the more stationary ones were the favorite instruments of accompaniment, making possible a more complex harmonic and general musical structure for the blues. The more stationary use was often in a church, in a musical type called the spiritual, in which some of the same performance characteristics were utilized, even though the content of the blues was regarded as sinful. Well into the twentieth century, Black preachers continued to use vocal devices like raspy voice which were also in use in jazz and blues singing, although for very different purposes.

In many cases, where the blues were concerned, the traditional **aab** stanza form was retained, and it can be heard on blues recordings made at least as late as the 1960s. But the **aa**-repetition at the beginning is in principle what the refrain is in more conventional European music and poetry—a repetition, even though it comes at the beginning rather than at the end. It was a comparatively slight shift to the end-repetition, making for refrain songs which still had many characteristics—both in words and in music—of the old blues. Many of the better bluesmen, like the above-mentioned Lightning Hopkins, use the older **aab** form and the refrain form with equal facility and familiarity.

The refrain form and the more general popular song type came to be associated with the "feeling" of the blues as the singers moved into St. Louis, Chicago, New York, and other metropolitan areas. Although not strictly speaking the same thing as a sad popular song, the blues tended to mix with that tradition and even, in its urban manifestation, to be swallowed up in the popular laments for lost loves and general troubles. A quite traditional blues singer in many respects, Bessie Smith sang in the old **aab** pattern and also in forms more generally associated with American popular music in recordings she made in the 1920s and 1930s. A retention of the "blues feeling," along with blue notes, seems to be what characterized the singing of Billy Holiday, always mentioned among the leading blues vocalists and considered by some to be the epitome of blues singing. The general American notion of *blues* as the virtual equivalent of sadness seems to apply by this stage, and a "happy blues" seems like an outright contradiction in terms. Only historical tracing could establish any connection between her music and the work songs from which the blues descended; cotton fields, mules, abusive foremen or "captains" and such are replaced by entirely citified concerns. Nevertheless, the audience for the blues seems almost unanimous in considering "Lady Day" to be a leading exponent of the blues.

Throughout the different stages and styles of jazz performance, the blues has remained as a kind of base from which operation is possible. There was an anecdote of how, in the highly individualistic "bop" or "bebop" movement led by Charlie Parker and Dizzy Gillespie, a saxophonist led the band into a song which virtually no one in the combo had ever heard before. There was hardly a moment of pause to show astonishment or embarrassment; a veteran trumpet player with a New Orleans background transformed the tune into the blues pattern and the whole group was off on its improvisatory way.

From the unaccompanied work songs to the use of improvised percussion instruments to the favored guitar, the blues has proved adaptable to any technical conditions. Where portability was not a question, the piano, played by a blues singer like Memphis Slim with or without rhythm accompaniment, often replaced the guitar. Today, some purists prefer the acoustic guitar to the electric; but working bluesmen seem not to care especially. Blues techniques and blues feeling can be fully realized wherever there are musicians who know the blues.

As the blues players and singers—and the jazz players and singers who in some sense derived from them—moved more nearly into the biracial mainstream, mixture with the forms and devices of the popular song was inevitable. In many cases, the blues stanza was simply abandoned, since popular songs had a different stanza form. What made these songs still blues, in addition to the oft-cited "feeling," was the fairly consistent use of the blue notes.

Nevertheless, the difference between the blues and "jazzed up" popular song often tended to blur out. The popular sense of *blues* was also mixed in; a "blues" could be simply a sad song, as in "St. Louis Blues" and "Memphis Blues."

The term for a popular song with a sad theme, usually of disappointed love, was *torch song*, based upon the metaphor that someone longing for a departed lover was "carrying a torch." It is not always possible to make a simple distinction between blues and the torch song, since the same singers performed both of them with great distinction. Perhaps one difference is that the torch song basically repeated the singer's supposed sad feelings whereas the blues was a way of doing something about them.

Summary

The blues may be formally defined in terms of harmonic and stanzaic (**aab**) structure. The feeling of sadness associated popularly with the word blues is also a frequent feature, but there are exceptions—"happy blues," songs of protest, etc. The harmonic if not the stanzaic character of the blues was basic to early jazz and remained influential even among highly experimental types of jazz which developed in the last few decades. In popular use, the blues became associated with the "torch song," with its lyric of lost or unrequited love. Some performers use enough of both traditions almost to eliminate the distinction.

Questions

1. Why is popular music not the same as the blues?
2. How do jazz musicians utilize the blues?
3. What is the relationship of the blues to spirituals?
4. To what degree is the wording of a blues stanza (**aab**) spontaneous and creative?

VOCABULARY LESSON

The purpose of this exercise is to help you review and deepen your knowledge of the ten general vocabulary words you worked with at the beginning of this chapter.

A. Structural Analysis—Affixes and Root Words
   1. Underline the suffix of the following word: *Familiarity*
   2. Find the dictionary definition of the root word of the word above and write the definition below:

   _____

B. Use of Context: Read the last paragraph of "Some Historical Background of the Blues" in which the following word appears, and in your own words write a definition: *Traditional*

C. Multiple Meanings of Words: Circle the definition below of the word *content* as it is used in this chapter. (See the last paragraph of the section "Some Historical Background of the Blues.")
   1. Subject matter, as of a book
   2. All that is contained in a receptacle

D. Synonyms and Antonyms: List one synonym (same meaning) and one antonym (opposite meaning) for each of the following words:

Word	Synonym	Antonym
Complex		
Urban		

E. Generate Your Own Language
   1. If someone received a *consolation* prize, did the person win or lose?
   2. If a decision is *unanimous*, how many people voted against it?
   3. If you are reading a difficult textbook chapter, would *familiarity* with the subject help or hurt you?
   4. In what *urban* area of the United States would you like to live? Why?
   5. What health rules do you follow *consistently*?
   6. What *distinctive* qualities should a good student possess?
   7. When have you found a friend making *contradictory* remarks about an issue that is important to you?

VOCABULARY EXTENSION

The purpose of this exercise is to help you see to what degree you know the ten general vocabulary words you worked with at the beginning of this chapter. Matching a word with its definition is the beginning of knowing a word. Using the word in your speaking and writing is full knowledge.

A. List the vocabulary words from this lesson that you can now use in both your speaking and writing.

B. List the vocabulary words from this lesson that you can now use in writing but are still not comfortable using in speaking.

C. List the vocabulary words from this lesson that you cannot use yet but will recognize in reading.

D. List general vocabulary words from this lesson that are still difficult to understand.

E. Use *five* vocabulary words from this lesson in a five-sentence paragraph on the topic of this lesson.

F. Illustrate the meaning of *one* of the vocabulary words from this lesson through some form of artwork or a cartoon. (This exercise is for right-brain students who enjoy drawing better than writing!)

EXTENDED READING ACTIVITIES

The purpose of this section is to give you a variety of options for independent study or investigation of the chapter topic. Reading is a skill that must be practiced each day if progress is to take place. These activities are designed to give you a variety of reading experiences through which you can improve your general vocabulary and increase your higher-level comprehension skills.

Your instructor may wish to (a) assign one or more activities to the class as a whole, (b) assign various activities to small groups, (c) assign one or more activities to individual students, or (d) let students choose to do the activities or not.

PROGRESS CHECK

A. List things you are doing outside of class that are helping you read on a higher level and improve your general vocabulary.

B. Approximately how many words have you added to your written vocabulary?

C. What new words have you used in conversations with others?

D. What ideas have you encountered through your reading that made you think about issues or ideas in a different way?

E. What gave you support or reinforcement for ideas and issues that are important to you?

ACTIVITIES

A. Weekly Reading Report: Continue keeping a weekly report of your daily reading. Use the form in Appendix C if you wish. In college one of the great freedoms is that it is alright to look intelligent and interested in academic matters, so check out sections of your library that you would not have been caught dead in when you were a high school student. You will not hyperventilate!

B. Attend your Reading Lab: Continue attending the reading lab on your campus. Are you working on your reading rate? Have you increased your words per minute? What topics slow you down? Which topics are faster reading?

C. Read your Novel: Continue reading your novel or choose a new one. Richard Peck's *Are You in the House Alone?* is scary and Jerry Spinelli's *There's a Girl in my Hammerlock* is about a girl in a man's sport who has lots of obstacles to overcome. You may also want to read a biography about one of the musicians mentioned in this chapter.

D. Read with your child
1. Judith Viorst, *If I Were in Charge of the World and Other Worries*
2. Paul Fleischman, *Joyful Noise: Poems for Two Voices*
3. Jill Bennett (collector), *Tasty Poems*
4. Mirra Ginsburg, *The Chinese Mirror* (adapted from a Korean Folktale)
5. Thomas Handforth, *Mei Li*

E. Reading/Writing Connection: Continue keeping your first year college journal. Has your taste in music changed since arriving on campus? Do your friends at home like the same music as your friends on campus? What have you heard on campus that is new to you? What does music do for you? Do you listen to music when you study? Write your responses in your journal. Use a new vocabulary word in your responses.

F. Use the Internet: Look up the *blues*, *jazz*, or one of the musicians, such as *Bessie Smith* or *Jelly Roll Morton*, mentioned in this chapter.

G. Vocabulary Journal: Continue keeping your vocabulary journal. Use the form in Appendix C if you wish.

H. Magazine/Journal/Newspaper Reading: Continue reading magazines, journals, and newspapers. Read about the fine arts and humanities for this lesson: (a) record what you read, (b) write a summary of one of the articles, and (c) write a paragraph about your opinion of the article. List any new vocabulary words you encounter and find dictionary definitions that match the way the words are used in the article. Use the form in Appendix C if you wish.
1. Fine arts: *American Craft, American Theatre, Performing Arts Journal, Art Journal, American Artist, Art in America, Art and Perception, Artforum International, Ceramic Review, American Ceramics, Ceramics, Ceramics Monthly, Sculpture, Opera News, Piano & Keyboard, Journal of Research in Music Education, Journal of the American Musicological Society, Photography, Print, Architectural Digest*
2. Humanities: *The Hiram Poetry Review, The Hudson Review, Humanities, The Sewanee Review, Southern Review, Literature Film Quarterly, Philosophy of Science, Philosophy and Literature, American Poetry Review, American Speech, Antioch Review, Billboard, Daedalus (Journal of American Academy of Arts and Sciences), English Today*

REFLECTION

MIND REVOLUTION

Hopefully, you have become interested in music you knew little about. The history of the blues, the explanation of blue notes, the differences in the European and African scales, the influence of the blues on other types of music are all areas for further exploration. This chapter gives you a historical point of view. What kind of blues is being played today? How is it connected to traditional blues? What about the type of guitars used, acoustic or electric? What are the arguments or issues over their use? Where do you stand?

VOCABULARY

The general vocabulary words should not cause reading difficulty in this chapter. The technical vocabulary words can. In the first section, *lyrics* is familiar enough, but *heptatonic* and *pentatonic* probably were alien. One easy way of thinking about them is that hepta = seven and penta = five. Seven and five tones will help define the scales. It is a beginning. *Octave, scales,* and *harmonic* are probably familiar but possibly hazy if you have no musical training. In the second section, *percussion* and *fifes* were possibly familiar. The information surrounding *fifes* helped you understand what kind of instrument is discussed. In the third section, *stanza* is the only new technical word and since it is also more generally used, it was possibly familiar.

COMPREHENSION

Three areas that can cause comprehension difficulty are (1) lack of background knowledge and experience, (2) assumptions on the part of the author, and (3) lack of interest in the topic.

Background knowledge of music could help you or hurt you in your understanding of this chapter. Reading the graphic on the two scales as well as the discussion that follows can be difficult to follow if you have little musical background. The European scale is probably familiar with its eight notes. If the African scale is not familiar, try to find an African finger piano and play it. The difference in the two scales becomes obvious when you hear the instrument played.

Another source of difficulty is the author's assumptions about his audience. He assumes the reader knows something about the technical side of music and about the African culture and American slavery. He also assumes that the reader knows about the migration of African Americans to the northern cities. He assumes that the reader knows the musicians and singers he refers to throughout the chapter. All of this can cause difficulty in reading the chapter.

Lack of interest can also cause difficulty. Many times we are set in our ways and are rather inflexible about the music we enjoy. We grow up with certain types of music that through the years brings comfort and memories of home. We have also often absorbed our generational music which gives us a sense of place and belonging, of mutual enjoyment and understanding. Many times our generational music expresses our emotions, our needs, our ideas, and it sets us apart from our parents and other generations. Listening to music that is different from that of family and peers can be dangerous. It also takes energy and time; it can cause alienation from those who are important in our lives. Sometimes, it just hurts our ears and we do not have the patience to listen long enough to learn what to listen for or what others hear in the music. Listening to the blues may be in this last category. Is it possible to expand your taste and interest in music to include the blues? You do not have to lose what you already enjoy; you can simply add some more to your list.

American English:
Does American English Have a History?

Overview

Reflection
    Mind Revolution
    Vocabulary
    Comprehension

VOCABULARY/METACOGNITION

The purpose of this exercise is to help you become aware of when you know the meaning of a word and to help you know when you do not know the meaning of a word. This is metacognition awareness.

On a scale of 1–5 (see below), rate your knowledge of the following vocabulary words from "Does American English Have a History?" After matching words with definitions on page 364, check your answers and then check your number *ones* and *fives* below. Did you know when you really knew a word and when you really did not know the word?

Scale

1. I absolutely do not know.
2. I do not think I know.
3. There's a 50/50 chance I have seen or heard it.
4. I think I know it.
5. I know the word and can use it.

Words

_____ 1. Discern (discernible)
_____ 2. Superficial
_____ 3. Fledgling
_____ 4. Paramount
_____ 5. Diffuse (diffused)
_____ 6. Tenuous
_____ 7. Facetious
_____ 8. Homogeneous
_____ 9. Diversity
_____10. Aegis

Go to page 364. See if you can match the right definition with the word and then write sentences for any five words in the list.

Words	Definitions
_____ 1. Discern (discernible)	A. Protection; sponsorship
_____ 2. Superficial	B. Composed of parts of the same kind
_____ 3. Fledgling	C. Widely spread
_____ 4. Paramount	D. Not deep or thorough
_____ 5. Diffuse (diffused)	E. (1) Essential difference; (2) variety
_____ 6. Tenuous	F. Superior to all others
_____ 7. Facetious	G. (1) Not legally binding; invalid; null; (2) having no contents; vacant
_____ 8. Homogeneous	H. Humorous; joking
_____ 9. Diversity	I. Young and inexperienced
_____10. Aegis	J. Distinguish by the eye of the intellect; perceive; discriminate

Write five words from the list and your own sentences that show you know how to use the words. Choose words that you marked a *five* if possible.

1. Word _____

   Sentence _____

2. Word _____

   Sentence _____

3. Word _____

   Sentence _____

4. Word _____

   Sentence _____

5. Word _____

   Sentence _____

PRE-READING THE TEXTBOOK CHAPTER

OVERVIEW

The purpose of this *first* of three steps in your reading plan is to suggest things to do *before* you read. First, as part of your pre-reading, read the Prior Knowledge section beginning on page 365. When you finish, return to this section and continue your pre-reading. The Academic Study Skills section will be used as your instructor wishes. You may want to skim it as a part of your pre-reading.

ACTIVITIES

    A. Tap experience and prior knowledge about the title of this chapter.

    B. Predict what you will read.

    C. Overview by reading the summary and the questions at the end of the chapter. Write the main headings of the chapter below.

Does American English Have a History?

I.   _____

II.   _____

III.   _____

IV.   _____

V.   _____

PRIOR KNOWLEDGE

This section, part of your pre-reading, presents a model to show you what will help you comprehend this chapter by using your own background knowledge. If you know much of the following information, you have a better background for reading this chapter. This section will suggest helpful kinds of background information and help you activate what you know; do not try to look up or learn everything listed. Ask yourself what you need to know before you read and what you already know that will help you to understand this chapter. Your instructor may want to use this section for a whole-class or small group discussion or have you read it silently.

CHAPTER SECTIONS

I.   The Traditional View

    A. Vocabulary

        1. Discernible

        2. Ecclesiastical

        3. Superficial

        4. Superimposed

    B. Recognition of Writing Patterns or Arrangement of Ideas and Devices

        1. No general-to-specific introduction pattern

        2. Chronological pattern—early to late

        3. Contrast/comparison pattern (paragraphs two and three)

    C. Concepts/Background Knowledge and Experience

        1. Density of Concepts: First paragraph gives a condensed history of British English. It doesn't stop for examples. The author does not

give examples because they would introduce too much complexity as to knowledge about language. It would be helpful if the readers had taken a course in English literature in high school.

    2. Ask yourself: "What is the traditional view of American English?"

II. Exploration and Early Settlement

    A. Vocabulary

        1. Aegis

        2. Abortive

        3. Acculturated

        4. Void

        5. Approximations

        6. Fledgling

        7. Paramount

    B. Recognition of Writing Patterns or Arrangement of Ideas and Devices

        1. Expository

    C. Concepts/Background Knowledge and Experience

        1. Condensed American history that assumes background knowledge of American history. It would be helpful to have taken a course in high school in American history.

        2. Helpful knowledge: Puritans, Pilgrims, geography

        3. Questions to ask yourself: (a) "How have exploration and early settlement played a part in the history of American English?" (b) "How did the Puritans communicate with Native Americans?" (c) "What is the importance of the interaction of the Native Americans with fishing vessels?"

III. Language Contact Factors

    A. Vocabulary

        1. Solidarity

        2. Diffused

        3. *Lingua franca*

        4. Deprecated

        5. Heterogeneous

        6. Maritime

        7. Creolization

    B. Recognition of Writing Patterns or Arrangement of Ideas and Devices

        1. Expository

        2. Use of examples

    C. Concepts/Background Knowledge and Experience

        1. Language history and terms to describe various languages, such as Pidgin English or creolization would be helpful. Simply knowing that English has changed since the beginning of the country and that various groups have influenced it would be helpful. Knowing something about slavery and the development of Black English would be helpful.

2. Ask yourself: (a) "What are language contact factors?" (b) "When people speak many different languages, how do they communicate?" (c) "What is Pidgin English? Who uses it?" (d) "What was English like around the time of the Revolutionary War?" (e) "How did English change in the nineteenth century? Why?" (f) "How was language different for house and field slaves?" (g) "How did African slaves often communicate with each other?" (h) "What is creolization?" (i) "Where did Black English come from?"

IV. Development of Regional Dialects

  A. Vocabulary

    1. Affected

    2. Regionalization

    3. Articulations

    4. Locale

    5. Tenuous

    6. Jargon

  B. Recognition of Writing Patterns or Arrangement of Ideas and Devices

    1. Chronological

  C. Concepts/Background Knowledge and Experience

    1. Knowing about the various ethnic groups that have immigrated to the country

    2. Knowing that the languages that these groups spoke influenced English

    3. Recognizing the names of (or better, having read) the literature to which the author refers

    4. Having heard the terms Chinese pidgin and Hawaiian pidgin

    5. Having a time line "in your head" of the nineteenth century as far as American history is concerned. This section begins with the early nineteenth century, moves to the 1860s, and then to the third quarter of the nineteenth century.

    6. Ask yourself: (a) "When did regional dialects develop?" (b) "What other languages influenced English?"

V. Standardization and Retention of Differences

  A. Vocabulary

    1. Superordinated

    2. Facetious

    3. Gradations

    4. Spatial

  B. Recognition of Writing Patterns or Arrangement of Ideas and Devices

    1. Expository

  C. Concepts/Background Knowledge and Experience

    1. Understanding what it means that language can be standardized and have differences at the same time

    2. The influence of radio and television on language

    3. British English is different from American English

    4. Understanding that Native American, African, European, and other groups have influenced American English

    5. Ask yourself: (a) "If you wanted a national network radio or television job, what language (dialect) would you need to speak?" (b) "What are superordinated people?" (c) "Which would probably be more likely to be misunderstood by a speaker of Standard American English, British or Gullah?"

    6. Briefly outline the history of American English.

VI. Chapter Summary

  A. Vocabulary

    1. Homogeneous

    2. Diversity

    3. Sanctioned

VII. Chapter Questions

  A. Vocabulary

    1. Distinctiveness

    2. Prominent

    3. Innovative

  B. Types of Questions

    1. The first three of the four questions are inferential. You have to gather information from more than one place to answer them. You also have to make judgments and draw conclusions.

    2. The fourth question is a text-based critical/creative one. You can gather information from the chapter and then add information to it from your own knowledge and observation about language.

ACADEMIC STUDY SKILLS

DIRECTIONS

You have a wide variety of study strategies at your disposal for this eleventh reading selection. Decide, based on the work you have done for the previous ten lessons and on your use of these strategies in your other classes, which one(s) would help you better understand the information in this chapter. Rank the strategies in the order of importance to you:

  A. SQ4R ("The Study of Your Own Language")

  B. Modified SQ4R ("Travel and Language in Its Cultural Context")

  C. Strategy for Placing Information in Long-Term Memory ("Some Problems with Columbus's 'Discovery' of America")

  D. Annotation or making notes in the margins of your textbook ("Two Views of the Study of Society and Culture")

  E. Underlining or Highlighting ("The Fiction of Chinua Achebe")

  F. Visual Mapping ("The Blues")

Use the strategy that you ranked highest for help in understanding and remembering information. If guided practice would be helpful, see exercises for the SQ4R study plan, memory, annotation, underlining/highlighting, and visuals in Appendix D, under Chapter 11. The following study skill will be used as your instructor wishes.

STUDY SKILL: NOTE TAKING DURING LECTURES

Another study strategy that you may find helpful with information like the kind presented in this chapter is taking notes during your professor's lecture. Below is a guide for lecture note taking:

A. Why should you take lecture notes? Lecture notes help you learn and remember course material. The process of writing should help you place the material in long-term memory. The notes should also be useful for review and study before an exam.

B. What causes problems with lecture note taking? If you have not had good experiences with note taking in the past, you may want to consider the course content, the concept load, the lecture organization, and the physical act of note taking as possible culprits or interference to your learning. All four can cause you to miss important information.

   1. If you are not familiar with the content of the course, you may need to read easier material on the course topics to build your knowledge base. If the content does not interest you, try to find ways to make it interesting; for example, talk to a classmate who seems excited about the material and try to understand what he/she gets out of the course.

   2. We have worked on concept load in previous lessons and pointed out how it can be difficult. Ask yourself what it is you are supposed to know before coming to class. What assumptions does the professor make about your knowledge of course material? You may need to read supplementary materials to build your background. Go to your professor for help and suggestions.

   3. How does the professor organize the lecture? Do you recognize the pattern? Is a cause/effect or a comparison/contrast pattern evident? Each lesson in our textbook has a writing pattern identified for the chapter. Review these patterns for help. If you are taking a composition course, your textbook probably identifies writing patterns and has writing exercises suggested for practice. Review that information.

   4. Problems can also occur during note taking. For example, if the professor is going too fast for you, you may find yourself writing meaningless notes. If such a problem occurs, try to write only the key concepts as you can identify them. Later use textbook information to fill out the needed information. You may also feel free to ask the professor to repeat information or to slow down.

If you feel that trying to write notes is interfering with your comprehension, you may want to quit taking notes and listen carefully for awhile. Advice from the experts is mixed on this issue with some suggesting continuing to write until information becomes clearer rather than stopping your note taking. You can try both ways and see what works for you.

C. What will help you focus on what to write? What considerations are there that will help you focus on what to write? You are probably going to be tested in some way on your textbook reading and on your professor's lectures. If you know ahead of time what kind of test you can expect, that information will help you to gear your note taking for that test. Taking a multiple choice, fill in the blanks, or short answer test can require you to know or recognize detailed information. If you are expecting an essay test, you will have to generate and organize the information in a meaningful way.

D. What is the best way to use your notes? If you enjoy studying with a group or an individual, compare your notes and talk through the information. Decide if you agree on what is the most important information and its support. Next, talk through the information to each other. If you can put information into your own words, you should understand it. If you find yourself repeating the professor or the textbook's words, you may need to delve further into the information. The group member with the most background and interest in the course may be very helpful at this point. You have had some practice in this process through the Reciprocal Teaching lessons in this textbook and through some of the steps of the study plans in the first two lessons. Review frequently.

E. What plan should you use? Several plans can be used successfully, and one that has been around for many years is the Cornell Method. Other reading and study skills experts have added to plans like the Cornell Method by suggesting various ways of marking different types of ideas and by suggesting lists of abbreviations. All of these are good advice. The one I decided to use is a simple one, one used in John E. Readence, Thomas W. Bean, and R. Scott Baldwin's *Content Area Reading: An Integrated Approach, third edition*. It is called the VSPP (Verbatim Split Page Procedure). Divide your note taking paper vertically with a 40/60 split. Forty percent of the paper is on the left-hand side and sixty percent is on the right. During the lecture, take notes on the left-hand side. The creators of this procedure suggest spending your energy listening, not writing. They also suggest taking notes verbatim during the lecture. Organize your notes during lecture pauses and immediately after the lecture on the right-hand side of your paper. Use an outline format, put the notes in your own words, expand them, and write out abbreviations before you forget what they stand for. I like this approach for several reasons. First, if there is a comprehension problem, emphasis on listening instead of writing should help by focusing and keeping it simple. Second, there is not a lot to remember about the note taking procedure while taking notes. If you are trying to remember too many details for note taking (the *how*) while taking notes on difficult material, your concentration may be on procedure instead of content (the *what*). Third, I like a simple plan that allows me a way to develop my individual procedure for note taking. Last, I like using pauses in lectures and time immediately after the lecture for expanding and clarifying information.

ACTIVE QUESTIONING

OVERVIEW

Your first step of the three-part reading plan was pre-reading. In pre-reading, you activated your prior knowledge, predicted what you would read, and overviewed the chapter before reading.

As the second step in this three-part reading plan, you will read this chapter by using the Active Questioning reading plan as explained below. An alternative plan, Reciprocal Teaching, is in Appendix B. In both plans you break up the chapter in sections and read and think about each as you read. The purpose of both plans is to keep you reading actively.

GENERAL DIRECTIONS

When using active questioning, write questions on the literal, inferential, and creative/critical levels. Although your last Active Questioning Reading Plan provided no teacher-made questions as models, this plan provides them just in case being independent on the last lesson was too difficult.

ASSIGNMENT

A. Read section one, "The Traditional View," and ask one text-explicit question (literal), one text-implicit question (inferential), and one experienced-based question (critical/creative) each on this section. Please answer all three questions. Do not ask a question that you cannot answer.

1. Text-explicit (literal level): A question that requires the reader to read the line. The answer will come from one line of print. Model text-explicit question: When is the history of English believed to have begun?

Your text-explicit question _____

Answer _____

2. Text-implicit (inferential level): A question that requires the reader to read between the lines. The answer will come from more than one line of print. You will need to make judgments and draw conclusions. Model text-implicit question: What languages are thought to influence English?

Your text-implicit question _____

Answer _____

3. Experience-based (critical/creative level): A question that requires the reader to read beyond the lines. Apply what you have learned to your world. Question what you have read. Model experience-based question: What sounds and vocabulary differences have you noticed that set American English apart from British English?

Your experience-based question _____

Answer _____

B. Read the second section, "Exploration and Early Settlement," and ask one text-explicit question, one text-implicit question, and one experience-based question each on this section. Please answer all three questions. Do not ask a question that you cannot answer.
1. Model text-explicit question: In what year did the Puritans land on or near Plymouth Rock?

Your text-explicit question _____

Answer _____

2. Model text-implicit question: Who were the various groups of people mentioned in this section of the chapter and what languages did they speak?

Your text-implicit question _____

Answer _____

3. Model experience-based question: If you decided to live in a country with a language very different from your own, what kinds of problems would you encounter before you learned the language?

Your experience-based question _____

Answer _____

C. Read the third section, "Language Contact Factors," and ask one text-explicit question, one text-implicit question, and one experience-based question each on this section. Please answer all three questions. Do not ask a question that you cannot answer.
1. Model text-explicit question: What are "pidgins"?

Your text-explicit question _____

Answer _____

2. Model text-implicit question: What major language contact factors influenced American English?

Your text-implicit question _____

Answer _____

3. Model experience-based question: Around the time of the Revolutionary War, American English was mostly uniform, but with the Westward Movement beyond the Cumberland Gap in the

nineteenth century, it became diverse. Why were the terms "mistakes" and "defects" used during the latter period?

Your experience-based question _____

Answer _____

D. Read the fourth section, "Development of Regional Dialects," and ask one text-explicit question, one text-implicit question, and one experience-based question each on this section. Please answer all three questions. Do not ask a question that you cannot answer.

1. Model text-explicit question: When did regional varieties begin developing?

Your text-explicit question _____

Answer _____

2. Model text-implicit question: Name groups that contributed to regional dialects.

Your text-implicit question _____

Answer _____

3. Model experience-based question: Can you tell the differences today in regional varieties? Do you believe American English is becoming more uniform or more diverse? Does mass communication (e.g., television, radio, Internet) make a difference?

Your experience-based question _____

Answer _____

E. Read the fifth section, "Standardization and Retention of Differences," and ask one text-explicit question, one text-implicit question, and one experience-based question each on this section. Please answer all three questions. Do not ask a question that you cannot answer.

1. Model text-explicit question: What are "superordinated persons"?

Your text-explicit question _____

Answer _____

2. Model text-implicit question: How do we know that American English does have a history?

Your text-implicit question _____

Answer _____

3. Model experience-based question: How aware are you of language differences of people on television and how do you judge people appearing on television who do not speak Network Standard American English?

Your experience-based question _____

Answer _____

POST-READING THE TEXTBOOK CHAPTER

OVERVIEW

In the second part of your three-part reading plan, you practiced reading your textbook chapter section by section and asked and answered questions.

In this third part of the three-part reading plan, you will find suggestions for what to do after you read. Your task is to compare what you predicted with what you actually read as an aid to comprehension, to add what you have learned to your file of information on the topic, and to think about it.

ASSIGNMENT

A. Compare what you predicted you would read with what you actually read. Did anything you predicted cause you a problem with comprehension? What? How?

B. What did you learn from the reading that you did not know about before working on this lesson?

C. Look at the words and phrases that you listed as your prior knowledge in the pre-reading section of this lesson. Group them below with relevant information in "B" above and make up your own headings. This is your new file of information on American English. (The ability to group ideas and to see relationships requires more complex comprehension than merely memorizing isolated facts.)

D. What have you learned from this chapter that is important?

E. What do you already know that you can relate to it?

F. What do you see differently as a result of reading this chapter?

Your Headings	Words and Phrases from Pre-Reading	Relevant Information from "B"

DOES AMERICAN ENGLISH HAVE A HISTORY?

The Traditional View

In the most simplistic sense, American English is an offshoot of the language of England. The history of the language itself is usually considered to begin in the middle of the fifth century A.D., although there are very few texts prior to the eighth century and not an abundance until the tenth. Between the *Beowulf* manuscript (copied around the year 1000 A.D.) and the Prologue to Chaucer's *Canterbury Tales* (around 1385) there are easily discernible differences in such simple matters as the words used and the endings attached to them to make grammatical differences like singular/plural and subject/object/possessive. Between that time and the time of Shakespeare (around 1600), further such changes are abundant and easily described. Early Modern English, which was in some sense the ancestor of American English, is still not quite what is spoken at the beginning of the twenty-first century, although matters like word endings haven't changed very much in nearly 400 years. Specialists debate how much the Celtic languages which were spoken on the islands when the Germanic peoples came over around the middle of the fifth century, the Norse which the Vikings brought around the ninth century, the French language which came with the Norman conquest in 1066, and the educated and ecclesiastical use of Latin may have contributed to the process of change. But changes are obvious.

The historian's task is in a sense more difficult for American English. There is hardly an example of a word ending peculiar to American speech. Although we have a greatly different vocabulary, specialists can persuade themselves to consider that factor superficial. The sound of American English isn't that of British, either, but they are closer together even in that respect than either is to any foreign language—German for example.

With such considerations dominant, it has been easy for language historians to overlook the fact that the same factors that made for change in England—large populations speaking other languages in intimate contact, conquest of one group by another and superimposed government, and extensive migration to name only a few—have existed in America to an even greater degree than in England.

Exploration and Early Settlement

Overlooking the possibility that the explorations of John Cabot and others under the aegis of the British crown brought some English to the northern parts of North America, the abortive colony of Sir Humphrey Gilbert before the end of the sixteenth century probably represents the first semi-permanent use of the language on our continent. But that group of adventurers failed to establish a permanent colony; so did the Roanoke expeditions of the 1580s, although local historians in the area still have fun debating whether the Lumbees, a mixed group of uncertain origin, somehow represent survivors of the colony which had disappeared when John White returned looking for it in 1590. John Smith finally led a successful attempt to found a permanent, English-speaking settlement in 1607.

The Puritans who landed on or near Plymouth Rock in 1621 get most of the attention from historians, and perhaps that focus is justified. Many attempts, none of them satisfactory, have been made to determine just what regional dialect of England the Pilgrims spoke. In fact, the Pilgrim fathers did not come to North America directly from England but from the Netherlands, where they had been strongly acculturated to Dutch ways and language practices. One of the reasons they decided to leave Holland was that they were afraid of losing their language. Once in the New World, they quickly came into contact with the Dutch from New York; it seems that Governor William Bradford, when he communicated with the other European group, had to make use of his knowledge of Dutch. Dutch remained very influential, especially in New York and New Jersey, throughout the nineteenth century.

The Puritans did not move into a linguistic void. There were Native Americans, regularly miscalled "Indians," in great numbers there; and those people were very advanced in many ways. The Puritans had to learn about the plants and animals of the region from the Indians, and the words were often English speakers' approximations of the Indian words. Only a few dozen of those words survive into modern American English, but that doesn't mean others were not used in the seventeenth and eighteenth centuries. A favorite term was *netop* 'friend'. Still more important may have been the pidgin English which the Indians who befriended the Pilgrims, Samoset and Squanto (or Tisquantum), seem to have picked up in the course of interaction with fishing vessels on the coast.

Until well after the Revolutionary War, the thirteen colonies and fledgling nation were stretched along the coast of North America, from Canada (in British hands) to Florida (controlled by the Spanish or the French). Maritime activity, like whaling, was of paramount importance to the colonies and early states, and seafaring terms were very widespread. Not only British, French, Spanish, and Dutch sailors were in contact with the American English speakers but even such today virtually unknown groups as the Basques, who conducted very important fishing and whaling operations from a time which might go back even to before Columbus, who ranged from Newfoundland to the coast of Florida, and who were famous for their ability to communicate with Indian tribes who remained mysterious to other Europeans.

Language Contact Factors

These sailors, including the Basques, used maritime contact languages because of the great number of different languages with which they were constantly in contact. We can call those languages "pidgins," although they weren't the crude languages we often think of when we use that term and not necessarily even entirely simple. After some of the Romance-based contact languages, depending upon the earlier experience of European sailors in the Mediterranean, Pidgin English developed into a dominant sailors' language for the areas and even came ashore for use in contact with Indians like Waban, the "justice peace" of a New England town of so-called praying Indians. When baseball developed from several other games in the early nineteenth century, the still-maritime areas adapted seagoing terms for that sport: on *deck* "the next batter," *in the hol (d)* "the next batter after that," *skipper* "manager."

Around the time of the Revolutionary War, the England-derived Americans developed a sense of solidarity which is reflected in their language. British visitors around 1775 report the "amazing uniformity" of the American variety of English. Tories, those who remained loyal to English rule, didn't go along with the process, but many of them were run away to Canada. The most distinctive Canadian vowel pattern, approximately *moose* and *aboot* for "mouse" and "about," is a likely result of that forced migration. British regional forms, already hard to pin down among the Pilgrims, became so diffused during the Revolutionary period that it became virtually meaningless to say that a certain word, word form, or pronunciation came from a specific area of England.

When speakers of this remarkably uniform language variety moved out beyond the Cumberland Gap in the nineteenth century, the situation changed drastically. New groups of Native Americans were met, and special language strategies were used. As writers like James Fenimore Cooper and many others make clear, Pidgin English became the *lingua franca* (language which can be used with anyone) of the frontier. Words like *squaw* and *papoose*, respectable approximations of Indian words for 'wife' and 'child' back in the Northeast, became ethnic slur words further west. Terms like *squaw man* "consort of Indian women" and *squaw side* "wrong side" were added to the western vocabulary. Within forty years, British visitors did not marvel at the "astonishing uniformity" of American speech but deprecated its frontier "mistakes" and with General Ethan Allen Hitchcock noted its "border defects." Except for a few easily impressed Easterners, who began trying to imitate the British by saying *cah* for "car" and *Bahston* for "Boston," Americans were splendidly unconcerned about what English visitors, even famous ones like Charles Dickens, thought.

Joining the many different tribal and language groups of Native Americans as early as 1619 had been another of equally heterogeneous linguistic nature, the Africans. Brought in as slaves, they were separated from their tribal groups; their African languages disappeared, as only a few of the American Indian languages did. House servant slaves often spoke exactly like their masters—and sometimes spoke a couple of languages which the masters didn't know—but the field hands had a tougher life linguistically as well as otherwise. Abundant documentary evidence shows that they used the maritime pidgin English as their lingua franca, primarily to communicate among themselves. This pidgin English went through a process called creolization—being adopted as a native language and acquiring many new words and expressions—to form what by the middle of the eighteenth century was called "Black English." An approximation of the creole stage (Geechee or Gullah) is still spoken in the Low Country (Sea Islands) of Georgia and South Carolina, as well as around Bracketville, Texas. Most of the Low Country people, and probably all of the black Texans, also speak a dialect closer to that recognized as characteristic of their region.

Development of Regional Dialects

It seems that regional varieties began developing in the United States in the second or third decade of the nineteenth century. Black speakers were prominent among those who moved west from the Old South, and in some documented cases the blacks taught English to white masters in Louisiana who had up to that point spoken only French. Scotch Irish and other Irishmen poured into the United States, especially after the potato famine of 1845–1848, and they had a great influence on the regions in which they settled. German immigrants into Pennsylvania and nearby states, called "Pennsylvania Dutch," remained separate from other parts of the population in customs as in dialect, and spoke a dialect fully as distinct as Black English. Dutch influence remained strong around New York and New Jersey, Scandinavians affected the speech of the upper midwest, and Cajun and Creole French were the dominant influences in Louisiana. The cotton trade from New Orleans along the coast all the way to New York spread what is stereotypically known as "Brooklynese" (in which, approximately, *bird* is "boid" and *shirt* is "shoit") sporadically along the way among selected occupational groups, but the dominant influence was in the direction of regionalization.

By the Civil War, division into "Yankee" and "Rebel" accents, easily discernible by the presence of drawl in the latter and of articulations like that of /s/ in *greasy* for the former, was quite plain. Freed Blacks, like Frederick Douglass, were often noted for losing "the slave accent"; but some of them, including Douglass, reported on the "imperfectly spoken" English of the plantations—in Maryland, in Douglass's case. Southerners, especially the aristocratic ones who had been assigned Black play children on the plantations, spoke a variety strongly influenced by Black English.

After the war, a very heterogeneous population spread into the West. Although some of the men preferred to be known only by their locale of origin, contact with the dialect and the customs of their birthplaces became slight and relationships tenuous. Spanish remained a strong influence on the jargon of the cattle industry, and a special maritime variety which had been transferred to the cattle trade in Florida even before the Texans learned *rodeo* and all those terms from the Mexicans had some influence. But Western soon became, and still remains, the hardest variety of modern American English to separate out into small regional groups.

Anyone who reads the American literature of the third quarter of the nineteenth century—perhaps a little earlier and a little later in some cases—can see the separation into regional varieties: New England, with some "re-Anglicization" because of high regard for England, Southern (with varieties of "deep" South speech), Black Southern (with some hints as late as James Thurber of Black Northern), Middle West and Upper Middle West, French-influenced deep Louisiana (especially George Washington Cable, Lafcadio Hearne), and Western. Chinese coming in for the railroads and the mining work brought their own version of the maritime pidgin English which already, greatly transformed, was a factor. Richard Henry Dana's *Two Years Before the Mast* represents Hawaiians already speaking their version of that pidgin English in the California coastal shipping trade by about 1820. Mark Twain, who actually tried his hand at mining, expresses the opinion in the "Buck Fanshaw's Funeral" episode from *Roughing It* that a virtually universal "slang" had been concentrated in the lingo of the miners; many others have written approximately the same for the cattlemen.

Standardization and Retention of Differences

When a standardizing influence did come to American English, it did not come as expected from New England. That dialect remained too much beyond the capabilities of anyone not born in the region. But the Chatauqua, the Lyceum, publishing, and the schoolmarm with her roots in Noah Webster soon spread an ideal of "good" English free of localism and identifying social features. When radio arrived on the scene, no one could get a job in that promising medium (except as a comedian or, later, a sportscaster) unless he spoke what soon became known as Network Standard. Television only intensified the influence which the radio had begun. Although politicians, television evangelists, and other superordinated (not subjected to the leveling pressures that affect most of us) persons carry their local characteristics into TV, that medium reflects to an amazing degree the leveling influences which have been the most striking characteristic of the history of American English in the twentieth century. Ambitious younger speakers often speak a dialect—Network Standard American—which sets them far apart from their parents.

Standard American English and R[eceived] P[ronunciation] British are mutually intelligible, even if perceptibly quite different. Dylan Thomas's facetious "up against the barrier of the same language" says something about American and British, but the difficulty of getting over that barrier should not be exaggerated. Americans tend to say *apartment* and *teevee* rather than *flat* and *telly*, but few from either country are confused when the other's word turns up in something like a motion picture. When it comes to some of the dialects, on the other hand—say, Gullah for American English and Yorkshire for British—intelligibility is hardly more than it is for Spanish and Italian or for Danish and Swedish. Between these extremes (perceptions of basic sameness and bewilderment in the face of difference) there are several gradations within which understanding is undoubtedly possible but much confusion is as likely.

After about 400 years of the speaking of English on the North American continent, we see changes from what we believe Early Modern English (the language of Shakespeare, roughly) was like. The language as spoken in England has undergone some of the same changes, but in many areas it has changed differently. We can probably conclude that the mere fact of spatial separation is responsible for only a tiny part of the difference which can be perceived. Without accounting for the many different language groups—Native American, African, European and other—who have contributed, we have only a hazy idea of how the change came about. In that respect, we would have to conclude that American English does after all have a history.

Summary

Because American English does not differ much in word forms from Early Modern English as it was spoken in England, some have assumed that the history of American English is negligible. Looking at the influence of language contact, however, one can discern a rich history. Early American colonists leveled their regional differences to produce a strikingly homogeneous speech, and a variety sometimes called "pidgin" was used by and with native Americans and West Africa–derived slaves, all of whom had languages of their own which were seldom learned by the Europeans. Contact with the Dutch, French, and Spanish colonies was linguistically influential from the beginning. Immigration in the nineteenth century brought influences from Irish English, German (including Yiddish), and other European languages. These influences were usually localized in specific areas. Along with these tendencies toward diversity, there has always been a semi-officially sanctioned tendency toward the development of a standard variety for public and formal use. This last variety is closer to the standard variety of British English spoken today than any social or regional dialect of American English.

Questions

1. Basically, why does American English differ from British English?
2. What are some of the groups that contributed to the distinctiveness of American English?
3. What factors are prominent in the development of regional varieties of American English?
4. In what ways has English been innovative in America?

VOCABULARY LESSON

The purpose of this exercise is to help you review and deepen your knowledge of the ten general vocabulary words you worked with at the beginning of this chapter.

A. Structural Analysis—Affixes and Root Words
 1. Underline the suffixes of the words below:
  a. Diffused _____
  b. Discernible _____
 2. Find the dictionary definition of the root word of each of the above words and write the definitions by the words above.
B. Use of Context: Read line four of the second paragraph in the fifth section, "Standardization and Retention of Differences," in which the word *facetious* appears. In your own words write a definition for it.

_____

C. Multiple Meanings of Words: Circle the definition below of the word *fledgling* that fits the way the word is used in this chapter on page 376:
 1. A young bird just able to fly
 2. Young, inexperienced
D. Synonyms and Antonyms: List one synonym (same meaning) and one antonym (opposite meaning) for each of the following words:

Word	Synonym	Antonym
Superficial		
Paramount		
Homogeneous		

E. Generate Your Own Language
 1. If reading is *paramount* to your success at school, should you spend more or less time doing it?
 2. During the Christmas season light is diffused throughout neighborhoods. What types of lights are *diffused* throughout your neighborhood?
 3. If your position at work is *tenuous*, should you relax or work harder?
 4. What *diversity* in style of dress do you notice on campus?
 5. Under whose *aegis* would you want to be if you were a sports star?

VOCABULARY EXTENSION

The purpose of this exercise is to help you see to what degree you know the ten general vocabulary words you worked with at the beginning of this chapter. Matching a word with its definition is the beginning of knowing a word. Using the word in your speaking and writing is full knowledge.

    A. List the vocabulary words from this lesson that you can now use in both your speaking and writing.

    B. List the vocabulary words from this lesson that you can now use in writing but are still not comfortable using in speaking.

    C. List the vocabulary words from this lesson that you cannot use yet but will recognize in reading.

    D. List general vocabulary words from this lesson that are still difficult to understand.

    E. Use *five* vocabulary words from this lesson in a five-sentence paragraph on the topic of this lesson.

    F. Illustrate the meaning of *one* of the vocabulary words from this lesson through some form of artwork or a cartoon. (This exercise is for right-brain students who enjoy drawing better than writing!)

EXTENDED READING ACTIVITIES

The purpose of this section is to give you a variety of options for independent study or investigation of the chapter topic. Reading is a skill that must be practiced each day if progress is to take place. These activities are designed to give you a variety of reading experiences through which you can improve your general vocabulary and increase your higher-level comprehension skills.

    Your instructor may wish to (a) assign one or more activities to the class as a whole, (b) assign various activities to small groups, (c) assign one or more activities to individual students, or (d) let students choose to do the activities or not.

PROGRESS CHECK

Many times students walk around campus acting like powerless victims of an alien system or world. Hopefully, by this time you can see how to help yourself improve your reading and academic study skills. You know by now that you must read every day to improve.

    A. Analyze your reading reports. Are you reading a variety of material that includes difficult reading for a longer period of time than when you began your course?
Yes___   No___   I'm Improving a Little___   I Will___

    B. Look over your vocabulary journals. Could you pass a test, at least an objective one in which you had to match a definition with a word, over the words you have listed?
Yes___   No___   Almost___   Over a Few___

    C. Are you reviewing the words on a regular basis? If you have to make a dentist or medical doctor visit, what do you do in the waiting room? Look around bored? Sigh and groan? Take your vocabulary words and review them. Test yourself.

I review the words during the following times and places:

_____

_____

D. List study strategies you have used in your other difficult classes. How have you adapted the strategies to fit your needs?

E. Have you finished your novel?   Yes___   No___   Almost___

    1. Would you want to read another one by the same author? Yes___   No___

    2. List what you have learned about human behavior and life itself from the novel.

       _____

       _____

    3. Will any of the characters live in your head for long? Why?

    4. What do you wish had been different?

F. If you consider yourself one of those people who *can* read but just do not like to read, has anything you have read in class or out of class changed your attitude? Sometimes when such students encounter new ideas or new writing styles, such a change occurs.

Activities

A. Weekly Reading Report: Continue keeping your weekly reading report. Use the form in Appendix C if you wish. Are you reading about more than sports and ax murders?

B. Attend a Reading Lab: Continue working in your campus reading lab. If you have worked on your comprehension in your reading lab, can you now identify types of questions on exams in your other classes? Do you recognize differences in text-explicit (literal), text-implicit (inferential), and experience-based (critical/creative) questions and know what you must do to answer them on these exams?

C. Read your Novel: Continue reading your novel or choose a new one. Paul Zindel's *Loch* is a frightening adventure story that you might enjoy. Karen Cushman's *Catherine Called Birdy* is a historical novel about an independent young lady in the Middle Ages who does not want her father to choose her husband and she outsmarts him. Two other novels are very popular with my students: Patricia MacLachlan's *Sarah, Plain and Tall* and Katherine Paterson's *Bridge to Terabithia*. Use the extra fiction report form in Appendix C if you wish.

D. Read with your child

    1. Jon Scieszka & Lane Smith, *The Stinky Cheese Man and Other Fairly Stupid Tales* and *The True Story of the 3 Little Pigs!* (By A. Wolf)

    2. Jon Scieszka & Steve Johnson, *The Frog Prince Continued*

    3. Eric Carle, *The Secret Birthday Message, The Very Hungry Caterpillar,* and *Do You Want to Be my Friend?*

    4. Mercer Mayer, *There's a Nightmare in my Closet*

     5.   Judith Viorst, *Alexander and the Terrible, Horrible, No Good, Very Bad Day*

     6.   Maurice Sendak, *Where the Wild Things Are*

     7.   Tomie dePaola, *Little Grunt and the Big Egg: A Prehistoric Fairy Tale*

E.   The Reading/Writing Connection: Continue keeping your college journal. Reread your journal entry on language for the Chapter 5 reading selection. What is the same? What is different? What is your ethnic background? Would some of your ancestors have belonged to some of the groups mentioned in this chapter? Has your family always lived in the same area of the country or have they moved frequently? How did either make a difference on your language? Write your insights in your journal. Use one new vocabulary word in your responses.

F.   Use the Internet: Look up *Old English*, *Middle English*, and *American English* or one of the groups mentioned in this chapter.

G.   Vocabulary Journal: Continue keeping your vocabulary journal. Use the form in Appendix C if you wish.

H.   Magazine/Journal/Newspaper Reading: From your campus or public library continue to read magazines, journals, and newspapers in your major. If you find the reading boring, you may want to consider a change of majors. Some reading can be difficult because it is meant for seniors or professionals already in the field. If you are interested in business and computers, read from the following list: *Sales and Marketing Management, Byte, Computer Graphics World, Internet World, Compute, Macworld, PC Computing, PC Magazine, Computer Science Education, Business Week, Forbes, Money, Journal of Business Strategy, Nation's Business, Business America, Business and Economics, Business and Economic Review, Business Daily, Business Horizons, Business Marketing, Journal of Business Ethics, Journal of Business Venturing, The Accounting Review, The CPA Journal, Legal Assistant Today, National Paralegal Reporter, Advertising Age, The American Enterprise*

REFLECTION

MIND REVOLUTION

The history of American English is complicated partly because of the influence of many other languages. Although English is presently the informal official language of the United States, many other languages are spoken throughout the country, especially in the large cities. When you visit other places, listen for different English and other languages.

VOCABULARY

Specialized vocabulary should not have been a serious problem in this chapter. Words like *lingua franca, creolization, regionalization,* and *superordinated* were probably the most difficult. The first two words have been used in previous chapters and should at least be vaguely familiar. The general vocabulary words, other than the vocabulary words used for this chapter, are also rather mainstream and used in general magazine and newspaper articles. *Superimposed, void, approximations, solidarity, deprecated, heterogeneous, maritime, affected, locale, jargon, gradations, sanctioned, distinctiveness, innovative, prominent*, and *spatial* seem to be rather common. Other general vocabulary words that might be less familiar are *ecclesiastical, abortive* (as used in this chapter), *acculturated*, and *articulations*. Reflect on your level of knowing each category of words. Do you recognize them? Recognize them in your reading? Use them in your writing? Use them in your speech? Watch for the words in your general reading as well as in your academic reading. Listen for them on radio and television and in others' speech.

COMPREHENSION

Comprehension difficulty comes from (1) lack of background knowledge, (2) density of concepts, and (3) the author's assumptions about your background knowledge. Part of the background knowledge you need in reading this chapter with understanding is a sense of time and a concept of historical time beginning in fifth century A.D. For example, in the first paragraph, you are given an historical overview whose purpose is to show you that English language changes are obvious. If you can keep this purpose in mind, then you have a better chance of having the support (examples) fall in place. If you read this paragraph thinking the significance is in the details, then you probably lost the purpose.

Lack of background knowledge as to American history in the second section of this chapter may make the reading more difficult for you. The concept of encounters with other languages probably was not as difficult as in the first section because of your American history framework. The concept, not elaborated upon, of the importance of maritime activity may be difficult for you. Thinking of the colonies being along the coastline may be new, not that you did not know, but that you never thought about its importance to language change.

The third section probably went up the scale in difficulty if you began reading it thinking *pidgins* are birds! The author assumes the reader has some background knowledge of pidgin languages and does not stop to discuss them. He goes briskly on to detailed information about them ("Romance-based") and their use. The examples he uses may also cause difficulty. *Waban* may not be a part of your American history background and you may not be a baseball fan or knowledgeable about the sport's vocabulary.

Another cause of difficulty is that the author offers no elaboration or explanation in his historical overview. If you begin this chapter not knowing that English has changed to the point of your not being able to read Old or Middle English without the help of a German or French background, then that can cause you difficulty. The author assumes a certain background on your part that may not be there. The rest of the first section gives you a breather. The material does not hit you with one piece of historical information after another. You end with similarities in factors that cause language change in American and British English.

The next concept for which you may not have knowledge is that of uniformity of language. You would probably need to have read about the history of the English language before attempting the reading of this chapter. Hopefully, from the second sentence you get some idea of the significance of uniformity of language. The example of the Tories may or may not shed additional light at this point, again depending on your American history framework.

Another concept is that of tracing language use to a specific area of England. You may well be surprised that someone would want to do it. If you have seen the television series on PBS, *The Story of English*, you may have noticed that no linguist would appear and pretend to trace American English back to areas of England. Luckily, this is supportive information, not a main idea, and is important in support of the idea that American English was uniform around the time of the Revolutionary War.

We move in time, to the nineteenth century, and use what we have previously learned in this chapter. *Pidgin English* should at least be familiar as we move west. Again, part of your understanding is based on your America history framework. We find that English is no longer uniform in this period. Language on the frontier changed through its various encounters. Any knowledge of the American West would probably increase your understanding of this section and historical period.

In the last part of this section, you can use your background knowledge on African American history from "The Blues," so this section should sound somewhat familiar. A new concept for which you may have no background knowledge is the process of *creolization*. An explanation is given but it may not be enough to make you comfortable. In a scale of one to ten, with one being high, your degree of knowing may be a seven at this point. The importance of this information is to show American English has changed and this is support for that main idea.

In the fourth section you are given a listing of different regional dialects with reinforcement in the last paragraph from American literature of the nineteenth century. This is probably the easiest section to read unless you get tangled up in names and writers of various literary works. Concepts should be familiar. For example, did you grow up identifying people by their speech? Have you ever asked people where they are from? Did you correctly guess California, Northeast, or South?

The fifth section is probably not difficult to understand since the concept of radio and television influence on the standardization of American English is familiar. Do you, for example, notice a national television newscaster's speech if it differs from the rest of the newscasters? Background from the first section of the chapter helps with the understanding of this section. You come back full circle with a comparison/contrast of factors that helped British and American English change. The chapter began with the question of whether or not American English has a history and completes the chapter with a positive answer. The material presented supports this position.

Religious Studies: Sociolinguistics and the Crucifixion Narrative

Overview

Progress Check
Activities
Reflection
Mind Revolution
Vocabulary
Comprehension

VOCABULARY/METACOGNITION

The purpose of this exercise is to help you become aware of when you know the meaning of a word and to help you know when you do not know the meaning of a word. This is metacognition awareness.

On a scale of 1–5 (see below), rate your knowledge of the following vocabulary words from "Sociolinguistics and the Crucifixion Narrative." After matching words with definitions on page 388, check your answers and then check your number *ones* and *fives* below. Did you know when you really knew a word and when you really did not know the word?

Scale

1. I absolutely do not know.
2. I do not think I know.
3. There's a 50/50 chance I have seen or heard it.
4. I think I know it.
5. I know the word and can use it.

Words

_____ 1. Skepticism
_____ 2. Virtually
_____ 3. Verify (verification)
_____ 4. Tentative (tentatively)
_____ 5. Explicit
_____ 6. Deign (deigned)
_____ 7. Correspond (correspondence)
_____ 8. Status
_____ 9. Consummate
_____10. Precise (precisely)

Go to page 388. See if you can match the right definition with the word and then write sentences for any five words in the list.

Words	Definitions
_____ 1. Skepticism	A. Bring to completion or perfection
_____ 2. Virtually	B. Condescend; stoop (to an act)
_____ 3. Verify (verification)	C. Inclination to doubt; questioning nature
_____ 4. Tentative (tentatively)	D. (1) Relative standing; (2) position, condition
_____ 5. Explicit	E. (1) Existing in power or effect, but not actually; (2) equivalent to though somewhat different or deficient
_____ 6. Deign (deigned)	F. (1) Exactly defined; definite; accurate; (2) punctilious; formal; (3) exact; identical
_____ 7. Correspond (correspondence)	
_____ 8. Status	G. (Of words, ideas) fully or clearly expressed, not merely implied; definite
_____ 9. Consummate	H. Ascertain or prove to be true
_____10. Precise (precisely)	I. Based on or done as a trial; experimental
	J. (1) Be similar or analogous; (2) conform; match; fit; (3) communicate by letter

Write five words from the list and your own sentences that show you know how to use the words. Choose words that you marked a *five* if possible.

1. Word _____

  Sentence _____

2. Word _____

  Sentence _____

3. Word _____

  Sentence _____

4. Word _____

  Sentence _____

5. Word _____

  Sentence _____

PRE-READING THE TEXTBOOK CHAPTER

OVERVIEW

The purpose of this *first* of three steps in your reading plan is to suggest things to do *before* you read. First, as part of your pre-reading, read the Prior Knowledge section beginning on page 389. When you finish, return to this section and continue your pre-reading. The Academic Study Skills section will be used as your instructor wishes. You may want to skim it as a part of your pre-reading.

ACTIVITIES

A. Tap experience and prior knowledge about the title of this selection.
B. Predict what you will read.
C. Overview by reading the summary and the questions at the end of the chapter. Write the main headings of the chapter below.

Sociolinguistics and the Crucifixion Narrative

I. _____

II. _____

III. _____

PRIOR KNOWLEDGE

This section, part of your pre-reading, presents a model to show you what will help you comprehend this chapter by using your own background knowledge. If you know much of the following information, you have a better background for reading this chapter. This section will suggest helpful kinds of background information and help you activate what you know; do not try to look up or learn everything listed. Ask yourself what you need to know before you read and what you already know that will help you to understand this chapter. Your instructor may want to use this section for a whole-class or small group discussion or have you read it silently.

PREVIEW

A. Have you heard of the following languages: Papiamentu, Koiné Greek, Classical Greek, Hebrew, Dutch, English, Pidgin English, Aramaic (a Semitic contact language used from 7 B.C.–7 A.D.), Ewondo, French, Creole?
B. Do you know where the following places are: Curaçao, Aruba, Bonaire, Venequela, ABC Islands, Holland, Jerusalem, Israel, Yaoundé, Cameroun?
C. Are the following technical vocabulary words and phrases meaningful to you: sociolinguistics, narrative, microlinguistic structure, typology of function?
D. Are the following Biblical verses familiar? Acts 21:37; 21:40; 26:14; Matthew 16:18; 27:11–14; Mark 15:2–5; Luke 23:1–3; John 18: 33–38; 19:20. These verses are offered as evidence for the position taken on languages in this chapter.

Chapter Sections

I. Language in the New Testament Period
   A. Vocabulary
      1. Paragraph One
         a. Skepticism
         b. Consummate
         c. Verification
         d. Tentatively (tentative)
      2. Paragraph Two
         a. Explicit
         b. Alternation
         c. Polyglot (adjective)
         d. Deigned (deign)
   B. Recognition of Writing Patterns or Arrangement of Ideas and Devices
      1. Paragraph One
         a. States the problem (skepticism)
         b. Part of the solution to the problem and thesis statement are the last sentence
      2. Paragraph Two
         a. Thesis statement is the first sentence
         b. Support by five specific examples—the rest of the paragraph
   C. Concepts/Background Knowledge and Experience
      1. The Old Testament was written in Hebrew with some in Aramaic roughly from 1400–400 B.C.
      2. The New Testament was written in Koiné Greek except for a few (five to six) words in Hebrew or Aramaic, usually quotes.
      3. In 1611 the King James version of the Bible was written by a group of scholars who wanted a definitive version of the Bible in English.
      4. Be familiar with Biblical scholarship. For example, the Slavonic translation of Josephus's *The Jewish War* refers to Jesus; the earlier Latin version has no mention of Jesus. Josephus lived in the first century A.D. He also wrote *Antiquities of the Jews*.

II. Types of Language Function
   A. Vocabulary
      1. Paragraph Three
         a. Typology
         b. Vernacular
   B. Recognition of Writing Patterns or Arrangement of Ideas and Devices
      1. The purpose of this section of the chapter is to support the main idea by examples of types and functions of various languages in other multilinguistic societies.

        a.   Background information

        b.   Specific examples

  C. Concepts/Background Knowledge and Experience

    1. See above.

III. The Inscription on the Cross and the Languages of Israel

  A. Vocabulary

    1. Paragraph Five

        a.   Koiné

        b.   Status

    2. Paragraph Six

        a.   Notoriously (notorious)

        b.   Virtually

        c.   Precisely (precise)

  B. Recognition of Writing Patterns or Arrangement of Ideas and Devices

    1. Paragraph One

        a.   Thesis statement (main idea) is sentence one. The rest of the paragraph supports the statement through the use of specific details.

    2. Paragraph Two

        a.   The paragraph poses a question/problem and elaborates on it

    3. Paragraph Three

        a.   This paragraph provides the answer to paragraph two's question/problem. Sentences one and two state the answer whereas sentence three to the end of the paragraph gives examples from contemporary times and from two different cultures.

  C. Concepts/Background Knowledge and Experience

    1. See above.

Academic Study Skills

Overview

In the previous lessons you have improved the management of internal factors such as memory, developed effective note taking methods for lectures, developed various levels of textbook strategies such as (a) the complex rehearsal strategies of underlining and highlighting, (b) the complex elaboration strategy of notetaking from textbooks through annotation, (c) the complex organizational strategies of outlining and mapping and organizing information, and (d) comprehension monitoring strategies, or metacognitive strategies, through SQ4R. For guided practice for many of these study skills, see Appendix D. The following study skill will be used as your instructor wishes.

STUDY SKILL: COLLABORATIVE LEARNING

In this lesson you will continue to develop your collaborative learning skills through the use of group work and work with a partner. You will continue to work constructively and efficiently in small groups in class and demonstrate your ability to form a study group. Below are the guidelines for forming your groups. Your instructor may wish to alter them.

A. Form groups of four to five members by random numbering off by group number. For example, if you plan on having five groups, go around the room numbering off one through five.

B. When forming these groups, arrange your chairs so that members of the groups can comfortably see each other and work together.

C. Take time to briefly introduce yourselves to each other. Questions to ask as an ice breaker might be (a) What high school did you attend? (b) Are you here right out of high school? (c) What are you planning to major in? (d) What other courses are you taking? (e) How do you feel about being in college?

D. After you are comfortable with each other, choose a *scribe* to do the group's writing and a *speaker* for the group's spokesperson for whole-class discussions. You can rotate both jobs among group members as you wish.

E. During discussions be sure everyone is included. Contribute your share of information to the group.

F. Respect and explore all opinions. Everyone has the right to voice his/her opinion.

G. Stay on task. Do not distract the group by too much wandering off the topic. Consider the good of the group over your own.

H. If you continue with the same group, meet as a study group outside of class when assignments require it.

ACTIVE QUESTIONING

OVERVIEW

Your first step of the three-part reading plan was pre-reading. In pre-reading, you activated your prior knowledge, predicted what you would read, and overviewed the chapter before reading.

As the second step in this three-part reading plan, you will read this chapter by using the Active Questioning reading plan as explained below. An alternative plan, Reciprocal Teaching, is in Appendix B. In both plans you break up the chapter in sections and read and think about each as you read. The purpose of both plans is to keep you reading actively.

General Directions

When using active questioning, write questions on the literal, inferential, and creative/critical levels. Models are provided for guidance.

Assignment

A. Read section one, "Languages in the New Testament Period," and ask one text-explicit question (literal), one text-implicit question (inferential), and one experienced-based question (critical/creative) each on this section. Please answer all three questions. Do not ask a question that you cannot answer.

1. Text-explicit (literal level): A question that requires the reader to read the line. The answer will come from one line of print. Model text-explicit question: What might be relevant to historical verification?

Your text-explicit question _____

Answer _____

2. Text-implicit (inferential level): A question that requires the reader to read between the lines. The answer will come from more than one line of print. You will need to make judgments and draw conclusions. Model text-implicit question: What languages were possibly spoken by those mentioned in the New Testament?

Your text-implicit question _____

Answer _____

3. Experience-based (critical/creative level): A question that requires the reader to read beyond the lines. Apply what you have learned to your world. Question what you have read. Model experience-based question: The author refers to the disciples as a "… roving band in a polyglot nation." What contemporary polyglot countries have you visited or which ones do you know about? Is the United States a polyglot nation? Support your answer.

Your experience-based question _____

Answer _____

B. Read the second section, "Types of Language Function," and ask one text-explicit question, one text-implicit question, and one experience-based question each on this section. Please answer all three questions. Do not ask a question that you cannot answer.

1. Model text-explicit question: What is the vernacular language on the island of Curaçao?

Your text-explicit question _____

Answer _____

2. Model text-implicit question: List the four types of language that most linguistic situations will utilize.

Your text-implicit question _____

Answer _____

3. Model experience-based question: What do you think about the English Only Movement in the United States? If you are Hispanic, would you feel differently about the movement than an Anglo would feel? If you lived in a multilingual city, would you feel differently from a person who lived in a monolingual town? What languages do citizens of the United States speak besides English?

Your experience-based question   _____

Answer   _____

C. Read the third section, "The Inscription on the Cross and the Languages of Israel," and ask one text-explicit question, one text-implicit question, and one experience-based question each on this section. Please answer all three questions. Do not ask a question that you cannot answer.

1. Model text-explicit question: What was the official language of the Roman occupiers of Jerusalem and its area?

Your text-explicit question _____

Answer _____

2. Model text-implicit question: What three languages were used in the writing of Jesus's cross? What language was left out? Why is knowing about these languages important to our historical understanding of the events in the four gospels?

Your text-implicit question _____

Answer _____

3. Model experience-based question: What differences in spoken English do you hear on your campus? What kinds of expressions and grammatical structures that you hear would not be written on an English paper? Have you ever seen one of the tourist-type books on hillbilly or southern English? How did you feel about it?

Your experience-based question   _____

Answer _____

POST-READING THE TEXTBOOK CHAPTER

OVERVIEW

In the second part of your three-part reading plan, you practiced reading your textbook chapter section by section and asked and answered questions.

In this third part of the three-part reading plan, you will find suggestions for what to do after you read. Your task is to compare what you predicted with what you actually read as an aid to comprehension, to add what you have learned to your file of information on the topic, and to think about it.

ASSIGNMENT

A. Compare what you predicted you would read with what you actually read. Did anything you predicted cause you a problem with comprehension? What? How?

B. What did you learn from the reading that you did not know about before working on this lesson?

C. Look at the words and phrases that you listed as your prior knowledge in the pre-reading section of this lesson. Group them below with relevant information in "B" above and make up your own headings. This is your new file of information on religious studies. (The ability to group ideas and to see relationships requires more complex comprehension than merely memorizing isolated facts.)

D. What have you learned from this chapter that is important?

E. What do you already know that you can relate to it?

F. What do you see differently as a result of reading this chapter?

Your Headings	Words and Phrases from Pre-Reading	Relevant Information from "B"

SOCIOLINGUISTICS AND THE CRUCIFIXION NARRATIVE

Languages in the New Testament Period

Skepticism about the Christian message has often taken the form of doubt as to the historicity of the books of the Bible, especially the four Gospels according to Matthew, Mark, Luke, and John. Virtually no one has denied that these books, if capable of being taken literally, report a matter of consummate importance. They are, as is well known, essentially consistent with each other, with just those differences in detail which might be expected to occur in records kept by different persons. Independent verification seems, however, to be restricted to the writings of the contemporary historian Josephus, in the Slavonic version of *The Jewish War* and in *Antiquities of the Jews*. For materials often dealing with the miraculous, objective tests according to known historical conditions are difficult to perform, although the Gospels certainly fit into the known historical situation. It is tentatively suggested here that some information about the languages and language use of first century A.D. Israel might be relevant to historical verification.

Like most other documents of its time, the New Testament says little about the language being used; in fact, the biblical accounts are just slightly more explicit than one accustomed to classical texts would expect. In Acts 21:37 Paul is identified by a Roman officer as knowing Greek, then proceeds to speak to the people of Jerusalem in the Hebrew language (21:40). In Acts 26:14, Paul identifies the appearance of Jesus on the road to Damascus in terms of the use of Hebrew. For Jesus's own usage, the assumption that he "spoke Aramaic" is often made. There are, however, indications in his reading in the synagogue(s) that he knew "letters" (i.e., Hebrew writing), and there is the much-debated alternation between

petros   "(small) rock"

and

petra   "broad expanse of rock"

in Matthew 16:18 which is more fully meaningful in terms of the disciples' (a roving band, after all, in a polyglot nation) conversing in Greek with their Master. It has been pointed out that no interpreter is mentioned in Jesus's confrontations with Pontius Pilate (Matthew 27:11–14, Mark 15:2–5, Luke 23:1–3, John 18:33–38), who would probably have insisted upon Latin or at the very most have deigned to communicate in (koiné) Greek.

Types of Language Function

Scholars in the United States are handicapped in their interpretation of such materials by their thorough familiarity with an exceptionally monolingual environment. In many other places—generally places lacking the military and economic dominance of the United States—even ordinary people characteristically use more than one language in their daily routines. As the discipline of sociolinguistics has long since pointed out, those languages—although virtually unrestricted in terms of microlinguistic structure—tend to take on a typology of function. Virtually any linguistic situation will utilize a vernacular language.

In some cases, as indicated in the popular usage of the term *vernacular*, a dialect may serve this function as against other functions for other dialects. The vernacular, dialect or language, is seldom identical with the official language.

Where trade relationships with outside groups are important and the vernacular or official language does not enjoy the worldwide prestige of English, there is often a trade language. (The trade language may be related to the official language, as in the case of Pidgin English and more standard English, or it may be totally unrelated.) Especially where education and literary culture have been sponsored from the outside, there may well be a classical language. Again, the classical language may be historically related to the official or the vernacular language(s); or there may be no clear relationship.

The island of Curaçao is a fairly typical case. The vernacular language is Papiamentu, a Spanish- (some say Portuguese-) based creole language used on that island, in Aruba, and in Bonaire but virtually nowhere else. In more recent years, Papiamentu has assumed more and more official functions, but in the past Dutch (the language of the colonial power in the area) had a great deal of that function. Spanish (especially from Venezuela), English (internationally), and Dutch are also much used in trade. Since these have historically been prestigious languages in the ABC islands as well as in a worldwide context, they might all be said to compete for the role of trade language. Citizens of Aruba and Curaçao often pursue their higher education in Holland or in the United States, so that Dutch and English compete for the status of

language of education—similar to, but not quite identical to, a classical language. That there is not a perfect fit of language and functional category is perhaps more usual on a worldwide scale than those places where the correspondence (language and function) is exact.

The Inscription on the Cross and the Languages of Israel

According to John 19:20, the inscription of Jesus's cross—along with other evidence—reveals an amazing correspondence of language to functional category. The official language of the Roman occupiers of Jerusalem and its area was of course Latin; any inscription would be expected to have that language. The trade language was koiné Greek; it is also said to have been present on the inscription. The classical (in this case, as not seldom) and also religious language was Hebrew, which is also represented. Only Aramaic, the vernacular in Israel at the time although an official language in other areas, was not used. But there is often a tendency to omit the vernacular from writing—to treat it as though it were not appropriate for such use. If (classical) Greek had not had a status as a classical language—a use of which educated Romans of the time were highly conscious—it is not likely that (koiné) Greek would have been included.

The case of the not-included language, Aramaic, is in some ways the most interesting here; certainly, it is the most problematic, arguments from silence being notoriously difficult to deal with. Virtually all commentators who have said anything about the matter agree that Aramaic was the most-used language in that time and that place. Why, then, would precisely that language be the one to be left off the inscription?

The answer is quite possibly that vernacular languages, no matter how widely used, are not typically the varieties used in writing. Where the vernacular is a dialect of the official language, the tendency to avoid putting the vernacular in writing is perhaps even stronger. Even in the strikingly monolingual United States, writing instruction from the very beginning tends to be in standard English, which may be somewhat different from the dialect (vernacular) which the students use outside the classroom—or inside, when not writing. In Yaoundé, Cameroun, in 1963–1964, the only written use of Ewondo, the local vernacular, was in signs warning passersby to beware of the dog or not to smoke. Almost all the other signs were in French, the official language. The only newspaper available, like most printed material also, was French. In fact, in many places there has long been a tendency to avoid the vernacular language in writing. Militant action in the last few decades has changed the situation somewhat, but there are still strong evidences of this tendency in many places.

Summary

The distribution of languages may provide some evidence for the historicity of the four Gospels and thereby of the validity of the Christian religion. The Gospels specify that Pontius Pilate had written over the cross "Jesus of Nazareth, King of the Jews." John specifies that the message was written in Latin, Greek, and Hebrew. Latin may be called the official language, Greek the trade language, and Hebrew more or less the classical language of Israel during this period. Aramaic, the vernacular language, was not included in the written material because vernacular languages are often not used in writing. Comparison with the distribution of Dutch, Spanish, English, and Papiamentu on the island of Curaçao reveals a similar if not identical distribution. Other multilingual societies have a similar distribution of language function, and the statement in John rings true in a general pattern of such distributions.

Questions

1. What are possible objections to the use of the four Gospels as evidence for the life, including the crucifixion, of Jesus?
2. Why is parallel evidence like the writings of the contemporary historian Josephus important?
3. How conclusive is the evidence from parallel sources?
4. How can patterns of language distribution provide evidence for drawing a conclusion?

VOCABULARY LESSON

The purpose of this exercise is to help you review and deepen your knowledge of the ten general vocabulary words you worked with at the beginning of this chapter.

A. Structural Analysis—Affixes and Root words
   1. Underline the suffix of the following word: *Virtually* _____
   2. Find the dictionary definition of the root word of the word above and write it by the word.

B. Use of Context: Read the first paragraph of this chapter in which the words *skepticism* and *consummate* appear, and in your own words write a definition for each below:
   1. Skepticism _____
   2. Consummate _____

C. Multiple Meanings of Words: Circle the definition below that fits the way the word *correspondence* is used in this chapter on page 397.
   1. Be similar or analogous
   2. Conform; match; fit
   3. Communicate by letter

D. Synonyms and Antonyms: List one synonym (same meaning) and one antonym (opposite meaning) for each of the following words:

Word	Synonym	Antonym
Precisely		
Tentatively		

E. Generate Your Own Language
   1. If your best friend expressed *skepticism* about your winning the lottery, what would your reaction be?
   2. If you have *tentatively* planned on spending the break in Florida, what preparations have you probably made?
   3. Describe your social *status*.
   4. How could you *verify* your age?
   5. In the reading lessons in this textbook, have you found it easier to write and answer *explicit* or implicit questions? Why?
   6. When has an older family member *deigned* to let you drive his or her new automobile?

VOCABULARY EXTENSION

The purpose of this exercise is to help you see to what degree you know the ten general vocabulary words you worked with at the beginning of this chapter. Matching a word with its definition is the beginning of knowing a word. Using the word in your speaking and writing is full knowledge.

A. List the vocabulary words from this lesson that you can now use in both your speaking and writing.

B. List the vocabulary words from this lesson that you can now use in writing but are still not comfortable using in speaking.

C. List the vocabulary words from this lesson that you cannot use yet but will recognize in reading.

D. List general vocabulary words from this lesson that are still difficult to understand.

E. Use *five* vocabulary words from this lesson in a five-sentence paragraph on the topic of this lesson.

F. Illustrate the meaning of *one* of the vocabulary words from this lesson through some form of artwork or a cartoon. (This exercise is for right-brain students who enjoy drawing better than writing!)

Extended Reading Activities

The purpose of this section is to give you a variety of options for independent study or investigation of the chapter topic. Reading is a skill that must be practiced each day if progress is to take place. These activities are designed to give you a variety of reading experiences through which you can improve your general vocabulary and increase your higher-level comprehension skills.

Your instructor may wish to (a) assign one or more activities to the class as a whole, (b) assign various activities to small groups, (c) assign one or more activities to individual students, or (d) let students choose to do the activities or not.

Progress Check

A. List what you are doing outside of class that you know is helping you improve your comprehension and vocabulary. How do you know?

B. List what you will continue to do after you complete this course.

C. List what has made you aware that you need to improve your comprehension and vocabulary.

D. List what activities you have recommended to classmates as being helpful. Could you tutor someone in reading? Could you lead an SI (Supplemental Instruction) session?
    Yes___   No___   I'll Think About It___

Activities

A. Weekly Reading Report: Continue keeping a weekly report of your reading. Use the form in Appendix C if you wish. What have you read this week that you knew nothing about at the beginning of the quarter?

B. Attend a Reading Lab: Have you picked up new vocabulary words? Does reading them in context help you to understand them?

C. Read your Novel: If you have completed your novel, have you found another one to read? Have you recommended the one you finished to a classmate or a friend? Has a classmate recommended reading (or not reading) a novel to you? Do you think you will read more fiction during your leisure time? If you are very busy at this time of the year, a very short but powerful novel that may interest you is Marion Dane Bauer's *On My Honor*. If you enjoy fantasy and have ever wished for a fairy godmother, then you may enjoy Gail Carson Levine's *Ella Enchanted*. Use the novel report form in Appendix C if you wish.

D. Read to your child
    1. Peter Spier, *Noah's Ark*
    2. Tomie dePaola, *Francis the Poor Man of Assisi*
    3. Tomie dePaola, *The Clown of God*
    4. Simms Taback, *Joseph Had a Little Overcoat*
    5. Beni Montresor, *May I Bring a Friend?*
    6. Sorche Nic Leodhas, *Always Room for One More*
    7. Tomie dePaola, *Pancakes for Breakfast* (wordless)
    8. Jan Ormerod, *Sunshine* (wordless)
    9. David Wiesner, *Tuesday* (almost wordless)
    10. Bill Martin, Jr. & John Archambault, *Chicka Chicka Boom Boom*
    11. Bill Martin, Jr. & Eric Carle, *Brown Bear, Brown Bear, What Do You See?*

E. Reading/Writing Connection: Continue your college journal. Has campus life influenced your spiritual or religious life? How? How do you feel about having historical background and proof for your spiritual or religious views? How are your spiritual or religious views different from or similar to those of your family? Write your insights in your journal. Use one new vocabulary word in your responses.

F. Use the Internet: Look up the *New Testament* or the four gospels (*Matthew, Mark, Luke, John*), or any major religions or philosophies in which you are interested.

G. Vocabulary Journal: Continue keeping a vocabulary journal. Use the form in Appendix C if you wish. How many of the words you have used in your vocabulary journals have you seen in print? Have they been in mainstream magazines? textbooks? Have you heard them used on television or in films?

H. Magazine/Journal/Newspaper Reading: Read in your campus or local library from the following list of magazines and journals in math and science. Use the form in Appendix C if you wish.
    1. Mathematics: *Mathematics Magazine, The Mathematical Intelligences, Mathematics and Computer Education, Journal of Recreational Mathematics, American Journal of Math, The College Math Journal, Interdisciplinary Science Reviews for Research in Mathematics Education*
    2. Natural Sciences: *Astronomy, American Journal of Physics, The American Naturalist, American Scientist, Scientific American, Analytical Chemistry, The Biological Bulletin, BioScience, Bulletin of Science, Technology, and Society, Journal of Geoscience Education, Science News, Nature, Natural*

History, New Scientist, North American Birds, The Bulletin of the Atomic Scientists, Chemical and Engineering News, Chemical Engineering, Ecology, Environmental Politics, Environmental Science and Engineering, Geology, Geotimes, The Journal of Cell Biology, National Geographic Journal, Discover (the World of Science), Science, Pollution Prevention Review

REFLECTION

MIND REVOLUTION

Perhaps the most important idea from this chapter is to question authority. We find that the historical authenticity of the four gospels is questioned and then we find one way to help verify their authenticity. How can this apply to our lives? First, we have the right to question the validity of significant information that affects our lives. In the age of fast communication and reporting of anything that looks halfway significant, we must identify the sources of information and then seek verification of facts. Second, we have the right to know. We should not be made to feel dumb or insignificant when we ask questions. We do live in a free society.

VOCABULARY

Surprisingly, this chapter does not overwhelm the reader with technical vocabulary. Koiné is probably the most difficult. Fortunately, the sentence in which it is used helps us with the meaning (… to communicate in (koiné) Greek). Interestingly, place names could be troublesome (Curaçao, Aruba, Bonaire, ABC islands, and Yaoundé, Cameroun) as well as names of people (Matthew, Mark, Luke, John, Paul, and Pontius Pilate). One could wonder what some of the last names were and why they are omitted. How were naming practices different?

COMPREHENSION

Probably the areas of concern as to comprehending this chapter would be background knowledge and experience and interest in the subject. On the surface the chapter deals with religion and one could get lost in the many scripture quotes. If you have no background knowledge or experience or interest in the New Testament, you may have had difficulty understanding what you read. If you find religious discussion offensive, you could also let your emotions interfere with your comprehension. If you are an atheist, agnostic, or member of one of the other great religions of the world, you may have resented reading about the New Testament.

If you are a member of one of the Christian churches that does not discuss historical context of the Bible, you could have found this chapter puzzling. Historical authenticity of the New Testament possibly has not come up as a topic of discussion in your church. You may ask why anyone would even think in such terms. Again, seeing the significance of such a discussion could have caused difficulty in reading the chapter. If you have a vast knowledge of New Testament scripture, you may have been comfortable with the quotes but then found yourself lost in the discussion. The reason, if this happened, could be a mismatch of expectations and material. You may have expected a religious discussion of the crucifixion instead of a discussion proving the historical authenticity of the New Testament. Being aware of such interference can help you adjust as you read.

Aside from religious background and interest, a lack of background knowledge and experience in languages could interfere with comprehension. For example, if you have been to a large city in the United States, had dinner in a nice restaurant where you heard several languages being spoken at surrounding tables, then the concept of the people of one country speaking several languages may have seemed normal. One of the joys of visiting Washington, D.C., is having such an experience, especially if other people are dressed in native dress and even if you are in an ethnic restaurant where you may not be completely comfortable and do not know quite how to attack the food. Those who have traveled extensively in the United States and abroad will have a variety of experiences visiting multilingual places to draw upon to help them feel that what they are reading is familiar and comfortable.

Patterns of organization should have been easy to follow, especially with the prior knowledge section of the lesson. Once you get the idea that we are proving that the languages written in the inscription over the cross were significant to verifying the historical authenticity of the gospels, no more concepts should have interfered with your comprehension as long as you did not get lost in the language examples. Knowing the writing pattern and seeing the examples as support should have helped you through.

Physical Education/Sports Management: Ethnicity and the National Pastime

Overview

Vocabulary/Metacognition
Graded Individual Classroom Assignment
    Checklist
Academic Study Skills
    Overview
    Study Plan
    Memory
    Annotation
    Highlighting or Underlining
    Visual Maps
    Collaborative Learning
    Learning Communities and Supplemental Instruction (SI)
Textbook Chapter: "Ethnicity and the National Pastime"
Vocabulary Lesson
Vocabulary Extension
Extended Reading Activities
    Progress Check
    Activities
Reflection
    Mind Revolution

Vocabulary
Comprehension

VOCABULARY/METACOGNITION

The purpose of this exercise is to help you become aware of when you know the meaning of a word and to help you know when you do not know the meaning of a word. This is metacognition awareness.

On a scale of 1–5 (see below), rate your knowledge of the following vocabulary words from "Ethnicity and the National Pastime." After matching words with definitions on page 406, check your answers and then check your number *ones* and *fives* below. Did you know when you really knew a word and when you really did not know the word?

Scale

1. I absolutely do not know.
2. I do not think I know.
3. There's a 50/50 chance I have seen or heard it.
4. I think I know it.
5. I know the word and can use it.

Words

_____ 1. Recapitulates
_____ 2. Obscure (obscured)
_____ 3. Emerge (emerging)
_____ 4. Satire (satirical)
_____ 5. Bruit (bruited)
_____ 6. Titillate (titillated)
_____ 7. Erudition
_____ 8. Delve
_____ 9. Assimilated
_____10. Typical (atypical)

Go to page 406. See if you can match the right definition with the word and then write sentences for any five words in the list.

Words	Definitions
_____ 1. Recapitulates	A. (1) Vague; not clearly expressed; (2) murky, dim; (3) remote; hidden
_____ 2. Obscure (obscured)	B. (1) Dig; (2) carry on laborious and continued research
_____ 3. Emerge (emerging)	C. Conforming to a type; being a representative specimen
_____ 4. Satire (satirical)	D. Make known publicly, as by rumor
_____ 5. Bruit (bruited)	E. (1) Summarize; review; (2) repeat (past stages of evolution) in development
_____ 6. Titillate (titillated)	F. The use of irony; ridicule
_____ 7. Erudition	G. Knowledge gained by study; learning
_____ 8. Delve	H. Rise out, as from water; come forth from something that conceals; become apparent
_____ 9. Assimilate (assimilated)	I. Excite agreeably; tickle
_____10. Typical (atypical)	J. (1) Take in and incorporate; absorb and digest; (2) make similar; bring into conformity; adapt

Write five words from the list and your own sentences that show you know how to use the words. Choose words that you marked a *five* if possible.

1. Word _____

   Sentence _____

2. Word _____

   Sentence _____

3. Word _____

   Sentence _____

4. Word _____

   Sentence _____

5. Word _____

   Sentence _____

GRADED INDIVIDUAL CLASSROOM ASSIGNMENT

This is a class assignment and may take more than one class period. Please do not work on it out of class. Turn in the complete lesson when finished.

A. To prepare for this assignment, review the three-part reading lessons that you have completed in this textbook. Use them as references as you work.

B. Do the Vocabulary/Metacognition Exercise.

C. Write a three-part reading lesson for the chapter.
  1. For pre-reading, be sure that you (a) tap experience and prior knowledge, (b) predict what you are going to read, and (c) overview the chapter.
  2. For reading, follow Reciprocal Teaching or Active Questioning.
  3. For post-reading, be sure to come full circle by (a) comparing/contrasting what you predicted with what you actually read and (b) incorporating what you read into long-term memory. Use previous work for guidance.

D. Complete the reading lesson you have written.
  1. Answer all parts of your lesson. If you have difficulty answering part of your lesson, improve it.
  2. Write a model of prior knowledge that a general reader would need in order to understand the chapter. What will be difficult? What should you already know before reading this chapter? See previous models for guidance.
  3. Divide the chapter into two to four sections. Write titles (main headings) for each section and write the first sentence of each new section with its page number.

E. Complete the Vocabulary Lesson and the Vocabulary Extension exercises.

CHECKLIST

A. Completed Vocabulary Exercise and Check on Metacognition ___
B. Prior Knowledge model ___
C. Titles (main headings) of divisions with first sentence and page number of beginning sections ___
D. Pre-reading section of three-part lesson
  1. Tap prior knowledge and experience section ___
  2. Predict ___
  3. Overview ___
E. Reading section (Reciprocal Teaching or Active Questioning) ___
F. Post-reading section
  1. Comparing/contrasting with prediction ___
  2. Placed in long-term memory ___
G. All parts of three-part lesson have been answered ___
H. Vocabulary Lesson and Vocabulary Extension completed ___

ACADEMIC STUDY SKILLS

OVERVIEW

In the previous lessons you have improved the management of internal factors such as memory, developed effective note taking methods for lectures, developed various levels of textbook strategies such as (a) the complex rehearsal strategies of underlining and highlighting, (b) the complex elaboration strategy of note taking from textbooks through annotation, the complex organizational strategies of outlining and mapping, and organizing information, and (d) comprehension monitoring strategies, or metacognitive strategies through SQ4R and a modified plan. You have also continued to work on collaborative learning by working with a partner or in a group. Complete the exercises below that you find helpful.

STUDY PLAN

Practice using SQ4R with this chapter.

A. **Survey** (or overview) by reading the summary, questions at the end of the chapter, chapter title, and your titles of main headings.

B. **Question** by turning each major heading you read into a question:

1. Question _____

2. Question _____

3. Question _____

4. Question _____

(If you divided the chapter into more than four parts, add the additional questions below.)

_____

_____

C. **Read** the chapter section by section as indicated by your headings above.

D. **Record** information by making visual maps for each section after each section is read:

1. Visual map

2. Visual map

3. Visual map

4. Visual map

(If you divided the chapter into more than four parts, add the additional visual maps below.)

E. **Recite** information for each section after you finish reading and recording for that section and before going on to the next section.

F. **Review** the chapter by answering the questions you wrote above. Also review the work you did on the lesson for this chapter.

1. Answer _____

2. Answer _____

3. Answer _____

4. Answer _____

(If you divided the chapter into more than four parts, add the additional answers below.)

_____

_____

MEMORY

A. Select one important idea that you wish to remember from each section of the chapter. Write each idea in your own words below:

1. Idea _____

2. Idea _____

3. Idea _____

4. Idea _____

(If you divided the chapter into more than four parts, add the additional ideas below.)

_____

_____

B. Ask yourself why it is important to remember these ideas. If you have no clue, then change the information. Focus on the purpose of the chapter, to show that baseball mirrors the development of the immigrant U.S. population.

C. What are the connections among the ideas? What do they lead to? Are the ideas building up to a point? Do they support each other?

D. Self-check at this point. Do you understand the main ideas you have chosen? Can you talk out loud about them in your own words? Could you write about them? What is the significance of the ideas? What do you really know and what is it that you thought you knew but do not at this point?

E. Identify your own prior knowledge and experience about the ideas you have chosen as important. What do you already know that helps you understand the new material? Any knowledge of the game or immigration patterns will be beneficial. What prior knowledge or experience conflicts with your new knowledge? For example, I did not realize that other African Americans had played baseball in the major leagues before Jackie Robinson. I was only dimly aware of the Negro league and of Spanish-speaking Blacks.

F. Connect your prior knowledge with the new information to create a new file of information that provides support for baseball's mirroring immigration patterns. Store this information in your long-term memory.

The more you use the new file, the better you will remember the information in it. You may want to share the information with friends while attending a game. If you are in a history class or a sports-related class that discusses historical background, discuss the new file of information with your professor or classmates. The idea of becoming upward mobile socially through sports may be a new way of seeing the society in which you live. Be creative in your use of your new file. In storing the file in your long-term memory, think of several categories under which to file it. Category titles that are personally important to you would be helpful. Store the file under as many categories as are meaningful to you. For me, *social mobility* will be the most important. Others would be *baseball, ethnic background and opportunity*, and *prejudice*.

G. What rewards will you receive for having a new file of information? For me, I will no longer think of the United States as a melting pot for all people; I will think of it as a salad bowl with people maintaining their distinctive features while adding to the flavor of the whole. I will think of ways our citizens have to rise socially, what opportunities and what barriers exist for them. I will transfer my new knowledge about the rise of ethnic groups to the rise of other groups like women.

ANNOTATION

A. In your textbook margin, write in your own words the most important idea in each paragraph of this chapter.

B. In your textbook margin, write in your own words any significant examples that support the most important ideas.

HIGHLIGHTING OR UNDERLINING

So far in this study skills lesson you have had the opportunity to create a study plan, work on ideas to place in long-term memory, and annotate the text through finding most important ideas and their support. Review the work you have done and then highlight (or underline) the most important idea in each section of the chapter. Write key words below that indicate what you chose:

A. Key word_____

B. Key word_____

C. Key word_____

D. Key word_____

(If you divided the chapter into more than four parts, add the additional key words below.)

_____

_____

Visual Maps

In your SQ4R study plan you created a visual map for each section of the chapter. Review the maps. Review the chapter by talking yourself through the maps. If you find yourself stuck, is it because the map is not clear or because you have changed your mind about what is important in the chapter? Can you fix the map? Would a different form be more helpful? Be sure your maps are not cluttered and that information of equal importance is equally represented. Below, draw a visual map of your choosing that shows the importance of the sections of the chapter to each other:

Collaborative Learning

You will continue to work constructively and efficiently in small groups in class and demonstrate your ability to form a study group. In this lesson you will continue to develop your collaborative learning skills through the use of group work and work with a partner. Use the self-check below to judge the amount of progress you have made in working with a partner or in a group:

A.   I contribute my share of information and work.
       Yes____   No____   Maybe____   I Will Work On This____

B.   I consider the good of the partnership or the group over my own good.
       Yes____   No____   Maybe____   I Will Work On This____

C.   I stay on task and do not distract my partner or my group from the assignment.
       Yes____   No____   Maybe____   I Will Work On This____

D.   I feel comfortable disagreeing with others and voice my opinion.
       Yes____   No____   Maybe____   I Will Work On This____

Learning Communities and Supplemental Instruction (SI)

Become a detective. Find out if learning communities have been formed on your campus and investigate them. Also find out if Supplemental Instruction is being offered next quarter or semester for a section of a difficult course that you plan to take. For this quarter or semester join any study groups organized on campus (or organize one) for courses that are now difficult.

ETHNICITY AND THE NATIONAL PASTIME ◄≡

Whether baseball is the "national pastime" or not, its history roughly recapitulates some of the history of the United States. An eastern seaboard game in the beginning—a fact somewhat obscured by the Cincinnati Redstockings' becoming the first salaried franchise in 1869—the personnel of the game in the nineteenth and twentieth centuries tended to reflect the immigrant structure of the emerging United States. But there was no change so great as when the color line was broken in the mid-twentieth century and black players began to play with whites.

Baseball apparently developed in the early nineteenth century through an amalgamation and leveling out of the traits of a few British games like one called One Old Cat. (Insofar as the leveling out of differences goes, the game tends to parallel the cultural and even the linguistic developments among the European immigrants to the United States.) Abner Doubleday is sometimes credited with the "invention" of the game, in 1839, but it seems clear that bat-and-ball games had been developing well before that time. It was a northeastern game; Union soldiers apparently practiced it to some degree during the Civil War, but not the Confederates. Abraham Lincoln may have shown some interest in the game. Before the War Between the States, playing primarily for spectators had already developed.

In the twentieth century, the origins of baseball on the East Coast were somewhat obscured by movements of clubs and by the introduction of so-called expansion teams in places like San Diego and Seattle. Until after World War II, there were only eight teams in the National League and eight in the American. There were three teams in Greater New York, two in Boston, two in Philadelphia. Inland cities were represented only by St. Louis (the Cardinals of the National League, and earlier the Browns of the American), Detroit (the Tigers of the American League), Cincinnati (the Reds of the National League), and Cleveland (the Indians of the American).

In the movement of franchises, the Philadelphia Athletics went to Oakland, California; the team variously called the Bees or the Braves from Boston to Atlanta; the New York Giants to San Francisco; and the Brooklyn Dodgers to Los Angeles. The last was the most calamitous of the moves, although the predicted wave of suicides in Brooklyn never developed. Brooklynites missed their beloved "bums" and were deprived of their standard end-of-the-season slogan: "Wait until next year!" There was a partial restitution through the early expansion team called the New York Met[ropolitan]s, with their slogan "Let's go, Mets!" Casey Stengel, lured out of retirement to manage the Mets after a very successful career with the Yankees and players like Mickey Mantle and Roger Maris, is supposed to have moaned, at an early Mets practice session, "Don't nobody here know how to play this game?" But with a pitching staff headed by Tom Seaver (and with Nolan Ryan primarily riding the bench because of his early wildness), the Mets quickly became champions. It was Ryan, by the way, who either innovated or popularized the slogan "Play me or trade me!"

The nineteenth century, the century in which baseball began, was also the century of wholesale

European immigration to the United States. The Dutch had been in New York and New Jersey even before the Englishmen came in, and other small European groups had been in various places along the eastern seaboard. As early as 1619, West Africans came into the general area—unwilling immigrants and slaves. Germans, Irish, Jews, and Italians arrived in the cities of the east coast during the nineteenth century and were integrated into the general population of what has been called the melting pot. Africans were, obviously, not so readily integrated; their case disrupts any smooth picture which one might wish to develop for progressive immigration and integration. In the middle of the nineteenth century, Chinese and Japanese began arriving in great enough numbers to be called the "yellow peril." They, too, were integrated only very slowly if at all. It is interesting that there had hardly been an oriental among baseball players before 1995 All-Star pitcher Okenoa Nomo of the Los Angeles Dodgers, although in Japan itself the sport is known to be highly popular and to be played with great proficiency.

There have been some Native American players, many of them stereotypically nicknamed Chief in their day: Charles Albert Bender, John Meyers, John L. (Pepper) Martin, among others. More recently, Cincinnati Reds catcher Johnny Bench is in baseball's Hall of Fame and is sometimes called the best in baseball history at his position. The amazing athlete Jim Thorpe added a brief stint in professional baseball to his other activities. But a Penobscot Indian who tried to play for Cleveland in the late nineteenth century drew satirical whoops from other participants; the team name, Indians, now one borne proudly (as in the case of the Atlanta Braves) was apparently a scornful one in the beginning. Native Americans were not subjected to as much prejudice as African Americans, however;

in the 1890s at least one black player managed to remain in segregated white baseball by passing as an Indian. Native Americans are still inclined to protest the "tomahawk chop" practiced by Atlanta fans as racist in nature.

Among the famous old players, the names usually bruited about in the histories of baseball are those like Tyrus Raymond (Ty) Cobb, Cap Anson, Walter Johnson, Tris Speaker, Cy Young, Christy Mathewson, and Grover Cleveland Alexander—ethnically uncomplicated if not necessarily "Anglo Saxon." Into the 1930s, Jerome Herman, Paul Dean, Enos (Country) Slaughter, and others were onomastically typical.

Irishmen had been perhaps first among the nineteenth-century immigrant groups to become prominent in baseball. There was a formerly famous Kelly, the one addressed in "Slide, Kelly, Slide." Indeed, Kelly is said to have been the originator of that now ubiquitous baseball maneuver, and spectators were apparently titillated at his innovation. Although he is hardly remembered today, Connie Mack (born Cornelius A. McGillicuddy), a catcher and then for a time the most famous of managers, was practically Mr. Baseball in the 1920s. Other famous managers of transparently Celtic ancestry were the New York Giants' John Jacob McGraw (called a "Napoleonic genius") and the Yankees' Joe McCarthy. One could as hardly mistake the ancestry of "Iron Man" McGinnity, who astonished the baseball world by the consecutive games he pitched in 1900.

The German immigrations beginning in the seventeenth century eventually led to the presence of dominant players in major league baseball. John Wagner (called Honus as an apparent imitation of German Hans), Ludwig Heinrich (Lou) Gehrig, and Warren Spahn are in the record books and in all the histories of the game, but it is George Herman (Babe) Ruth who really dominates the German contribution. Although his names do not necessarily suggest ethnicity, they are not too far from Georg Hermann; and it has been said that Ruth spoke German. Ruth, whose 714 career home runs and 60 in one season were once thought insuperable records, was an outstanding left-handed pitcher before the New York Yankees bought his contract from the Boston Red Sox and converted him to an outfielder in order to take advantage of his hitting. There may still be those who consider Ruth the greatest all-around baseball player of them all, although Ty Cobb was considered a strong competitor in the old days and Willie Mays would certainly deserve a lot of consideration in more recent times. Not too many Dutchmen have been in major league baseball, but Johnny Vander Meer astounded the sporting world by pitching two consecutive no-hit games in 1938.

In New York City, with a large Italian population, Babe Ruth became the Bambino—an obvious translation into an ethnic language. (No such honor seems to have been accorded other Babes, like Babe Herman of the old Brooklyn Dodgers.)

There were Italians who were prominent, especially after about 1930. Ernie Lombardi, Frank Crossetti, Dolph Camilli, and Phil Rizzuto all had outstanding major league careers. On Ruth's own Yankee team from 1926 was "Poosh 'em up" Tony Lazzeri, possibly named from an Italian dialect instruction to a bartender "Poosh 'em [i.e., beers] upa, Tony." Little Italian came into the baseball talk which was reported to radio listeners (and later television watchers) and sports column readers, but there may well have been more down on the field. Carl Furillo, a Brooklyn Dodger teammate of the famous Jackie Robinson and not a notably fast runner, was known as Skooj, from the Italian for "snail." Joe

DiMaggio, one of the great Yankee heroes, spoke Italian, as did probably his brothers Vince and Dom, both of whom played outfield in the major leagues, although not so famous as Giuseppe. There can seldom have been any more ethnic pride than New York Italian fans had in "Jolting Joe," and it seems reasonable that the association of the Italian language with baseball got a big boost. It would be fascinating to know just how much more of the Italian language was used down on the playing field, hardly finding its way into the broadcast booths and press boxes.

Jewish players were perhaps never outstandingly prominent among baseball players, perhaps because the Jewish culture tended to stress education rather than athletics. But Henry Greenberg, a right-handed home run slugger for the Detroit Tigers between 1930 and 1947, with 1942–1944 out for World War II, had a loyal following among Jewish fans. In the leveling process characteristic of baseball, little was made of Greenberg's racial/religious background; his nickname was "(Big) Hank," a form which was also given to the black hitter who ultimately beat Ruth's career record, Henry Aaron. Sandy Koufax, a left-handed pitcher who had the second greatest number of no-hit games behind Nolan Ryan, was also Jewish, but one would have to delve into background material to acquire the information. Little was made of it publicly. Ken Holzman, Moses Solomon, and Sid Schacht were also Jewish big leaguers, as was Moe Berg, better known for his erudition than his abilities as a catcher or a hitter.

There was all along a sprinkling of Slavic names among those of major league players. Stan Musial, perhaps the outstanding player among them, is not so easily recognized as of Slavic provenience because of the tendency to pronounce his name with three syllables rather than the more authentic two. Home-run slugger and fancy fielding first baseman Ted Kluszewski has a more easily recognizable Slavic name like his teammate on the Cincinnati Reds of the 1950s, Ray Jablonski.

Until about the time of World War II, white baseball players made up almost the entire personnel of the major leagues. Baseball fans' heroes were Ted Williams, the most recent batter to hit over .400 in a major league season, and Bob Feller, much touted as an Iowa farm boy and thus characteristic of middle America. Another who came into the major leagues young like Feller, Schoolboy Rowe, typified the American dream (a color-specific dream, some would perhaps say) of an all-around, "All-American" boy arriving in the Big Leagues. It was the stuff that movies were made of. But Jackie Robinson's arrival on the Brooklyn Dodgers' team in 1947 as the first clearly African-American major leaguer was one of the most important events in the history of baseball.

Black players, provided they spoke Spanish, had been around before. Luis Olmo and Hiram Bithorn (the latter famous enough on his home island to have a stadium named after him) were black Puerto Ricans playing in the major leagues in 1940. Dolf Luque was a pitcher from Cuba, where the color line has never been so aggressively drawn, around 1912. Between that date and the arrival of Jackie Robinson, there were about 40 Latin American players in the majors, most of them rather dark-skinned. Cuban Tony Perez, who was one of the four outstanding players on the Cincinnati Big Red Machine of the 1970s, exemplified the Latin (or Caribbean) contribution to major league baseball. Other Cuban players, almost all of them with at least some African ancestry, have included Tito Fuentes, Tony Taylor, Camilo Pascual, Tony Gonzalez, Pedro Ramos, Tony Oliva, Rene Arocha, Ariel Prieto, Rey Ordoñez, Osvaldo Fernandez, Livan

Hernandez, and increasingly large numbers in more recent years.

Even before Portsmouth, Ohio native Branch Rickey brought Jackie Robinson into the major leagues, and certainly before other blacks arrived on the scene to turn the National League from what threatened to become another minor league into a strong competitor with the American league, black ability in the sport tended to be an open secret. An attempt was made to smuggle Charles Grant into the major leagues as an "Indian" as early as 1900, but the move was defeated by racist protests. The Negro baseball league had produced players who were legendary by word of mouth, if not prominent on the sports pages. Cool Papa Bell, for example, was said to be so fast that he could hit the electric switch and be in bed before the light went out. Other players had equally well-known abilities. There is speculation as to how catcher and slugger Josh Gibson could have established hitting records if he had been allowed to play in the all-white major leagues. But perhaps the best of all was Leroy "Satchel" Paige, a pitcher who did make it to the major leagues late in his career—too old to show what he really could have done. "Dizzy" Dean, an Arkansas native who almost typified the Anglo-Saxon contribution to the sport, is reported to have said that Paige was the best pitcher he had ever seen, better than Dean himself, who won thirty games in one major league season (1934).

The black players who followed Robinson into major league baseball may have been the best of the lot, but a very good best they were. Early stars like centerfielder Larry Doby of the Cleveland Indians (the first black player in the American league), pitcher Don Newcombe, and catchers Roy Campanella and Elston Howard were obvious All-Star material from the very beginning. Other players like Monte Irvin and

Joe Black were also obviously outstanding. After the pioneering "generation" came outstanding black players like Willie McCovey, Bill White, Bob Gibson (who holds more St. Louis Cardinals team records than Dean), Curt Flood, Vada Pinson, John Roseboro, Willie Stargell, Maury Wills, and Lou Brock.

Today, fifty-three years after Robinson's entry into the National League, Black and "Latin" players come close to dominating the sport. In many cases, "Latin" is not distinct from Black, since many of the players come from the Caribbean and are dark in color if Spanish-speaking. Puerto Rico has furnished players like Roberto Clemente, Juan Pizarro, and Orlando Cepeda; the Dominican Republic, Rico Carty, Felipe Alou (with Matty and Jesús Alou). That island's Sammy Sosa, who lost the 1999 "home run derby" to Mark McGwire by a slight margin, may be the most likely player to break not only McGwire's record of seventy home runs in a season but also Hank Aaron's career record of 758. (Barry Bonds has already beaten the first record, and there are those who believe he will beat the second.)

With the advent of non-Hispanic black players, especially, it is no longer possible to judge ethnicity in terms of names in the box scores—even without the traditions of name changing which affected non–Anglo-Saxon populations in the United States during a period of its history. The color line seems never to have been so fixed in the Latin American countries (including Puerto Rico and the Dominican Republic), and a name like Tony Gonzalez (a Black player of the 1950s) or Alex Rodriguez, a Hispanic drafted out of high school in 1993, says nothing about the skin color of its bearer. Muslim names like Mohammed are exemplified among football and basketball players—and are usually taken by African Americans—but seem rare in baseball.

Because freed slaves in the American South often took the surnames of their former owners, a name like Johnson is equally unrevealing as to the ancestry of the person so named. Certainly no one thought of Willie (Stretch) McCovey as being of Celtic parentage.

Black players furnish an obvious exception to the pattern that sons or grandsons of immigrants go immediately into professional sports, with the result that there is—in the case of the Irish, Germans, Italians, and to some extent Jews—a period in which a given ethnic group is prominent and then a succeeding period in which another group replaces it in prominence in the sport. In the usual pattern, as the immigrant group is more fully assimilated into mainstream American culture, its talented members go into business, politics, law, and the other professions. But African-American athletes seem to be immune to this pattern of periodicity. Because of slavery, segregation, and prejudice, they had been denied entrance into baseball (and other professional sports) in the first generation or two after their atypical immigration. Unlike Irish, Italians, Germans, or Jews, they had developed their own parallel big league with its own World Series—of about the same quality as the more mainstream major leagues. Postseason games between (white) major leaguers and Negro League teams quite often resulted in victories for the latter. Not having been absorbed into mainstream American culture at the same rate as the other ethnic groups, they do not seem ready to lose their dominance in baseball as quickly as did other groups.

Spanish-named big leaguers furnish a partial parallel—even without the same influence from segregation. Some of the Latin American countries or islands had their own leagues. Mexico attracted some major league players, most notoriously catcher Mickey Owen, who had been a National League All-Star. (In the 1960s and 1970s, Japan also hired away big league players at higher salaries than they could get in the United States.) In the Caribbean, with its nearly uniform year-round climate, baseball was played all year. In the winter, some major league players played on Puerto Rican teams, where the color line was never so dominant. The seeds of racial integration in baseball were sown long before the time of Jackie Robinson, but its full flowering has come only in the last three or four decades.

Hispanic. It was a major change, however, when Jackie Robinson became the first non-Hispanic Black in the major leagues in 1947. Forced immigrants as slaves as early as 1619, the blacks were prevented from assimilating into the mainstream through the period of segregation, and they had formed their own leagues. They had developed as high a level of proficiency as the white major leaguers; they had a long tradition of playing, and they did not seem likely to relinquish their dominance in baseball.

Summary

Although modeled to some degree on games of England, baseball is in many ways an originally American sport which mirrors the development of the immigrant U.S. population. Few Native Americans (Indians) have been prominent in the sport, and the earliest of them were subject to rather offensive stereotyping. Irishmen, Italians, and Germans have had their periods of dominance, and Jews have from time to time been highly successful players, as have individuals from Slavic and other ethnic backgrounds. The most persistent and perhaps most successful ethnic group has, however, been the African Americans. Black baseball players had found their way into professional baseball, especially Santo Domingans and Puerto Ricans who were considered

Questions

1. What is the possible relationship between ethnicity and proficiency in sports?
2. What did you already know about Branch Rickey that helped your understanding of this chapter?
3. Do you think some people develop proficiency in sports as a compensation for social inequality?
4. What more recent major league players confirm or contradict the trends outlined in this chapter?
5. What do you think is the future of Asians in major league baseball?
6. To what extent are the statements made about baseball true of football?
7. To what extent are the statements made about baseball true of basketball?

Vocabulary Lesson

The purpose of this exercise is to help you review and deepen your knowledge of the ten general vocabulary words you worked with at the beginning of this chapter.

A. Structural Analysis—Affixes and Root Words
   1. Circle the prefix of the following word: *Atypical* _____
   2. Find the dictionary definition of the root word of the word above and write the definition by the word.
   3. How does the prefix change the meaning of the word?
   4. Underline the suffix of the following word: *Erudition*
   5. Find the dictionary definition for *erudition* above and then write your own definition for the root word *erudite*. _____
   6. How does the suffix change the meaning of the word?

B. Use of Context
   1. Read the first paragraph of the chapter (page 412) in which the word *recapitulates* appears, and in your own words write a definition for it below:

      _____

   2. Read the sixth paragraph of the chapter (page 413) in which the word *satirical* appears, and in your own words write a definition for it below:

      _____

   3. Read the twentieth (next-to-last) paragraph (page 416) of the chapter in which the word *assimilated* appears, and in your own words write a definition for it below:

      _____

C. Multiple Meanings of Words: Circle the definition below of the word *obscure (obscured)* that fits the way it is used in the first paragraph (page 412):
   1. Vague, not clearly expressed
   2. Murky, dim
   3. Remote; hidden

D. Synonyms and Antonyms: List one synonym (same meaning) and one antonym (opposite meaning) for each of the following words:

Word	**Synonym**	**Antonym**
Emerge (emerging)		
Titillate (titillated)		

E. Generate Your Own Language
   1. If the meaning of a word is *obscure*, what should you do?
   2. Why are Americans *titillated* by comics who depend on four-letter words for their humor?
   3. What kind of *atypical* behavior have you demonstrated in your family?

4.   When was the last time you and a group of friends *bruited* about the topic of best baseball teams? What teams do you like?

5.   When you and your friends *delve* into the mysteries of the universe, what do you usually discuss?

VOCABULARY EXTENSION

The purpose of this exercise is to help you see to what degree you know the ten general vocabulary words you worked with at the beginning of this chapter. Matching a word with its definition is the beginning of knowing a word. Using the word in your speaking and writing is full knowledge.

A.   List the vocabulary words from this lesson that you can now use in both your speaking and writing.

B.   List the vocabulary words from this lesson that you can now use in writing but are still not comfortable using in speaking.

C.   List the vocabulary words from this lesson that you cannot use yet but will recognize in reading.

D.   List general vocabulary words from this lesson that are still difficult to understand.

E.   Use *five* vocabulary words from this lesson in a five-sentence paragraph on the topic of this lesson.

F.   Illustrate the meaning of *one* of the vocabulary words from this lesson through some form of artwork or a cartoon. (This exercise is for right-brain students who enjoy drawing better than writing!)

EXTENDED READING ACTIVITIES

The purpose of this section is to give you a variety of options for independent study or investigation of the chapter topic. Reading is a skill that must be practiced each day if progress is to take place. These activities are designed to give you a variety of reading experiences through which you can improve your general vocabulary and increase your higher-level comprehension skills.

Your instructor may wish to (a) assign one or more activities to the class as a whole, (b) assign various activities to small groups, (c) assign one or more activities to individual students, or (d) let students choose to do the activities or not.

PROGRESS CHECK

A.   List what skills you are using from this class for another class.

B.   Circle what you are doing outside of class that you know is helping you improve your comprehension and vocabulary. How do you know?

1.   Reading for other courses

2.   Reading challenging leisure-time materials, including novels

3. Reading interesting topics on the Internet
4. Keeping a weekly reading report
5. Attending a reading lab
6. Keeping a private journal that includes reactions to what I have read
7. Reading magazines and journals that help me understand my chosen major
8. Reading magazines, journals, and newspapers for general information
9. Keeping a vocabulary journal and using new words in my writing and speech
10. Others

C. List what you will continue to do after you complete this course.
D. What has made you aware that you need to improve your comprehension and vocabulary?
E. List activities you have recommended to classmates as being helpful.
F. If you have completed your novel, have you found another one to read? Have you recommended the one you finished to a classmate or a friend? Has a classmate recommended reading (or not reading) a novel to you? Do you think you will read more fiction during your leisure time? If you have a child, have you spent time reading to him/her?

ACTIVITIES

A. Weekly Reading Report: Continue keeping a weekly report of your reading. Use the form in Appendix C if you wish.
B. Attend a Reading Lab: Continue using the reading lab at your school. Are you still increasing your general vocabulary? How aware are you of the denotation and connotation of the words you encounter?
C. Read your Novel: If you are looking for another novel to read, you might enjoy the wonderful J. K. Rowling's *Harry Potter and the Sorcerer's Stone*. A word of warning! Once you get into this fantasy, it is difficult to put down. If you are ready for a more serious novel, one about how one's friend having cancer can alter a friendship, then you may enjoy Davida Wills Hurwin's *A Time for Dancing*. Use the novel report form in Appendix C if you wish.
D. Reading/Writing Connection: Continue keeping your beginning year college journal. What sports do you enjoy on campus? Do you participate? Observe? Describe the best sports experience you have ever had. How have your interests in sports changed over the years? Are athletes treated fairly on campus? How? How not? Write your insights in your journal. Use one new vocabulary word in your responses.
E. Read to anyone's child
1. Harve & Margot Zemach, *Duffy and the Devil*
2. William Steig, *Sylvester and the Magic Pebble*
3. Bill Martin, Jr. & John Archambault, *White Dynamite and Curly Kidd*
4. Arthur Yorinks & Richard Egielski, *Hey, Al*

  5. Alice & Martin Provensen, *The Glorious Flight Across the Channel with Louis Bleriot*

  6. Arthur Ransome & Uri Shulevitz, *The Fool of the World and the Flying Ship* (A Russian tale)

  7. Margaret Hodges & Trina Schart Hyman, *Saint George and the Dragon*

  8. Russell Hoban & Lillian Hoban, *A Baby Sister for Frances*

F. Use the Internet: Look up articles on Cuban baseball players defecting to the United States. For example, there are articles from 1997-2000 on CNN and *The Sporting News* over the Internet. Try the addresses below:

http://europe.cnn.com/WORLD/9803/24/cuba.defectors/

http://www.sportingnews.com/baseball/articles/19980113/38706.html

http://www.time.com/time/magazine/archive/1996/dom/960729/cuba.html

http://www.netspace.org/herald/issues/102097/edit.f.html

http://www.sportserver.com/newsroom/ap/bbo/1998/mlb/arz/feat/archive/090798/arz46944.html

G. Vocabulary Journal: Continue keeping a vocabulary journal. Use the form in Appendix C if you wish.

H. Magazine/Journal/Newspaper Reading: Read in your campus or local library from the following list of magazines and journals: *Journal of Sport & Exercise Psychology, Sporting News, Athletic Business, Sports Illustrated, Sport Marketing Quarterly, Sport Psychologist, The Physician Sports Medicine, Sports and the Courts, Athletic Management, Fitness, Journal of Sport Management, Journal of Sport Rehabilitation*

REFLECTION

MIND REVOLUTION

The big issue introduced in this chapter is how sports help various ethnic groups to rise socially. Think about ways you and your family have risen and what changes happened as a result. What people do you know who are better off than their parents and their grandparents? What does "better off" mean to them? to you? When you rise socially, what price do you pay? What do you lose? What do you gain? What new ethnic groups now have trouble being accepted into the mainstream culture?

VOCABULARY

The vocabulary used was not filled with highly technical or specialized words. A newspaper article describing a game, for example, can be so filled with the jargon of the sport that a person not knowledgeable about the sport may finish reading the article and wonder who won and how. Sports has a special language all its own. This chapter did not depend on that special language.

Comprehension

The greatest difficulty may come from the author's assumption that you share his knowledge and interest in the history of the sport. His cataloging of names of teams and players may have overwhelmed you if you know little about the sport or if your interest lies only in present-day games. You may have begun the chapter hazily thinking that *ethnicity* was not going to be the focus of the chapter. If so, you may have read without understanding until the focus of the chapter finally hit you. Hopefully, a light bulb went on if this is so. Once you see that the chapter is organized by ethnic groups you should be able to read with better understanding.

Another problem with reading this chapter could come from having no main headings marked for you. This is the first chapter that has not been divided into sections and part of your task was to make those divisions for yourself. Reading the summary and questions at the end of the chapter should have been helpful as you divided the chapter for yourself.

Other areas of difficulty could come from having no historical overview of immigration patterns for the United States or not knowing that many ethnic groups have had difficulty being accepted into mainstream U.S. culture.

Your background knowledge and interest in baseball also help determine how easily you read the chapter. If the teams and names of players mentioned are mostly familiar, you probably read the chapter with little difficulty.

Alternative Reading Plans
for Part I, Chapters 1–4

The following reading lessons may be used instead of the Reciprocal Teaching or Active Questioning plan in the Chapters 1–4 lessons. The only lesson with teacher-made models is the first. The lessons may be used with teacher guidance as an oral whole-class lesson, or they may be used in small groups. Students are probably not ready to follow the reading plan independently or with only a partner at this stage in the course.

Chapter 1: Computers

Active Questioning

Overview

As the second step in this three-part reading plan, you will read this chapter by using an alternative plan, the Active Questioning reading plan, as explained below. The Reciprocal Teaching reading plan is in Chapter 1. In both plans you break up the chapter in sections and read and think about each as you read. The purpose of both plans is to keep you reading actively.

General Directions

Complete all parts of the pre-reading lesson before doing this lesson. When you finish, go to the post-reading part of the reading plan.

A. The purpose for writing questions on three levels of comprehension is to first get the facts and basic information to understand the meaning on a literal level.

B. From there you move to using this information in the chapter and your own prior knowledge to synthesize information, draw conclusions, and make judgments.

C. The last level of comprehension gives you the opportunity to incorporate the information you have learned into your own life. Answers to questions on the last two levels of comprehension take more time to process and sometimes you may feel insecure about your answers. The literal level is easier because you can copy the answer from the text. Many times you can get this answer right without really understanding what you are reading. You need to be able to do something with the literal-level information, to see its importance or significance, and that is why working on the other two levels is important.

Assignment

When using active questioning, write questions on the literal, inferential, and creative/critical levels. You may answer the questions provided or write and answer your own.

A. Read section one, "1.1 The Information Society," and ask one text-explicit question (literal), one text-implicit question (inferential), and one experience-based question (critical/creative) each on this section. Please answer all three questions. Do not ask a question that you cannot answer.

    1. Text-explicit (literal level): A question that requires the reader to read the line. The answer will come from one line of print. Model text-explicit question: For what do we use the term IT?

Your text-explicit question _____

Answer _____

    2. Text-implicit (inferential level): A question that requires the reader to read between the lines. The answer will come from more than one line of print. You will need to make judgments and draw conclusions. Model text-implicit question: Look at the list of things IT-competent people will be able to do and then list them in the order of importance to you. Justify your choices.

Your text-implicit question _____

Answer _____

    3. Experience-based (critical/creative level): A question that requires the reader to read beyond the lines. Apply what you have learned to your world. Question what you have read. Model experience-based question: Are you presently afraid of computers or were you when you first learned to use them? Did becoming competent in using them help rid you of the fear? Describe your feelings/experiences.

Your experience-based question _____

Answer _____

B. Read the second section, "1.2 Networking: Bringing People Together," and ask one text-explicit question, one text-implicit question, and one experience-based question each on this section. Please answer all three questions. Do not ask a question that you cannot answer.

    1. Model text-explicit question: What is turning the world into a global village?

Your text-explicit question _____

Answer _____

    2. Model text-implicit question: What are the two ways of gaining access to the Internet? Which do you think is best? Why?

Your text-implicit question _____

Answer _____

    3. Model experience-based question: What are the advantages in belonging to a global village?

Your experience-based question _____

Answer _____

C. Read the third section, "1.3 Computers: The Essentials," and ask one text-explicit question, one text-implicit question, and one experience-based question each on this section. Please answer all three questions. Do not ask a question that you cannot answer.

    1. Model text-explicit question: What are the names of the four basic components of a computer system?

Your text-explicit question _____

Answer _____

    2. Model text-implicit question: Look at Productivity Software as listed in Figure 1.5 on page 38 and then list below the software you use from most used to least used. Are any of the ones you do not use interesting to you? Will you use them in the future?

Your text-implicit question _____

Answer _____

    3. Model experience-based question: How will you use computers in your new job when you graduate from college? Is computer knowledge or competency going to be important in your future profession?

Your experience-based question _____

Answer _____

D. Read the fourth section, "1.4 Personal Computers to Supercomputers," and ask one text-explicit question, one text-implicit question, and one experience-based question each on this section. Please answer all three questions. Do not ask a question that you cannot answer.

    1. Model text-explicit question: What is a platform?

Your text-explicit question _____

Answer _____

    2. Model text-implicit question: Name the two major types of personal computers and their operating systems. Which would you choose for your own computer? Why?

Your text-implicit question _____

Answer _____

    3. Model experience-based question: How could one of the personal digital assistants (PDAs) support your personal information management system as a student? Which one would you choose? What features?

Your experience-based question _____

Answer _____

E. Read the fifth section, "1.5 A Computer System at Work," and ask one text-explicit question, one text-implicit question, and one experience-based question each on this section. Please answer all three questions. Do not ask a question that you cannot answer.

1. Model text-explicit question: What two operations do computers perform?

Your text-explicit question _____

Answer _____

2. Model text-implicit question: Rank the list of computer strengths in order of importance to you. Justify your list.

Your text-implicit question _____

Answer _____

3. Model experience-based question: The computer has two processing operations: computation and logic. How will these operations be beneficial to you in your major field? If you plan to major in business, for example, how will you use them?

Your experience-based question _____

Answer _____

F. Read the sixth section, "1.6 How Do We Use Computers?" and ask one text-explicit question, one text-implicit question, and one experience-based question each on this section. Please answer all three questions. Do not ask a question that you cannot answer.

1. Model text-explicit question: What do you combine to create an information system?

Your text-explicit question _____

Answer _____

2. Model text-implicit question: Name several CBT programs available and then list ones that you would be interested in taking via the computer. Why would you rather take them by computer than in a traditional classroom?

Your text-implicit question _____

Answer _____

3. Model experience-based question: Have you taken any CBT classes or classes through distance learning? If so, describe your experiences. If not, which do you feel works best for you, traditional classrooms or CBT/distance learning classes. Learning does not have to be an either/or situation. You may want to combine the two.

Your experience-based question _____

Answer _____

CHAPTER 2: PSYCHOLOGY

RECIPROCAL TEACHING

OVERVIEW

Complete the lesson below after you finish all parts of pre-reading. As the second step in this three-part reading plan, you will read this chapter by using an alternative plan, the Reciprocal Teaching reading plan, as explained below. The Active Questioning reading plan is in Chapter 2. In both plans you break up the chapter in sections and read and think about each as you read. The purpose of both plans is to keep you reading actively. When you finish this part, go to part three, post-reading. There are no teacher models in this lesson. You may want to do this lesson as a whole-class assignment or in small groups instead of with partners.

GENERAL DIRECTIONS

The concept of Reciprocal Teaching outlined here is adapted from Palinscar and Brown, 1986. See Bess Hinson, ed., *New Directions in Reading Instruction Revised* (Newark, DE: International Reading Association, 2000), p. 23, for an updated version. In the updated version, the steps are the same, but the order changes to (1) predict, (2) question, (3) clarify, and (4) summarize. Also see Chapter 3, page 140.

    A.   Both partners read a section under a subheading at a time. Take turns summarizing the section in as few sentences as possible.

    B.   Take turns asking a high level question or two on each section (inferential or critical/creative).

    C.   Explain or clarify difficult parts to each other. Practice repeating main ideas and supporting details in your own words.

    D.   Read the next subheading and predict what the section will be about. Discuss (exchange) ideas.

ASSIGNMENT

    A.   Read the first section, "Roles and Rules," and follow the directions below.

        1.   Write a summary of the first major section.

Your summary _____

_____

_____

        2.   Write one question on this section. Try to write an inferential or a critical/creative question. If you can't, write a literal-level question.

Your question _____

Your answer _____

        3.   Orally explain or clarify an important idea.

Your idea _____

4. Predict what you will read in the second major section, "Social Influences on Beliefs."

Your prediction _____

B. Read the second section, "Social Influences on Beliefs."
1. Summarize this second major section.

Your summary _____

_____

_____

2. Write one question on this section. Try to write an inferential or a critical/creative question. If you can't, write a literal-level question.

Your question _____

Your answer _____

3. Orally explain or clarify an important idea in this section.

Your idea _____

4. Predict what you will read in the third major section of the chapter, "Individuals in Groups."

Your prediction _____

C. Read the third section, "Individuals in Groups."
1. Summarize this third major section.

Your summary _____

_____

_____

2. Write one question on this section. Try to write an inferential or a critical/creative question. If you can't, write a literal-level question.

Your question _____

Your answer _____

3. Orally explain or clarify an important idea in this section.

Your idea _____

4. Predict what you will read in the fourth major section of the chapter, "Group Conflict and Prejudice."

Your prediction _____

D. Read the fourth section, "Group Conflict and Prejudice."
1. Summarize this fourth major section.

Your summary _____

_____

_____

2. Write one question on this section. Try to write an inferential or a critical/creative question. If you can't, write a literal-level question.

Your question _____

Your answer _____

    3.   Orally explain or clarify an important idea in this section.

Your idea   _____

    4.   Predict what you will read in the fifth major section of the chapter, "The Question of Human Nature."

Your prediction _____

E.   Read the fifth section, "The Question of Human Nature."
    1.   Summarize this fifth major section.

Your summary   _____

    _____

    _____

    2.   Write one question on this section. Try to write an inferential or a critical/creative question. If you can't, write a literal-level question.

Your question   _____

Your answer _____

    3.   Orally explain or clarify an important idea in this section.

Your idea   _____

CHAPTER 3: SOCIOLOGY

ACTIVE QUESTIONING

OVERVIEW

As the second step in this three-part reading plan, you will read this chapter by using an alternative plan, the Active Questioning reading plan, as explained below. The Reciprocal Teaching reading plan is in Chapter 3. In both plans you break up the chapter in sections and read and think about each as you read. The purpose of both plans is to keep you reading actively.

GENERAL DIRECTIONS

Complete all parts of the pre-reading lesson before doing this lesson. When you finish, go to the post-reading part of the reading plan.

A.   The purpose for writing questions on three levels of comprehension is to first get the facts and basic information to understand the meaning on a literal level.

B.   From there you move to using this information in the chapter and your own prior knowledge to synthesize information, draw conclusions, and make judgments.

C.   The last level of comprehension gives you the opportunity to incorporate the information you have learned into your own life. Answers to questions on the last two levels of comprehension take more time to process and sometimes you may feel insecure about your answers. The literal level is easier because you can copy the answer from the text. Many times you can get this answer right without really understanding what you are reading. You need to be able to do something with the literal level information, to see its importance or significance, and that is why working on the other two levels is important.

Assignment

When using active questioning, write questions on the literal, inferential, and creative/critical levels.

A.   Read section one, "The Social Meaning of Race and Ethnicity," and ask one text-explicit question (literal), one text-implicit question (inferential), and one experience-based question (critical/creative) each on this section. Please answer all three questions. Do not ask a question that you cannot answer.

1.   Text-explicit (literal level): A question that requires the reader to read the line. The answer will come from one line of print.

Your text-explicit question _____

Answer _____

2.   Text-implicit (inferential level): A question that requires the reader to read between the lines. The answer will come from more than one line of print. You will need to make judgments and draw conclusions.

Your text-implicit question _____

Answer _____

3.   Experience-based (critical/creative level): A question that requires the reader to read beyond the lines. Apply what you have learned to your world. Question what you have read.

Your experience-based question _____

Answer _____

B.   Read the second section, "Majority and Minority: Patterns of Interaction," and ask one text-explicit question, one text-implicit question, and one experience-based question each on this section. Please answer all three questions. Do not ask a question that you cannot answer.

1.   Your text-explicit question _____

Answer _____

2.   Your text-implicit question _____

Answer _____

3   Your experience-based question _____

Answer _____

C. Read the third section, "Race and Ethnicity in the United States," and ask one text-explicit question, one text-implicit question, and one experience-based question each on this section. Please answer all three questions. Do not ask a question that you cannot answer.

1. Your text-explicit question _____

Answer _____

2. Your text-implicit question _____

Answer _____

3   Your experience-based question _____

Answer _____

D. Read the fourth section, "Race and Ethnicity: Looking Ahead," and ask one text-explicit question, one text-implicit question, and one experience-based question each on this section. Please answer all three questions. Do not ask a question that you cannot answer.

1. Your text-explicit question _____

Answer _____

2. Your text-implicit question _____

Answer _____

3   Your experience-based question _____

Answer _____

CHAPTER 4: ENVIRONMENTAL GEOLOGY

RECIPROCAL TEACHING

OVERVIEW

Complete all parts of the pre-reading lesson before doing this lesson. When you finish, go to the post-reading part of the reading plan. As the second step in this three-part reading plan, you will read this chapter by using an alternative plan, the Reciprocal Teaching reading plan, as explained below. The Active Questioning reading plan is in Chapter 4. In both plans you break up the chapter in sections and read and think about each as you read. The purpose of both plans is to keep you reading actively.

GENERAL DIRECTIONS

Read the chapter based on the old model listed below or the updated model in which the steps are predict, question, clarify, and summarize. Use the version that works best for you. No teacher models are given in this lesson. The concept of Reciprocal Teaching outlined here is adapted from Palinscar and Brown, 1986.

A. Both partners read a section under a subheading at a time. Take turns summarizing the section in as few sentences as possible.
B. Take turns asking a high level question or two on each section (inferential or critical/creative).
C. Explain or clarify difficult parts to each other. Practice repeating main ideas and supporting details in your own words.
D. Read the next subheading and predict what the section will be about. Discuss (exchange) ideas.

ASSIGNMENT

A. Read "Case History: Ducktown, Tennessee," and follow the directions below.
   1. Write a summary of this major section.

Your summary _____

_____

_____

   2. Write one question on this section. Try to write an inferential or a critical/creative question. If you can't, write a literal-level question.

Your question _____

Your answer _____

   3. Orally explain or clarify an important idea.

Your idea _____

   4. Predict what you will read in the next major section.

Your prediction _____

B. Read "1.1 Introduction to Environmental Geology."
   1. Summarize this major section.

Your summary _____

_____

_____

   2. Write one question on this section. Try to write an inferential or a critical/creative question. If you can't, write a literal-level question.

Your question _____

Your answer _____

    3.   Orally explain or clarify an important idea in this section.

Your idea _____

    4.   Predict what you will read in the next major section of the chapter.

Your prediction _____

C.   Read "1.2 How Geologists Work: The Scientific Method."
    1.   Summarize this major section.

Your summary _____

_____

_____

    2.   Write one question on this section. Try to write an inferential or a critical/creative question. If you can't, write a literal-level question.

Your question _____

Your answer _____

    3.   Orally explain or clarify an important idea in this section.

Your idea _____

    4.   Predict what you will read in the next major section of the chapter.

Your prediction _____

D.   Read "1.3 Culture and Environmental Awareness."
    1.   Summarize this major section.

Your summary _____

_____

_____

    2.   Write one question on this section. Try to write an inferential or a critical/creative question. If you can't, write a literal-level question.

Your question _____

Your answer _____

    3.   Orally explain or clarify an important idea in this section.

Your idea _____

    4.   Predict what you will read in the next major section of the chapter.

Your prediction _____

E.   Read "1.4 Environmental Ethics."
    1.   Summarize this major section.

Your summary _____

_____

_____

2.　Write one question on this section. Try to write an inferential or a critical/creative question. If you can't, write a literal-level question.

Your question　_____

Your answer　_____

3.　Orally explain or clarify an important idea in this section.

Your idea　_____

4.　Predict what you will read in the next major section of the chapter.

Your prediction　_____

F.　Read "1.5　The Environmental Crisis."
　　1.　Summarize this major section.

Your summary　_____

_____

_____

2.　Write one question on this section. Try to write an inferential or a critical/creative question. If you can't, write a literal-level question.

Your question　_____

Your answer　_____

3.　Orally explain or clarify an important idea in this section.

Your idea　_____

4.　Predict what you will read in the next major section of the chapter.

Your prediction　_____

G.　Read "1.6　Fundamental Concepts of Environmental Science."
　　1.　Summarize this major section.

Your summary　_____

_____

_____

2.　Write one question on this section. Try to write an inferential or a critical/creative question. If you can't, write a literal-level question.

Your question　_____

Your answer　_____

3.　Orally explain or clarify an important idea in this section.

Your idea　_____

Alternative Reading Plans for Part II, Chapters 5–12

CHAPTER 9: WEST AFRICAN LITERATURE
> Active Questioning
>> Overview
>> Assignment

CHAPTER 10: MUSIC
> Active Questioning
>> Overview
>> Assignment

CHAPTER 11: AMERICAN ENGLISH
> Reciprocal Teaching
>> Overview
>> Assignment

CHAPTER 12: RELIGIOUS STUDIES
> Reciprocal Teaching
>> Overview
>> Assignment

The following reading lessons may be used instead of the Reciprocal Teaching or Active Questioning plan in the chapter lesson. The lessons may be used with teacher guidance as an oral whole-class lesson, or they may be used in small groups. Some students are probably ready to follow the reading plan independently or with a partner at this stage in the course. For those who continue to need more guidance, Chapter 7 contains model questions for the first section and Chapter 9 contains model questions for all three sections.

CHAPTER 5: LINGUISTICS

ACTIVE QUESTIONING

OVERVIEW

As the second step in this three-part reading plan, you will read this chapter by using an alternative plan, the Active Questioning reading plan, as explained below. The Reciprocal Teaching reading plan is in Chapter 5. In both plans you break up the chapter in sections and read and think about each as you read. The purpose of both plans is to keep you reading actively.

GENERAL DIRECTIONS

Complete all parts of the pre-reading lesson before doing this lesson. When you finish, go to the post-reading part of the reading plan. Review the General Directions for Active Questioning for Chapter 1, Appendix A, page 424, if needed.

When using active questioning, write questions on the literal, inferential, and creative/critical levels. Review model questions in Chapters 2 and 4. Also look at the model questions in the Reciprocal Teaching lesson for this chapter.

ASSIGNMENT

A. Read section one, "Differences about Language in the Academic World," and ask one text-explicit question (literal), one text-implicit question (inferential), and one experience-based question (critical/creative) each on this section. Please answer all three questions. Do not ask a question that you cannot answer.

1. Text-explicit (literal level): A question that requires the reader to read the line. The answer will come from one line of print.

   Your text-explicit question _____

   Answer _____

2. Text-implicit (inferential level): A question that requires the reader to read between the lines. The answer will come from more than one line of print. You will need to make judgments and draw conclusions.

   Your text-implicit question _____

   Answer _____

3. Experience-based (critical/creative level): A question that requires the reader to read beyond the lines. Apply what you have learned to your world. Question what you have read.

   Your experience-based question _____

   Answer _____

B. Read the second section, "A Simple Illustration of the Differences," and ask one text-explicit question, one text-implicit question, and one experience-based question each on this section. Please answer all three questions. Do not ask a question that you cannot answer.

1. Your text-explicit question _____

   Answer _____

2. Your text-implicit question _____

   Answer _____

3. Your experience-based question _____

   Answer _____

C. Read the third section, "A Third View: Sociolinguistics," and ask one text-explicit question, one text-implicit question, and one experience-based question each on this section. Please answer all three questions. Do not ask a question that you cannot answer.

1. Your text-explicit question   _____
    Answer _____

2. Your text-implicit question   _____
    Answer _____

3. Your experience-based question _____
    Answer _____

CHAPTER 6: CULTURAL STUDIES

RECIPROCAL TEACHING

OVERVIEW

Complete all parts of the pre-reading lesson before doing this lesson. When you finish, go to the post-reading part of the reading plan. As the second step in this three-part reading plan, you will read this chapter by using an alternative plan, the Reciprocal Teaching reading plan, as explained below. The Active Questioning reading plan is in Chapter 6. In both plans you break up the chapter in sections and read and think about each as you read. The purpose of both plans is to keep you reading actively. There are no teacher models in this lesson. You may want to do this lesson as a whole-class assignment or in small groups instead of with partners.

GENERAL DIRECTIONS

The concept of Reciprocal Teaching outlined here is adapted from Palinscar and Brown, 1986.

A. Both partners read a section under a subheading at a time. Take turns summarizing the section in as few sentences as possible.
B. Take turns asking a high level question or two on each section (inferential or critical/creative).
C. Explain or clarify difficult parts to each other. Practice repeating main ideas and supporting details in your own words.
D. Read the next subheading and predict what the section will be about. Discuss (exchange) ideas.

ASSIGNMENT

A. Read the introduction and the first section, "The Special Problem of Food in Ecuador," and follow the directions below.
    1. Write a summary of the first major section.
    Your summary _____

    _____

    _____

2.   Write one question on this section. Try to write an inferential or a critical/creative question. If you can't, write a literal-level question.

Your question _____

Your answer _____

3.   Orally explain or clarify an important idea.

Your idea _____

4.   Predict what you will read in the second major section, "A *Faux pas* in the Cameroun."

Your prediction _____

B.   Read the second section, "A *Faux pas* in the Cameroun."
1.   Summarize this second major section.

Your summary _____

_____

_____

2.   Write one question on this section. Try to write an inferential or a critical/creative question. If you can't, write a literal-level question.

Your question _____

Your answer _____

3.   Orally explain or clarify an important idea in this section.

Your idea _____

4.   Predict what you will read in the third major section of the chapter, "Eating Problems in Burundi."

Your prediction _____

C.   Read the third section, "Eating Problems in Burundi."
1.   Summarize this third major section.

Your summary _____

_____

_____

2.   Write one question on this section. Try to write an inferential or a critical/creative question. If you can't, write a literal-level question.

Your question _____

Your answer _____

3.   Orally explain or clarify an important idea in this section.

Your idea _____

4.   Predict what you will read in the fourth major section of the chapter, "Problems in Traveling, Even Close to Home."

Your prediction _____

D.   Read the fourth section, "Problems in Traveling, Even Close to Home."
1.   Summarize this fourth major section.

Your summary _____
_____
_____

    2.   Write one question on this section. Try to write an inferential or a critical/creative question. If you can't, write a literal-level question.

Your question _____

Your answer _____

    3.   Orally explain or clarify an important idea in this section.

Your idea _____

CHAPTER 7: AMERICAN HISTORY

ACTIVE QUESTIONING

OVERVIEW

As the second step in this three-part reading plan, you will read this chapter by using an alternative plan, the Active Questioning reading plan, as explained below. The Reciprocal Teaching reading plan is in Chapter 7. In both plans you break up the chapter in sections and read and think about each as you read. The purpose of both plans is to keep you reading actively.

GENERAL DIRECTIONS

Complete all parts of the pre-reading lesson before doing this lesson. When you finish, go to the post-reading part of the reading plan. Review the General Directions for Active Questioning for Chapter 1, Appendix A, page 424, if needed.

    When using active questioning, write questions on the literal, inferential, and creative/critical levels. Model questions are given for the first section only.

ASSIGNMENT

    A.   Read introduction and section one, "Cosmopolitan Nature of Columbus and the Crew of His First Voyage," and ask one text-explicit question (literal), one text-implicit question (inferential), and one experience-based question (critical/creative) each on this section. Please answer all three questions. Do not ask a question that you cannot answer.

        1.   Text-explicit (literal level): A question that requires the reader to read the line. The answer will come from one line of print. Model text-explicit question: What important minority group outfitted the Santa Maria?

Your text-explicit question _____

Answer _____

2. Text-implicit (inferential level): A question that requires the reader to read between the lines. The answer will come from more than one line of print. You will need to make judgments and draw conclusions. Model text-implicit question: With what languages was Columbus familiar?

   Your text-implicit question _____

   Answer _____

3. Experience-based (critical/creative level): A question that requires the reader to read beyond the lines. Apply what you have learned to your world. Question what you have read. Model experience-based questions: Why is it important to know that the Basques, a Spanish minority group, made significant contributions to Columbus's first voyage, especially in light of the introduction of this chapter? Why is it still important to know about contributions to society by minority groups?

   Your experience-based question _____

   Answer _____

B. Read the second section, "Problems in Documenting Columbus's First Voyage," and ask one text-explicit question, one text-implicit question, and one experience-based question each on this section. Please answer all three questions. Do not ask a question that you cannot answer.

   1. Your text-explicit question _____

      Answer _____

   2. Your text-implicit question _____

      Answer _____

   3. Your experience-based question _____

      Answer _____

C. Read the third section, "Certain and Possible Pre-Columbian Voyages to the Americas," and ask one text-explicit question, one text-implicit question, and one experience-based question each on this section. Please answer all three questions. Do not ask a question that you cannot answer.

   1. Your text-explicit question _____

      Answer _____

   2. Your text-implicit question _____

      Answer _____

   3. Your experience-based question _____

      Answer _____

D. Read the fourth section, "The Effects of Columbus's Voyages," and ask one text-explicit question, one text-implicit question, and one experience-based question each on this section. Please answer all three questions. Do not ask a question that you cannot answer.

1. Your text-explicit question _____

    Answer _____

2. Your text-implicit question _____

    Answer _____

3. Your experience-based question _____

    Answer _____

CHAPTER 8: ANTHROPOLOGY AND SOCIOLOGY

RECIPROCAL TEACHING

OVERVIEW

Complete all parts of the pre-reading lesson before doing this lesson. When you finish, go to the post-reading part of the reading plan. As the second step in this three-part reading plan, you will read this chapter by using an alternative plan, the Reciprocal Teaching reading plan, as explained below. The Active Questioning reading plan is in Chapter 8. In both plans you break up the chapter in sections and read and think about each as you read. The purpose of both plans is to keep you reading actively. There are no teacher models in this lesson. You may want to do this lesson as a whole-class assignment or in small groups instead of with partners.

GENERAL DIRECTIONS

The concept of Reciprocal Teaching outlined here is adapted from Palinscar and Brown, 1986.

A. Both partners read a section under a subheading at a time. Take turns summarizing the section in as few sentences as possible.
B. Take turns asking a high level question or two on each section (inferential or critical/creative).
C. Explain or clarify difficult parts to each other. Practice repeating main ideas and supporting details in your own words.
D. Read the next subheading and predict what the section will be about. Discuss (exchange) ideas.

ASSIGNMENT

A. Read the introduction and the first section, "The Nature of Anthropological Research," and follow the directions below.
    1. Write a summary of the first major section.

Your summary _____

_____

_____

   2.   Write one question on this section. Try to write an inferential or a critical/creative question. If you can't, write a literal-level question.

Your question _____

Your answer _____

   3.   Orally explain or clarify an important idea.

Your idea _____

   4.   Predict what you will read in the second major section, "Cultural and Linguistic Relativism."

Your prediction _____

B.   Read the second section, "Cultural and Linguistic Relativism."

   1.   Summarize this second major section.

Your summary _____

_____

_____

   2.   Write one question on this section. Try to write an inferential or a critical/creative question. If you can't, write a literal-level question.

Your question _____

Your answer _____

   3.   Orally explain or clarify an important idea in this section.

Your idea _____

   4.   Predict what you will read in the third major section of the chapter, "The Nature of Sociological Research."

Your prediction _____

C.   Read the third major section of the chapter, "The Nature of Sociological Research."

   1.   Summarize this third major section.

Your summary _____

_____

_____

   2.   Write one question on this section. Try to write an inferential or a critical/creative question. If you can't, write a literal-level question.

Your question _____

Your answer _____

   3.   Orally explain or clarify an important idea in this section.

Your idea _____

CHAPTER 9: WEST AFRICAN LITERATURE

ACTIVE QUESTIONING

OVERVIEW

As the second step in this three-part reading plan, you will read this chapter by using an alternative plan, the Active Questioning reading plan, as explained below. The Reciprocal Teaching reading plan is in Chapter 9. In both plans you break up the chapter in sections and read and think about each as you read. The purpose of both plans is to keep you reading actively.

ASSIGNMENT

Model questions are provided for all three sections of the chapter. If you cannot write and answer your own questions, answer the models.

A. Read the introduction and section one, "The Initial Period of Nigerian–British Contact," and ask one text-explicit question (literal), one text-implicit question (inferential), and one experience-based question (critical/creative) each on this section. Please answer all three questions. Do not ask a question that you cannot answer.

1. Text-explicit (literal level): A question that requires the reader to read the line. The answer will come from one line of print. Model text-explicit question: What is the name of Chinua Achebe's first novel?

Your text-explicit question _____

Answer _____

2. Text-implicit (inferential level): A question that requires the reader to read between the lines. The answer will come from more than one line of print. You will need to make judgments and draw conclusions. Model text-implicit question: Give examples that support the idea that the relationship between the Ibo and the Europeans is complicated and seemingly hopeless.

Your text-implicit question _____

Answer _____

3. Experience-based (critical/creative level): A question that requires the reader to read beyond the lines. Apply what you have learned to your world. Question what you have read. Model experience-based questions: Has the United States ever dealt with polygyny? Would citizens be open to a polygynous society? How do Americans seek status in their culture? Would Nigerians condemn the American ways? With what taboos do you live in your culture?

Your experience-based question _____

Answer _____

B. Read the second section, "Novels Dealing with the More Recent Situation in Nigeria," and ask one text-explicit question, one text-implicit question, and one experience-based question each on this section. Please answer all three questions. Do not ask a question that you cannot answer.

   1. Model text-explicit question: Name three of Achebe's later writings.

Your text-explicit question _____

Answer _____

   2. Model text-implicit question: Trace Odili Samalu's maturity.

Your text-implicit question _____

Answer _____

   3. Model experience-based questions: Relate Obi Okonkwo's downfall to any public servant you know about or have read about in your state. How can a person's downfall be ennobling or how can the downfall be good for him/her? When corrupt politicians are ousted from power, Achebe's country doesn't appear to be better or worse off. Could this happen in your state or in the United States? What makes a difference in the welfare of the people of any country?

Your experience-based question _____

Answer _____

C. Read the third section, "The Style of Achebe's Fiction," and ask one text-explicit question, one text-implicit question, and one experience-based question each on this section. Please answer all three questions. Do not ask a question that you cannot answer.

   1. Model text-explicit question: Describe Achebe's writing style.

Your text-explicit question _____

Answer _____

   2. Model text-implicit question: List elements of the "African flavor" of Achebe's novels.

Your text-implicit question _____

Answer _____

   3. Model experience-based questions: The author states that Achebe is concerned about his people and their problems and presents them objectively "so that sympathy doesn't become sentimentality." What does this mean? How would a writer about your culture do that?

Your experience-based question _____

Answer _____

Chapter 10: Music

Active Questioning

Overview

As the second step in this three-part reading plan, you will read this chapter by using an alternative plan, the Active Questioning reading plan, as explained below. The Reciprocal Teaching reading plan is in Chapter 10. In both plans you break up the chapter in sections and read and think about each as you read. The purpose of both plans is to keep you reading actively.

Assignment

This lesson contains no teacher models.

A. Read section one, "Defining the Blues," and ask one text-explicit question (literal), one text-implicit question (inferential), and one experience-based question (critical/creative) each on this section. Please answer all three questions. Do not ask a question that you cannot answer.

    1. Text-explicit (literal level): A question that requires the reader to read the line. The answer will come from one line of print.

    Your text-explicit question _____

    Answer _____

    2. Text-implicit (inferential level): A question that requires the reader to read between the lines. The answer will come from more than one line of print. You will need to make judgments and draw conclusions.

    Your text-implicit question _____

    Answer _____

    3. Experience-based (critical/creative level): A question that requires the reader to read beyond the lines. Apply what you have learned to your world. Question what you have read.

    Your experience-based question _____

    Answer _____

B. Read the second section, "Some Historical Background of the Blues," and ask one text-explicit question, one text-implicit question, and one experience-based question each on this section. Please answer all three questions. Do not ask a question that you cannot answer.

    1. Your text-explicit question _____

    Answer _____

    2. Your text-implicit question _____

    Answer _____

3. Your experience-based question _____

Answer _____

C. Read the third section, "More Modern Manifestations of the Blues Tradition," and ask one text-explicit question, one text-implicit question, and one experience-based question each on this section. Please answer all three questions. Do not ask a question that you cannot answer.

1. Your text-explicit question _____

Answer _____

2. Your text-implicit question _____

Answer _____

3. Your experience-based question _____

Answer _____

Chapter 11: American English

Reciprocal Teaching

Overview

Complete all parts of the pre-reading lesson before doing this lesson. When you finish, go to the post-reading part of the reading plan. As the second step in this three-part reading plan, you will read this chapter by using an alternative plan, the Reciprocal Teaching reading plan as explained below. The Active Questioning reading plan is in Chapter 11. In both plans you break up the chapter in sections and read and think about each as you read. The purpose of both plans is to keep you reading actively. When you finish this part, go to part three, post-reading. There are no teacher models in this lesson. You may want to do this lesson as a whole-class assignment or in small groups instead of with partners.

Assignment

A. Read the introduction and the first section, "The Traditional View," and follow the directions below.

1. Write a summary of the first major section.

Your summary _____

_____

_____

2. Write one question on this section. Try to write an inferential or a critical/creative question. If you can't, write a literal-level question.

Your question _____

Your answer _____

   3.   Orally explain or clarify an important idea.

Your idea   _____

   4.   Predict what you will read in the second major section, "Exploration and Early Settlement."

Your prediction _____

B. Read "Exploration and Early Settlement."

   1.   Summarize this second major section.

Your summary _____

_____

_____

   2.   Write one question on this section. Try to write an inferential or a critical/creative question. If you can't, write a literal-level question.

Your question   _____

Your answer _____

   3.   Orally explain or clarify an important idea in this section.

Your idea   _____

   4.   Predict what you will read in the third major section of the chapter, "Language Contact Factors."

Your prediction _____

C. Read "Language Contact Factors."

   1.   Summarize this third major section.

Your summary _____

_____

_____

   2.   Write one question on this section. Try to write an inferential or a critical/creative question. If you can't, write a literal-level question.

Your question   _____

Your answer _____

   3.   Orally explain or clarify an important idea in this section.

Your idea   _____

   4.   Predict what you will read in the fourth major section of the chapter, "Development of Regional Dialects."

Your prediction _____

D. Read "Development of Regional Dialects."

   1.   Summarize this fourth major section.

Your summary _____

_____

_____

   2.   Write one question on this section. Try to write an inferential or a critical/creative question. If you can't, write a literal-level question.

Your question   _____

Your answer   _____

     3.   Orally explain or clarify an important idea in this section.

Your idea   _____

     4.   Predict what you will read in the fifth major section of the chapter, "Standardization and Retention of Differences."

Your prediction _____

E.   Read "Standardization and Retention of Differences."

     1.   Summarize this fifth major section.

Your summary   _____

_____

_____

     2.   Write one question on this section. Try to write an inferential or a critical/creative question. If you can't, write a literal-level question.

Your question   _____

Your answer   _____

     3.   Orally explain or clarify an important idea in this section.

Your idea   _____

CHAPTER 12: RELIGIOUS STUDIES

RECIPROCAL TEACHING

OVERVIEW

Complete all parts of the pre-reading lesson before doing this lesson. When you finish, go to the post-reading part of the reading plan. As the second step in this three-part reading plan, you will read this chapter by using an alternative plan, the Reciprocal Teaching reading plan as explained below. The Active Questioning reading plan is in Chapter 12. In both plans you break up the chapter in sections and read and think about each as you read. The purpose of both plans is to keep you reading actively. There are no teacher models in this lesson. You may want to do this lesson as a whole-class assignment or in small groups instead of with partners.

ASSIGNMENT

A.   Read "Languages in the New Testament Period," and follow the directions below.

     1.   Write a summary of this first major section.

Your summary _____

_____

_____

2. Write one question on this section. Try to write an inferential or a critical/creative question. If you can't, write a literal-level question.

Your question _____

Your answer _____

3. Orally explain or clarify an important idea.

Your idea _____

4. Predict what you will read in the second major section, "Types of Language Function."

Your prediction _____

B. Read " Types of Language Function."
    1. Summarize this second major section.

Your summary _____

_____

_____

2. Write one question on this section. Try to write an inferential or a critical/creative question. If you can't, write a literal-level question.

Your question _____

Your answer _____

3. Orally explain or clarify an important idea in this section.

Your idea _____

4. Predict what you will read in the third major section of the chapter, "The Inscription on the Cross and the Languages of Israel."

Your prediction _____

C. Read "The Inscription on the Cross and the Languages of Israel."
    1. Summarize this third major section.

Your summary _____

_____

_____

2. Write one question on this section. Try to write an inferential or a critical/creative question. If you can't, write a literal-level question.

Your question _____

Your answer _____

3. Orally explain or clarify an important idea in this section.

Your idea _____

Extended Reading Activities Forms

The following forms are for work introduced in the textbook chapters. These forms are provided for your convenience should you wish to continue doing the activities. If you plan to work throughout the course on any of the activities, you should photocopy multiple copies of the forms you plan to use. They provide a fast and easy way to record the work you are doing and give you a record of your reading efforts. Your instructor may wish to assign some of these activities on a regular basis and may require your turning in the appropriate forms on a schedule.

Weekly Reading Report

Content Area Report

Weekly Vocabulary Journal

Weekly Magazines/Journals/Newspapers Reading Report

Reading in Your Major Journal Report

Fiction Report

Weekly Reading Report

Your Name _____

Directions: The purpose of this reading report is to make you aware of how much you are reading. Please answer as accurately as possible. I strongly suggest that you record everything you read daily.

A. List each course you are currently taking under the appropriate subject and what you have read for those courses during this week.

Subjects	Chapters	Topics
English		
Math		
Social sciences		
Business/computers		
Natural sciences		
Health sciences		
Technical courses		
Other		

B. List all pleasure reading you have done this week (e.g., magazines, journals, books, newspapers). Also list the topics you read about.

_____

_____

_____

_____

_____

C. List one interesting topic you read about this week. Briefly, tell why it interested you. Be specific.

_____

_____

_____

_____

_____

D. Reflection. How has your reading improved? Are you spending more time reading? Thinking deeper? Reading more high-level content?

Content Area Report

Your Name _____

  A. Overview

      1. Choose a textbook for a subject you are now taking or for your major.

         a. Title: _____

         b. Author: _____

      2. Summarize the message of the preface in your own words:

_____

_____

      3. List the first ten chapter titles in the Table of Contents below:

_____

_____

_____

_____

_____

_____

_____

_____

_____

_____

      4. What pages are the index on? _____

      5. Does it have a glossary? _____

      6. Are there chapter

         a. Introductions? _____

         b. Stated objectives? _____

         c. Summaries? _____

         d. Review questions? _____

  B. Choose a chapter from the textbook.

      1. List the major headings:

_____

_____

_____

      2. Give the subheadings for one major heading:

_____

_____

  C. Choose a paragraph and copy it on a separate sheet of paper. You may photocopy it if you wish. Write the following below the paragraph:

      1. Main idea

      2. Supporting details for the main idea

  D. Outline or draw a visual map of the chapter on the back of this paper. (See directions in Extended Reading Activities, letter F, page 63.)

Weekly Vocabulary Journal

Your Name _____

Directions: The purpose of this vocabulary journal is to help you deepen your knowledge of words you vaguely know. The directions are as follows: (1) Skim your own pleasure and school (academic) reading to find words you know vaguely but feel you cannot define adequately. (2) Write the words in the context in which they were found. In other words, write at least the phrase or sentence in which the word was used. Give the source for the word. (3) Write what you think the word means as it is used. (4) Check your guess against a dictionary definition and write the dictionary definition down. If you cannot find the word in your dictionary, check your spelling, look for the root word, or use a larger dictionary.

A. Word: _____
   1. Source: _____
   2. Sentence in which word is used: _____
   3. What word means in sentence: _____
   4. Dictionary definition:_____

B. Word: _____
   1. Source: _____
   2. Sentence in which word is used: _____
   3. What word means in sentence: _____
   4. Dictionary definition:_____

C. Word: _____
   1. Source: _____
   2. Sentence in which word is used: _____
   3. What word means in sentence: _____
   4. Dictionary definition:_____

D. Word: _____
   1. Source: _____
   2. Sentence in which word is used: _____
   3. What word means in sentence: _____
   4. Dictionary definition:_____

E. Word: _____
   1. Source: _____
   2. Sentence in which word is used: _____
   3. What word means in sentence: _____
   4. Dictionary definition:_____

Weekly Magazines/Journals/Newspapers Reading Report

Your Name _____

Directions: Read thirty minutes a day for this class. You may spend one hour a week reading from the magazines, journals, and newspapers listed in the Extended Reading Activities. Most of them can be found in your campus library, hometown public library, or on-line.

A. List the names of magazines, journals and/newspapers you have read:

_____

_____

_____

_____

_____

B. List the titles of articles that you have read:

_____

_____

_____

_____

_____

C. Summarize the most interesting article you read this week:

_____

_____

_____

_____

D. Give your opinion about the article you summarized:

_____

_____

_____

_____

E. List *two* new vocabulary words you found in the articles you read and write their dictionary definitions:

1. Word _____

    Definition _____

2. Word _____

    Definition _____

Reading in Your Major Journal Report

Your Name _____

Your Major _____

Directions: Choose journals in your major and read as many articles as you have time. Report on one of them below by providing the information indicated. Some journals in your major may be too difficult for you at this time. You may need advanced knowledge in the field to understand the articles. Browsing through them can still be fun just to see what you will be able to talk about in a year or two. If everything you encounter is too boring to read, you may want to consider another major.

    A. Bibliographical information:
        1. Article title _____
        2. Author(s) _____
        3. Journal's name _____
        4. Date of journal _____
        5. Page numbers of article _____
    B. Topic (subject) of the article:

        _____
        _____

    C. I learned the following about this topic (state main ideas):

        _____
        _____

    D. The information above related to what I already knew about the topic in the following way:

        _____
        _____

    E. I would rate my level of interest in this topic as
        high___   average___   low___
        because:

        _____
        _____

    F. This topic is important to my major in the following way:

        _____
        _____

    G. I have changed my ideas about my major in the following ways as a result of reading this article:

        _____
        _____

Fiction Report

Your Name _____

A. Title of Novel _____

   Author _____

B. Check the appropriate major conflict or theme:

___ Person vs. Person (e.g., two people battling for the same position)

___ Person vs. Nature (e.g., a person surviving in a forest)

___ Person vs. God (e.g., a person fighting against fate or Divine Will)

___ Person vs. Himself/Herself (e.g., a person's greatest enemy is within.)

C. Plot (Choose C1 or C2 below).

   1. What happened in the work?

      a. What was the normal situation at the beginning?

      b. How was the status quo upset? What changed? Did someone move? Lose his/her job? Was someone killed or attacked? Did someone fall in or out of love? Get divorced? Did someone begin an adventure?

      c. What adventures or experiences occurred?

      d. How did the work end?

         _____

         _____

   2. Plot the action. Let the content dictate the form. (See examples a–g.)

      a. Boy meets Girl.

      b. Boy falls in love with Girl.

      c. Boy and Girl are engaged.

      d. Boy goes out with Girl's best friend.

      e. Girl finds out and breaks engagement.

      f. Boy regrets his decision. He performs unselfish act to redeem himself, such as saving a child from a fire at great personal risk.

      g. Boy and Girl are reconciled and marry.

         _____

         _____

D. Characters.

   1. List the name(s) of the major character(s).

      _____

      _____

   2. Do these characters change by the end of the story? Yes___   No___ How do they change? How do you know? What do they do? How does the author describe their change?

      _____

      _____

3. Are any of these characters types of people you recognize in any work of fiction or movie?   Yes___   No___
   What do you recognize about them? Are they courageous like John Wayne, the underdog like Woody Allen, tough and ruthless like Clint Eastwood, alienated like Holden Caulfield, dependent on the physical like Rambo?

   _____

   _____

E. Setting.
   1. Physical Setting. The main place the work takes place is (circle the appropriate response):
      a. city
      b. country
      c. fantasy world
      d. science fiction world
      e. other _____

   2. Psychological Setting: The place is not really identified and would be unimportant to the story.   Yes___   No___

   3. Time Setting. Circle the appropriate response:
      a. Present (modern, post-twentieth century) How is it identified?_____
      b. Past. What century?   _____
         How is it identified?   _____
      c. Future. How is it identified? _____

F. Mood. Circle the response that reflects the predominant mood of the work:
   1. dark and gloomy
   2. fearful and terrifying
   3. light-hearted and comical
   4. serious
   5. everyday atmosphere
   6. other _____

G. Narrator and Point of View.
   1. Who is telling the story? Circle the appropriate response:
      a. a person in the story
      b. a person outside of the story
   2. What is the point of view? Circle the appropriate response:
      a. First person narrator (Uses "I")
      b. Third person narrator (Uses "They")

H. Style. How would you describe the author's style? Circle the appropriate response:
   1. lots of description
   2. long sentences

3. digressions
4. direct, straightforward
5. other _____

I. In twenty-five words or less, describe the most memorable scene in the story:

_____

_____

_____

_____

_____

J. Reflection.
1. Look at the title of this work. Look back at your identification of the theme of the story on the first page of this report. Now answer these questions:
    a. What did you think the story would be about, based on the title?

    _____

    b. What was different from what you expected?

    _____

    c. How does the story fit the theme you chose?

    _____

    d. What experiences—real or vicarious—have you had that you can relate to this theme?

    _____

2. What did you already know about the setting? Have you been there? Have you seen pictures? Do you know someone who lived or visited there?

    _____

    _____

3. How was the setting different from anything you knew about? How did the author help you to visualize it? At what point did you accept it as familiar?

    _____

    _____

4. What "real" people or characters that you have seen in movies or on television behave very much like the characters in the story? How are they alike? What do they do? Are they also different in a significant way?

    _____

    _____

5. Review your answers on setting, style, mood, and characters. Did recognition of the theme, setting, style, mood, and/or characters help you understand what you read? Yes____   No____
    Did such recognition help keep you interested in what you read? Yes____   No____

K. Response.
    1. If you were bored by the work, identify the reason(s):
        a. Reading too difficult
            (1) couldn't figure out what was happening
            (2) didn't make sense
            (3) too many difficult words
            (4) too many complicated sentences
            (5) couldn't tell when something was happening; time jumped around
            (6) other (please identify) _____
        b. Genre, theme, plot, setting, characters were uninteresting
            (1) ideas not easy to relate to my values, life style, culture
            (2) didn't like what happened
            (3) didn't like the characters
            (4) didn't like this type of story
            (5) didn't like this type of setting
            (6) didn't like the writing style
            (7) took too long to get to the point
            (8) other (please identify) _____
    2. If you enjoyed the selection, identify reason(s):
        a. easy to read
        b. could personally relate to the theme and/or character
        c. discovered something new
            (1) new way of "seeing" situations/new solutions
            (2) interesting characters
            (3) interesting style
            (4) interesting "different world"
            (5) other (please identify) _____

L. Rating.
    1. On a scale of 1–10, with 10 as the highest, how would you rate this work? ____
    2. Review your answers to the above questions. Based on your responses, give one specific reason for your rating:

    _____

    _____

    _____

Academic Study Skills
Practice Lessons for Part II

Overview

The following optional exercises are written to give you further guidance in learning to use and practice the various study skills presented in Part II of the textbook. You have been introduced to each in the chapter lessons.

You were introduced to using SQ4R and a modified study plan in Chapters 5 and 6. If you wish to continue to use these study plans, study plan exercises for Chapters 7 through 12 are listed in Part I of this appendix. You were introduced to memory improvement in Chapter 7; the memory exercises for Chapters 8 through 12 are listed in Part II of this appendix. You were introduced to annotation in Chapter 8; the annotation exercises for Chapters 9 through 12 are listed in Part III of this appendix. You were introduced to underlining/highlighting in Chapter 9; the underlining/highlighting exercises for Chapters 10 through 12 are listed in Part IV of this appendix. You were introduced to creating visuals in Chapter 10; the visual exercises for Chapters 11 and 12 are listed in Part V of this appendix.

By the time you reached Chapter 13 you should have had enough guidance and practice to decide for yourself which study skills are most helpful to you. Chapter 13 contains guided practice for all the study skills learned in Part II of the textbook. Choosing the most helpful one(s) is your independent level of learning.

PART I: SQ4R AND MODIFIED SQ4R STUDY PLANS

CHAPTER 7

MODIFIED SQ4R STUDY PLAN

A. Pre-Reading—Survey: You have already surveyed this lesson. What is still difficult?

1. _____
2. _____
3. _____

B. Reading—Questioning/Reading/Recording: Reread the chapter one section at a time and list the most important idea in each below:
1. The most important ideas:
   a. "Cosmopolitan Nature of Columbus and the Crew of His First Voyage"
   b. "Problems in Documenting Columbus's First Voyage"
   c. "Certain and Possible Pre-Columbian Voyages to the Americas"
   d. "The Effects of Columbus's Voyages"
2. Significant support for most important ideas: How are these ideas supported? In your own words briefly state the support below:
   a. "Cosmopolitan Nature of Columbus and the Crew of His First Voyage"
   b. "Problems in Documenting Columbus's First Voyage"
   c. "Certain and Possible Pre-Columbian Voyages to the Americas"
   d. "The Effects of Columbus's Voyages"

C.   Post-Reading—Recite/Review

1. Review the work you have already completed for this chapter, including the questions you have written and the important ideas from the previous section. Below write questions and answers that better reflect the important information in each section.

2. Recite the information you have learned with a partner. Use the summary and questions at the end of the chapter, your questions and answers, and tell each other the significance of the information you are discussing.

3. Ask yourself what you know and what you do not know. Monitor your own learning much like you have done on the vocabulary exercises for the chapter lesson. Reflect on what you have learned, especially on how you connected information to your own life. Add new thoughts to the post-reading section of the Reciprocal or Active Questioning lesson you completed.

    a. "Cosmopolitan Nature of Columbus ..."

    Question: _____

    Answer: _____

    b. "Problems in Documenting Columbus's First Voyage"

    Question: _____

    Answer: _____

    c. "Certain and Possible Pre-Columbian Voyages to the Americas"

    Question: _____

    Answer: _____

    d. "The Effects of Columbus's Voyages"

    Question: _____

    Answer: _____

CHAPTER 8

MODIFIED SQ4R STUDY PLAN

A. Pre-Reading—Survey: You have already surveyed this chapter by skimming the Prior Knowledge section, by tapping into your prior knowledge and experience, by predicting what you will read, and by overviewing the chapter. From your overview, briefly write below in your own words what will be difficult:

1. _____

2. _____

3. _____

B. Reading—Questioning/Reading/Recording: You have already read this chapter by the Reciprocal Teaching lesson or by the Active Questioning lesson. In both lessons you have read the chapter section by section. In both lessons you asked questions about the material and answered them. Reread the chapter one section at a time and list the most important idea in each:

1. The most important ideas:
    a. "The Nature of Anthropological Research"
    b. "Cultural and Linguistic Relativism"
    c. "The Nature of Sociological Research"
2. Significant support for most important ideas: What supports these ideas in each section? Your summaries (Reciprocal Teaching lesson) and your questions should help you.
    a. "The Nature of Anthropological Research"
    b. "Cultural and Linguistic Relativism"
    c. "The Nature of Sociological Research"

C. Post-Reading—Recite/Review

1. Review the work you have already completed for this chapter, including the questions you have written and the important ideas from the previous section. Below write questions and answers that better reflect the important information in each section.
2. With a partner recite the information you have learned. Use the summary and questions at the end of the chapter, your questions and answers, and the work you have done on this academic study skills lesson for guidance on the significance of the information you are discussing.
3. Ask yourself what you know and what you do not know. Monitor your own learning much like you have done on the vocabulary exercises for the chapters. Reflect on what you have learned, especially on how you connected information in the chapter to your life. Add new thoughts to the post-reading section of the Reciprocal Teaching or Active Questioning lesson you completed.
    a. "The Nature of Anthropological Research"

    Question: _____
    Answer: _____
    b. "Cultural and Linguistic Relativism"

    Question: _____
    Answer: _____
    c. "The Nature of Sociological Research"

    Question: _____
    Answer: _____

CHAPTER 9

MODIFIED SQ4R STUDY PLAN

A. Pre-Reading—Survey: You have already surveyed this chapter by tapping into your prior knowledge and experience, by predicting what you will read, and by overviewing the chapter. From your overview, briefly write in your own words what will be difficult:

1. _____

2. _____

3. _____

B. Reading—Questioning/Reading/Recording: You have already read this chapter by the Reciprocal Teaching lesson or by the Active Questioning lesson. In both lessons you have read the chapter section by section. In both lessons you asked questions about the material and answered them. Reread the chapter one section at a time and list the most important idea in each below:

1. The most important ideas.
   a. "The Initial Period of Nigerian–British Contact"
   b. "Novels Dealing with the More Recent Situation in Nigeria"
   c. "The Style of Achebe's Fiction"

2. Significant support for most important ideas: What supports these ideas in each section? Your summaries (Reciprocal Teaching lesson) and your questions should help you.
   a. "The Initial Period of Nigerian–British Contact"
   b. "Novels Dealing with the More Recent Situation in Nigeria"
   c. "The Style of Achebe's Fiction"

C. Post-Reading—Recite/Review

1. Review the work you have already completed for this chapter, including the questions you have written and the important ideas from the previous section. Below write questions and answers that better reflect the important information in each section.

2. With a partner recite the information you have learned. Use the summary and questions at the end of the chapter, your questions and answers, and the work you have done on this academic skills lesson for guidance on the significance of the information you are discussing.

3. Ask yourself what you know and what you do not know. Monitor your own learning much like you have done on the vocabulary exercises for the chapters. Reflect on what you have learned, especially on how you connected information in the chapter to your life. Add new thoughts to the post-reading section of the Reciprocal Teaching or Active Questioning lesson you completed.

   a. "The Initial Period of Nigerian–British Contact"

   Question: _____

   Answer: _____

   b. "Novels Dealing with the More Recent Situation in Nigeria"

   Question: _____

   Answer: _____

   c. "The Style of Achebe's Fiction"

   Question: _____

   Answer: _____

CHAPTER 10

MODIFIED SQ4R STUDY PLAN

A. Pre-Reading—Survey: You have already surveyed this chapter by tapping into your prior knowledge and experience, by predicting what you will read, and by overviewing the chapter. From your overview, briefly write below in your own words what will be difficult:

1. _____

2. _____

3. _____

B. Reading—Questioning/Reading/Recording: You have already read this chapter by the Reciprocal Teaching lesson or by the Active Questioning lesson. In both lessons you have read the chapter section by section. In both lessons you asked questions about the material and answered them. Reread the chapter one section at a time and list the most important idea in each below:

1. The most important ideas.
   a. "Defining the Blues"
   b. "Some Historical Background of the Blues"
   c. "Some Modern Manifestations of the Blues Tradition"

2. Significant support for most important ideas: What supports these ideas in each section? Your summaries (Reciprocal Teaching lesson) and your questions should help you.
   a. "Defining the Blues"
   b. "Some Historical Background of the Blues"
   c. "Some Modern Manifestations of the Blues Tradition"

C. Post-Reading—Recite/Review

1. Review the work you have already completed for this chapter, including the questions you have written and the important ideas from the previous section. Below write questions and answers that better reflect the important information in each section.

2. With a partner recite the information you have learned. Use the summary and questions at the end of the chapter, your questions and answers, and the work you have done on this academic skills lesson for guidance on the significance of the information you are discussing.

3. Ask yourself what you know and what you do not know. Monitor your own learning much like you have done on the vocabulary exercises for the chapters. Reflect on what you have learned, especially on how you connected information in the chapter to your life. Add new thoughts to the post-reading section of the Reciprocal Teaching or Active Questioning lesson you completed.
   a. "Defining the Blues"

   Question: _____

   Answer: _____

b. "Some Historical Background of the Blues"

Question: _____

Answer: _____

c. "Some Modern Manifestations of the Blues Tradition"

Question: _____

Answer: _____

CHAPTER 11

SQ4R STUDY PLAN

A. Survey (or overview) by reading the summary, questions at the end of the chapter, chapter title, and titles of main headings.

B. Question by turning each major heading listed below into a question:

1. The Traditional View

Question _____

2. Exploration and Early Settlement

Question _____

3. Language Contact Factors

Question _____

4. Development of Regional Dialects

Question _____

5. Standardization and Retention of Differences

Question _____

C. Read the chapter section by section as listed by headings above.

D. Record information by highlighting the most important ideas and then recording key words that show what you highlighted below for each section:

1. The Traditional View

2. Exploration and Early Settlement

3. Language Contact Factors

4. Development of Regional Dialects

5. Standardization and Retention of Differences

E. With a partner recite information for each section after you finish reading and recording for that section and before going on.

F. Review the chapter by answering the questions you wrote in "B" above. Also review the work you did on the Reciprocal Teaching or Active Questioning lesson for this chapter.

1. The Traditional View

Answer _____

2. Exploration and Early Settlement

Answer _____

3. Language Contact Factors

Answer _____

    4. Development of Regional Dialects

Answer   _____

    5. Standardization and Retention of Differences

Answer   _____

CHAPTER 12

SQ4R STUDY PLAN

  A. Survey (or overview) by reading the summary, questions at the end of the chapter, chapter title, and titles of main headings.

  B. Question by turning each major heading listed below into a question:

    1. Languages in the New Testament Period

Question _____

    2. Types of Language Function

Question _____

    3. The Inscription on the Cross and the Languages of Israel

Question _____

  C. Read the chapter section by section as listed by headings above.

  D. Record information by making visual maps (on a separate sheet of paper) for each section.

  E. With a partner recite information for each section after you finish reading and recording for that section and before going on.

  F. Review the chapter by answering the questions you wrote above. Also review the work you did on the lesson for this chapter.

    1. Languages in the New Testament Period

Answer   _____

    2. Types of Language Function

Answer   _____

    3. The Inscription on the Cross and the Languages of Israel

Answer   _____

PART II: EXERCISES ON MEMORY

CHAPTER 8

MEMORY

In Chapter 7 of this textbook, you worked on memory and placing material in your long-term memory. Review your work on that lesson.

  A. Select one important idea that you want to remember from each section of the chapter. Write each idea in your own words:

1. The Nature of Anthropological Research
   Idea _____
2. Cultural and Linguistic Relativism
   Idea _____
3. The Nature of Sociological Research
   Idea _____

B. Ask yourself why it is important to remember these ideas. If you have no clue, then change the information. Focus on the purpose of the chapter, a comparison/contrast of the ways anthropologists and sociologists study society and culture.
   Why I will remember the three pieces of material I have listed:

   _____

   _____

C. What are the connections among the ideas you have chosen? Are the ideas building up to a point? Do they support each other?
   How the three pieces of material I have chosen to remember are connected:

   _____

   _____

D. Self check at this point.
   1. Do you understand the most important ideas you have chosen? Can you talk out loud about them in your own words? Could you write about them?
   2. What is the significance of the ideas?
   3. What do you really know and what is it that you thought you knew but do not at this point?

E. Identify your own prior knowledge and experience about the ideas you have chosen as important. What do you already know that helps you understand the new material? For example, for my prior knowledge I have taken sociology courses but not anthropology as an undergraduate. My prior experience does include having an anthropologist as a personal friend and watching television documentaries about various cultures.
   My prior knowledge:

   _____

   _____

   Conflicts between my prior knowledge and what I read:

   _____

   _____

F. Connect your prior knowledge with the new information to create a new file of information that provides support for the most important idea in this chapter, that of the similarities and differences in ways of studying society and culture by anthropologists and sociologists. Store this information in your long-term memory. The more you use this file the better you will remember the information in it. For example, the next time you see a television documentary about a different culture, perhaps one of the Amazon Basin tribes, note whether or not an anthropologist is part of the research team. What about a sociologist? Are the researchers speaking the language of the native people or dependent on interpreters? How long has the team been with the native people? Is the project extended over several visits? What are the researchers investigating? Do the researchers use untrained observers or informants? In judging by the comments made by the narrator of the documentary, would you guess the narrator to be a cultural relativist or a deficit theory proponent? On what do you base your opinion? What is the sociologist using to gather information? Is the research team providing objective information about the culture being studied? These are points of interest that may come for you from reading this chapter.

I will connect my prior knowledge and the new information I read and then store it in my long-term memory by doing the following things:

———————————————————————

———————————————————————

Think of several categories for storage so that you can retrieve the information from more than one place. What can you add to this list? *anthropology, sociology, society, culture, research methods, untrained observers, fiction, history of literature, speaking languages, living in another culture, questionnaires, statistical information, visiting other cultures*

I will use the following categories to store the file:

———————————————————————

———————————————————————

G. What rewards will you receive for having a new file of information? The most important reward for me would be having new ways to see things. The questions I can now ask myself as I view a documentary as stated in "F" above give me a depth of observation that I have not had before. I have also never compared/contrasted the two fields of study before. Just having a basis for such a project is a reward. As an English teacher, I also find it rewarding to see a different use for literature, of seeing it used for verification for cultural observations.

My rewards for learning and remembering this new information and connecting it with what I already knew will be:

———————————————————————

———————————————————————

Chapter 9

Memory

In Chapter 7 of this textbook, you worked on memory and placing material in your long-term memory. You also had an opportunity to work on memory in the eighth chapter. Review your work on either lesson.

A. Select one important idea that you want to remember from each section of the chapter. Write each idea in your own words:

    1. The Initial Period of Nigerian–British Contact

Idea _____

    2. Novels Dealing with the More Recent Situation in Nigeria

Idea _____

    3. The Style of Achebe's Fiction

Idea _____

B. Ask yourself why it is important to remember these ideas. If you have no clue, then change the information. Focus on the purpose of the chapter, how Achebe's novels reflect a West African–European culture clash.

Why I will remember the three pieces of material I have listed:

_____

_____

C. What are the connections among the ideas? What do they lead to? Are the ideas building up to a point? Do they support each other?

How the three pieces of material I have chosen to remember are connected:

_____

_____

D. Self check at this point.

    1. Do you understand the most important ideas you have chosen? Can you talk out loud about them in your own words? Could you write about them?

    2. What is the significance of the ideas?

    3. What do you really know and what is it that you thought you knew but do not at this point?

E. Identify your own prior knowledge and experience about the ideas you have chosen as important. What do you already know that helps you understand the new material? For example, for my prior knowledge I have read many of the novels discussed in the chapter and I have a friend who has traveled and written about West Africa. I enjoy television documentaries about Africa and I have seen Achebe interviewed on television.

My prior knowledge:

_____

_____

Conflicts between my prior knowledge and what I read:

_____

_____

F. Connect your prior knowledge with the new information to create a new file that provides support for the most important idea in this chapter, the reflection of the culture clash of West Africans and Europeans in Achebe's novels. Store this information in your long-term memory. The more you use this file the better you will remember the information in it. For example, the next time you see a documentary on television on Africa or a movie about African people, you may remember to look for culture clash as an important part of the film. Are there conflicts between groups of people? What causes the conflicts? Different ways of doing things? Value systems? Do the people in the documentary or film misunderstand each other because they do not know each other's history and traditions? Are the people and situations complex? Do the good guys have faults and the bad guys have good character traits? Is any of the history shown in the documentary or movie similar to the history in Achebe's novels?

I will connect my prior knowledge and the new information I read and then store it in my long-term memory by doing the following things:

_____

_____

Think of several categories for storage so that you can retrieve the information from more than one place. What can you add to this list? *Chinua Achebe, West Africa, African history, European dominance of various African countries, types of characters, themes in novels, important literary awards*

I will use the following categories to store the file:

_____

_____

G. What rewards will you receive for having a new file of information? Having new information about a favorite author and something new to think about would be the most important rewards for me. When I reread the novels, I will have a better background for understanding. I usually read for plot (what happens) and to meet interesting characters, but now I can read the novels from a historical background, one that shows clashes between West Africans and Europeans, and one that shows problems within the tribes, among the people themselves.

My rewards for learning and remembering this new information and connecting it with what I already knew will be:

_____

_____

CHAPTER 10

MEMORY

In Chapter 7 of this textbook, you worked on memory and placing material in your long-term memory. Review your work on that lesson.

A. Select one important idea that you want to remember from each section of the chapter. Write each idea in your own words below:
1. "Defining the Blues"
Idea _____
2. "Some Historical Background of the Blues"
Idea _____

        3.   "Some Modern Manifestations of the Blues Tradition"
        Idea _____

    B.   Ask yourself why it is important to remember these ideas. If you have no clue, then change the information. Focus on the purpose of the chapter, the definition, history, and influence of the blues.

    C.   What are the connections among the ideas? What do they lead to? Are the ideas building up to a point? Do they support each other?

    D.   Self-check at this point. Do you understand the most important ideas you have chosen? Can you talk out loud about them in your own words? Could you write about them? What is the significance of the ideas? What do you really know and what is it that you thought you knew but do not at this point?

    E.   Identify your own prior knowledge and experience about the ideas you have chosen as important. What do you already know that helps you understand the new material? For example, for my prior knowledge I listen to old blues recordings and discuss the music with friends. I am familiar with the history of African Americans.

    F.   Connect your prior knowledge with the new information to create a new file of information that provides support for the most important idea in this chapter, the definition, history and influence of the blues. Store this information in your long-term memory. The new information that I will add has more to do with the influence of the blues on modern types of music and on the definition of the blue note. I now have a file that has information about blue notes that I can connect to the sounds I can play on a finger piano in my home, names of blues singers and musicians that I have heard play in performance or on recordings, a history of the blues, and the influence of the blues on jazz and torch songs. I also have more information on differences in types of music. Think of several categories for storage so that you can retrieve the information from more than one place. What can you add to this list? *blues, blue notes, blues and African slaves, house and field hands on plantations, musicians, singers, jazz, torch songs*

    G.   What rewards will you receive for having a new file of information? The new file provides me with more technical information on what makes the blues the blues. When I listen to the recordings of some of my favorite musicians like Jelly Roll Morton, my reward will be that I will listen more intelligently. I also have a base of information on blue notes to which I can add.

Chapter 11

Memory

In Chapter 7 of this textbook, you worked on memory and placing material in your long-term memory. Review your work on that lesson.

    A.   Select one important idea from each section of the chapter. Write each idea in your own words:

1. The Traditional View
    Idea _____

2. Exploration and Early Settlement
    Idea _____

3. Language Contact Factors
    Idea _____

4. Development of Regional Dialects
    Idea _____

5. Standardization and Retention of Differences
    Idea _____

B. Ask yourself why it is important to remember these ideas. If you have no clue, then change the information. Focus on the purpose of the chapter, language contact has helped American English to have a rich history.

C. What are the connections among the five ideas? What do they lead to? Are the ideas building up to a point? Do they support each other?

D. Self-check at this point. Do you understand the main ideas you have chosen? Can you talk about them in your own words? Could you write about them? What is the significance of the ideas? What do you know and what did you think you knew but do not know at this point?

E. Identify your own prior knowledge and experience about the ideas you have chosen as important. What do you already know that helps you understand the new material? I have taken American history courses throughout my life and I have read American history as background for the literature courses I have taken and taught. I have taken linguistics courses that involved pidgin languages. What prior knowledge or experience conflicts with your new knowledge? For example, from Chapter 5 in this textbook, on the study of English, I had some background knowledge about formal and informal English. I was not sure how this fit in with the section in this chapter on Network Standard American.

F. Connect your prior knowledge with the new information to create a new file of information that provides support for American English having a rich history. Store this information in your long-term memory. The more you use the new file, the better you will remember the information in it. If you are in a history class or a literature class that discusses historical background of literary pieces, discuss the new file of information with your professor or classmates. Be creative in your use of your new file. In storing the file in your long-term memory, think of several categories under which to file it. Category titles that are personally important to you would be helpful. Store the file under as many categories as are meaningful to you. For me, *language contact factors, American English, American history, language history, language leveling, language diversity,* and *regional dialects* are helpful categories.

G. What rewards will you receive for having a new file of information? Having a better overview of language development will be my first reward. As a southerner, I have been ridiculed for my accent and in the past have been self-conscious about it. With a better overview, especially of the influence of so many languages, my perspective will be broader and I will not take offense as easily as I have done in the past.

CHAPTER 12

MEMORY

In Chapter 7 of this textbook, you worked on memory and placing material in your long-term memory. Review your work on that lesson.

A. Select one important idea that you want to remember from each section of the chapter. Write each idea in your own words below:

1. Languages in the New Testament Period
Idea _____

2. Types of Language Function
Idea _____

3. The Inscription on the Cross and the Languages of Israel
Idea _____

B. Ask yourself why it is important to remember these ideas. If you have no clue, then change the information. Focus on the purpose of the chapter, support for the historical authenticity of the four Gospels.

C. What are the connections among the three ideas? What do they lead to? Are the ideas building up to a point? Do they support each other?

D. Self-check at this point. Do you understand the main ideas you have chosen? Can you talk about them in your own words? Could you write about them? What is the significance of the ideas? What do you know and what did you think you knew but do not know at this point?

E. Identify your own prior knowledge and experience about the ideas you have chosen as important. What do you already know that helps you understand the new material? Any knowledge of the New Testament or of the need for verification of historical accuracy will be beneficial. What prior knowledge or experience conflicts with your new knowledge? For example, from the chapter in this textbook on Columbus, I knew that the copy of Columbus's journal has not been verified as his and that for historical researchers this was an important issue. I transferred this knowledge to this chapter.

F. Connect your prior knowledge with the new information to create a new file of information that provides support for historical authenticity of the four Gospels. Store this information in your long-term memory. The more you use the new file, the better you will remember the information in it. If you attend a Christian church, you may want to share the information with friends there. If you are in a history class or a literature class that discusses historical background of literary pieces, discuss the new file of information with your professor or classmates. The idea of having to verify historical records of any kind may give you new ways of seeing information in your other courses. Be creative in your use of your new file. In storing the file in your long-term memory, think of several categories under which to file it. Category titles that are personally important to you would be helpful. Store the file under as many categories as are meaningful to you. For me, *historical verification of records* will be the most important. Others would be *multilingual countries, types of languages spoken by multilingual people,* and *biblical history.*

G. What rewards will you receive for having a new file of information? For me, I will be more alert to the importance of verifying historical events. When I see or hear some important new discovery from our dark historical past, I will ask myself what the sources are and how many sources there are for the new information. I will ask how the information was verified and how the reporter knows the information is authentic.

PART III: EXERCISES ON ANNOTATION

CHAPTER 9

ANNOTATION

Annotating is making notes in the margins of your textbook, a skill that you practiced in the Chapter 8 lesson. For this practice exercise, write your annotations on this sheet of paper.

A. In your own words, write the main ideas for each section of the chapter below:
1. The Initial Period of Nigerian–British Contact

   _____

2. Novels Dealing with the More Recent Situation in Nigeria

   _____

3. The Style of Achebe's Fiction

   _____

B. In your own words, write any examples that support the most important ideas below:
1. The Initial Period of Nigerian–British Contact

   _____

2. Novels Dealing with the More Recent Situation in Nigeria

   _____

3. The Style of Achebe's Fiction

   _____

C. After identifying main ideas and their support, do you have any questions about the material? Write any questions you have about the sections below:
1. The Initial Period of Nigerian–British Contact

   _____

2. Novels Dealing with the More Recent Situation in Nigeria

_____

3. The Style of Achebe's Fiction

_____

D. Review the information you have learned from the reading lesson and from your annotation of the text. Write a formal outline of this information by using the main headings provided in the chapter.

CHAPTER 10

ANNOTATION

Annotating is making notes in the margins of your textbook, a skill that you practiced in the previous lesson. For this practice exercise, write your annotations on this sheet of paper.

A. In your own words, write the main ideas for each section of the chapter below:
1. Defining the Blues

_____

2. Some Historical Background of the Blues

_____

3. Some Modern Manifestations of the Blues Tradition

_____

B. In your own words, write any examples that support the most important ideas below:
1. Defining the Blues

_____

2. Some Historical Background of the Blues

_____

3. Some Modern Manifestations of the Blues Tradition

_____

C. After identifying main ideas and their support, do you have any questions about the material? Write any questions you have about the sections below:
1. Defining the Blues

_____

2. Some Historical Background of the Blues

_____

3. Some Modern Manifestations of the Blues Tradition

_____

CHAPTER 11

ANNOTATION

A. In your textbook margin, write in your own words the most important idea in each of the five sections of this chapter.
   1. The Traditional View
   2. Exploration and Early Settlement
   3. Language Contact Factors
   4. Development of Regional Dialects
   5. Standardization and Retention of Differences
B. In your textbook margin, write in your own words any significant examples that support the most important ideas.
   1. The Traditional View
   2. Exploration and Early Settlement
   3. Language Contact Factors
   4. Development of Regional Dialects
   5. Standardization and Retention of Differences

CHAPTER 12

ANNOTATION

A. In your textbook margin, write in your own words the most important idea in each of the three sections of this chapter.
   1. Languages in the New Testament Period
   2. Types of Language Function
   3. The Inscription on the Cross and the Languages of Israel
B. In your textbook margin, write in your own words any significant examples that support the most important ideas.
   1. Languages in the New Testament Period
   2. Types of Language Function
   3. The Inscription on the Cross and the Languages of Israel

PART IV: EXERCISES ON UNDERLINING/HIGHLIGHTING

CHAPTER 10

UNDERLINING/HIGHLIGHTING

Review the work you have done on highlighting in Chapter 9's featured selection, "The Fiction of Chinua Achebe." In Chapter 10's featured selection, "The Blues," highlight the most important idea in each of the three sections of the chapter. Do not highlight too much or too little. Write key words for what you highlighted in each section of the chapter:

A. Defining the Blues
B. Some Historical Background of the Blues
C. Some Modern Manifestations of the Blues Tradition

Chapter 11

Underlining/Highlighting

Highlight (or underline) the most important idea in each section of Chapter 11. You will have a total of five parts highlighted. Write key words below that indicate what you chose:

A. The Traditional View
B. Exploration and Early Settlement
C. Language Contact Factors
D. Development of Regional Dialects
E. Standardization and Retention of Differences

Chapter 12

Underlining/Highlighting

Review the work you have done on this chapter and then highlight (or underline) the most important idea in each section of Chapter 12. You will have a total of three parts highlighted. Write key words below that indicate what you chose:

A. Languages in the New Testament Period
B. Types of Language Function
C. The Inscription on the Cross and the Languages of Israel

Part V: Exercises on Visual Mapping

Chapter 11

Visual Mapping

This chapter lends itself to visual mapping. Below are a few suggestions that may be helpful.

A. Time Line: In this chapter we move rapidly from fifth century A.D. to modern times. A time line, a horizontal line with major dates and events identified, is one way to see an overview of the information. Draw a horizontal in the middle of a piece of paper and add the information below to it in a meaningful way. Do not clutter or try to write too much information on the time line. Also be sure that you can read what you have written.

1. Fifth century A.D.
2. 1000 A.D. (Beowulf)
3. 1385 (Prologue to the *Canterbury Tales*)
4. 1600 (Shakespeare and Early Modern English)
5. 1607 (John Smith—shift to America)
6. 1621 (Puritans)
7. 18th century (Revolutionary War and uniform language)
8. 19th century (Westward movement and language diversity)
9. 1619 (Africans)
10. 18th century (Black English)
11. 19th century, second or third decade (Regional varieties)
12. 19th century, Civil War (Yankee and Rebel languages)
13. 19th century, after the Civil War (Emphasis on West)
14. 20th century (Influence of radio and television on language)
15. Contemporary, after about 400 years (Can now see changes from Early Modern English of Shakespeare's time)

B. A Comparison/Contrast Visual: the T: Several forms for showing how things are alike and different are useful, including one you may have used in another class, the Venn Diagram, in which interlocking circles provide a center (where they overlap) for likenesses and outer parts of circles provide space for differences. Because of the nature of the likenesses and differences in the information in this chapter, I have chosen a simpler approach. On a sheet of paper, draw a T. Several spaces above the horizontal line, write the name of this visual comparison, "Factors for Change in British and American English." On the left-hand side on the horizontal line write the word *ALIKE* and on the right-hand side on the horizontal line write the word *DIFFERENT*. The vertical line provides the point of separation. Below is a list of factors that you may use by writing them in the appropriate places:

1. Alike
    a. Large population speaking other languages in intimate contact
    b. Conquest of one group by another and superimposed government
    c. Extensive migration
2. Different
    a. Sound of language
    b. Some vocabulary
    c. Dialects become difficult to understand to other English-speaking groups

What other information could you add to the visual comparison above? Would examples help you to remember various parts? What other shape could you use? Remember to write just enough information to be helpful and not to clutter your visual.

C. Relationship through the Use of Clusters and Circles: I would hate to try to explain why circles appeal to me, but they do, so the last visual I want to suggest that may help get all this information under control involves drawing circles. The point of these visuals is to see what is the most important information or idea and what supports or contributes to it. In this chapter we have many languages listed as contributors to British and American English. The following visuals show this relationship:

1. Celtic, Norse, French, and Latin have influenced British English. In the center of a piece of paper draw a circle with "British English" written inside it. In an outer group of four circles, write the names of the languages that influenced British English.

2. American English has been influenced by several other languages, (a) the Dutch of Holland and New York, (b) Native American languages, (c) French, (d) Spanish, (e) African languages and Black English, (f) Scotch Irish, (g) German, and (h) Scandinavian languages. In the center of a piece of paper draw a circle with "American English" written inside it. In an outer group of eight circles, write the names of the languages that influenced American English.

3. Nine American regional dialects are discussed in this chapter. In the center of a piece of paper, draw a circle with "American Regional Dialects" written inside. In an outer group of nine circles, write the names of the regional dialects. Review the fourth section of this chapter to find the names. You may want to use these visuals for review of the material. With a partner or a study group, note the overview of the material. Next, call out parts and see what you can say out loud in your own words about the material. When you find you do not remember enough about the material, review the work you have done on the lesson and reread parts of the chapter for help.

Chapter 12

Visual Maps

In your SQ4R study plan, you created a visual map for each section of the chapter. Review the maps. Review the chapter by talking yourself through the maps. If you find yourself stuck, is it because the map is not clear or because you have changed your mind about what is important in the chapter? Can you fix the map? Would a different form be more helpful? Be sure your maps are not cluttered and that information of equal importance is equally represented. Draw a visual map of your choosing (on a separate sheet of paper) that shows the importance of the three sections of the chapter to each other.

Index